PARADIGM OF

SENSE

PARADIGM OF

SENSE

a guide to the consciousness of the fifth dimension

CAVALHER

for Daimón

If I should succeed — and I hope I shall not — in taking all of you up to viśuddha, you would certainly complain; you would stifle, you would not be able to breathe any longer, because there is nothing you could possibly breathe. It is ether. In reaching viśuddha, you reach the airless space, where there is no earthly chance for the ordinary individual to breathe. So it seems to be a very critical kind of adventure.

(Carl Gustav JUNG. *The psychology of Kundalini Yoga*)

TABLE OF CONTENTS

ACKNOWLEDGEMENTS

To my Masters. João Bosco Assunção. Carlos Alberto Goursand. Geraldo Magela Araújo. Ciro Álvaro de Faria. For being my masters.

To Helena Angelini. For being with me since always. For being with me exactly as I am, with all my perfection and all my imperfection. For having discussed ethics with me when we were only twenty years old, and since then, a myriad of other spiritual themes which were crucial for my development; our conclusions are valid to this day. For having killed me and for calling me back.

To Tatiane Vesch and Ana Paula Moreira. For teaching me about friendship. For not accepting my isolation. For going into the unfathomable abyss with me. For showing me that everything was real.

To Heloisa de Souza Rodrigues Pereira, Lívia Anna Maria Marchisio, Lúcia Carlota Tomaz de Aquino, Nair Hatuko, Regina Uno and Tânia Regina de Araújo. For being my mothers and for loving me in the darkest and the most luminous hours.

To Valerya Carvalho. For seeing me. For believing in me. For demanding that I write this book. For pushing me forward.

To the Vertente. For being my school, my laboratory, my work, my battlefield, my grave and the place where I made some of the deepest friendships I am honoured to have. To my friends: Adriana Angelelli, Agatha Cavalher, Ana Paula Moreira, Andrei Branco, Erik Vesch, Fabiana Gonçalves, Hélcio Pereira, Helena Angelini, Heloisa de Souza Rodrigues Pereira, Izilda Borges, Lívia Anna Maria Marchisio, Lúcia Carlota Tomaz de Aquino, Maica Alves, Márcia Padovan, Nair Hatuko, Paula Caju, Paulo Freitas, Rafaela Ferreira, Regina Uno, Renan Fragale, Rúbia Mattos, Simone Padovan, Tatiane Vesch, Thaisa Ishimine and Valerya Carvalho. For loving me. For teaching me so much. For saving my life so many times.

To my beloved daughter, Agatha Cavalher, and my love, Paulo Freitas. For continually loving and encouraging me. For understanding and helping me when I needed to dedicate myself to this work instead of being with them.

To my parents, Debora Anne Peterson Cavalher and Fernando José Campos Cavalher. For giving me my life. For all the love I have received. For the thorough education I was given.

To my enemies. For making my life heroic. For the honour and the greatness they have entrusted me with.

5D TEAMWORK

Fifth-dimensional *Images* are immense and too complex to be held by a single person. It requires the union of various consciousnesses in order to *Manifest*. Fifth-dimensional *Images* about fifth-dimensional *Images* – particularly when they are about a paradigm – are exponentially complex. I had the honour of meeting people who had the necessary consciousness complexity to walk the path with me. However, despite their notable intelligence, it was love that united us.

I met Fabíola Conceição working: she chose to develop her consciousness with me. Our relationship rapidly turned into a friendship. My dream of publishing my work in English was added to her brilliant intelligence, and thereby emerged the perfect scenario to work together.

When we initiated this work, the *Image* started to behave in a way which is typical of the fifth dimension: its complexity constantly increased. The complexity continued to increase throughout, to a point where we started to refer to the work as "the infinite book". We finished the work with the knowledge that a second edition is nothing but absolutely necessary.

In searching for excellence, we agreed to dedicate ourselves to various hard tasks. However, amongst them all, the one which struck me the most was the recreation of language. The *Paradigm of Sense*, for its own nature, demanded the creation of a fifth-dimensional language which is characterized by unity, different to the typical duality of the Portuguese and the English language. It also demands to be expressed in a multi-paradoxical manner. Strongly influenced by the extraordinary consciousness of Friedrich Nietzsche, Carl Jung and Lama Anagarika Govinda, besides the Greek culture, I wanted to highlight the etymological meaning and the historical weight of the words themselves. Fabíola was able to make that possible, with exceptional results.

My wish to converse with the consciousness of great authors of humanity lead us to the extensive research of their indelible works, and the construction of one of my proudest achievements: the over 600 references present in this book. When this new level of complexity emerged, Love brought more consciousnesses to work with us. Now, I have the honour of working with my mother, Debora A. P. Cavalher. I was hugely impressed by the dedication, diligence, and motherly love that she brought to the work. When we used to end our calls, I was never sure whether I was more impressed by her technical excellence or by the beauty of the love which came from her. Often, I would cry a little.

Alongside my mother, Heloisa S. R. Pereira and Lívia A. M. Marchisio also worked in the research of the English version. They shone by working alone in the research of the original version in Portuguese, and once again, were indispensable and admirable in the construction of the English version. Finally, in the final stages of the research for this version, Andrew Weightman brought us important contributions which were often incredibly hard to find.

At the end of the research, my mother told me something that touched me deeply and still touches me whilst I write these words. She acknowledged the work of Fabíola as a translator and told me that the English version of the book is better than the original book I wrote in Portuguese – and she is my mother. She is right.

For that reason, my sincerest acknowledgements to these brilliant people. I know we will walk together in these newly opened paths.

FOREWORD FROM THE TRANSLATOR

Most people are transformed by the books they read, in one way or another, whether they are works of fiction made to entertain, or, as it is the case with the present work, their content inspires an unprecedented revolution in the way one perceives life and living. The language of this book, although mostly based on terminology well-known to those familiar with Analytical Psychology and Greek Mythology, has also often had to be created, in the search for meaning that expressed the author's creation of a new Paradigm. It took several months of reviews, discussions and exchanges between the author and the translator, to arrive at a level of understanding where logical and lexical semantics could faithfully express the novel and intricate thoughts and ideas of the author. The search for the appropriate balance between signifiers (words, phrases, signs and symbols) and what they stand for in reality was a real labour of love and dedication to language and meaning. The lengthy discussions, over weekly video calls – since the author and the translator lived in different countries – involved not only detailed linguistic matters such as sense and reference, analysis of meanings and the relationship between the words, but also explanations about the complex psychological concepts that the translator needed to understand before finding the words which were the best fit to express certain ideas. Being proficient in both Portuguese and English, as well as undergoing a process of consciousness development with the author, simultaneous to performing the translation, were invaluable to the interpretation, understanding and translation of the author's ideas as closely as possible to its originally intended meaning. This may have been impossible without the knowledge of the cultural differences and idiosyncrasies of both languages, and perhaps an unattainable challenge for other translators. This intense experience and the synergy between author and translator, a rich and transformative experience for both, resulted in the English version of the Paradigm of Sense, which will certainly be reflected in the carefully crafted pages you are about to read and be transformed by.

PREFACE

The translation of the present book was performed from the original in Portuguese. It is the result of lengthy discussions between the Author and the Translator, about the meaning of several concepts and the words which were best suited to describe their intended meaning, given the complex and often novel ideas presented here. Some of the published works cited throughout the present book had never been translated to the English Language, or a translation was not found, despite exhaustive searches. In these cases, the Translator of the present book performed the translation from their Portuguese versions (when this was the case, it is indicated on the footnotes). In other cases, although the work cited had an English version (or its original was written in English), the citation was still not found, and therefore had to be translated by the Translator of the present book, for the sake of completeness of the argument presented. This is particularly relevant at the time when the translation was finalized, in 2020, as only digital searches were possible due to restrictions of movement and closure of public spaces, which hindered the possibility of a physical library search. When this was the case, it is clearly indicated as "Translated from the Portuguese version". The Translator apologizes to these authors for any incorrectness that may occur in the translation from the Portuguese version, and assures that every step was taken to retain the meaning intended by those authors.

INTRODUCTION

The central figure on a series of dreams which put me in a state of panic for some years was a boy of eight years old. There were several oneiric situations experienced by this boy, but the most frequent one was being in a free-falling elevator. Although it took me years to understand what this series of dreams was trying to tell me, the reason for the presence of this eight-year-old boy was very clear: when I was around eight years old, a religious conflict exploded inside me at full force.

I was raised in Campanha, a small city of the Brazilian state of Minas Gerais. As with many cities in Brazil, Campanha has a cathedral in the centre of town, besides several other churches. The presence of Catholicism was determining. The worldview of Campanha's inhabitants is solidly Catholic, as is its moral system. Catholicism not only governed people's consciousness: their imagery is also strongly composed by Catholic images. Catholicism was present inside my house through my Catholic father. This whole scenario was all there. I did not even have an objective consciousness about this; and precisely for that reason the Catholic worldview was hegemonic inside me.

However, a simultaneous tendency sneakily grew inside me. My mother had come from a Methodist family and belonged to that religion. My maternal grandparents were Methodist missionaries who had immigrated to Brazil from the USA: my grandfather, a pastor of the Methodist Church, and my grandmother a professor of Ethics and Philosophy at a Methodist university. The Methodist worldview also existed in my house, through my mother.

At the age of eight, I already had a very good understanding that there were two different worldviews and I also knew some of their divergences. I remember very well a catholic priest arriving at our house to talk to my grandfather, a Methodist pastor, about religious dogmas. They respected each other, and the conversations were very exciting. Evidently, I wanted to be part of these moments, and, to my surprise and everyone else's, I had very strong opinions to offer. With the typical naivety of children, I directly questioned both the Catholic and the Methodist dogmas. The fact that my parents belonged to different religions and encouraged the harmonious co-existence of representatives of both, determined – already then – some striking facts of my personality: a strong religious impulse, an affinity with controversy and the freedom to express my points of view.

This harmony ended very quickly when I became more interested in religion and decided to have catechism lessons. The same freedom of expression that the priest and my grandfather admired in me shocked the pious women who taught these lessons. To defend themselves from the harsh questions I would ask in front of everyone, they used the fact that I had been baptized in the Methodist Church to try and stop me from having the First Communion in the Catholic Church. Their fanaticism, combined with their sanctimonious behaviour, made me realise something about them that I could only name much later: hypocrisy.

This event broke the impartiality that there was inside me, and for the first time, I started to believe that one religion was better than another. I veered towards Methodism. But there were no Methodist churches in my city, so I had to wait until my family went to other localities in order to go to church. At first, the anger I felt for those pious women pushed me towards a religious fervour inside the Methodist Church. But this blew off rapidly in face of the monotony of Methodism. I did not find there any deeper questions, simply a more pleasant kind of fanaticism, and, in a way, a more tired one. Other than that, the same hypocrisy.

This second disappointment completely destroyed my inclination to be part of an organized religion, at the same time as it made me separate myself completely from the religions in my family. It was a first movement of independence.

Now, however, I had no guiding authority for my development. The effect of this was to fall into the whole pseudo-knowledge offered by esotericism. I read hundreds of esoteric books. When I started to read those, the aura of mysticism in the texts, and a subtext suggesting that those were occult pieces of knowledge, made me feel like one of the chosen few, who had the immense honour to access that knowledge – a complete nonsense. But, for a teenager seeking to affirm himself through spirituality, esotericism was the perfect seduction. I became involved with some esoteric schools, believing that I had finally found the way, only to become disappointed again and again.

The ability to analyse, discuss and be critical I had learned with my parents thankfully prevailed. After a few years, I had realised that an esoteric book is just an almanac, a grouping of curiosities of dubious sources. I started to ask myself: 'What have I actually learned with this book?'. The answer was always invariably nothing or almost nothing. Pragmatism put an end to this matter. When I started to ask myself 'How can I use this knowledge in practice?' and the answer was 'This knowledge is useless', I realised that esotericism was just a factory of products selling pseudo-knowledge, little witches dressed in purple and symbols stolen from legitimate spiritual traditions, misunderstood by the consumer. I started to walk in and out of book shops without buying a single book, because I didn't know what to read. I was seventeen years old.

However, one of these failed trips to a bookshop in Belo Horizonte was the stage of one of the most significant meetings of my life. I was crouching down, looking at the books closer to the lowest shelf, when I noticed a man standing behind me. I looked back to speak to him, and the depth of his gaze touched me profoundly; in a way that was unfathomable to me, he saw me. Although he did not know me, he showed a great admiration for me and I felt analysed in a remarkably correct and profound manner. His name was João Bosco Assunção. I say 'was' because our time together was very short, no more than ten meetings. I never saw him again and I have no idea what happened to him. Even so, to this day, I still consider him my great initiator, my Master, because everything that came from him proved to be true countless times, and still guides me.

One of the most generous acts of João Bosco was introducing me to one of his friends, Carlos Alberto Goursand. João Bosco did not have a lot of patience with me. And I can understand why; I was very young and my idealization of him must have tired him somewhat. But Goursand was an older man, a professor, and more dedicated. It was him who introduced me to the explosive philosopher: Friedrich Nietzsche.

It is a fact that I had already become disappointed with Christianity as a whole – Catholicism, Methodism and esotericism (yes, esotericism is a disguise for the worst of Christianity) had been enough to cause that. But Nietzsche was an express train in that direction. He launched in my life the work I have dedicated myself to for the last twenty years: the meticulous destruction of all moralism I find within myself. More than that, Nietzsche finally managed to show me something sufficiently vast, profound and true, which was enough to fill the gap left by Christianity, and place me back into movement: myself. I still remember Goursand's statement: "When you study Plato, you understand Plato. When you study Kant, you understand Kant. When you study Nietzsche, you understand yourself."

I owe my first contact with Carl Gustav Jung to a footnote, from the page of a book about Nietzsche, whose author I no longer recall the name. Although I had already come across Jung's name before, only when I saw it associated to Nietzsche, I decided it was worth studying him. During the first days of reading *Man and his symbols* (JUNG. C. G., 1964) I had an extremely numinous dream:

> I'm crossing a long pedestrian overpass that links the coach station in Belo Horizonte to a metro station. I see a tall slim woman, covered in rags, her olive skin body exposed, with dark straight hair. She carries a round-based bucket filled with water, placed on a supporting base. She offers to read my destiny. The price is only 75 cents. I'm fascinated by her, and I promptly accept. I look inside the bucket.
>
> Immediately, I'm in a completely different place. I see a square portal, made entirely of old stones, covered in Egyptian hieroglyphs. It is not possible to see anything inside the portal, as it is filled with darkness. I know I have to enter it, but I am scared.
>
> The vision fades away and I realise that I had that vision from looking into the water. The woman is looking at me with an expression that says 'Your time is up. Go.' I continue to cross the overpass.

For the eight years during which I was involved with religion, and afterwards, with esotericism, I had never experienced anything of that magnitude. The veracity and intensity of the dream's image, as well as its closeness with the contents of the book about *anima* were so strong that, when I woke up, I already knew that Jung was a real master. I started to devour Jung's complete works, and other authors at the same time, such as Marie-Louise von Franz, Aniela Jaffé, James Hillman, Edward Edinger, Erich Neumann, James Hollis, Adolf Guggenbühl-Craig, Rafael López-Pedraza, James Hollis, John Sanford, Aldo Carotenuto and Eugene Monick; they started to become part of my life. With Nietzsche's and Jung's presence, I had taken a fundamental step. I was no longer searching for the correct religion or philosophical school. I was walking in the direction of my own self.

It amazed me how much Nietzsche's and Jung's universes were compatible. I noticed very quickly that both authors would constantly refer to classic Greek culture. My first serious contact with that brought on an immediate passion. The Greek gods transcend the rigid western division between good and evil. The gods are very different among themselves, therefore their cosmology is much wider than Christian theology. The idea that human beings can have different gods as divine ancestors is, for me, extremely liberating, as it allows people to have strongly diverse personality tendencies, and none are wrong or worse than the other. The idea that human beings can fight with the gods also makes me very comfortable to be myself, since my relationship with the Transcendence is extremely tempestuous. The notions of *hýbris* and *hamartía* make much more sense to me than the notion of sin, a source of repression. The ideas of *Moîra* and *kairós* show us a much more aesthetic cosmos than the eternal petty rivalry between divine grace and individual merit. My passion for Greek culture is strong because it seeks to see reality as it is, not as it should be. It does not try to overwrite society with dogmas and unobservable ideas, which are, ultimately – and thankfully – unreachable. It does not try to force the human being to be what it is not. Greek culture performs a sanitation from hypocrisy.

As I delved deeper into the Greek word, however, a new element emerged: the body. In Greece, the gods are nature itself, there is no division. The stunning and sexually attractive anthropomorphic bodies appear. The statues of Dionysius arouse lust, his gaze is seductive. In Greece, human beings are intensely corporeal, and even the Greek philosophers, whose area of work is considered abstract in our era, possess bodies which are literally sculptural. However, I did not notice my own body.

The contact with the book *Incest and Human Love* (STEIN, R. 1973) opened another huge chapter in my life, and moved me even more intensely in the direction of the body. Stein's ideas are, in my view, indisputable, and became guidelines for me. For instance, the notion that the therapist should be their client's equal, never on a superior level to them. But it was the idea that an intact relationship with the archetype of incest leads to a perfect equivalence between love – of a spiritual nature – and lust – of a corporeal one –, started an irreversible process of destroying the abstractionism in me. Reading Stein made me progressively more comfortable with my muscles, my phallus, my lust, my instincts.

It became progressively clear that the heated conflict between various religions, schools of thought, psychological schools and ethical positionings was not the crucial question. There was a much deeper conflict going on within me: a division between body and soul. When the conflict was sufficiently advanced, I dreamed that the eight-year-old boy was in the lift, and, for the first time, instead of falling, the doors opened and on the wall immediately in front of it, there was a picture of the god Hades, naked, laying over clouds on a clear sky. A few days later I dreamed that the eight-year-old was again in a falling lift, but this time it fell until the second level underground, and the boy was having a panic attack, shaking violently and very scared. When I woke from this dream, I finally understood that I was in a panic about my own body. I carried out a few processes of active imagination and talked to the boy, caringly but firmly, and told him that I would stay with him, and that the body is a blessing we can enjoy. I never dreamed with the boy again. To offset the process of moral destruction within me, I continued to develop the process of destroying the abstractionism – for me, a series of physical exercises have as much spiritual value as reading a book, completing a psychological integration or going through a transcendental experience. Certain personality traits that I already had were over-emphasized: like the scientific spirit of testing, the pragmatism and the search for results. Knowledge, for me, is not consciousness – action is.

I had been analysing my dreams and also having had them analysed by other people for approximately ten years already, when in 2008 something really odd happened: there was someone whose dreams made no sense. I could not interpret them at all. The dreamer was an extraordinarily advanced person who had noticeably overcome the moral limits by integrating her dark aspects and was in a frank relationship with the archetypal world and intimately related to her own Self. She had concluded a consciousness design process conducted by me a few years back and was a diligent observer of her own series of dreams, working towards resolving the problems brought up to the surface, and applying the solutions pragmatically. However, despite this diligence and dedication, her dreams no longer made sense.

This strongly sparked my interest, and I dedicated myself to the dreamer and her dreams, seeking to understand what was happening. To my surprise, I started to find in my own dreams the same pattern as I found in the woman's dreams, the same deviation in relation to the dreams of everyone else I knew. The dreams seemed to have a low or no level of symbology. They literally depicted situations of physical life. There were several dreams about the same physical life, however with different versions for the end. In face of the same life situations, the dreams seemed to be simultaneously in favour, totally contrary, and completely neutral to it. Several of these dreams with various versions of reality would suddenly stop at an intense point, as many dreams do, however clearly leaving the ego in a position where it had to choose. Until the choice was made, the dream would reappear in different formats, always stopping at a point where the ego had to make a choice for one of the versions of reality presented.

Faced with that, we started to feel deeply anguished, because we realised that the guiding character of the Self was no longer present. In a usual series of dreams, it is clear that, however tumultuous the psychological situation, the Self pushes the ego in a certain direction, guiding the ego's positioning. In our series of dreams, however, the Self was not guiding in any direction. The total lack of guidance left us literally disoriented and anxious, having been used to trust the guiding character of the Self and its symbology, after years of dedication to the psychological work. We felt abandoned by the Self.

Despite the huge anguish, at certain point, the dreamer and I, each in our own story and psychological reality, finally realised that we had to make a choice among the various versions of reality presented in the dreams. We were shocked to notice that, immediately after our decisions, our dreams incorporated our choices. We started to have dreams that would develop the version of reality we had chosen, highlighting that the choice we had made had been incorporated into that reality – similar to a password that is able to reset a computer system. All the other dreams with other versions of reality disappeared after that point. The chosen reality would solidify and from there, the cycle would repeat itself: new possibilities with new unravelling would appear and again, choices had to be made. These were only some of the oddities present in our dreams.

It was not possible to say that Jung and Jungian professionals were wrong, because the dreams of all the other people I knew had exactly the same structure: symbolic, full of psychological conflicts which demanded ethical conflicts. For everyone else, the Self remained a strong guide. So, I was forced to abandon the comfortable situation of someone who had found an all-inclusive, all-serving worldview. Up to that point, Jung's view was enough to clarify all phenomena I could observe. But suddenly there were two people who functioned on a different key, and this caused a deep conflict in me. The mere possibility of being in front of something beyond the colossal worldview of Jung was extremely disturbing, and I made a huge effort to repress this idea. For a while, I still tried to believe that I was getting something wrong, that I did not know the mechanism of a certain archetype, that some inconsistency of mine was interfering in my understanding. However, one day, an idea hit me like lightening: what if the dreamer and I were experiencing a different paradigm? And what if Jung was right, once again? What if what was happening to me and the dreamer was, in fact, not an exception, but the pattern for those who had succeeded in their processes of individuation?

That idea stayed with me irretrievably. I then started to try to understand which pattern would this be, through the observations I was making of the dreamer, of myself and of the other few people who started to appear in the same situation.

A year and a half later, there was another great milestone in my history – the book *Jung and the Alchemic Imagination* (RAFF, J. 2000). Various affirmations made by the author were entirely in line with what I had observed. Raff affirmed that there was a "transpsychic" reality, which was simultaneously psychic and physical, which he called a psychoid reality. This could explain, for example, the dreams that showed physical realities which were simultaneously significant and literal. But the idea from Raff that had the biggest impact on me was the affirmation that there is a "manifested Self" and a "psychoid Self", each existing in their own reality, with their own way of functioning and interacting between themselves. Raff showed that the psychoid Self is beyond the manifested Self, existing as a kind of "Self of the Self", as a more complex structure of the Self. Considering the scope of Jung's work, Raff affirmed that the manifested Self promotes the second *coniunctio*, whereas the psychoid Self promotes the third *coniunctio*. It was instantly clear to me that the strange phenomenon that I had observed was the manifestation of the psychoid Self. I was witnessing processes of the third *coniunctio*, processes that aimed at reaching the *Unus Mundus*.

Around the same time, I came across another of Jung's book, *The psychology of Kundalini Yoga* (JUNG, C. G., 1996). In that book, Jung analyses the *cakras* (in English, it is normally written "*chakra*"), and shows that the psychological structure of those who have their consciousness guided by each of these *cakras* is very diverse. I remembered various parts of his work where Jung mentions that, not only the ego is modified through the contact with the Self, but also the Self is modified from time to time, when the ego experiences large integrations. Adding it all up, I concluded that, in each *cakra*, the Self is configured in a specific manner, based on specific laws, behaving in specific ways and requiring specific developments from the ego. In each *cakra*, the Self establishes a new **paradigm**.

The term paradigm is especially dear to the present work. According to the *Merriam-Webster Dictionary*, it originates from the Greek *paradeigma*, from *paradeiknynai*, to show side by side, from *para + deiknynai*, to show. The term is used to refer to a model, a pattern to be followed. It is a matrix idea, guiding a long development to come, whose objective is to elaborate the matrix idea and the questions it generates, as well as finding solutions or conclusions for those questions.

The term paradigm becomes easier to understand in science. Nicholas Copernicus and Galileo Galilei established Heliocentrism as a paradigm. Isaac Newton established paradigms that guided Physics for approximately 300 years, but Albert Einstein established a new paradigm in physics: Relativity. Charles Darwin established as a paradigm the Evolution of Species. Gregor Mendel established as a paradigm the transmission of hereditary factors and became the father of Genetics. There are many other examples that could be listed here. For this work, however, there is still one other example that needs to be highlighted: Sigmund Freud established a new paradigm in psychology when he demonstrated the existence of the Unconscious.

A paradigm is, therefore, a formulation so strongly innovative, so diverse from all others that already exist, and arises so many questions that it becomes a guidance for a long phase of development. We can see this in all the examples listed above.

Nothing, however, stops us from applying this concept to other contexts. In a theological scenario, for example, it is perfectly possible to affirm that Confucius, Siddhartha Gautama, Moses, Jesus Christ and Mohammed established new paradigms. In arts, each school has established a new paradigm: Renaissance, Baroque, Impressionism, Expressionism, Cubism and Surrealism are just a few examples.

Paradigms do not necessarily need to happen in succession throughout time. For example, in politics, Monarchy is a paradigm and Republic is another. Nowadays, both exist concurrently, and are, each in their own way, functional.

A paradigm is a basic law that determines all others.

Reading *The psychology of Kundalini Yoga* led me to realise that each *cakra* is guided by a paradigm. However, applied to the psychological context, the term paradigm has an infinitely higher meaning. Given that the human psychological structure determines how the whole reality is going to be perceived, interpreted and experienced, **a psychological paradigm defines the whole reality**. A change in paradigm, in turn, implies that the **whole reality changes**, since, from then on, it will be perceived, interpreted and experienced in a radically different way. For example, it is impossible to affirm that the worldview of someone who is not aware of the existence of the unconscious is similar to the worldview of someone who has found the unconscious within themselves. A whole new layer of reality appears with the discovery of the unconscious. Although they live in the same planet, these two people live in completely different realities. The difference in perception is so radical that we can safely affirm that they are in **different dimensions**, dimensions which interpenetrate, but still are totally different.

That way, inspired by Jung's book, it was possible to notice that the consciousness structure in each *cakra* follows a specific paradigm, defined by a specific manifestation of the Self, which determines a certain reality, a certain worldview and a group of specific experiences. "Each *cakra* is a whole universe" (JUNG, C. G. 1996). Each *cakra* is a dimension. In the present book, the dimensions are numbered according to the *cakras* that define them.

Jung also offers a very useful guidance. He affirms that most of humanity is experiencing the third *cakra*. He points out that the discovery of the Self as *puruṣa* (the Self as an internal "Other"), is typical of the fourth *cakra*, and, with that, albeit indirectly, he positions his own psychological model, the Analytical Psychology, as structurally belonging to that dimension. In effect, Jung clearly says that the fifth *cakra* is too ethereal for him, that it is difficult for him to comprehend, and therefore, explain. The *paradigm of sense* tries to perform this herculean task: comprehend the fifth *cakra* and offer pragmatic applications.

Jung's analysis of Kundalini Yoga, among other factors, drew me closer to eastern schools of thought, particularly Tibetan Buddhism. Having contact with the book *Foundations of Tibetan Mysticism* (GOVINDA, A. 1975) was another milestone in my life – a milestone difficult to experience, since it took me almost four years to fully comprehend it. The eastern parameters of perception and interpretation of reality are hugely different from western ones. They open an entirely new worldview and offer the opportunity to see the western worldview from the outside and relativize it. It becomes evident in Govinda's texts that *cakras* are centres of consciousness, which is much more comprehensive and profound than the tiresome relationships between *cakras*, colours and glands offered by esotericism.

Besides, esotericism is a worsened version of Christianity, and has inherited certain ideas which are noxious to the comprehension of the human psychological structure. For example, it has absorbed ideas such as being superior is better than being inferior, that it is possible and desirable to reach perfection though the absence of faults, that development is a finite process that ends when this perfection is reached, as well as the Christian sectarianism. By doing that, esotericism has created a huge confusion by mixing eastern and Christian thinking and has developed the hollow belief that the more evolved the *cakra*, the better it is, as if the coronary *cakra* were better than the rest and the root *cakra* the worst. Consequently, those who have reached the development of more cranial *cakras* would be better people than those who worked towards more caudal *cakras*. This esoteric speech promotes the mediocre, mean and foolish worldview where there is a stupid competition for the one who has developed more *cakras*. In addition to that, in preaching an increasing evolution in the direction of the cranial *cakra*, esotericism promotes an abstractionist worldview and proposes an escape from this world, which would certainly make Nietzsche accuse it of the most current type of nihilism.

Govinda's work is elegant and goes beyond esotericism by far and large. Evidently, the more *cakras* developed will result in more consciousness. However, the author makes it clear that the heart *cakra* is more developed than the coronary *cakra* because a higher level of spirituality achieved in the physical realm is more developed than just interior spirituality. This simultaneously destroys the esoteric abstractionism and its useless competition for the one with more *cakras* developed.

Govinda also shows that relationships are cosmically ruled by equality. In a very simplified way, equality is the idea according to which each being is extremely vast and their various parts are in direct relationship with the people around them, and ultimately, with all humanity. This idea resonates with the concept of projection adopted by Freud and used by Jung. The idea of equality combined with the acknowledgement that each person is at a given phase of development leads to a great perception: that the various parts that compose the immense being that makes up each one of us, are at different phases of development. This means that it is not possible to affirm that a certain person is entirely in the dimension of this or that *cakra*. Much more appropriate is to notice that parts of our beings have reached the level of development of the fourth *cakra*, but that many parts are still dedicated to the third, second and first *cakras*. Once again, Govinda's view goes far beyond the view of esotericism.

Govinda's work cleansed my being by overcoming various prejudices that I had absorbed from esotericism. However, more than that, Govinda presents ideas which are much more advanced, without which it would have been impossible to formulate the Paradigm of Sense. The idea of universality, according to which each and every element that appears is part of the totality and part of my being, for example, allows for the formulation of the concepts of *Imponderable* and *Evolution*. The idea of equality, mentioned above, is fundamental for the notion of *Collective Ego*. There are many examples, but these are enough to demonstrate that the Tibetan Buddhism is fundamental to the comprehension of the psychological structure of the fifth *cakra*.

The encounter with these authors and their work were great milestones in my life, and indispensable for the construction of my worldview and the formulation of the paradigm I am proposing. Achieving the formulation of the *Paradigm of Sense*, however, confronted me with a dilemma.

The reaction of the pious women from Campanha – full of fanaticism, hypocrisy and rejection – was only the first of a long series of similar situations that I experienced, and that depicts the huge difficulty that human beings have to relativize their points of view when diverging worldviews appear. I was psychologically scarred by this experience, and I learned to hide. Keeping my ideas for myself was the way I found to avoid suffering rejection and ostracism. This relatively unconscious factor has undoubtedly contributed towards my choice to, only now, after twenty years of work, express my ideas and creations. Other more conscious needs, such as maturing my creation and developing a language to express it, also contributed to it. However, all this has been achieved, and once again life places me in front of another dilemma: whether or not to expose my creations. Finally, I have opted for transposing this neurotic limitation and it is in that spirit that I make my work public.

* * * * *

Paradigm of Sense is a book that aims at describing the reality experienced by those who have succeeded in their processes of individuation and integrated the Self. For such, it shows reality from the psychological perspective of the fifth *cakra*, the fifth dimension, the fifth paradigm.

In order to offer a new view of reality, it was necessary to develop a unique language, so I wrote the book in the form of a dictionary. Most of the chapters have a type of entry as a title, such as "*Spirit*", "*Body*", "*Demon*", "*Macroimage*", "*Force*" and so on. However, the structure of languages is usually dual. Therefore, in order to refer to the unified reality – which is non-dual – of the fifth dimension, I wrote the words that refer to fifth-dimensional structures in a specific format in italic. Here are most of the 5D terms used in this book: *Action with no Guarantee, All-the-times, Body, Collective, Creation, Demon, Education, Enigma, Evolution, Force* and *Dynamic Force, Free-will, Grail, Greatness, Human, Image, Imbalance, Imponderable, Inspiration, Instinct, Interference, Joy, Karma, Macroimage, Manifestation, Multi-dimensionality, Obvious, Plenitude, Pneûma (Pneûmata* and *Pneumatic), Relationship* (when applied to *Evolution), Repetition, Resurrection, Sense, Soul Retreat, Spirit* (and *Holy Spirit), Truth, Universe, Unus Mundus, Verse* and *Perverse,* and *Word.* – However, it is important to notice that foreign words and titles of books are also in italic.

Since, according to Jung, the whole humanity is developing the third *cakra*, that Analytical Psychology has its gravity centre in the fourth *cakra*, and that the present work describes the reality of the fifth *cakra*, I will primarily deal with these three *cakras*. For that reason, most chapters develop their themes in three, four and then finally five dimensions. At those points where it became indispensable, the first, the second and the sixth *cakras* were also mentioned.

This is a plural book, inserted mainly in the context of Jung's and Jungian's Analytical Psychology, but with equally strong roots in the philosophy of Nietzsche, Tibetan Buddhism and Kundalini Yoga.

Altogether, it becomes imperative in order to facilitate comprehension, to present terms of equivalence between the language of the various schools that contributed to the present work.

TABLE OF EQUIVALENTS

Dimension	1D	2D	3D	4D	5D	6D
Paradigm	-	Paradigm of Civilization	Paradigm of Self-Affirmation	Paradigm of Balance	Paradigm of Sense	-
Cakra (chakra)	*mūlādhāra* (root)	*svādhiṣṭhāna* (umbilical)	*maṇipūra* (solar plexus)	*anāhata* (heart)	*viśuddha* (throat)	*ājñā* (frontal)
Symbol	grey elephant	whale or crocodile	sheep	deer	white elephant	winged seed
Self	1D *Self*	2D *Self*	3D *Self*	4D *Self*: Soul	5D *Self*: Spirit	6D *Self*
Behaviour of the *Self*	-	encompasses society	latent	victory over the ego: guiding	abandons the ego: retreat of the Soul	-
Philosopher's Stone	-	-	-	1st Philosopher's Stone	2nd Philosopher's Stone	-
Coniunctio	-	-	1st *coniunctio*: *unio mentalis*	2nd *coniunctio*	3rd *coniunctio*: *Unus Mundus*	-
Basic Law	-	life in society	development of the ego	relationship with the archetypes and with the *Self*	creative ego	-
Criteria	-	social	moral	ethics	creation	-
Type of consciousness	-	duality	duality	acknowledged duality	unity	-
Main product	consciousness	human civilization	strong ego	balance (all archetypes are balanced and integrated to consciousness)	personal sense	-
Climax	expulsion from Paradise	ego independent from society	moral defeat	crucifixion	Grail	*I Am IRon man*

INTEGRATION OF THE SELF

Although the notion of the unconscious already existed, it was through the brilliant mind of Sigmund FREUD, the father of Psychology, that the **unconscious** became an actual concept[1,2].More than that, the unconscious was understood as a practical and accessible reality. FREUD, one of the creators of the 20th century, demonstrated that the ego is not the centre of the human psyche. On the contrary, the ego is but a small psychic instance amidst the infinitude of the unconscious.

Carl Gustav JUNG. Swiss psychiatrist. Creator of Analytical Psychology. The man in whose story the unconscious was realised.

JUNG had the honour of spending time with FREUD, to whom he wisely pays homage and shows recognition in various points of his works[3,4,5]. As it was the case for all of humanity, JUNG received, from the father of psychoanalysis, the concept of the unconscious. From then on, however, JUNG trod a completely individual path, as all great creators do. Based on individual experiences, or **psychological facts**, as he would later call them, he constructed his own definitions of the unconscious, ego, psychological energy, unconscious complex, neurosis, etc. Evidently, in redefining the basic concepts of psychoanalysis, JUNG described a completely new model of the psychological structure and dynamics, and the way the human psyche, particularly the unconscious, functions. However, as he stated himself, JUNG never abandoned the concept of reductive therapy[6] conceived by FREUD[7], despite working on a totally different basis. In fact, JUNGrealised that the beginning of a successful psychological process must start with the confrontation of the consciousness with what was later perceived as the **personal unconscious**.

Any psychological development process must essentially start with a **strong ego**[8,9]. The unconscious is infinite and powerful. Although it contains the possibility of a desirable direct and conscious contact with the Transcendence, the unconscious also possesses within itself extremely dangerous regressive dimensions that can dissolve the ego. To increase the chances of a successful psychological development and confrontation with the unconscious, it is essential that the ego is strong[10] and has been realised with a well-rooted physical and material life. This is why JUNG states that, when it happens, the psychological development occurs with far greater frequency and safety during the second half of life[11,12].

However, once initiated, the psychological development must necessarily go through a reductive therapy. In this process, the ego will meet its neuroses, its unconscious complexes[13], which are found in the personal unconscious. The unconscious complexes are parts of the Self which could have been part of the ego complex[14], the consciousness, but for various reasons were repressed and remained unconscious. In the reductive therapy, the individual finds out that the unconscious exists, and experiences the first level of a relationship with it. They find various unconscious complexes and integrates them into the ego, the existing consciousness. The ego grows and becomes a much more complex psychological structure. The consciousness is now much more advanced.

While JUNG's vision about reductive therapy is original, the great breakthrough of Analytical Psychology is to note the existence of **archetype**[15,16,17]and the **collective unconscious**[18,19,20,21]. JUNG tells that, whilst treating a patient, at the end of the reduction therapy he believed that the patient was ready to be released from treatment. However, the unconscious continued to produce symbols that evidenced a much bigger dimension than the one present in the unconscious complexes. JUNG noticed that this bigger dimension showed the same psychological contents symbolized by the gods, goddesses, heroes and heroines present in the mythology of every culture[22]. It was evident that the gods, goddesses, heroes and heroines were being manifested through constant and timeless symbols – whichwere standardized, therefore archetypical – directly on the individual psyche of every person. These supra-human contents, or divine, are the archetypes. Together, they make up the collective unconscious.

In noticing the presence of archetypes in the human psyche, JUNG demonstrated that the nature of the psyche is fundamentally spiritual[23,24,25,26]. The archetypes are indeed divine and supra-human. They do not, however, intend to remain at an unreachable superior instance. On the contrary, the archetypes try hard to be noticed by the consciousness and, ultimately, become part of it through a progressive and infinite process. The divine archetypes want to be part of the human consciousness. The archetypes want to be **humanized**. Noticing these facts, JUNG went beyond the reductive therapy and created the synthetic therapy[27,28,29], a process by which **the gods are humanized, i.e., the archetypes can be integrated into the consciousness**[30].

However, no other finding by JUNG is more complex and impressive than the **Self**. It is true that the Self is defined as an archetype. Nonetheless, JUNG makes it very clear, throughout his work, that the Self is an archetype of a superior hierarchy in relation to the others. He calls it the central archetype, the archetype of totality[31,32], the regulating centre of the psyche[33]. The Self pre-exists the ego. Whereas the ego is defined as the **centre of consciousness**– and the consciousness is only a small part of the human psyche –, the Self is defined as the **centre of the totality of the Being**. It encompasses the whole of the collective unconsciousness, therefore all other archetypes, the personal unconsciousness, the consciousness, the ego and the physical body. The Self transcends even the limits of our individual psyches and our bodies, attracting certain relationships and repelling others, producing concrete life situations and defining the individual's destiny. Although there are countless elements composing the human psyche, the enormity of the Self is such that it is possible to understand the whole psychological development as being defined by the **relationship between the ego and the Self**[34].The Analytical Psychology is the science that studies this precious relationship and develops methods by which it can be experienced consciously and practically.

JUNG's unfathomable merit is precisely this: Analytical Psychology is a method, a reality, and it **works**.In fact, starting with a strong ego, it is **possible** to tangibly notice the existence of the personal unconscious and its unconscious complexes, confront them and **integrate** them.It is **possible** to tangibly notice the existence of the collective unconscious and the Archetypes, confront them and **integrate** them. It is **possible** to tangibly notice the existence of the Self, confront it and **integrate** it[35,36].

It is true that the unconscious, the archetypes, and especially the Self are **infinite** – a fact of unlimited **beauty**. However much we advance in the development of consciousness, the end will never be reached. However much the unconscious can be integrated and become part of the consciousness, this process never ends. However much each archetype can be integrated and become part of the consciousness, this process never ends. However much the Self can be integrated and become part of consciousness, the Self is infinite and can continue to be integrated forever[37].

Whilst it progresses in its infinite process of consciousness development, the ego grows and develops. The ego grows and develops to the point of integrating the Self. What is really impressive, to the point of being shocking, is that JUNG is correct. Analytical Psychology is correct, **the Self actually exists, and it can be integrated**. However infinite the process of integration of the Self, one cannot affirm that the integration of the Self never occurs.

All those who have dedicated themselves to the process of psychological development and built a conscious relationship with the Self reached a psychological reality which contains various paradoxes. In this reality, an idea that would normally be perceived as contrary to another – both, therefore, exclusive – starts to be perceived as paradoxically simultaneous to one another. An idea never excludes the other, but on the contrary, both are realities that compose a higher truth. That way, the fact that the process of integrating the Self is infinite **does not exclude the fact that the process of integrating the Self can be concluded. Jung is correct**, and for that reason, there is a moment when it can be affirmed: "**I have concluded the infinite process of integrating the Self**". The process of integrating the Self will continue infinitely, and **in the meantime, the conclusion of the integration of the Self opens a new phase on the psychological development.**

---

[1] JUNG, C. G. (1975) *The structure and dynamics of the psyche. On the nature of the psyche.* Chapter VIII; "The Unconscious in historical perspective". Translated by Hull, R. F. C. CW VIII/8. Bollingen Series XX. Princeton University Press.

[2] EDINGER, E. F. (2002) *Science of the soul: A Jungian perspective.* Canada: Inner City Books. Chapter 1.

[3] JUNG, C. G. (1972) *Two essays on Analytical Psychology. On the psychology of the unconscious.* Translated by Hull, R. F. C. 2nd edition. CW VII. Bollingen Series XX. Princeton University Press. §1 and §15.

[4] JUNG, C. G. (1975) *The structure and dynamics of the psyche. On psychic energy.* Translated by Hull, R. F. C. CW VIII/1. Bollingen Series XX. Princeton University Press. §35.

[5] JUNG, C. G. (1976) *Symbols of transformation. The concept of libido.* Translated by Hull, R. F. C. CW V/1. Bollingen Series XX. Princeton University Press. §194.

[6] JUNG, C. G. (1976) *Psychological types*. Appendix. Translated by Baynes, H. G. CW VI. Bollingen Series XX. Princeton University Press. §88.

[7] JUNG, C. G. *The structure and dynamics of the psyche*. Op. Cit. §93.

[8] "It is essential, in differentiating the ego from the non-ego, that a *man should be firmly rooted in his ego-function; that is, he must fulfil his duty to life, so as to be in every respect a viable member of the community*. All that he neglects in this respect falls into the unconscious and reinforces its position, so that he is in danger of being swallowed up by it. But the penalties for this are heavy." JUNG, C. G. (1972) *Two essays on Analytical Psychology. On the Psychology of the unconscious*. Translated by Hull, R. F. C. 2nd edition. CW VII Bollingen Series XX. Princeton University Press. §113.

[9] "The important fact about consciousness is that **nothing can be conscious without an ego to which it refers**. If something is not related to the ego than it is not conscious. Therefore you can define consciousness as a relation of psychic facts to the ego." JUNG, C. G. (1980) *The symbolic life*. Lecture 1. Translated by Hull, R. F. C. CW XVIII/1. Bollingen Series XX. Princeton University Press. §§18 and 19. [author's own highlights]

[10] "The self in its divinity (i.e., the archetype) is unconscious of itself. It can become conscious only within our consciousness. And it can do that only if the ego stands firm." JUNG, C. G. (1973) *Letters*, Vol. I. Edited and translated by Hull, R. F. C. Bollingen series XCV. Princeton University Press. p. 336.

[11] NEUMANN, E. (1962) *The origins and history of consciousness*, Vol II. "The Psychological Stages in the Development of the Personality". Item D "Centroversion and the Stages of life. New York: Harper Torchbooks.

[12] JUNG, C. G. (1975) *The structure and dynamics of the psyche. On psychic energy*. Translated by Hull, R. F. C. CW VII/1. Bollingen Series XX. Princeton University Press. §113.

[13] "According to Jung's definition every complex consists primarily of a "nuclear element", a vehicle of meaning, which is beyond the realm of the conscious will, unconscious and uncontrollable; and secondarily, of a number of associations connected with the nuclear element, stemming in part from innate personal disposition and in part from individual experiences conditioned by the environment. Supposing we take an image of the "paternal", of the Greek god Zeus, for example, in an individual's unconscious as such a "nuclear element". We can speak of a "father complex" in this individual only if the clash between reality and the individual's own vulnerable disposition in this respect, the clash between the particular inward and outward situation gives tis "nuclear element" a sufficiently high emotional charge to carry it out of a state of merely "potential" disturbance into one of actual disturbance. Once constellated and actualized, the complex can openly resist the intentions of the ego consciousness, shatter its unity, split off from it, and act as an "animated foreign body in the sphere of consciousness." Accordingly, Jung says: "Everyone knows nowadays that people 'have complexes'; what is not so well known [...] is that complexes can have us" [...]. JACOBI, J. (1971) *Complex/Archetypes/Symbol in the Psychology of C. G. Jung*. Chapter I "Complex". Translated by Manheim, R. Bollingen Foundation, Inc.

[14] "[Fundamental to Analytical Psychology] is the theory of complexes, which recognizes the complex nature of the unconscious and defines complexes as "living units of the unconscious psyche." It also **recognizes the complex nature of the ego, which, as the centre of consciousness, forms the central complex in the psychic system**. This

conception of the ego [...] is one of the distinctive features of analytical psychology: 'The ego complex is a content of consciousness as well as a condition of consciousness, for **a psychic element is conscious to me so far as it is related to the ego complex**. But so far as the ego is only the centre of my field of consciousness, it is not identical with the whole of my psyche, being merely one complex among other complexes." NEUMANN, E. *The origins and history of consciousness*, Vol II. Op. Cit. p. 261. [author's own highlights]

[15] JACOBI, J. (1971) *Complex/Archetypes/Symbol in the Psychology of C. G. Jung.* Chapter I: "Complex, Archetype, Symbol": "Archetype". Translated by Manheim, R. Bollingen Foundation, Inc.

[16] JUNG, C. G. (1977) *The archetypes and the collective unconscious.* Translated by Hull, R. F. C. CW IX/1. Bollingen Series XX. Princeton University Press. §5-§7.

[17] "The concept of the archetype [...] is derived from the repeated observation that, for instance, the myths and fairy tales of world literature contain definite motifs which crop up everywhere. We meet these same motifs in the fantasies, dreams, deliria, and delusions of individuals living today. These typical images and associations are what I call archetypal ideas. The more vivid they are, the more they will be coloured by particularly strong feeling tones... **They impress, influence, and fascinate us.** They have their origin in the archetype, which in itself is an irrepresentable, unconscious, pre-existent form that seems to be part of the inherited structure of the psyche and can therefore manifest itself spontaneously anywhere, at any time." JUNG, C. G. *Memories, dreams and reflexions.* Glossary. Translated by Winston, R. and C. Revised Edition. Vintage Books. (eBook) Available at: <http://www.venerabilisopus.org/en/books-samael-aun-weor-gnostic-sacred-esoteric-spiritual/pdf/200/265_jung-carl-memories-dreams-reflections.pdf> Access: April 23rd 2020. p. 473 [author's own highlights]

[18] JUNG, C. G. (1977) *The archetypes and the collective unconscious.* Translated by Hull, R. F. C. CW IX/I. Bollingen Series XX. Princeton University Press. §§88, 89, 90.

[19] JUNG, C. G. (1972) *Two essays on analytical psychology. The relations between the Ego and the unconscious.* Part I "The effects of the unconscious upon consciousness". Chapter I "The personal and the collective unconscious". Translated Hull, R. F. C. 2nd edition. CW VII/2. Bollingen Series XX. Princeton University Press.

[20] "[...] [the unconscious] includes not only *repressed* contents, but also all psychic material that lies below the threshold of consciousness. It is impossible to explain the subliminal nature of all this material on the principle of repression, for in that case the removal of repression ought to endow a person with a prodigious memory [...] We therefore affirm that in addition to the repressed material the unconscious contains all those psychic components that have fallen below the threshold, as well as subliminal sense perceptions. Moreover, we know, from abundant experience as well as for theoretical reasons, that besides this **the unconscious contains all the material that has not yet reached the threshold of consciousness. These are the seeds of future conscious contents**." Ibid. Appendix: "The structure of the unconscious". 1. "The distinction between the personal and the impersonal unconscious". [author's own highlights]

[21] JACOBI, J. (1971) *Complex/Archetypes/Symbol in the Psychology of C. G. Jung.* Translated by Manheim, R. Bollingen Series LVII. Princeton University Press.

[22] JUNG, C. G. (1980) *The symbolic life.* Translated by Hull, R. F. C. CW XVIII. Bollingen Series XX. Princeton University Press. §634.

23 "[...] that sexuality seems to us the strongest and most immediate instinct, standing out as the instinct above all others. On the other hand, I must also emphasize that the spiritual principle does not, strictly speaking, conflict with *instinct* as such but only with blind *instinctuality*, which really amounts to an unjustified preponderance of the instinctual nature over the spiritual. *The spiritual appears in the psyche also as an instinct*, indeed as a real passion, a "consuming fire," as Nietzsche once expressed it. It is not derived from any other instinct, as the psychologists of instinct would have us believe, but *is a principle sui generis, a specific and necessary form of instinctual power.* [...]" JUNG, C. G. *The structure and dynamics of the psyche. On psychic energy.* Op. Cit. §108.

24 "In a general psychological theory, however, it is impossible to use purely sexual energy, that is, one specific drive, as an explanatory concept, since psychic energy transformation is not merely a matter of *sexual dynamics.* Sexual dynamics is only one particular instance in the total field of the psyche." Ibid. §54.

25 "I am therefore of the opinion that, in general, psychic energy or libido creates the God-image by making use of archetypal patterns, and that man in consequence worships the psychic force active within him as something divine. We thus arrive at the objectionable conclusion that, from the psychological point of view, the God-image is a real but subjective phenomenon. (...)" JUNG, C. G. (1976) *Symbols of transformation. The song of the moth.* Translated by Hull, R. F. C. CW V. Bollingen Series XX. Princeton University Press. §129-§130.

26 JUNG, C. G. (1975) *Psychology and religion: West and East –A psychological approach to the dogma of the Trinity.* 4.2 "Christ as an archetype". Translated by Hull, R. F. C. 2nd edition. CW XI/2. Bollingen Series XX. Princeton University Press.

27 NEUMANN, E. (1962) *The origins and history of consciousness*, Vol II. Op. Cit. Item B "The separation of the systems" – "The synthetic function of the ego".

28 JUNG, C. G. (1985) *The practice of psychotherapy. Principles of practical psychotherapy.* Translated by Hull, R. F. C. 2nd edition. CW XVI Bollingen Series XX. Princeton University Press. §9.

29 JUNG, C. G. (1976) *Psychological types. Definitions.* Translated by Baynes, H. G. CW VI. Bollingen Series XX. Princeton University Press. §782.

30 "The achievement of a synthesis of conscious and unconscious contents, and the conscious realization of the archetype's effects upon the conscious contents, represents the climax of a concentrated spiritual and psychic effort, in so far as this is undertaken consciously and of set purpose. That is to say, the synthesis can also be prepared in advance and brought to a certain point – James' *"bursting point"* – unconsciously, whereupon it irrupts into consciousness of its own volition and confronts the latter with the formidable task of assimilating the contents that have burst in upon it, yet without damaging the viability of the two systems, i.e., of ego-consciousness on the one hand and the irrupted complex on the other. Classical examples of this process are Paul's conversion and the Trinity vision of Nicholas of Flüe." JUNG, C. G. (1975) *The structure and dynamics of the psyche. On the Nature of the Psyche* Translated by Hull, R. F. C. CW VIII. Bollingen Series XX. Princeton University Press. §413.

31 "As an empirical concept, the self designates the whole range of psychic phenomena in man. It expresses the unity of the personality as a whole. But in so far as the total personality, on account of its unconscious component, can be only in part conscious, the concept of the self is, in part, only *potentially* empirical and is to that extent a *postulate.*

In other words, it encompasses both the experienceable and the inexperienceable (or the not yet experienced). [...] In so far as psychic totality, consisting of both conscious and unconscious contents, is a postulate, it is a *transcendental* concept, for it presupposes the existence of unconscious factors on empirical grounds and thus characterizes an entity that can be described only in part but, for the other part, remains at present unknowable and illimitable. Just as conscious as well as unconscious phenomena are to be met with in practice, the self as psychic totality also has a conscious as well as an unconscious aspect. [...] Empirically, therefore, the self appears as a play of light and shadow, although conceived as a totality and unity in which the opposites are united." JUNG, C. G. (1976) *Psychological types. Definitions.* Translated by Baynes, H. G. CW VI. Bollingen Series XX. Princeton University Press. §902.

[32] JUNG, C. G. (1980) *Psychology and alchemy. Individual dream symbolism in relation to alchemy.* Translated by Hull, R. F. C. 2nd edition. CW XII. Bollingen Series XX. Princeton University Press. §44.

[33] "The Self is the ordering and unifying center of the total psyche (conscious and unconscious) just as the ego is the center of the conscious personality. Or, put in other words, the ego is the seat of *subjective* identity while the Self is the seat of *objective* identity. The Self is thus the supreme psychic authority and subordinates the ego to it. The Self is most simply described as the inner empirical deity and is identical with the *imago Dei*. [...]" EDINGER, E. F. (1992) *Ego and archetype.* Boston and London: Shambhala. p. 3.

[34] "Since there are two autonomous centers of psychic being, the relation between the two centers becomes vitally important. The ego's relation to the Self is a highly problematic one and corresponds very closely to man's relation to his Creator as depicted in religious myth. (...)" Ibid. p. 4.

[35] "Is the individual ego, both man and God, ego and Self? Jung touches on this same question in his alchemical studies. He writes: '[...] with their sun symbol they (the alchemists) were establishing an intimate connection between God and the ego.' After noting that the alchemists were dealing with unconscious projections which are natural phenomena beyond interference by the conscious mind, he then reaches the conclusion that: '[...] nature herself is expressing an identity of God and ego.' [...] Hence the implication is that the Western psyche is rooted in a myth which equates man with God, the ego with the Self." Ibid. p. 155.

[36] "In this transformation process – which not only occurs in the conscious form of the individuation process, but, through the self-regulation of the psyche, also governs the maturation of all personality – the ego reaches consciousness of the self. With the growing self-awareness of the ego, **the self evolves out of its unconscious activity and arrives at the stage of conscious activity**. NEUMANN, E. (1962) *The origins and history of consciousness*, Vol II. New York: Harper Torchbooks. p. 412. [author's own highlights]

[37] "[...] There is little hope of our ever being able to reach even approximate consciousness of the self, since however much we may make conscious there will always exist an indeterminate and indeterminable amount of unconscious material which belongs to the totality of the self. Hence **the self will always remain a supraordinate quantity**." JUNG, C. G. (1972) *Two essays on analytical psychology. The relations between the ego and the unconscious.* Translated by Hull, R. F. C. 2nd edition. CW VII. Bollingen Series XX. Princeton University Press. §274 and §275. [author's own highlights]

PSYCHOLOGICAL DIMENSIONS

In face of the complexity of the human consciousness, multiplied by the infinitude of the Self, the number of variables is infinite, and each human being is revealed as an entirely new universe, unique and unknown. For that reason, the classification of human beings in hermetic categories, or a classification determined by points in tests is always a simplistic evaluation, exercised by small systems.

Although everyone has a unique psychological composition, different from all the others, the main concern of psychology is with the phases of human development[38]. This happens not only because the interaction with a person **must** consider where they are in terms of their human development – after all, the way to interact with a child must be different from the way to interact with an adult –, but also because in many cases the psychological problems are rooted in phases of human development previous to the one they find themselves now. Amongst others, these reasons led JUNG and his school of thought to study and correlate the phases of cultural development among the various levels of social organization, on one hand, and the phases of individual development on the other[39]. For example, old matriarchal societies are studied at the same time as the first phases of the individual development, when the child is intensely related to the mother, living the maternal dynamics[40].

Amongst the vast literature that covers this topic, one of them arouses particular interest: *The Psychology of Kundalini Yoga*, a compendium of notes made from a seminar given by JUNG in 1952[41]. There, JUNG deals with the *cakras*[42] as symbols of the psychological development, the degree of psychic complexity achieved by societies and individuals. Each *cakra* symbolizes a specific psychological structure, and although this structure is of great complexity, it is entirely based on a **single, specific and**

defining paradigm of that psychological structure, which is sparked by a specific psychological event. "Each *cakra* is a whole world." [43] The structure proposed by JUNG in this work, as well as the content of this and various other works inspired the creation of a division system of the human psychological development into paradigms. The aim of this chapter is to begin presenting this system, particularly the paradigms related to the second, third and fourth *cakras*, preparing the reader for an understanding of the paradigm related to the fifth *cakra* – object of this book – in the subsequent chapters.

From this point forward, it is suggested that the reader is familiarized with the framework "Psychological Dimensions", presented in the Introduction, as it contains the necessary wording for such understanding.

However, before starting this analysis, a question needs to be resolved. Given the complexity of JUNG's thought, it is not easy for the reader of *The Psychology of Kundalini Yoga* to understand whether the encounter with the unconscious occurs in the structure defined by the second or the fourth *cakras*. Let us analyse this point first.

Considering its symbology, JUNG says that "[*Svādhiṣṭhāna*] must be the unconscious."[44] This and other affirmations lead us to infer that a consciousness structured around this centre is characterized by a direct and conscious experience of the Self. However, only later in his seminar, JUNG, talks about the fourth *cakra*, *anāhata*, and declares that in this level "you discover the Self; you begin to individuate. So, in *anāhata* individuation[45,46] begins."[47] After all, does the experience of the unconscious start when the psychological development reaches the levels of the second or the fourth *cakras*?

The word "or" is not adequate to treat the unconscious. Full of ambiguity and paradoxes, the unconscious cannot be described by a logical, dualist language, where something has a definition that excludes its contrary. Due to the totality of its nature, the unconscious naturally presents situations in which the definitions are given by coexisting contraries. The language that JUNG uses throughout his work is compatible with the nature of the unconscious, reflecting with dexterity its ambiguities and paradoxes. That way, we can interpret the *cakras* by saying that, **for those who are engaged in a process of consciousness expansion and investigation of the unconscious**, the structure of the second chakra, *svādhiṣṭhāna*, implies a conscious experience of the unconscious. We could **also** come up with an **equally valid** interpretation stating that, **for those who are not engaged in a process of consciousness expansion and investigation of the unconscious**, the structure of the second chakra, *svādhiṣṭhāna*, does imply a prominence of the unconscious, however this prominence is experienced **unconsciously**. Only within the structure of the fourth *cakra anāhata*, there is a conscious contact with the unconscious. This work uses this point of view.

Now that this question has been resolved, we can move forward to the ordered analysis of the various psychological dimensions, starting with the dimension related to the second *cakra*.

The consciousness structure of the **second** *cakra*, *svādhiṣṭhāna*, is based on the prominence of the unconscious and its basic mechanisms of identification and projection, with a preponderance of the latter. In this type of consciousness, the level of *participation mystique*[48] is extremely high and a large quantity of psychological material is projected onto others. Reflecting a matriarchal society[49], the person does not exist separately, but only as part of the clan[50]. There is no social mobility and the person is not allowed or able to freely engage in any activity considered important to his or her life: they should only perform those activities which are inherent to their roles inside the clan. For example, the tribe's witchdoctor is responsible for managing the spiritual life and heal the other people in the clan, but he does not hunt. The hunters, on the other hand, are responsible for hunting and feeding meat to all the others in the clan, but they do not interfere in the others' spiritual life. It is all about casts. The various parts of the person – caring for the spiritual life, hunting, planting, sowing, etc. – are distributed around the clan, each cast performing one of them, and each person maintains only a certain position or role. In a way, it could be said that the whole society is one person, with all its parts. We will call the psychological dimension reached in the **second** *cakra* **second dimension**, or **2D**.

Although this type of structure can seem obsolete in view of the present structures, to look at it that way would be a mistake. This structure enables the construction of societies, and ultimately, the existence of culture and civilization. Even though present societies are structured in a different way, it cannot be said that the existence of societies, cultures and civilizations is "obsolete". The rise of other psychological structures, symbolized by the next *cakras* (more cranial), does not delete structures already formed. Besides, the psychological structures which appear at each phase of the development, symbolized by more cranial *cakras*, are not better than the structures already formed, symbolised by the more caudal *cakras*. When the psychological structure is developed enough to reach the level symbolized by a more cranial *cakra*, this new level is **not better** than the previous levels, in the same way that the abdomen is **not better** than the hips. The appearance of a new level of consciousness adds

an extra dimension to the consciousness, and **modifies, without extinguishing**, the already existing levels of consciousness. The whole of the consciousness structure becomes **more complex.**

When we contemplate the psychological structure of a clan and the individuals that compose it, symbolised by *svādhiṣṭhāna*, we notice a **complexity inherent to this structure**. Indeed, the Jungian literature widely documents this complexity, analysing a large quantity of mythologies and related social rituals. For that reason, JUNG says that "Each *cakra* is a whole world"[51].

Nevertheless, this whole universe is contained in a **single** symbol, a **single** *cakra*. What does that mean? However numerous the elements of a universe, however bigger its variations and combinations, even then this universe has certain laws that will apply to all the elements, variations and combinations. The universe of situations, operations and psychological events inherent to the psychological structure symbolised by *svādhiṣṭhāna* is entirely contained in the **life in society**. The basic law that rules *svādhiṣṭhāna* is **life in society** and its final objective is the construction of a **civilization**. As we saw in the Introduction of this book, the term that refers to a basic law which defines all others is **paradigm**. Therefore, the paradigm for *svādhiṣṭhāna* is the **Paradigm of Civilization**.

Among the numerous rituals that compose the Paradigm of Civilization, one of them interests us the most: the scapegoat[52]. The main meaning of this ritual is the cyclical extermination of the **evil**, the purging of all that which is considered **alien** for that clan. The ritualistic action consists in expelling from society a human being or a goat, abandoning it in a desert or similar place. Expelling the alien element, the evil, the clan can **continue** to exist with only its **known** elements, which do not threaten the social order of the clan.

The existence of a ritual that purges evil out of society, therefore from the individuals themselves, shows that the Paradigm of Civilization includes evil and has a way of atoning it: the purging. Evil is a threat to the clan. However, the clan knows it, which makes evil **predictable**. They deal with it, which makes evil **controllable**. Even though it is a threat, evil does not relativize nor does it extrapolate the Paradigm of Civilization.

Which element, then, could provoke a strong enough leap of consciousness to extrapolate the psychological structure of *svādhiṣṭhāna* and reach the psychological structure symbolised by the third *cakra*, *maṇipūra*?

Consciousness is crime[53].

So, the question becomes: Which crime is serious enough to provoke the leap of consciousness to the next level?

The ritual of the scapegoat shows that this crime is not at all related to the practice of evil, since the evil is simply purged, and the Civilization continues to be the Paradigm.

The crime against the Paradigm of Civilization is committed when someone with a second-dimension ego (2D ego) acquires enough consciousness to recognise that they have, **inside themselves**, the ability and desire to occupy different positions to that occupied in the clan, as well as an ability and desire to perform different functions to that performed in the clan[54]. In discovering that, this person is freed from the social structure of the clan. It is not impossible anymore, not a taboo anymore, to perform the functions of other people in the clan. It is not a taboo anymore to be free from the casts and achieve social mobility. Strictly speaking, that person no longer **depends entirely** on the society. However pleasant, or even more productive, it might be to remain in society, the psychological structure of that person is no longer entirely based on the society. Having inside them the same strength of a whole society, instead of being purged, this person has committed a big enough crime to become **king**.

Life in society is no longer the basic law. The person has realised that they are the centre of their own lives, not the society. It no longer makes sense to put their personal lives behind the needs of society. On the contrary, the personal life becomes a priority which only indirectly interacts with society, and will, maybe, contribute to it.

The structure of consciousness in the **third** *cakra, maṇipūra*, is based on the prominence of the ego – **and it is at this level that the great majority of society is today**[55]. In this type of consciousness, the whole psychological dynamic is invested in the construction of a progressively stronger ego. A person with a third-dimension ego (3D ego) wants to be able to occupy various social positions and accumulate a large number of roles and abilities, in order to increase their independence. These positions, functions and abilities are psychologically associated to the ego itself; they start to become part of the conscious personality and are used as characteristics that **describe** the ego.

The unconscious moves to the second plan. Given that the ego occupies such a central position, now it is the identification with the energies of the unconscious that preponderate. An unconscious process, identification is interpreted by the consciousness as a great strength possessed by the ego. The ego does not realise that the sensation of grandiosity and strength is

47

derived from the identification with an unconscious complex or archetype. It sees grandiosity and strength as its own achievements.

In a way, the 3D ego is correct. We know that the Self is the Archetype of Totality, the central power of the psyche, and that it can, at any time, use its primacy to beat the ego and take command. Therefore, if the 3D ego can remain in control of the psyche, ignoring the unconscious and believing its own supremacy, this can only occur because, in this phase, **the Self allows the ego to ignore it**. Why does the Self do that?

The very permission for the ego to exist is already a very curious fact. At first sight, given that the unconscious includes the totality, there would be no reason to create anything **other than totality**, particularly a structure that denies, or at least does not notice, totality. However, in order to be totality, it is necessary that it also contains, within it, all parts. The ego is a part, and a very important part: the consciousness. The Self moves towards creating the only thing that itself and the unconscious "are not": the **consciousness**, the **ego**[56]. Therefore, the relationship between the Self and the Ego is essential for the psyche: the Self depends on the ego and vice versa[57]. Edward Edinger dedicates an entire book, a magnificent one, to this theme: *Ego and Archetype*[58]. Knowing that the Self dedicates so much energy to the creation of the ego, it becomes easier to understand why it allows the ego to ignore it throughout its whole development in the third dimension, *maṇipūra*'s dimension. This allows the ego to become **as strong as possible**, without worrying about the unconscious or the Self. The increased strength of the ego, which is central in the third dimension, will become even more important in the following dimensions.

The whole universe of situations, operations and psychological events inherent to the psychological structure symbolized by *maṇipūra* is totally contained in the **development of the ego**. The basic law that rules *maṇipūra* is the **development of the ego** and its final goal is the construction of **an ego capable of progressively affirming itself in relation to the unconscious, in relation to life.** Therefore, the paradigm of *maṇipūra* is the **Paradigm of Self-Affirmation**. Humanity is presently at this level of consciousness.

In this process, the contrast established by the 3D ego between itself and the unconscious is entirely based on a **dualist consciousness.** The characteristics that the ego perceives as being its own, which it attributes to itself and uses to describe itself, are defined as "**me**". These characteristics are in close relationship with the psychological content with which the ego is identified. The characteristics that the ego perceives as incompatible, contrasting or opposed to its own are defined as "**not-me**". These characteristics are projected on other people. That way, simultaneously to the construction of a **self-affirmative ego** in the third dimension, the second dimension continues to exist and functions normally through the **group of psychological characteristics** that this 3D ego **projects** on other people. The difference is that the experience of the projections in the second dimension was interpreted as 'other people who are part of the **same society** that I am', whereas the experience of projections in the third dimension is interpreted as 'other people who are **different from me'**. The contrast and the distance in relation to the other is accentuated. The three-dimensional reality is strongly **dualist**.

The result of that is a **strong ego**. The stronger the ego, the more self-affirming, the closer the individual is from concluding the consciousness structure of the third *cakra, maṇipūra.* At some point, the level of strength and self-affirmation will be enough. When that happens, which element, then, will cause a strong enough leap of consciousness to extrapolate the *maṇipūra* psychological structure and reach the psychological structure symbolized by the fourth *cakra, anāhata*?

Consciousness is crime.

Once again, the question is: Which crime is serious enough to cause a leap of consciousness to the next level?

Once again, **evil** has nothing to do with that. Evil is also **predicted** in the third dimension, and it is **controllable**. In the third dimension, evil is all that which deviates from the dominant morality in the society where one lives. More than that, once the ego is developed, based on characteristics that it sees as "good", to the point of using them to describe itself proudly, the "bad" characteristics are projected on the others. Therefore, in the third dimension, evil are the others.

Once developed, the 3D ego has become capable of resolving its problems through its own abilities. When this ability is strong enough, when the ego is strong enough, the Self, previously asleep, awakes. Nothing that the ego does, however, can "awake" the Self. Transcendental and autonomous, the Self is not determined by the ego. It was with the Self's permission that the ego could behave as the king of the psyche, ignoring the unconscious. It is also the Self that determines that the 3D ego is sufficiently developed and that it is time the ego recognises the Self.

This moment of psychological development is brilliantly described by JUNG in *Answer to Job*[59]. According to him, the Self causes a situation which is **contrary to the interests of the ego**, a situation that generates **pain**. In fact, Jehovah allows Job to be attacked by Satan with such intensity that there is no possibility of defending himself. The ego suffers an **inexorable defeat**. As the ego, throughout the whole third dimension, sought to develop itself by emphasizing characteristics that it considered good – regardless of whether or not they were aligned with the social morals in place – the ego considers itself **good**. And, **even then**, the ego is attacked by the Self and will be inexorably defeated. That's why JUNG says that the ego goes through a **moral defeat**[60].

Nothing in this situation is caused by the 3D ego. On the contrary, the ego would prefer to continue evolving and becoming even stronger. However, the Self autonomously **takes evil action against the ego**, and, as JUNG shows in *Answer to Job*, this harm is **unfair**, since it's not a consequence of moral failures committed by the person with a three-dimensional ego[61]. But, after all, why has the Self chosen to show itself through an **evil** and **unfair** act? If the Self was to act with fairness, its actions would be determined by the good behaviour of the ego, and the Self would then be determined by the ego, that is, only reacting to the ego. If the Self was to act by doing **good**, the ego, accustomed, throughout the whole development of the third dimension, to not noticing the Self, would see this goodness as one more of its own achievements, **a success of the ego**, and would continue to not notice the Self. On the other hand, the **evil and unfair** action of the Self generates a situation which the ego **cannot** solve, and the expectation of the ego that its good behaviour leads to good and fair consequences is **frustrated**. The ego starts to recognise the existence of the Self and is shocked with the perception that "God" is completely different from everything it had imagined. The image of a **good and fair** God now needs to exist simultaneously with the image of an **evil and unfair** God. God is not loyal. And, despite all the pain, a **conscious contact has been established with the Self**. "[In *anāhata*], you discover the Self." [62]

The crime against the Paradigm of Auto-affirmation is perpetrated when someone with a third-dimensional ego (3D ego) acquires enough consciousness to recognise that **God is inside oneself, being directly revealed in one's heart**; when someone has the courage to say that they are **consciously talking to God**; when someone has the courage to say that they are a **Child of God** and that **"I and The Father are ONE"** [63]. This crime is considered terrible to the point of being finally punished with the crucifixion, whether this is two thousand years ago or in the 21st century.

The life centred around a strong ego is no longer the basic law. The individual has realised that the Self is the centre of one's life, not the ego. It no longer makes sense to place one's personal life around the ego. On the contrary, the psychological life and the conscious contact with the Self are priority for the well-being of the ego or society.

The consciousness structure of the **fourth** *cakra, anāhata*, is based on the autonomy and primacy of the Self, the ego moving, against its will, to another level. "The recognition that the psyche is a self-moving thing, something genuine and not yourself, is exceedingly difficult to see and to admit."[64] In this type of consciousness, every psychological dynamic is invested in the conscious contact between the ego and the Self and the psychological restructuring that this implies. An individual with a fourth-dimension ego (4D ego) progressively **surrenders** to the Self, abdicating its egoic power more and more in view of the evident supremacy of the Self.

The unconscious reclaims its place on the first level. Differently from what happens in the second dimension, the ego establishes a **conscious relationship** with the unconscious in the fourth dimension. However, it is necessary to clarify that a "conscious relationship" does not mean that the ego knows the whole of the unconscious – a false supposition, a typical view that people from the third dimension have of the fourth-dimensional structure. Quite the contrary, a conscious relationship with the unconscious is dependent on the perception that the unconscious exists, and that it is **actually unconscious**. It will, therefore, demand an enormous and invariably increasing effort to relate to the unconscious, and ultimately, to the Self.

As if admitting to being secondary to the Self in the psyche was not sufficiently destructive for the pride inherited by the 4D ego from its three-dimensional structure, other extremely hard and painful tasks will still need to be realised. The 4D ego discovers that the personality traits that it used to describe itself and of which it was so proud, are, in their great majority, neurotic defences against unconscious complexes. These personality traits will need to be relativized, probably to a point where they will no longer matter. And even then, that's not enough. The contact with the various Archetypes will prove to the 4D ego that life and spirituality are completely different from all that it had imagined. For example, the contact with the Shadow will show that morality, so very much preached by the 3D ego as being its greatest achievement, is in fact ignorance about other aspects of life, equally valid. These aspects were previously projected onto people considered inferior or onto enemies, and now, the 4D ego realises that it is not morally superior to "inferior people" or "enemies". What was previously seen as moral integrity and superiority is now portrayed as **self-repression**.

The universe of situations, operations and psychological events inherent to the psychological structure symbolised by *anāhata* is entirely contained in the **relationship of the ego with the various Archetypes,**

and, ultimately, with the Self. The basic law that rules *anāhata* is the **relationship of the ego with the Archetypes and the Self** and its final objective is the construction of **an ego capable of equally relating to all Archetypes**, honouring all gods and goddesses, **reaching a balance among all archetypes and manifesting them in all its actions**. Therefore, the paradigm of *anāhata* is the **Paradigm of Balance**.

This long, complex and profound four-dimensional path of establishing a conscious relationship between the 4D ego and the personal unconscious, the Archetypes and the Self, was brilliantly described by JUNG and Jungian authors, and constitutes the wonder of Analytical Psychology.

The way in which this was registered seems to indicate that JUNG believed that, just as the Self is infinite, so is the work of consciousness, of the ego, of the integration of the Self. The integration of the Self extends, therefore, forever. And it is true; it really does so.

However, in the same way as **life in a 2D society** does not stop evolving with the conclusion of the Paradigm of Civilization and the appearance of a **self-affirming 3D ego**; in the same way as the **self-affirming 3D ego** does not stop evolving with the conclusion of the Paradigm of Self-Affirmation and the appearance of a **4D relationship between the ego and the Self**; the **4D relationship between the ego and the Self** does not stop evolving, does not stop deepening infinitely, with the conclusion of the Paradigm of Balance.

How then, does the Paradigm of Balance ends?

In many moments of its work JUNG analyses the symbol of the Christ as a symbol of the Self[65]. For example, Christ in the centre of a circle with the four evangelists, or the twelve apostles around him. This formation of a *mandala* shape represents totality both as unity (Christ in the centre), and as quaternity (figures in multiples of four in the surroundings).

Paradoxically, Jesus' life is often the symbol for the experience of someone who is in progressive contact with the *Self*. When Jesus says "Father, if you are willing, take this cup from me. Nevertheless, let your will be done, not mine." [66], he demonstrates that his **sacrifices of the desires of the ego** and his surrender to the archetypical reality, his **surrender to the Self**, is so complete that he is willing to do it, even if that means feeling the unsurmountable pain that is also included in the totality that is the Self.

When Jesus says "the Father and I are one"[67], he goes even further, demonstrating that there is such great harmony between him – the ego –, and the Father – the Self –, that both can be considered as a whole unit. In placing himself in unison with the Father, Jesus affirms that he has

surrendered so much that through him any aspect of the Father can be manifested, whether luminous or dark, making it clear that he is capable of maintaining the **Balance** between the various archetypical aspects.

As the Crucifixion approached, Jesus goes through a terrible process of humanization, going from a state of strong self-confidence to a state of extreme agony. From absolute proximity with the Father, in a state of unity, to a state of complete separation, which Jesus expresses pungently: "My God, my God, why have you forsaken me?"[68]. And even then, *in extremis,* he maintains the **surrender to the Self**, saying, in his final moments, "Father, into your hands I commit my spirit."[69]

With the 4D ego is conscious of the characteristics of all Archetypes, capable of manifesting them through its actions, in perfect **Balance**, without choosing between them, in complete **surrender** to the desires of the Self, the Paradigm of the Balance is completed.

However, consciousness is crime.

Another crime will be necessary, a crime serious enough to promote a leap of consciousness, catapulting the ego to the next paradigm, a penta-dimensional paradigm, the **Paradigm of Sense**. This crime involves going beyond Christ, for he said himself: "In all truth I tell you, whoever believes in me will perform the same works as I do myself, and will perform even greater works, because I am going to the Father." [70]

---

[38] LIMA FILHO, A. P. (2002) *O pai e a psique.* Chapter 1: "Os Ciclos Arquetípicos". São Paulo: Editora Paulus.

[39] "In the course of its ontogenetic development, the individual ego consciousness has pass through the same archetypal stages which determined the evolution of consciousness in the life of humanity. The individual has in his own life to follow the road that humanity trod before him [...]" NEUMANN, E. (1962) *The origins and history of consciousness*, Vol II. Translated by Hull, R. F. C. New York: Harper Torchbooks. "Introduction." p. 2.

[40] NEUMANN, E. *The origins and history of consciousness*, Vol II. Op. Cit. "Introduction." p. 2.

[41] JUNG, C. G. (1996) *The psychology of Kundalini Yoga. Notes on the seminar given in 1932.* Bollingen Series XCIX. Princeton University Press.

[42] In Portuguese this word is usually written using "ch": chakra.

[43] JUNG, C. G. *The Psychology of Kundalini Yoga.* Op. Cit. p. 13.

[44] Ibid. p. 15.

[45] "I use the term 'individuation' to denote the process by which a person becomes a psychological 'individual', that is, a separate, indivisible unity or 'whole."

"Individuation means becoming a single, homogeneous being, and, in so far as 'individuality' embraces our innermost, last, and incomparable uniqueness, it also implies becoming one's own Self. We could therefore translate individuation as 'coming to selfhood' or 'self-realization'"

"But again and again I note that the individuation process is confused with the coming of the ego into consciousness and that the ego is in consequence identified with the self, which naturally produces a hopeless conceptual muddle. Individuation is then nothing but ego-centeredness and autoeroticism. But the Self comprises infinitely more than a mere ego... It is as much one's Self, and all other Selves, as the ego. Individuation does not shut one out from the world, but gathers the world to oneself." JUNG, C. G. *Memories, Dreams and Reflexions.* Glossary. Translated by Winston, R. and C. Revised Edition. Vintage Books. (eBook) Available at: <http://www.venerabilisopus.org/en/books-samael-aun-weor-gnostic-sacred-esoteric-spiritual/pdf/200/265_jung-carl-memories-dreams-reflections.pdf> Access: December 7th 1919. p. 477.

[46] Although in *The Psychology of Kundalini* Yoga, Jung suggests that there are various dimensions in the human psyche, in his work as a whole, he does not adopt the system of various psychological dimensions. When, however, we analyse the concept of individuation of Jung, we see that he refers specifically to the process that he himself defines as regarding the fourth *cakra*. Therefore, the process of individuation occurs in the psychological dimension of the fourth *cakra*.

[47] JUNG, C. G. (1996) *The Psychology of Kundalini Yoga.* Lecture II. Bollingen Series XCIX. Princeton University Press. p. 39.

[48] "*Participation mystique* is a term derived from LÉVY-BRUHL. It denotes a peculiar kind of psychological connection with objects, and consists in the fact that the subject cannot clearly distinguish himself from the object but is bound to it by a direct relationship which amounts to partial *identity* (q.v.). This identity results from an *a priori* oneness of subject and object. *Participation mystique* is a vestige of this primitive condition. It does not apply to the whole subject-object relationship but only to certain cases where this peculiar tie occurs. It is a phenomenon that is best observed among primitives, though it is found very frequently among civilized peoples, if not with the same incidence and intensity. Among civilized peoples it usually occurs between persons, seldom between a person and a thing. In the first case it is a transference relationship, in which the object (as a rule) obtains a sort of magical – i.e. absolute – influence over the subject. In the second case there is a similar influence on the part of the thing, or else an *identification* (q.v.) with a thing or the idea of a thing." JUNG, C. G. (1976) *Psychological types.* Definitions. Translated by Baynes, H. G. CW VI. Bollingen Series XX. Princeton University Press. §781.

[49] NEUMANN, E. (2002) *The origins and history of consciousness, Vol I.* Part I "The Mythological Stages in the Evolution of Consciousness. A: "The Creation Myth". II "The Great Mother". Translated by Hull, R. F. C. London: Routledge. Kindle eBook. Available at:

<https://www.amazon.com/Origins-History-Consciousness-International-Psychology-ebook/dp/B019P2PSDM>. Access: April 26th 2020.

[50] "Woman was entrusted with the care of the captive young animals; she was the tamer of domestic beasts and the founder of cattle breeding. What is more, she domesticated the male through the taboos that she imposed on him, and so created the first human culture. In exacting the domination, curtailment, and sacrifice of the instinctual drives, the Lady of the Beasts represented more than the principle of the natural order. She was more than a protectress and breeder of beasts. Thus the formative power of the Feminine that is realized in the connection starts from the narrowest confines of the family, tribe or clan. But here it does not remain. [...]" NEUMANN, E. (1963) *The great mother — an analysis of the archetype.* Chapter 14 "The lady of the beasts". Translated by Manheim, R. Bollingen series XLVII. Princeton University Press. p. 280.

[51] JUNG, C. G. (1996) *The Psychology of Kundalini Yoga.* Lecture I. Bollingen Series XCIX. Princeton University Press. p. 13.

[52] "Today we use the term "scapegoat" easily in discussions of collective morality. We have become attuned to finding the phenomenon of scapegoating in social psychology, and there are many studies of the scapegoat pattern in small groups, in families, in ethnic and national politics. We apply the term "scapegoat" to individuals and groups who are accused of causing misfortune. This serves to relieve others, the scapegoaters, of their own responsibilities, and to strengthen the scapegoaters sense of power and righteousness." BRINTON PERERA, S. (1986). *The scapegoat complex – Toward a mythology of shadow and guilt.* "Introduction". University of Toronto Press, Canada. p. 8.

[53] "The myth depicts the birth of consciousness as a crime which alienates man from God and from his original preconscious wholeness. [...] It is the fruit of the tree of the knowledge of good and evil which means that it brings awareness of the opposites, the specific feature of consciousness. Thus according to this myth and the theological doctrines that rest on it, consciousness is the original sin, the original *hybris*, and the root cause for all evil in human nature. [...] The acquisition of consciousness is a crime, an act of *hybris* against the powers-that-be; but it is a necessary crime, leading to a necessary alienation from the natural unconscious state of wholeness." EDINGER, E. F. (1992) *Ego and archetype.* Boston: Shambhala. p. 18.

[54] "The history in Egypt enables us to trace in a unique way how the ego grows out of its original collective identity and how the Great Individual, as carrier for the projection of the collective self, paves the way for the formation of each individual ego, and initiates and assists the process. Whereas in a collective composed of incomplete individuals the god-king is the archetypal representative of the group's totality, this figure gradually develops a mediatory function, that is, it gives up more and more of its mana to the group members [...]" NEUMANN, E. (1954) *The Origins and History of Consciousness.* Vol. II. New York: Harper Torchbooks. p. 429.

[55] [...] "one must consider the fact that it is hard to talk of these things, because most people are still identical with *maṇipūra.*" JUNG, C. G. (1996) *The psychology of Kundalini Yoga.* Lecture 2. Bollingen Series XCIX. Princeton University Press. p. 36.

[56] "The Self gives birth to the ego initially – the unconscious Self gives birth to the ego – which is then the major seat of consciousness for a period of time." EDINGER, E. F. (1994) *The mystery of the coniunctio.* Canada: Inner City Books. Picture 10 "Resurrection of the United Eternal Body".

[57] "The Philosopher's Stone [...] emphasizes the crucial importance of the ego for the success of the opus, and this is one of the special features of the whole alchemical enterprise that is unique of the Western psyche. Even when the alchemists maintain that the opus will only succeed *Deo concedente*, God willing, and with an appropriate religious attitude, nevertheless there's no question that the opus will ever take place by itself; it has to have an alchemist, an ego. [...] Ibid.

[58] EDINGER, E. F. (1992) *Ego and archetype.* Boston: Shambhala.

[59] JUNG, C. G. (1975) *Psychology and religion: West and East – Answer to Job.* Translated by Hull, R. F. C. 2nd edition CW XI. Bollingen Series XX. Princeton University Press.

[60] "The self, in its efforts at self-realization, reaches out beyond the ego-personality on all sides; because of its all-encompassing nature it is brighter and darker than the ego, and accordingly confronts it with problems which it would like to avoid. Either one's moral courage fails, or one's insight, or both, until in the end fate decides... you have become the victim of a decision made over your head or in defiance of the heart. From this we can see the numinous power of the self, which can hardly be experienced in any other way. For this reason, *the experience of the self is always a defeat for the ego.*" JUNG, C. G. (1977) *Mysterium coniunctionis. The conjunction.* Translated by Hull, R. F. C. 2nd edition. CW XIV. Bollingen Series XX. Princeton University Press. §778. And still: "There are numerous descriptions of religious experiences, which typically are preceded by what St. John of the Cross called "the dark night of the soul", what Kierkegaard called "despair", and what Jung called "defeat of the ego". EDINGER, E. F. (1992) *Ego and Archetype.* Boston: Shambhala. p. 49.

[61] "The victory of the vanquished and oppressed is obvious: Job stands morally higher than Yahweh. In this respect the creature has surpassed the creator". JUNG, C. *Psychology and religion: West and East – Answer to Job.* Op. Cit. §640.

[62] JUNG, C. G. (1996) *The Psychology of Kundalini Yoga.* Bollingen Series XCIX. Princeton University Press. p. 39.

[63] "The myth of Jesus Christ is unique in its assertion of the paradoxical double aspect of Christ. He is both God and man. As Jesus he is a human being living a particular, limited, historical existence in space and time. As Christ, he is the "anointed one", the king, the Logos that has existed from the beginning beyond space and time, the eternal deity itself. Understood psychologically, this means that Christ is simultaneously a symbol for both the Self and the ideal ego." EDINGER, E. F. (1992) *Ego and archetype.* Boston: Shambhala. p. 131.

[64] JUNG, C. G. *The psychology of Kundalini Yoga.* Op. Cit. p. 54.

[65] JUNG, C. G. (1979) *Aion – researches into the phenomenology of the self.* Translated by Hull, R. F. C. 2nd edition. CW IX /2. Bollingen Series XX. Princeton University Press. §70.

[66] *The New Jerusalem Bible.* Luke 22:42

[67] Ibid., John 10:30

[68] Ibid., Mathew 27:46

[69] Ibid., Luke 23:46

[70] Ibid., John 14:12

THE PARADIGM OF SENSE

RETREAT OF THE SOUL

The Paradigm of Balance reaches its climax at the pungent symbol of Crucifixion.

Symbol of the 4D ego, Jesus took the **unification with the Father** – "The Father and I are one"[71] – to the ultimate consequences. He had numerous opportunities to abandon the path he knew to be his. Pilatus saw no crime in his actions and gave him repeated chances to defend himself. "Have you no reply at all?[72]" But Jesus remained silent, waiting for the events that would lead him to his Destiny.

The **surrender** that Jesus was capable of grew proportionally to the **brutality** of the situation. Brutal was Pilatus, knowing that he was standing before an innocent man and still washed his hands off. Brutal were the priests, who protected their positions and status, claiming to be spiritual whilst defending the torture of a truly spiritual man until death. Brutal were the people, who followed Jesus and praised him as a king just a week before they chose his death to that of Barabbas. However, above all, brutal was God[73], demanding the sacrifice of His own son, in the humiliating altar of the Cross, through torture and death. The Self commits an act of brutality against the 4D ego, demanding its total surrender to Transcendence, through psychological torture and the complete loss of its personality.

At the Cross[74], the Paradigm of Balance reaches its climax. "Father, into your hands I commit my spirit. [75]" The **surrender** is so complete to the point of becoming death[76]. The 4D ego is entirely in the hands of the Self.

The symbol is clear: there is not way out of the fourth dimension without the death of the 4D ego.

Before any confusion is established, let's make a digression. This is not about the farce of the death of the ego preached by many spiritualists and holistic people at the change of the 20th century. This refers to the death of the ego as if it was something that the individual could do himself/herself. It suggests that people should kill their egos. With that attitude, they only reveal their ignorance about Psychology, since the "individual" and the "ego" are not two separate things, which can kill one another and yet continue to exist. The belief these spiritualists and holistic people have, however, is not surprising. What they are doing is trying to understand the fourth-dimensional structure of the Paradigm of Balance in terms of the three-dimensional psychological structure of the Paradigm of Self-Affirmation; this is not possible. In 3D, it is the ego that conducts the process of psychological development, where the mistaken belief that the ego can make the decision of killing itself derives from. Besides, in 3D, God is always seen as **good**, independently of the individual's notion of good, even if this notion includes absurdities such as God being able to influence the victory of their football team, for example. Therefore, these spiritualists and holistic people attribute to God their own egoic definitions of **good**. In trying to live in a paradigm to which they have no access, they betray the three-dimensional supremacy of their egos through their hypocritical and passive-aggressive behaviours, as well as their moralism, through their childish and selfish belief in an exclusively benevolent God, a God whose good corresponds exactly to their expectations. That's the simulacrum of the ego's death.

It is not the ego that kills the ego. The Self morally defeats the ego so that it can enter the fourth dimension. The Self completely destroys the ego, kills it, so that it can leave the fourth dimension. The Self is brutal: it defeats and destroys the ego.

This needs to be clear: the fact that it is a symbol does not mean that the experience is not absolutely real. The moral defeat is shameful for the ego, and its destruction implies an unbearable psychological pain, sometimes physical pain. There are no shortcuts for the human development.

Nobody can **cause** these phenomena.

Even in the Tibetan Buddhism, where the psychological development is the sole responsibility of the individual, the emergence of the Self in the consciousness structure of *anāhata* is a miracle that transcends the ego. [It is about] "re-orientation, the new attitude, the turning away from the outside world of objects to the inner world of oneness, of completeness –

the all-embracing universality of the mind. It is a new vista, 'a direction of the heart' (as Rilke calls it), an entering into the stream of liberation. It is the only miracle which the Buddha recognized as such and besides which all other *siddhis* are merely playthings.[77]"

At the Cross, the brutality of the actions that the Self has inflicted **against** the ego became the ultimate betrayal: it reached torture. It is precisely **because** the actions of the Self are **brutal**, it is precisely **because** the actions of the Self are **against** the ego, that the **absolute power** of the Self is evident to the ego. The Self is not bound by the moralist concepts (3D) which fantasize that God is exclusively good, or by the moralist concepts (3D) which try to say what God can or cannot do. The Self is autonomous and can do whatever it wants.

It is in the face of the absolute power of the Self, manifesting itself through the brutality of the torture imposed against the ego, that the 4D ego reaches the plenitude of the Paradigm of Balance through **surrender**. If the 4D ego is capable of still surrendering to the Self, even in face of the torture and death, this means that this ego is capable of accepting any archetypical constellation the Self produces, and acting according to them. If any archetypical constellation is accepted and put into practice, the **Balance between the Archetypes was reached by the 4D ego.**

However, the unlimited brutality of the Self conceals a nefarious surprise until the last minute. "My God, my God, why have you forsaken me[78]"? Despite the unmeasurable weight of perishing through the psychological torture imposed by a balanced constellation of all the Archetypes, the Self still abandons the 4D ego: the ego will perish **without** the Presence of the Self, alone.

The Paradigm of the Sense (5D) starts precisely at the moment when the Paradigm of the Balance reaches its climax: on the pungent symbol of Crucifixion. It starts with this infamous event: the Self **abandons** the ego the at the moment it needs it the most, i.e. the *Soul retreats*. We now know, exactly where the betrayal of Judas has come from in Jesus life: from God. God is **not** loyal.

The life centred on the surrender to the Self is not the basic law anymore: God has abandoned the ego. The individual has realised that the Self will abandon them and at the most tragic moments, and they will have to act alone. It no longer makes sense to organise the personal life around the unconscious. On the contrary, **the ego will have to choose without the supervision of the Self**. The consciousness structure of the **fifth** *cakra*, *viśuddha*, is based on the **choice of the ego**, with the ego moving to the first level, against its own will.

There is a great temptation of mistaking this with the three-dimensional structure, where the ego makes the choices independently of the Self. However, the 3D ego **believes** that it makes choices. It has this infimal degree of freedom, only because the Self is dormant and only whilst it is dormant. The 3D ego does not know the unconscious and does not even suspect that most of its personality is defined by games of identification and projection. It does not notice that its "choices" are determined by its unconscious complexes, by the Archetypes and, ultimately, by the Self.

In the same way as the supremacy of the unconscious is experienced unconsciously in the second dimension, and consciously in the fourth dimension, the choices of the ego are experienced unconsciously in the third dimension and consciously in the fifth dimension. The situation of the 5D ego is completely different. This ego already lives in society, has already built a life in the physical world through the development of its aptitudes, has already become a strong ego, has already been morally defeated by the Self, has already been possessed by various unconscious complexes which confronted it with identifications and projections. It has lost its personality traits by removing its repressions and prejudices, it has strongly relativized the loyalty of its friends and it has reconciled with its enemies, it has already got in touch with the Archetypes and was forced to recognise that there are transcendental powers capable of directing it. It has integrated the Archetypes that led it to have benevolent actions and be divinized by people, it has integrated Archetypes that led it to have very evil actions and be demonized by people. It has made contact with the Self and become one. It has had the courage to walk in the direction of death to fulfil the desire of the Self. And, above all, it has been abandoned by the Self in its most fragile moment...

Nobody escapes unscathed from such experiences. The 5D ego is not making choices because it has suddenly forgotten who has the primacy: the Self. The 5D ego is making choices because the one who had the primacy has simply abandoned it.

It is important to remember that the new-born 5D ego has just left a huge period of fourth-dimensional development, where the Self has guided him through dreams, through the perception of identifications and projections, synchronicities or even transcendental experiences, such as visions. The 5D ego is **used to being guided by the Self** in all circumstances; it was trained for that. However awkward has the moral defeat been, however dark have the paths been, however brutal has the crucifixion been, the Self was always present, guiding, in such a way that these experiences had **meaning**[79,80] and were, therefore, **bearable**.

Now, in the most tragic moment of life – the collapse of the structure of the ego – the Self has abandoned it. The 5D ego is no longer guided. If we are coherent with Analytical Psychology, we need to admit that, without the presence of the Self and its symbols, the experience has lost meaning and becomes immediately **unbearable**. The fourth dimension, with its terrible darkness, still relied on the presence of God and its meaning. However bad the directions determined by the Self, the 4D ego had (almost) certainty that it had to follow it, surrendering to the Self. Now, in the fifth dimension, the 5D ego waits for the guidance of the Self, it waits for it desperately, but it never comes. The 5D ego needs to deal with the void left by the abandonment of the Self. In this scenario, the first thing it can do is die, murdered by the Self.

The universe of situations, operations and psychological events inherent to the psychological structure symbolised by *viśuddha* is entirely contained in the **abandonment of the Self,** in the *Retreat of the Soul*. The basic law that governs *viśuddha* is the **creative action of the ego** and its final objective is the construction of a **personal sense**. Therefore, the paradigm of *viśuddha* is the **Paradigm of the Sense**.

---

[71] *The New Jerusalem Bible*. John 10:30.

[72] Ibid. Mark 15:4

[73] "But, to his horror, he has discovered that Yahweh is not human but, in certain respects, less than human, that he is just what Yahweh himself says of Leviathan (the crocodile): 'He beholds everything that is high /He is king over all proud beasts.' This symbolism explains Yahweh's behaviour, which, from the human point of view, is so intolerable: it is the behaviour of an unconscious being who cannot be judged morally. Yahweh is a *phenomenon* and, as Job says, "not a man." JUNG, C. G. (1975) *Psychology and religion: West and East – Answer to Job* Translated by Hull, R. F. C. 2nd edition. CW XI. Bollingen Series XX. Princeton University Press §599 and §600.

[74] "Psychologically understood, the cross can be seen as Christ's destiny, his unique life pattern to be fulfilled. To take up one's own cross would mean to accept and consciously realize one's own particular pattern of wholeness. The attempt to imitate Christ literally and specifically is a concretistic mistake in the understanding of a symbol. Seen symbolically, Christ's life will be a paradigm to be understood in the context of one's own unique reality and not as something to be slavishly imitated. JUNG has spoken clearly on this subject: 'It is no easy matter to live a life that is modelled on Christ's, but it is

unspeakably harder to live one's own life, as truly Christ lived his." EDINGER, E. F. (1992) *Ego and Archetype*. Boston: Shambhala. p. 135.

[75] *The New Jerusalem Bible*. Luke 23:46.

[76] "The drama of the crucifixion and the events leading up to it are a profound expression of the ultimate aspects of individuation. Individual experiences of scorn, disgrace and rejection take on meaning and majesty when related to their archetypal paradigm. Exemplary also is Christ's attitude in the Garden of Gethsemane: 'My Father, if it is possible, let this cup pass from me; not as I will, but as thou wilt.' (Luke 22:42). This is the classic statement of the ego attitude needed in the face of an individuation crisis. And with such an attitude, support from the archetypal psyche is usually forthcoming. Likewise, the experience of betrayal which has its ultimate agonized expression in the words: 'My God, my God, why hast thou forsaken me?' (Matthew 27:46) is a characteristic feature of crucial phases of individuation. At such times the ego feels utterly deprived of comfort and support, both from within and from without. Trust, based on projections and unconscious assumptions, is abruptly terminated. This state is a transition period. It is the limbo despair following the death of an old life orientation and preceding the birth of a new one. [...] The crucifixion was the culmination of Jesus' earthly life. In the course of being crucified, Jesus as ego and Christ as Self merge." EDINGER, E. F. *Ego and archetype*. Op. Cit. p. 149.

[77] GOVINDA, A. (1975) *Foundations of Tibetan mysticism*. New York: Samuel Weiser. p. 75.

[78] *The New Jerusalem Bible*. Matthew 27:46.

[79] "The least of things with a meaning is worth more than the greatest things without it." JUNG, C. G. (1933) *Modern man in search of a soul*. London: Kegan Paul, Trench, Trubner & Co LTD. p. 75.

[80] "The only thing that we cannot under any circumstances tolerate is the **lack of meaning**. Everything, even death and destruction, can be faced as long as it has meaning. Even in the midst of abundance and fullness, the lack of a sense of inner meaning is unbearable. In Jung's terms: "Common sense, firm human judgment, science as a compendium of common sense, all of this certainly helps us to travel a good part of the road, but it never takes us beyond the frontier of the most common realities of life, beyond what is merely everyday and normal. There is no answer to the question of psychological suffering and its profound **meaning**. A psychoneurosis must ultimately be considered as the suffering of a soul that has not discovered its **meaning**. But all creativity in the realm of the Spirit, as well as all psychic progress of man, arises from the suffering of the soul and the cause of suffering is spiritual stagnation or psychic sterility." WHITMONT, Edward C. (1969). *The symbolic quest*. Princeton University Press. New Jersey. P.74 [author's own highlights]

PARADOX

The psychological structures symbolised by the cakras *svādhiṣṭhāna* and *maṇipūra* are essentially **dualist**[81], that is, based on contrast. They separate the reality in two parts which are opposed to each other. Given that the level of psychological development of humanity only reaches, at most, the third dimension, the dualistic perspective is hegemonic.

On the Paradigm of Civilization, duality is manifested directly on the social structure. The social classes differ amongst themselves, and for that reason, they **separate**. Even though the prominence of the unconscious in the second dimension provides cohesion in society, this cohesion is enabled through difference. Someone with two dimensions only considers as socially valid a social class that is different from theirs if they do not have to be part of it. Other social classes should be composed by other people. The hunter admits that there are priests and even admires them, as long as he can continue to be a hunter and does not have to be the priest.

On the Paradigm of Self-Affirmation, the duality has reached its climax. The unconscious is no longer prominent, and social cohesion drastically decreases. To affirm itself, the ego greatly relies on the possibility of **denying** the different. Almost everything that exists in the world is perceived through dualist parameters, which are manifested from small daily situations to universal ones.

In the huge effort that the ego makes to define itself, the difference in relation to the other becomes fundamental. The conversations between people, for example, are entirely based on the comparison between them. If someone says, 'I like classical music', the other person will automatically respond with 'Well, I prefer pop'. In this hypothetical discussion, there is no intention to explore the other's point of view, to go deeper, to visit the alternative universe that is the other. For instance, continuing with the example of the classical music, nobody will ask why or what in the music is attractive, which are the styles or preferred periods of the classical music, which are the favourite composers and why, which sensations the other person experiences when listening to classical music, which are the reasons why a large part of the population does not listen to classical music, and an infinity of other questions that could be asked and discussed.

Instead of embracing a greater development, and the alternative universes that make up the conversation partner and classical music are simply **ignored**, and the only answer that comes to mind has **nothing to do** with classic music, or the topic of the conversation, but is simply concerned with establishing a contrast: the preference for pop music. A careful analysis of the great majority of conversations will show that people don't understand what others are saying because they don't think about what was said; they are not even paying attention to one another. The aim of the conversation is not to understand the other, but, if anything, to counter argue, since in most cases the aim is to just disagree, create the contrast, even if the reason for that is not clear, since whatever the other person has said has not been understood or even heard. If anyone presents an idea with any degree of complexity, the listener is often not even able to repeat what has been said, because whilst they were poising externally as though they were listening, internally they were busy formulating their disagreement. The ego affirms itself by using the difference from the other as a reference.

In the dualist conscious structure, it is not enough to establish a difference between people and things. It adds to it a **value judgement**. One person is necessarily **better** than the other, immediately implying that the other person is **worse**. This creates a series of partialities, and markedly its saddest consequence: prejudice. A difference in the skin colour is enough for white people to feel superior to black people. The reaction of black people is often a retaliation; for example, some black Americans refer to what they call "white trash".

Within the same ethnic background, men are not ashamed of their own chauvinism and treat women as though they are somehow inferior, often as people who should obey them or as their possession. It is extremely odd to observe a man affirming their heterosexuality and love for a woman but reacting with horror to the idea of being a woman. The idea of something being "good", as long as it's not me, predominates. Still in the sexual context, just as odd as chauvinism is homophobia, as are many other gender conflicts, as if the sexual preferences of the other were somehow relevant.

The list of prejudices against social classes is long. There are prejudices against those who did not go to college, even though it is accepted that the educational system has failed. On the same line, there are prejudices against those who are operational. It is relatively normal to boss the lower level staff around or even mistreat them. As it is clear, the Paradigm of Civilization keeps its sovereignty, despite having been overcome by the Paradigm of Self-Affirmation.

But it is in religion that duality becomes cruel. As dualist as any other organization, religion maximizes the value judgement, deifying people from the same creed and demonizing those from others. Akhenaton[82] considered himself enlightened by a superior spirituality, a **single** god, perhaps the first monotheism of humanity, and felt entitled to impose this view on the age-old culture of ancient Egypt, establishing a strong conflict with the priestly caste, only for it all to fall apart after his death. The Jews treated those adepts of other religions as inferior, worshipers of "false" gods, the idols, and believed that the '**only** true god', coincidently the god of Israel, would give them power to conquer other nations. Christianity has not learned anything with the persecution that it endured in the first centuries, and as soon as it became established, it fiercely persecuted "heresy", sent crusades against the Arabs and created the 'Holy' Inquisition. Some Muslims act in the same way.

Modern religions, such as science, capitalism and socialism also fiercely fight to exterminate heretics. Science fights to stop new discoveries from relativizing the status quo, sometimes making a fool of themselves: in 2012, after spending years and years affirming that acupuncture was fraudulent, doctors lobbied to keep a market reserve for the practice. Capitalism and socialism in turn, also created a holy war: The Cold War.

Why, however, is duality so powerful in the human psyche? Why is it so strong in the second and third dimensions? Despite its increasing exaggeration leading to the conclusion that duality is negative, it has an extremely important function: it creates opportunity for creation and development of the ego.

The unconscious includes the totality of the human characteristics. Even if two things are opposed and mutually exclusive, both are present in the unconscious[83,84]. We all have inside ourselves goodness and evil, masculinity and femininity, wisdom and naivety, etc. In an extremely simplistic way, it can be said that, without duality, without the capacity to **oppose** to the unconscious, the ego would be incapable of establishing a defined personality, which has some characteristics but not **others**. If all human beings were to manifest all the characteristics present in the unconscious, they would all have the exact same personality and humanity would reach a monotonous homogeneity.

Evidently, it is much more complex than that. Magnificent works such as *The Origins and History of Consciousness*, by Erich NEUMANN[85], describe each step of the formation of consciousness. It is the very all-encompassing unity[86] of the Self that initiates duality, creating the ego[87] and **separating it** from the unconscious, so that the consciousness can exist. From this moment, the unconscious promotes various other mechanisms that, in many phases of the psychological development, progressively increase this separation, all described by NEUMANN. One of these mechanisms is of special interest in the later stages of the present work: the Incest Archetype, described by Robert STEIN in *Incest and human love*[88], which, with its desire for incest being simultaneous to the natural taboo against incest, instils in the individual the progressive increase of its consciousness[89].

In summary, duality allows the ego to structure its consciousness into an **me** and **not-me**, into characteristics used to describe its own personality and reality itself, as well as into characteristics used to describe others and their reality, subtly (or not so subtly) considered inadequate. Duality is necessary for the ego to **be able to** maintain itself separate from the unconscious, strongly resisting to melt into it. As egos who have developed up until the third dimension are incapable of directly noticing the existence of the unconscious, they can only project it onto others, that way managing to keep separate from "the others" and strongly resisting to "others".

This is the level of development of society, which involves anything from fanatic and intolerant cultures **with their differences,** until extremely tolerant cultures also **with differences**: outdated tri-dimensional cultures and advanced tri-dimensional cultures, but nevertheless tri-dimensional and dualist.

The moral defeat imposed by the Self on the ego at the beginning of the fourth dimension, symbolized by the fourth *cakra, anāhata,* which opens the Paradigm of Balance, is a devastating quake for the dualist consciousness. Since this event only occurs to self-affirmative, strong and developed egos, which are successful in the third-dimensional structure, the moral defeat occurs in an extremely dualist scenario, where the personality is firmly established. The strength of the ego at this point is so intense that it believes to be capable of solving any psychological problems that appear. For that reason, JUNG affirmed that the ego can only acknowledge the existence of the Self after exhausting every attempt to solve a certain problem created by the Self[90]. Only when the ego sees itself **defeated** by the problem, it is ready to recognize the Self and seek therapy[91]. However powerful the ego is at that point, its power is scanty when compared to the power of the Self.

As the Archetype of Totality, the Self will confront the ego with various complexes existent in the personal unconscious. Someone who has as the central characteristic of its ego the desire for peace, will be forced to realise that it has been denying its aggression. Considering aggression as an inferior quality, maybe even a negative one, every time that this person has had to fight for its points of view, its objectives or for loved ones, they let the other's point of view, often unfair, to dominate. Claiming the defence of peace, they have given up on their objectives and hurt loved ones. Levels of output tend to appear, generally through passive-aggressive behaviour.

Someone with a central characteristic of its ego being chastity will be forced to realise that it has been denying its sexuality. Considering sexuality as something inferior, perhaps even sinful, that person represses its sexuality only to realise it only becomes stronger, that its desire and fantasizing increase. Levels of output tend to appear, some of them quite serious: it is not a coincidence that cases of child sexual abuse perpetrated by the "chaste" Catholic clergy have come to the public knowledge.

The simple emergence of unconscious psychological content, such as repressed aggressiveness and sexuality explained above, strongly relativizes the duality of the ego. It is **no longer possible** to attribute some characteristics to 'me' and the opposite characteristics to 'not-me'. It becomes clear that **all the characteristics**, however unconscious or evil they might be, are part of 'me'. It is no longer possible to believe that someone is a pacifist **or** aggressive, chaste **or** sexual – this perspective is third-dimensional. A fourth-dimensional consciousness is pacifist **and** aggressive, chaste **and** sexual.

The psychological transformation is so strong that it even changes the functional structure of the consciousness. In *Psychological Types*[92], JUNG demonstrated that the human being can be introvert and extrovert, and, besides that, can have one or two of four functions more developed: thinking, feeling, intuition or sensation. In view of the appearance of the Self and the development of the ego in the fourth dimension, an introvert can develop an extrovert structure, as well as a thinking type can develop to the point of becoming simultaneously a feeling type.

As the fourth-dimensional development progresses to even more advanced phases, overcoming the personal unconscious, the Self will confront the ego with the Archetypes. A simple study of Greek mythology with the twelve Olympic gods shows how incompatible they are. The truth of Ζεύς (Zeus) is incompatible with the half-truth of Έρμῆς (Hermes). The strategy of Ἀθηνᾶ (Athena) is incompatible with the immediate action of Ἄρης (Ares). The chastity of Ἑστία (Hestia) is incompatible with the beauty and sexuality of Ἀφροδίτη (Aphrodite). The protective father Ζεύς (Zeus) is incompatible with the destructive and mortal Ἅιδης (Hades). The perfection and clarity of Ἀπόλλων (Apollo) are incompatible with the ambiguity of Ποσειδῶν (Poseidon) and its taste for monstrosity. However, in four dimensions there is no incompatibility. As the ego synthetises each Archetype into its consciousness, the various Archetypes, before incompatible, now reach **Balance**, are humanized, and can express themselves through human consciousness. The ego stops defending a dualist personality, which accepts certain psychological energies and rejects others (3D ego). It starts to experience a sort of acknowledged duality, where there is space for truths and half-truths, chastity and sexuality, strategy and immediate action (4D ego).

But even this structure, the acknowledged duality, is still a simplistic formulation of the fourth-dimensional psychological structure. However more advanced is a consciousness capable of alternately manifesting personality characteristics which are opposed to each other (one characteristic once, an opposite characteristic another time), in comparison to a consciousness which is only capable of manifesting some of them (one characteristic but **never** the opposed one), the **alternate** manifestation of characteristics is still very dualist.

At some point of the ego's development, the Self will promote a direct confrontation between itself and the 4D ego. What occurred progressively throughout the whole fourth-dimensional development becomes now evident: the Self is a *coniunctio oppositorum*[93,94,95], a conjunction of opposites, and only through living this seventh alchemic operation[96] it is possible to integrate it. It is a **conjunction** of opposites, not an **alternation** of opposites.

There is no way of understanding this without considering one of the most important insights of JUNG: the **transcendent function**.

The logical reality of the third dimension assumes that, if someone is unaware of something, they can use their consciousness, in particular the thinking function of the consciousness, to learn this thing. This is valid for theories – in fact, the *Theory* is the first phase of the alchemic process of consciousness development[97]. But its validity stops there. Integrating an unconscious content into the consciousness is totally different from what is normally called "learning". The psychological reality of the fourth dimension assumes that, if someone is unconscious of something and this unconscious content constellates (is activated), it is necessary to apply consciousness in order to create a **tension** between a conscious and an unconscious content which is pressing. The tension is established, preventing the unconscious content to "leak", whether through behaviours resulting from identification or behaviours resulting from projection of this content. Prevented from "leaking", the energy of the unconscious content accumulates and its value increases. The effort made by the ego to prevent this unconscious content to "leak" increases proportionally. When this tension reaches a threshold established by the Self, the **transcendent function**[98] acts. As a result of this action, both previous elements **disappear** – the conscious and the unconscious element – and a **third element appears, transcendent, unpredictable**. This third element is a **paradox**.

Since most people tend to interpret a paradox from a third-dimensional perspective, and that even the first phases of the fourth dimension are insufficient for its correct apprehension, it is first necessary to define what **is not** a paradox.

A paradox is not a **false proposition**.

A paradox is not an opinion opposed to common sense; this is just an **unpopular opinion**.

A paradox is not a declaration or attitude contrary to what has been said or adopted previously; this is a **contradiction** or even an **incoherence**.

A paradox is not a lack of nexus or logic; this is just a **low quality logical formulation**.

A paradox, above all, is not something that admits various senses and generates doubts and confusion; this is **ambiguity**.

All these are 3D definitions of paradox.

From a 4D perspective, **a paradox is the simultaneous co-existence of two valid and opposed truths**. Even if this definition can be defined in logical terms, rationally, especially mathematically (as in a square root equation that simultaneously produces two valid and opposed results), the psychological experience and the understanding of this, and above all the ability to **act paradoxically,** only occurs when the Paradigm of Balance is about to conclude, expressing itself through the seventh alchemic operation, *coniunctio*, in intimacy with the Self.

Therefore, a conscious paradoxical action is not good, and then evil. A conscious paradoxical action is simultaneously good **and** evil. A conscious paradoxical action transcends the good-evil: it is amoral. For example, a 4D ego who employs a conscious paradoxical action, when talking to a friend about a problematic situation in their lives, being extremely frank and harsh, will cause on their friend a paradoxical sensation. The friend will feel strongly impacted by the reality exposed by the conversation and even hurt by its extreme harshness to the point of feeling a **deep hatred**. However, they will also **simultaneously** feel cared for by the impact of that reality exposed by the conversation, as well as attacked by its extreme harshness to the point of feeling a **deep love**. This is because the consciousness of an advanced 4D ego embraces good and evil, and their friend, **for the same reasons**, **simultaneously** experiences **opposite** sensations and reactions.

In the same way, a conscious paradoxical action is not masculine, and then feminine. A conscious paradoxical action is simultaneously masculine and feminine. A conscious paradoxical action transcends the masculine-feminine: it is androgynous. For example, a 4D ego that employs a conscious paradoxical action, when exposing a point of view in which it strongly believes during a discussion, will cause a paradoxical sensation on its listener, who will feel strongly impacted by the male ardour and individuality with which the point of view is defended to the point of becoming silent. Simultaneously its listener will feel strongly impacted by the openness and disposition for feminine relationships of the 4D ego with which they are called out to disagree, to the point of defending their own point of view. An authentically 4D ego does not admit that its points of view are ignored, and equally does not admit to winning the discussion, but it calls their listener out to fight for their own point of view. An authentically 4D ego does not want their point of view to be victorious neither do they want their listener to be victorious; they are willing to fight for their point of view (masculine) and relate to the other's point of view (feminine), until there is a transcendental point of view (androgynous).

For example, a 4D ego that employs a conscious paradoxical action, in exposing a point of view in which it strongly believes during a discussion, will cause a paradoxical sensation on his listener. This person will feel strongly impacted by the masculine firmness and individuality with which the point of view is defended, to the point of being **lost for words**. And **simultaneously**, this person will feel strongly impacted by the female receptivity and wiliness with which they are called to disagree, to the point of **defending their point of view**.

However, if a paradox and a conscious paradoxical action are the highest level of the fourth dimension, the apogee of the Paradigm of Balance, they are also the lowest level of the fifth dimension, the beginning of the Paradigm of Sense. In 5D, the paradox is the norm.

From a 5D perspective, a paradox is a **conscious Spiritual *Truth*** (= *Pneumatic*[99]), **which transcends any polarity**. The fifth dimension is **not** dual, it is **unified**.

The 5D ego has zero concern or need for its action to be good or evil, male or female or any other polarity: the meaning of the word "or" in 5D is totally different, and in no way implies division, opposition or polarity. Therefore, there is no duality, nor acknowledged duality, not even a conjunction of opposites: the transcendent function has **already fulfilled** its role.

What is important to understand is that the perception of reality is directly determined by the perception one has of himself. It is perfectly known that one cannot see outside oneself that which does not exist inside. **The 5D ego no longer defines itself in terms of characteristics**. The 3D ego is concerned with developing and strengthening those characteristics in itself that are admired, as well as in denying those considered damaging, not understood or not acknowledged. The 4D ego is concerned with transcending the personal characteristics that have been developed and strengthened, as well as those which, in the unconscious, complement and compensate them. The 5D ego has already done it all. For that reason, the 5D ego has whichever characteristics it wants and chooses. **The 5D ego is free to desire and choose whatever it wants**. For this reason, sometimes it chooses a conscious action where good prevails; but it knows that evil is as present in the action as good. Other times, it chooses a conscious action where evil will prevail; but it knows that good is as present in the action as evil.

Despite the fact that any sentence can be constructed for any polarity, the expression of these ideas in terms of good and evil has the advantage of allowing to mention, for the first time, that a 5D ego is beyond morals (3D), therefore beyond good and evil, as well as beyond ethics[100] (4D), therefore beyond the need to evaluate its actions in terms of being in harmony with the Soul (positivity) or in disharmony with the Soul (negativity). The criteria in the fifth dimension is different. As it is beyond moral, people will consider the action of a 5D ego as paradoxically moral and immoral at the same time. As it is beyond ethics, people will consider the actions of a 5D ego as paradoxically ethical and unethical at the same time, or even as angelical and demoniac at the same time.

As the 5D ego is not determined nor can it be defined by any characteristic or its opposite, nor by the simultaneity of these opposites or the transcendence of these opposites, being therefore beyond morals and ethics;

As the 5D ego acknowledges others and reality exactly as it acknowledges itself – not defined by any characteristic nor its opposites or simultaneity of these opposites, or even the transcendence of these opposites, therefore beyond morals and ethics;

As the 5D ego was abandoned by the Self during its Crucifixion; as the Soul has retreated and will not offer any guidance;

As the 5D ego lives in the Spiritual *Truth* – which transcends the multi-paradoxical archetypical reality of the Paradigm of Balance, where all the Archetypes, including the Self, were placed in balance and are integrated and **available for use**;

Then there is no pre-defined direction to follow and the 5D ego realises that it can **freely choose** how to live or what to do.

At precisely this moment, the colossal weight of freedom is felt and with it comes the realisation of the abyss it is in.

---

[81] "Duality, dissociation and repression have been born in the human psyche simultaneously with the birth of consciousness. This means simply that consciousness in order to exist in its own right must, initially at least, be antagonistic to the unconscious. This insight teaches us that all utopian psychological theories which assume that he human personality can be whole and healthy if only it is not subject to sexual and instinctual repressions in childhood are wrong. The innate and necessary stages of psychic development require a polarization of the opposites, conscious versus unconscious, spirit versus nature." EDINGER, E. F. (1992) *Ego and Archetype*. Boston: Shambhala. p. 20.

[82] Akhenaton was the pharaoh of the XVIII Dynasty of Egypt. He adopted this name in the fifth years of his ruling. Before that he was known as Amenhotep IV. He abandoned the traditional Egyptian polytheism and introduced the adoration to a single god, Aton, the god of sun.

[83] "[...] in the process of creating consciousness we shall at first be thrown back and forth between opposing moods and attitudes. Each time the ego identifies with one side of a pair of opposites the unconscious will confront one with its contrary. Gradually, the individual becomes able to experience opposite viewpoints simultaneously." EDINGER, E. F. (1984) *The creation of consciousness.* Chapter 1: "The new myth" Canada: Inner City Books. p. 18

[84] "[...] But the collective unconscious is not made up of individual experience; it is an inner correspondence to the world as a whole. What is overlooked is that the collective unconscious is of an entirely different nature, comprising all the contents of the psychic experience of mankind, the most precious along with the most worthless, the most beautiful with the ugliest; and it is also overlooked that the collective unconscious is in every respect "neutral", that its contents acquire their value and position only through confrontation with consciousness". JACOBI, J. (1971) *Complex/Archetypes/Symbol in the psychology of C. G. Jung.* Translated by Manheim, R. Bollingen Foundation, Inc. p. 60.

[85] NEUMANN, E. (1962) *The origins and history of consciousness*, Vol II. Translated by Hull, R. F. C. New York: Harper Torchbooks.

[86] "In the beginning is perfection, wholeness. This original perfection can only be "circumscribed" or described symbolically; its nature defies any description other than a mythical one, because that which describes, the ego, and that which is described, the beginning, which is prior to any ego, prove to be incommensurable quantities as soon as the ego tries to grasp its object conceptually, as a content of consciousness" NEUMANN, E. (2002) *The origins and history of consciousness, Vol I.* Part I "The Mythological Stages in the Evolution of Consciousness". "The Creation Myth". Chapter 1 "The Uroboros". Translated by Hull, R. F. C. London: Routledge. Kindle eBook. Available at:

<https://www.amazon.com/Origins-History-Consciousness-International-Psychology-ebook/dp/B019P2PSDM> Access: April 2020.

[87] [...] [the] "Self, the central source of life energy, the foundation of our being [...] NEUMANN, on the basis of mythological and ethnographical material, has depicted symbolically the original psychic state prior to the birth of ego consciousness as the *uroborus*, using the circular image of the tail-eater to represent the primordial Self, the original mandala-state of totality out of which the individual ego is born. FORDHAM, on the basis of clinical observations of infants and children, has also postulated the Self as the original totality prior to the ego." EDINGER, E. F. (1992) *Ego and archetype.* Boston: Shambhala. p. 4.

[88] STEIN, R. (1973) *Incest and human love.* Dallas, TX: Spring Publications.

[89] "The process of advancing from childhood to adulthood involves a gradual internalization of hierogamous images. The incest taboo and other rituals related to the mysteries of sexuality are fundamental to this process. [...] Although restrictions on the spontaneous manifestation of sexual desires and human development seem to go hand in hand, they are also responsible for throwing man into a state of conflict between his spiritual and animal-sensual natures. [...] **The limitations that the man imposed on his sexual instinct made it impossible for him to be completely free, sensual and physically, in his relationship with others. However, in the ever-expanding world of your imagination that is thus open, your spirit has unlimited freedom**. There is nothing to stop his imagination from doing anything or going anywhere he wants. He is free to transgress any sexual taboo and reconcile the conflict between his mind and his body. He can return again and again to his paradisiacal state of wholeness, before his spiritual and animal natures have been separated." STEIN, R. (1973) *Incest and Human Love.* "Incest and Wholeness". Los Angeles: Third Press. p. 38. [author's own highlights]

[90] "Let us return to conflict where it reaches the climax. There is a state of suspension where everything is stalled, the ego oscillates between Yes and No and there is the torture of a stagnated and sterile life. At this point the ego surrenders, stating that the conflict is unsolvable – a conflict that it cannot resolve – and that it will submit to

something objective, to a sign that becomes evident. We say that we will submit to what the dreams say." von FRANZ, M. L. *Shadow and evil in fairy tales*. [Translated from the Portuguese version: (1985) *A Sombra e o Mal nos Contos de Fada*. São Paulo: Editoras Paulinas. p.80]

[91] "Generally speaking the ego is a hard-and-fast complex which, because tied to consciousness and its continuity, cannot easily be altered, and should not be altered unless one wants to bring on pathological disturbances. The closest analogies to an alteration of the ego are to be found in the field of psychopathology, where we meet not only with neurotic dissociations but also with the schizophrenic fragmentation, or even dissolution, of the ego. [...] But if the structure of the ego-complex is strong enough to withstand their assault without having its framework fatally dislocated, then assimilation can take place. In that event there is an alteration of the ego as well as of the unconscious contents. Although it is able to preserve its structure, **the ego is ousted from its central and dominating position** and thus finds itself in the role of a passive observer who lacks the power to assert his will under all circumstances [...] This experience **paralyzes an over-egocentric will and convinces the ego that in spite of all difficulties it is better to be taken down a peg** than to get involved in a hopeless struggle in which one is invariably handed the dirty end of the stick. In this way the will, as disposable energy, gradually subordinates itself to the stronger factor, namely to the new totality figure I call the *self.* JUNG, C. G. (1975) *The structure and dynamics of the psyche. On the nature of the psyche.* Translated by Hull, R. F. C. CW VIII/2. Bollingen Series XX. Princeton University Press. §430. [author's own highlights]

[92] JUNG, C. G. (1976) *Psychological types*. Translated by Baynes, H. G. CW VI. Bollingen Series XX. Princeton University Press.

[93] "The coniunctio, and the process that creates it, I consider to represent the creation of consciousness, which is na enduring psychic substance **created by the union of opposites**." EDINGER, E. F. (1994) *The mystery of the coniunctio. Introduction to Jung's Mysterium Coniunctionis* Canada: Inner City Books. Page 35. [author's own highlights]

[94] "The common formulation says that the Self unites and reconciles the opposites. However [...] as it is implicit throughout the whole of alchemy, [...] the ego promotes the union of the opposites and that way creates the Self or, at least, causes it to manifest. This accentuates the supreme importance of the conscious ego. It must unite the opposites, which is no easy task. **To sustain the opposites is equivalent to simultaneously experience a paralysis that reaches the depths of a real crucifixion**." EDINGER, E. F. *Anatomy of the psyche: alchemical symbolism in psychotherapy.* [Translated from the Portuguese version: (2008) *Anatomia da psique*. São Paulo: Cultrix. p. 234.] [author's own highlights]

[95] JUNG, C. G. (1977) *Mysterium coniunctionis*. Part VI. "The conjunction". Translated by Hull, R. F. C. 2nd edition. CW XIV. Bollingen Series XX. Princeton University Press.

[96] Edward EDINGER. (1991) *Anatomy of the psyche: Alchemical symbolism in psychotherapy*. Open Court Publishing Company.

[97] "[...] Other alchemical texts did discuss the means by which the fish without bones might be snared. According to some texts, the magnet of the wise catches the fish, and Jung explains that this symbol refers to *theoria*, or a system of thought that governs the alchemical undertaking. *Theoria* means theory, and the magnet of the wise would symbolize the theory of the alchemist, which allows him to determine the nature of the self that he is seeking. This is na important idea for anyone beginning inner alchemy and

needs some explanation." RAFF, J. (2000) *Jung and the alchemical imagination.* Chapter 3 "The Creation of the Self". Florida: Nicolas-Hays, Inc. (Kobo ebook version).

[98] "But what can the ego do if there are opposed tendencies asking to be realized in terms of action? At this point, the ego is forced to perform one of its most valuable and heroic roles – maintain the tension between the opposites whilst stopping them to manifest in the world as action. It is a task that causes a great discomfort for the ego, designed to interact naturally in the world. But it still needs to be performed. When the tension of the opposites is successfully retained, the psyche is ready to manifest the transcendent function, allowing for **a symbolic solution where no logic solution is possible**. This was the reason why Jung considered the transcendent function a *tertium non datur*, "the third term not **logically** given". This solution frequently takes the form of a change in the tacit structure of the ego's identity, in such a manner that the tension between the opposites is no longer felt in its acute form. The tension **is not resolved; it is transcended into a more comprehensive vision**." HALL, J. A. (1986) *The Jungian experience.* [Translated from the Portuguese version: (1995) *A experiência jungiana.* São Paulo: Cultrix p. 109.] [author's own highlights]

[99] Pneumatic, from the Greek πνεῦμα (*pneûma*): wind, Spirit. PEREIRA, I. (1990) [Translated from the Portuguese version: *Dicionário Grego-Português e Português-Grego.* São Paulo: Apostolado da Imprensa Martins Fontes.]

[100] For a definition of moral and ethics, see Chapter 9 "Creation" (Part 1).

LILITH

In the same way that happens in previous Paradigms, there are myths that relate directly to the structure of the Paradigm of Sense. Throughout this book, we will focus on the mythology of the Τίτανες (Titans) – more adequate to the Paradigm of Sense than the Olympic mythology – with the God Διόνυσος (Dionysius) and the psychological interpretations of aspects of western religion (Christianity) and eastern religion (Tibetan Buddhism). No archetype, however, is more vital for the understanding of the Paradigm of Sense than Lilith. We will follow the steps of Roberto SICUTERI in his work *Lilith – a Lua Negra*[101], as well as the biblical extracts that the author uses, as an introduction to the mythology of this Goddess.

Lilith appears in the Babylonian mythology as a goddess with a close relationship to the beasts. Wild animals surround her, and parts of her body are theriomorphic. SICUTERI, citing Eric NEUMANN, describes a statue of Lilith:

> It is a hybrid standing figure, facing forward, with constantly open arms, elbows bent close to the flanks, in a prayer mode, open hands, fingers touching.
>
> The figure has an evidently round shape, big eyes well marked out and regular nose. The mouth is portrayed in a big smile, with an imperative fremitus of provocative sensuality; the whole expression is a presage of the archaic Greek plastic modality: impenetrable, severe, potent and ineffable.
>
> The style of the hair is impressive, according to the Mesopotamian or proto-Assyrian scheme: from the nape of the neck stem four superposed serpents forming a cone, whose heads, standing in an evidently phallic position, converge in the form of a split.
>
> The symbology reminds of **Kundalini emerging in the total realization**, as well as the gorgonian figures. From Lilith's back

descend, open in a straight angle, two wings sculpted with precision. The human energy seems concentrated precisely at the back and chest, where the breasts are cast wide and very round, with an evident and sombre seductive function.

Next to the figure are these traits which give it a notable lunar quality. The body is robust, very feminine until the ample hip and pubis. The legs, which gradually narrow down in the direction of the knees, lose the feminine plasticity and become beastly, potent; instead of feet, they are horrid and powerful vulture claws which emerge from the creepy wrinkled toes.

The coarse and woody malleolus give the impression of the wrinkled extremities of elephants and rhinos! The disposition of the claws is symmetrical, sloped, with a dominant accent; the whole powerful energy seems to emerge and flow over the bestial claws which land over the body of a two-headed beast, which looks like a crouching lioness. In her hands, Lilith holds two amulets which vaguely resemble the two hieroglyphic signs of the Scale, sceptres of power, initiation and justice. On the sides, below, slightly threatening the two-headed beast, there are two birds, sculpted the proto-Assyrian way, whose heads resemble an eagle or an owl or the Egyptian cats; they are in a fixed frontal position, claws united, rigid, totally resembling Lilith's.

They are vigilant animals which wind up the representation.[102] [author's own highlights]

SICUTERI continues: "In the Assyrian-Babylonian Pantheon of numerous inferior entities, as previously in the Sumerian-Acadian era, Lilith was seen as a female **demon**, a genius **of evil**."[103]

Although the author examines the archetypical images of Lilith in various mythologies and in astrology, it is in the Hebraic mythology that the myth of Lilith appears in a more tragic manner. Let us see some excerpts from SICUTERI's work.

The author uses biblical evidences and rabbinical cultural references to demonstrate that Lilith is created at the same time as Adam, **before** Eve.

"God said, 'Let us make man in our own image, in the likeness of ourselves,' [...] God created man in the image of himself, in the image of God he created **him**, male and female he created **them**." (*Genesis 1:26-27*)[104] [author's own highlights]

SICUTERI continues: "Therefore, in these three phases we see the appearance of man as an individual composed of two parts. The change of pronoun from singular to plural is revealing of the concept of hermaphroditism or androgyny, otherwise one must, surely, think that they were none less than the true distinct couple, Adam, and "the first companion", that is, Lilith. [...] Let us look now at the other phases, when the creation of Adam appears isolated, that is, with no feminine characters, and one where the creation of Eve follows as "the second companion"[105]:

> Yahweh God shaped man from the soil of the ground and blew the breath of life into his nostrils, and man became a living being. (*Genesis 2:7*) Yahweh God said, 'It is not right that the man should be alone. I shall make him a helper. (*Genesis 2:18*) The man gave names to all the cattle, all the birds of heaven and all the wild animals. But no helper suitable for the man was found for him. (*Genesis 2:20*)[106]

SICUTERI continues: "In this biblical extract, it is reconfirmed that Adam was alone and had given name to the animals, that is, that met them at mating. Only that way had he understood the need for differentiation. The obscure traces of a removed adamic bestiality are evident in the text. It is in this exact point of the myth that Adam abandons the element of identification with the divine expressed by androgyny and overcomes the animal sexuality as a living being. It is in this moment that a female companion is asked of God."[107]

Later: "Lilith, certainly, is connected to Genesis I. If we exclude androgyny as a celestial archetype reflected in terrestrial Adam, we must necessarily accept that it is Adam with a female companion. **And God blessed them**[108] [emphasis of this author], let us not forget. No doubt, in the Jehovah version, the first man and the first woman were in an animal state, their sexuality was undifferentiated; there was no disparity between both sexes. They were formless: "Created him as a formless mass". [...] "In Genesis II, 21 there is finally a description of creating the woman:"

> Then Yahweh God made the man fall into a deep sleep. And, while he was asleep, he took one of his ribs and closed the flesh up again forthwith.[109]

SICUTERI cites a comment from Rabi Shemuel:

> A bone between two ribs. It is not written in *his* place, but: in *their* place [...][110]

SICUTERI analyses this in the following way: "In his place" refers, on the contrary, to Adam as a singular, and the correction of the Rabi is in plural, it says *their*. Therefore, the part that was taken should result from both, that is, "two in one flesh." The rib (or the bone) mentioned is the symbol of a new entity that is born from *them*, that is, the *couple*. It is clear that this means that the couple already existed before the 'birth' of Eve.[111]

SICUTERI presents two more proofs of Lilith's existence before Eve.

> Male and female he created them. He **blessed them** and gave them the name Man, when they were created. (*Genesis* V:2) [author's own highlights]
>
> Yahweh God fashioned the rib he had taken from the man into a woman, and brought her to the man. And the man said: This one at last is bone of my bones and flesh of my flesh! (*Genesis* II:22-23)[112]

SICUTERI questions: "How not to notice Adam's astonishment and joy, as if he had been, finally, revived and reconciled with God, because "this time" [this one at last] the gift of a female is certain and beautiful! In this exclamation there is a confirmation of a "first time", referring to a previous woman. Or would it indicate that "this time" is about a human female and not an animal female that Adam had repudiated? In any case only the Comment of Beresit-Rabba helps us understand:"

> R. Jehudah said, on behalf of Rabi: *In the beginning, he created her*, but when the man saw her full of saliva and blood, he created her a second time, as it is written: "*This time*. This and that from the first time."[113]

Having demonstrated the evidence of Lilith's creation being **simultaneous** to the creation of Adam and **previous** to the creation of Eve, SICUTERI continues describing the myth of Lilith:

The love of Adam for Lilith, however, was soon disturbed; there was no peace between them because when they united in flesh, evidently in the most natural position – the woman underneath and the man on top – Lilith demonstrated impatience. And then asked Adam:

— Why do I have to lie down under you? Why do I have to open myself up under your body?

Maybe here there was silence or perplexity on the part of the companion. But Lilith insists:

— Why do I have to be dominated by you? However, I was also made of dust and for that reason, I am your equal.

She requests that they invert their sexual positions so that they can establish an evenness, a harmony that will mean equality between two bodies and two souls. Despite this request, still warm from its feverish supplication, Adam answers with a dry denial: Lilith is submitted to him, she must be symbolically under him, support the weight of his body. Therefore: there is an imperative, an order that must not be transgressed. The woman does not accept this imposition and rebels against Adam. **It is the breakdown of balance**.

Legitimate [...] was Lilith's claim. To Adam's refusal in conceding the inversion of positions in sexual intercourse, that is, his refusal to concede a significant evenness to his companion, Lilith irritably pronounces God's name, and accusing Adam, goes away.

Whilst this happens, Adam is taken by an anguished feeling of abandonment. It is sunset, and the first shadows of Saturday night are falling. Lilith has gone away. The man had opposed a "no" to his woman. And the darkness comes; for the second night the darkness comes, the same darkness of Friday when Jehovah created the demons. It is the moment of deep sleep, once again. The sleep is the beginning of the fall. "Nobody saw, nobody knew, nobody woke up."

Adam is afraid, he feels that the darkness oppresses him. He feels that things, all the good things, are spoiled. He wakes up, certainly looks around and does not see Lilith. Adam thinks that his companion has once again disobeyed his orders. He addresses God Jehovah, as the son who trusts the paternal experience and authority. "I sought in my bed, at night, the one who is the love of my soul; I sought her and could not find her."

Now there is despair, the bitterness for having lost Lilith. He asks the Father, and the Father wants to know the reason for the dispute and learns that the woman has challenged the man, and therefore, the divine.

After all, Lilith has fled far away, in the direction of the Red Sea margins, after having profaned the name of Father God.

In the crucial moment when Adam refused her desire, she fled in the direction of the Red Sea, now hateful of her spouse. God Jehovah proffered his order: The desire of the woman is for the husband. Go back to him".

Lilith does not answer with obedience, but with refusal: "I do not want anything to do with my husband". God Jehovah says: "Return to desire, return to desire your husband".

But Lilith's nature changed the moment she blasphemed against God, and there is no longer obedience.

Then God Jehovah sends a formation of Angels in the direction of the Red Sea. They reach Lilith: they find her in the deserted heathlands of the Arabic Sea, where the popular Hebraic tradition says that the waters call out, attracting like a magnet, all the demons and evil spirits. Lilith is transformed: she is no longer Adam's companion. **She is the demoniac manifested**, she is surrounded by all the perverted creatures arisen from the darkness. She is in a cursed place, where thorns and thistles are produced (*Genesis* 3:18); mosquitos, ticks, evil flies infect other beings; stinging nettles and brambles hurt the feet, dens of jackals are mistaken for stones, wild dogs meet hyenas and the satyrs call for each other in lascivious orgiastic seductions (*Isaiah* 34:13-15). [emphasis of this author]

The angels with the fire and the blazing sword shout to Lilith the order for her return to Adam, since, if she does not go, she will be drowned. But Lilith, deep down, is as bitter as wormwood, sharp as the double-edged sword (*Proverbs* 5:4) and answers: "How can I return to my man and live like a wife, after this gesture of mine and after living here?" But there is no space for doubt and hesitation: the angels even declare: "If you disobey and do not return, it will be death for you".

The dramatic tension of this even is extremely strong. There is total confrontation; the forces of the heavens are tested against the forces of the earth and darkness. A tension where, on one hand is the threat to the celestial authority, the sovereign destiny, and on the other, unravels the poisonous flower of scorn and affront. Lilith positions herself in the conflict, aware of her own role:

— How can I die, if God himself has entrusted me to deal with all the children who are born boys, until their eighth day of life, date of their circumcision, and of the girls until they are twenty?

Lilith refuses to follow the three angels and tells them: "If I see your three names or your semblance on a new-born, as a talisman, I promise to spare him."

> The angels, in a way, accept gratefully the bad luck and accept at least the partial concession offered by Lilith. They return to Eden, but God Jehovah had already decided to punish Lilith, exterminating her children.[114] [author's own highlights]

* * * * *

The tragicality of Lilith's myth impresses for its singularity: Lilith **successfully** confronts the sovereign powers of Cosmos, Jehovah, producing a cosmic crack that was never reconstituted, and a theological abyss so deep that could never be transposed. Lilith's action removes Jehovah's hegemony. In face of Lilith's refusal to obey Jehovah and return to Eden, **Jehovah retreats**, Lilith maintains her position and constitutes a parallel power in the *universe.* Even if the hegemonic power is always challenged in other mythologies, neither the context nor the consequences or the implications have ever been as devastating as they were in the myth of Lilith. If we take the Greek mythology as an example, both the victory of Κρόνος (Cronus) over Ούρανός (Uranus) and the victory of Ζεύς (Zeus) over Cronus have completely different characteristics. In these cases, Cronus is descendant and legitimate heir of Ouranós, so the same characteristics exist between Zeus and Cronus. These myths are perfectly in line with the mythologem of a young king eventually replacing an older king. Or even, when Προμηθεύς (Prometheus) steals the fire of the gods, awakening the fury of Zeus, the hegemonic power, he is chained and punished, and humanity must face deluge. However, at no point the hegemony of Zeus is at risk. On the contrary, Zeus is successful in the solution he finds to the problem. The cosmos continues as before. More than that, later, Prometheus is freed.

All this is very different in the myth of Lilith. The hegemonic power of the universe cannot solve the problem, and for that reason, immediately loses hegemony. The conflict becomes even more acute when taking into consideration the fact that Jehovah tried to be a monotheist god. Judaism and Christianity were built (and the universal spiritual history evolved) based on this awkward cosmic accident, so embarrassing to the point of carefully omitting Lilith from the Bible.

Whatever was responsible for causing this cosmic accident, this fact is primordial in the human psyche. It manifests itself in one of the oldest known civilizations, the Babylonian, and appearing in the Bible right on the first chapter of the first book, as a phenomenon taken place even before the end of Creation. SICUTERI places the first divorce of the universe before the end of the Seventh Day: "Everything happened between the sixth and the seventh day; if what is written about Adam is true: 'At the end of Saturday he lost his splendour and was expelled from the Garden of Eden'. [...] and the divine light existed only for the few hours of the sixth day and all of Saturday. In the end of the day when God rested, Adam had already consummated his relationship with Lilith, and therefore had known, in the darkness, an *awful truth*."[115]

Let us analyse carefully this cosmic wound, starting with the symbology of the Paradise of Eden, the environment where Lilith inhabits, in the beginning of the myth.

Edward EDINGER analysed this Symbol extensively[116]. According to him, in the centre of the Paradise is the Tree of Life, around which is the Tree of Knowledge of the Good and Evil, the latter blocking access to the former. God, in an extremely ambiguous act, calls the attention of Adam and Eve to that tree, only to forbid them to eat from it.

On top of the Tree of Knowledge of the Good and Evil is the Serpent (which Lilith uses as a crown). The Serpent's proposal is more than tempting, it is **clever**: knowledge, or even better, **consciousness**. Eve, showing her propensity for intelligence, accepted, probably instantly. In face of the disastrous possibility of having consciousness alone, she offered it to her companion. Adam, also intelligent, and perhaps having already learned with his experience with Lilith to not discard the woman's point of view too quickly, shared it. They were both expelled from Paradise. Archangel Michael is placed at his Gates, with his Flaming Sword, blocking the entry. Although this seems to be a disgraced fact, what is the alternative? Remain in the Paradise of Ignorance, promoted by God?

We have seen in the chapters "Psychological Dimensions" and "Paradox" that duality, specially the duality between good and evil, is absolutely fundamental to the creation and the development of the ego, therefore consciousness. The Serpent simply offers the duality, giving humanity the opportunity of consciousness.

Therefore, the Serpent, with its forked tongue, duality itself, the Consciousness of Good and Evil, is a landmark. Before it, there is no consciousness of duality. The encounter with the Serpent is the climax of the first dimension and the access to the duality of the second dimension. Therefore, in eating the apple, Eve and Adam entered the structure of consciousness *svādhiṣṭhāna,* the Paradigm of Civilization.

Since Lilith comes before Eve, Lilith begins her history in the **unity** of the Paradise of Eden – the nature of Eden is unity (first dimension) – before the **duality** and the Fall (second dimension). Always in close relationship with the Serpent – with which Lilith crowns itself and goes to live with after she leaves Eden – Lilith appears to feel the impulse towards Consciousness, even though she has never eaten from the Tree of Knowledge of Good and Evil. She asks to **invert** the sexual positions to establish **parity**. "Inversion" and "Parity" are ideas strongly related to duality. When inverting something, you place it in an **opposite** position, establishing duality. And nothing is more dual than a **pair**. In **denying** a request from Lilith, Adam has given to her everything she needed to establish duality and move forward: **opposition**.

Establishing a completely independent cosmic current, Lilith leaves the Paradise **because she wants to**, she was never expelled. On the contrary, when Lilith is incited to return through threats, she **refuses**. From then on, Lilith is demonized and remains so to this day.

Before we continue, let us make a small digression. We currently see spiritualist and feminist schools of thought that use Lilith as a symbol of female liberation. They defend that the Archetype of Lilith was banned by patriarchy to subjugate women, as if humanity had opted to ban Lilith and forget about her. This is not true. Quite the opposite, **Lilith freely opted for the exile**. Adam does not seem to be a very strong man; he is only doing what his father told him to do. Only **after** Lilith leaves Paradise, God tries to subjugate her, and even then, He fails. Therefore, it is much more honest and honourable to affirm that Lilith is a strong and independent Goddess, capable of powerful choices which she can sustain, even if her enemy is hegemonic in the universe. Considering these facts, we can conclude two things: First, given the reasons presented here, Lilith deserves the admiration of spiritualists and feminists even more. Secondly, patriarchy exists not due to men being evil beings, but because the Masculine Archetypes have strongly prevailed in the last few millennia. And yes, many unethical men took advantage of it. In the same way, the Archetype of Lilith was not maliciously banned **by humans. Exiling is part of the way the Archetype of Lilith works**: once again, Lilith leaves the Paradise **because she wants to**.

What does it mean, then, Lilith's exit from Paradise?

The Sumerian sculpted a partially therianthropic Lilith, with her head crowned by the Serpent, surrounded by animals. Adam sees a horrible Lilith, full of blood and saliva, also symbols of animality. The core of the relationship between Adam and Lilith is sexuality. SICUTERI demonstrates at various points that Lilith is with Adam when he experiments sexual intercourse with animals. Animals are often the symbol of the instinct.

Lilith is the archetype of *Instinct*.

Imagine now the psychological stage of humanity when Lilith appeared: the moment of its creation, the moment of the first steps of psychological development. If there is no duality at the time when Lilith in Paradise is constellated in the human psyche, then **there is no ego**. Without the ego, the ability to resist the unconscious is **zero**. Without ego, without consciousness, there is no possibility of choice. The person is totally dominated by the unconscious, reacting to every instinctual discharge that appears, setting them into action.

Add to that the fact that instinctual satisfaction causes pleasure. Resisting an instinct, on the other hand, generates frustration, spends energy, is tiring. Yes, resisting an instinct generates consciousness. But we know what the consequences are: when Adam and Eve achieve consciousness, they are expelled from the Paradise of Ignorance (which is delicious), they are exiled in the desert, they will need to work hard and feel pain. And there is still the Serpent...

Why would a human being opt to sacrifice pleasure for consciousness and pain?

The answer is simple: for no reason. The human being does not sacrifice pleasure for consciousness and pain.

Therefore, to forcibly push the human being to the path of psychological development, the archetypes constellated in a specific manner: the Celestial God prevailed over Lilith, **the Symbol prevailed over the Instinct.** With the Archetypes **determining** that God is **celestial and symbolic**, and **determining** that the permanence of *Instinct* is demoniac, the human being finally managed to sacrifice pleasure and unveil its consciousness. SICUTERI, citing REIK, says:

> This could be about the first experience of sexual orgasm in the natural level which would have triggered an unbearable anguish in mankind, since the sexual passion would distance them from divinity, with a regressive threat from which they still had an evolutive memory. Others come, in the conflict of Adam and Eve and her sin, an introjection of divinity through the totemic tree (REIK).[117]

SICUTERI continues:

> Whether this is about Lilith or Eve, it is nevertheless always a *tragedy of Eros and sex* that is consummated in *Genesis*. It is his *own*

libidinal totality that man played with for the first time, in a precise phylogenetic moment: and that becomes a taboo.[118]

It is interesting that SICUTERI used the term **taboo**. According to the above, Lilith's self-exile in the human psyche is not an option of the human being, but an autonomous archetypical movement. Therefore, Lilith's self-exile is not a **social taboo**, but a **natural taboo**.

In his monumental work *Incest and Human Love*[119], in my opinion an authentic breakthrough in global psychology, Robert STEIN analyses the Archetype of Incest. According to the author, and various anthropological studies cited by him, the prohibition of incest between brothers and sisters is the most radical and disseminated among all cultures. If the prohibition is so radical and so disseminated, there must be a powerful instinct behind it. From these conclusions, STEIN shows that the Archetype of Incest has a very different way of functioning to all other archetypes. Any archetype, when constellated, seeks to be noticed and demands that people's experiences and actions include its pattern. For example, when the Self constellates the archetype of the Hero, it wants the ego to embark on a heroic journey. Or, when the Self constellates the archetype of the Anima or Animus, it wants the ego to relate with other people **and** with the Self. The Archetype of the Incest does not work like that. When the Self constellates the Archetype of Incest, it intensely stimulates the desire of the brother for the sister, or the sister for the brother. **But this archetype, whilst it causes the desire, it also vigorously forbid it**[120]. The Archetype of Incest generates an enormous quantity of instinctual psychological energy (the incestual sexual desire), without allowing the energy to manifest itself in concrete actions. STEIN argues that this mechanism forces the energy to flow abstractly. In forcing its passage through more abstract psychological routes instead of allowing an instinctual discharge, the psychological energy develops more abstract routes of the human psyche[121].

Since the Archetype of Incest aims at stimulating the flux of psychological energy through abstract routes, in detriment of using the instinctual discharge, I ask myself if this archetype is not a mechanism intimately related to Lilith's archetype, as it facilitates self-exile, both being **natural taboos**. (This relationship between archetypes, however, is a mere hypothesis. I have no evidence to base it on.)

Lilith's self-exile immediately enabled the instinctual repression – or more correctly put, the subjection of the instinct to the Symbol – and the birth of consciousness. However, her self-exile remains. According to

SICUTERI, even mythology shows Lilith like that: a problem without solution.

> This is how Lilith's story is shown in the Hebraic culture. There is no conclusion: Lilith remains in freedom itself, possessed by the demon, perhaps even a Queen in the Demon's palace, with her feminine spirit. From the moment she declares war against the Father, and the Father subjects her to the role, she unleashes her destructive force and from then on, there is no more peace for mankind.[122]

Later on SICUTERI suggests that we should allow Lilith to return to consciousness, **without the demon**. I admit that the author's intentions are good. However, besides being of the opinion that this type of decision is not down to human beings, but the Self and its archetypical constellations, I strongly argue that, as we will see a few chapters ahead, when Lilith does return to the consciousness, she does that **with the demon**[123].

Why does the self-exile of Lilith remain?

If we accept that an archetypal constellation can destroy any social structure, however large, and that its constellation does not even have to be consciously noticed – on the contrary, the more unconscious, the more powerful and brutal – then we must admit that the continuity of Lilith's self-exile is not due to a patriarchal society, even if society can benefit from it. Lilith remains in self-exile because humanity still needs it. Or, to put it a different way, because the self-exile has still not fulfilled its role. We know the role of self-exile: to promote the instinctual repression and stimulate the development of consciousness in relation to the Symbol. So, to find out when the self-exile will end, we need to ask when the journey towards the Symbol will end.

Never. The answer is never. JUNG is correct: The Self is infinite, and we will integrate it forever.

However, the fact that a certain psychological dimension is infinite does not mean that the next dimension cannot be reached. And, when the next one is reached, the previous dimension does not stop developing. For example, the fact that a person reaches the Paradigm of Self-Affirmation and therefore prioritizes the development of their ego, does not mean that they stop developing life in society on the Paradigm of Civilization. In the same way, the fact that a person reaches the Paradigm of Balance and prioritizes the surrender to the Self and individuation does not mean that they stop developing the ego: the ego must submit itself to the Self while being strong enough to integrate it. In fact, people **must not** stop developing the previous dimensions because, without them, they will fall into abstractionism, dehumanization, isolation, they will start psychologizing and will develop much more serious psychological deformities.

Therefore, the fact that we need to recognize that the Self is infinite and that we need to integrate it forever does not mean that this process cannot reach a plenitude, or at least a sufficiency. In fact, it does. The Paradigm of Balance, another name for individuation, reaches its peak at Crucifixion, a process that we are all capable of living. Contemplating Crucifixion, we must admit that it is the climax of spiritualization. The psychological development towards the symbol is whole, and the ego manages to do exactly what the Self demands: "I and the Father are one"[124]. It does so even though the demands might be terrifying and even if it includes death: "Father, into your hands I commit my spirit."[125] The instinct is indeed experimented – individuation includes an adequate instinctual experience – however, **the instinct is invariably following a direction demanded by the Self, it is adequate to the Symbol.** In Crucifixion, the demand of adequacy to the Self is so immense that the instinct of survival itself is tested and "defeated".

When the instinct reaches **this psychological level**, it is completely spiritualized. There is no more risk of regression due to instinctual experiences. **At this level**, Lilith's self-exile is no longer necessary.

With the opening of the Paradigm of Sense, the Gates of Eden open and Archangel Michael allows Lilith to enter the Paradise again. The Serpent remains strong on the branches of the Tree of Knowledge of Good and Evil, as it has always been. Now, however, there is access to the Tree of Life. After all, we are talking of the resurrected.

The 5D ego experiments **the resurgence of the *Instinct*** as a spiritualized, healthy, useful and pleasurable energy. The *Instinct* is no longer guided by and submitted to the Symbol. On the contrary, **the *Instinct* is now the direction of the development of consciousness**. Its place in the Paradigm of Sense is absolutely fundamental because in the unified nature of the fifth dimension, the "internal world" is identical to the "external world". Additionally, it is the *Instinct* that maintains these dimensions perfectly united, since it is corporeal and transcendental at the same time. On one hand, the *Instinct* 'happens to the ego', it brings immediate and indispensable 'perceptions' to the ego, which in turn cannot (and does not want to) control it: it is transcendental. On the other hand, the *Instinct* acts directly on the physical *Body:* it is corporeal. The grey elephant of *mulādhāra* reappears as the white elephant of *viśuddha*: the *Instinct* has been redeemed[126].

Since at each psychological dimension reached, the speed of the consciousness increases – the more developed a consciousness is, the more psychological operations by unity of time it will perform – the fifth dimension is extremely fast. In this case, specifically, the speed is the most important factor of the fifth dimension, given that, as we will see later, this is the dimension of the **continuous movement**. Due to all that, it is fundamental that the 5D ego is extremely fast and has immediate actions. The *Instinct*, psychological instance that is manifested instantaneously and directly on the *Body*, enabling immediate actions, needs to be available and reliable: it is.

The experience that opens the Paradigm of Sense is the abandonment of God, the *Retreat of the Soul*. The 5D ego will need to make choices alone, without the demands and guidance of the Self. A fundamental factor for its choices is its *Instinct*, the element of harmony between the *Spirit* and the 5D ego.

Precisely at this point, the Sun rises: the *Spirit* appears.

---

[101] SICUTERI, R. *Lilith, la luna nera* [not published in English. Translated from the Portuguese version: (1985) *Lilith, a lua negra.* 3ª edicao. São Paulo: Editora Paz e Terra. p. 10].

[102] Ibid., p. 23.

[103] Ibid., p. 23.

[104] *The New Jerusalem Bible.* Genesis 1:26-27.

[105] SICUTERI, R. *Lilith, la luna nera.* Op. Cit. p. 10.

[106] *The New Jerusalem Bible.* Genesis 2:20.

[107] SICUTERI, R. *Lilith, la luna nera.* Op. Cit. p. 10.

[108] *The New Jerusalem Bible.* Genesis 5:2. See also note 12.

[109] SICUTERI, R. *Lilith, la luna nera.* Op. Cit. p. 13.

[110] Ibid., p. 14

[111] Ibid., p. 14

112 Ibid., p. 14

113 Ibid., p. 14

114 Ibid., p. 19

115 Ibid., p. 16

116 EDINGER, E. F. (1992) *Ego and archetype.* Part I "Individuation and the stages of development. "The inflated ego" 3. "Adam and Prometheus." Boston: Shambhala

117 SICUTERI, R. *Lilith, la luna nera.* Op. Cit. p. 16.

118 Ibid.

119 STEIN, R. (1973) *Incest and human love.* Dallas, TX: Spring Publications.

120 "[...] the longing for the incestuous union, although repressed, is as powerful as our horror of violating taboo. The more we repress it, more power it has over us, so much that we are continually fascinated and attracted by incestuous types of involvement. Ibid. Part II. "Incest". Chapter 4 "The incest wound". p. 45.

121 "More than anything else, the incest taboo forces mankind to become conscious of not being complete. [...] The longing to meet and be united to the mysterious other half of oneself is a direct consequence of the taboo between brother and sister. [...] He helped **stop the sexual impulse from being purely biological to become the supreme tool for the psychological development of mankind**. Above all else, in his desire to find his soul companion, mankind is finally able to **discover and mould their own soul**." Ibid. Part II. "Incest". Chapter 3. "Incest and wholeness". p. 38. [author's own highlights]

122 SICUTERI, R. *Lilith, la luna nera.* Op. Cit. p. 16.

123 See Chapter 13, "Demon"

124 *The New Jerusalem Bible.* John 10:30

125 Ibid. Luke 23:46

126 "In that moment, the unproductive fracture that finally demands a correction was psychologically reconfirmed: the serpent will no longer be crushed under the feet of the Good Mother, because the serpent is Eve herself. However, if we finally saw her as Lilith-Dark Moon, maybe the serpent, saved, would restore Sofia to us." SICUTERI, R. *Lilith, la luna nera.* Op. Cit. p. 78.

Paradigm of Sense

SPIRIT

"[...] the experience of the self is almost impossible to practically distinguish from the experience of 'what has always been referred to as God'".[127]

To JUNG, the importance of the Sun and the Moon is so big that he cites them as the magnificent symbols in the human psyche[128]. The grandiosity of the Sun and Moon encompasses the whole archetypal reality. This is the reality that appears, for example, in the *Rosarium Philosophorum*, alchemical illustrations analysed by JUNG[129]. These drawings show the relationship between **Brother Sun** and **Sister Moon**, an incestuous and mortal relationship which culminates in the great alchemical objective – the *coniunctio*, the conjunction between the Sun and the Moon.

Logos and Eros are intellectually formulated intuitive equivalents of the archetypal images of Sol and Luna. In my view the two luminaries are so descriptive and so superlatively graphic in their implications that I would prefer them to the more pedestrian terms Logos and Eros, although the latter do pin down certain psychological peculiarities more aptly than the rather indefinite "Sol and Luna."[130]

Why is this conjunction so important to the point of being the "final" objective?

Both the Sun and the Moon are Archetypes which symbolize both great psychological functions. The Sun is the cosmic principle Λόγος (*Lógos*)[131]. Creative, the Sun builds the Universe[132]. The Sun is the great guide of the Hero, encouraging it to defeat the night and fulfil its tasks, reaching consciousness[133,134]. Since its creation, the ego's consciousness is continuously stimulated by clarity, discrimination and discerning, emanated by the Sun[135,136]. The Sun is the male principle, promoter of individuality[137]. An excessive Sun, on the other hand, is scorching, produces a partial and individualist consciousness, incapable of relating to other people and to its own interior.

The Moon is the Great Mother[138]. The origin of everything, it is also the excessive regressive force that stops the movement of the Hero and needs to be defeated[139]. During the development of the ego, particularly the masculine ego, the Moon is denied by consciousness. But this *status quo* cannot last forever, otherwise there would be a consciousness with "excessive Sun", partial and individualist. As soon as a strong ego is established, it is necessary to start a relationship with the darkness of the unconsciousness[140]. A cosmic principle known as Ἔρος (Éros), the Moon will rule this phase[141]. The Hero faces the katabasis[142,143]. The success of this process leads, again, to the Sun, to the Self. The alternance between the principles of the Moon and the Sun culminates in simultaneousness, in its union, the *coniunctio*[144].

If reaching *coniunctio* was not complex enough, the process of *coniunctio* occurs three times, and it is wider and deeper each time it is completed. The first *coniunctio* is known as *unio mentalis*. It occurs precisely at the transition from the Paradigm of Self-Affirmation to the Paradigm of Balance. It is the moral defeat that the Self imposes to the ego, forcing it to recognise the existence of the psyche, the unconscious and its own.

The second *coniunctio* is much more complex. It requires a huge effort from the ego. Besides entering its personal unconsciousness and dealing with its neuroses, integrating its unconscious complexes, the ego will need to largely experience the archetypal world. The ego will reach the second *coniunctio* by going through all the phases described on the *Rosarium Philosophorum*, whose last illustration shows a being depicting the Sun and the Moon as integrated.

It is very difficult to explain, in logical terms, the consciousness of someone who has reached the second *coniunctio*. One could start by saying that this person has a **strong ego**. Just before the *unio mentalis*, having a strong ego means that the person was able to become accomplished in the physical world, having at least some achievements such as family, work, money etc. However, a strong ego experiencing the second *coniunctio*, is **much** more than that: this ego must be able to integrate the Sun and the Moon. To integrate the Sun is to have a wide enough consciousness that can remain distinct from the unconsciousness, without merging, reaching a deep individuality. The integration of the Sun implies a capacity to express the singularity of the Self in the consciousness and in the acts of the ego[145]. None of this is possible without the Moon. To integrate the Moon is to be able to open "inwards", to the unconscious, to the katabasis, to build a relationship with the Archetypes and, ultimately, with the Self[146]. It is also an opening "outwards", to build a relationship with other people, because as the Analytic Psychology clarifies, the relationship with the Soul is extremely similar, if not identical, to the relationship with other people[147]. "It [the soul] is therefore the very essence of relationship"[148].

Only a multi-paradoxical consciousness can understand this point of the development, being able to abandon dualism. Is the Moon the Mother from whom all else originates, being defeated by the Hero led by the Sun? Or is she the one who defeats the solar Hero, forcing him to enter the night again to perform katabasis? It is both. The Sun is the one who convinces the Hero to leave the Great Mother Moon behind, only to see it submerge in the katabasis? Or is the deeper individuality that appears when the Hero goes through the moonlit night of the unconscious? It is both.

These paradoxes, however, are easy. They could be seen as just phases of a development. A level of paradox slightly higher is to understand that an individuated being encompasses not only being an individuality (solar principle), but also relating to the unconscious (lunar principle), allowing itself to be strongly influenced – maybe even determined – by it. However, if our relationship with our interiority is **identical** to our relationship to other people, then an individuated being also encompasses the relationships that exist between its ego and other people. Ultimately, **an individuated being is also the other people** they relate to. Here, it is impossible not to ask: are the people who relate to an individuated being parts of him or completely distinct beings? **Paradoxically**, it is necessary to admit that it's both.

An even higher level of paradox appears when the concept of free-will is considered. Although, in my opinion, actual free-will is only possible in the Paradigm of Sense, it is necessary to relatively consider it here. Let us admit the perfect reflection, obviously lunar, of the relationship between the "interior" psychological figures and "external" people. What happens when the individuated being takes one more step in its never-ending process of integration of the Self? The configuration of their psyche changes: the arrangement of the unconscious complexes changes, the archetypical constellation changes. JUNG says that the psychological integration causes **even the Self to change** – which is already an immense paradox: how can something which is **perfect and eternal change**? Following this thought process, if the psychological configuration changes, the "exterior" people who precisely reflect this configuration must change in the **exact same way**. However, if they are people who are "exterior" to the individuated being, will they change only because they are a reflexion of the changing psychological structures of the individuated being, or will they change because they have their own free-will, and therefore, choose to change? **Paradoxically**, we must admit that it is both.

It is of utmost importance to say that a 4D ego that is experiencing the final phases of the Paradigm of Balance, close to its Crucifixion, **experiences this**, lives this type of reality in practice. This is not a belief or a mental exercise, but a fact, so concrete that it should – and must – be **purposely and consciously produced**. The 4D ego, in modifying the configuration of its psyche through a simple deidentification, the integration of an unconscious complex or even the more complex integration of an Archetype, **observes** that people around it, who were previously compatible to its earlier psychological setting, **change**, and they do so in order to perfectly adjust to the new psychological configuration reached by that 4D ego. However, if anyone asks these people why they have changed, they will answer with very personal reasons, coherent with their personal stories.

One more level of paradox is established due to the fact that Archetypes are transpersonal structures. The very definition of Archetype – that which is expressed in **all** human beings – is proof of its transpersonal nature. When an individuated being integrates an Archetype, this has an overarching transpersonal effect on humanity, which **is modified at the same time as the individuated being**. This means that, when it is said that humanity has changed, people who have no relationship whatsoever with the individuated being change too. Does this happen because of the psychological changes in the individuated being or due to their free-will? **Paradoxically**, we must admit that it is both. This is easy to see in the image of Christ: his life, and particularly his crucifixion, opened a New Era in humanity, establishing the birth of an entire culture. Tibetan Buddhism also teaches that, when a Buddha was illuminated, all of humanity was illuminated with him[149].

Finally, let us analyse one last important paradox for this point of our development. In various parts of his work, JUNG shows that, when a person integrates the Self, the Self is **humanized** and its intrinsic structure **changes**[150]. This becomes evident, for example, as the effect of the action from Job[151] and Jesus[152]. Despite the elevated nature of these names, I can categorically affirm that this type of action is not exclusive to them and is available to any human being who has reached the apogee of the fourth dimension: Balance. Without a doubt, JUNG was one of those who reached this level and changed the Self. **God changes, despite, paradoxically, being perfect and eternal**.

The integration of the Self – symbolized by the paradox of the *coniunctio* between the Sun and the Moon – is manifested at the apogee of the Paradigm of Balance on a 4D ego, which can support a level of consciousness that realizes and expresses, in corporeal actions, archetypal themes. This, in turn, determines the psychological progress of the whole humanity, maintaining its human individuality – which includes their failures and limitations – whilst at the same time relating to other people whose psychological changes are in total synchronicity with the psychological changes of the 4D ego, even if they retain their free-will. It is worth mentioning once again that this level of consciousness is not something which one **believes** in, but instead, a state of psychological development **experienced** by individuated beings, advanced 4D egos. Once again: Analytical Psychology is correct and works.

The Self, as it has been described here, is the **Human Soul**. In his work, JUNG uses the term Soul to refer to the unconscious, the archetypes and the Self[153,154,155,156]. The Human Soul can lead the 4D ego to this super specialized level: an individuated being with a multi-paradoxical consciousness.

Perhaps the main tool that the Human Soul uses to lead the ego is the σύμβολον (*sýmbolon*)[157]. The understanding of the concept of **Symbol** in Analytical Psychology is one of the most complex. Three characteristics, however, are fundamental here. The first is almost obvious: the Symbol is symbolic. A symbol can not be understood literally, it needs to be interpreted. When facing a Symbol, one should seek its **meaning**[158,159]. To put it very simply, in order to arrive at the meaning of a symbol in a dream, the analyst must access the list of associations of the dreamer, if this is a reductive analysis. Or, if on a synthetic therapy, the analyst must search for references directly from the mythologies. This process must be carried out with the awareness of the infinite creativity and variability of the unconscious, as well as remembering that a certain symbol will only make sense if the psychological context of the dreamer is observed. There is no dream dictionary, symbols must be interpreted one by one.

Besides being symbolic, the **Symbol also acts**. It is very common to see the symbol merely as a communicator of meanings. The symbol is seen as a road sign. When we see a road sign with an arrow pointing left crossed by a red line, we understand that it is not permitted to turn left. However, the decision to turn left or not is individual. The road sign will do nothing to the person if they continue ahead, turn left or right. For that reason, the road sign is not a symbol: it simply informs. An actual Symbol acts on the person in whose psyche it is constellated. If, for example, the Symbol of the Moon is constellated in a person's psyche, the **energy of the Symbol** will act, and exert a huge influence on the person and their life circumstances. Ultimately, sooner or later, it will force the person to integrate what the Moon means to their consciousness and life style.

Finally, **the Symbol is paradoxical**. Since we have already discussed paradox, it is easier to understand this. Is the Moon a regressive force that disturbs the development, or is it the force that promotes the contact with the unconscious and katabasis? Paradoxically, it is both. Is the Sun the force that pushes the Hero forward or is it the deep individuality? Paradoxically, it is both. Almost always, paradoxes are progressive. Besides being paradoxes, the Sun and the Moon, as we have discussed, come into conjunction, creating a **paradox of paradoxes**. This is a **multi-paradoxical consciousness**. Such is the complexity of Human Soul.

The Human Soul guides the 4D ego through the Paradigm of Balance until Crucifixion, when a multi-paradoxical consciousness is reached. At that point, as largely documented by Analytical Psychology, the Self is humanized and the Archetype of the Self **changes**. JUNG proves this, for example, by showing that God changes behaviour radically from the Old to the New Testament. After completely realising the Paradigm of Balance, Christ changed God's behaviour and, with that, brought the Era of Pisces to the whole Humanity, opening the way for every human being to reach and realise the Paradigm of Balance.

If everything that is being said about Christ is true, we need to admit that Christ reached a consciousness climax, that the Archetype of Self changed for Christ and changed the relationship between them – besides all other changes that this has brought to Humanity as a whole. More than that, we must also admit that the same ideas are valid for all those who experience their own Crucifixion, each in their own way, a way imposed by the Self.

Given that the Self has different behaviours in each dimension of psychological development, in each Paradigm, and that it is the Self that regulates the psyche in each dimension of development, we can now understand what was implicit: the nature of each dimension of development is emanated by the Self, already having in itself all those dimensions. Therefore, it becomes clear that the Self that determines the Paradigm of Civilization has two dimensions, the Self that determines the Paradigm of Self-Affirmation has three dimensions, the Self that determines the Paradigm of Balance has four dimensions. The Self that lead Christ to Crucifixion had four dimensions, a 4D Self. Crucified, Christ reached the apogee of a fourth-dimensional consciousness, integrated the Self, again modified, and became a Self with five dimensions, a 5D Self.

Christ himself mentions this transformation:

> "But now I am going to the one who sent me. Not one of you asks, 'Where are you going?' Yet you are sad at heart because I have told you this. Still, I am telling you the truth: it is for your own good that I am going, because **unless I go, the Paraclete will not come to you; but if I go, I will send him to you**. And when he comes, he will show the world how wrong it was, about sin, and about who was in the right, and about judgement: about sin: in that they refuse to believe in me; about who was in the right: in that **I am going to the Father and you will see me no more**; about judgement: in that the prince of this world is already condemned. **I still have many things to say to you but they would be too much for you to bear now. However, when the Spirit of Truth comes he will lead you to the complete truth,** since he will not be speaking of his own accord, but will say only what he has been told; and he will reveal to you the things to come."[160] [author's own highlights]

Christ presents the ***Spirit of Truth.*** Having spoken of himself as being in complete union with the Father, Christ would not need to differentiate himself from the *Spirit*, unless the Spirit was completely different from him. Therefore, the spiritual entity that is Christ is **different** from the spiritual entity that is the *Spirit*.

The emphasis on this difference is such that the time of the Spirit is necessarily posterior to the time of Christ: its arrival is conditioned to Christ's departure. Clearly, he says: "unless I go, the Paraclete will not come to you; but if I go, I will send him to you."[161] Well, we know that Christ's departure happens through Crucifixion. Therefore, Crucifixion is a necessary event for the Spirit's arrival. The Crucifixion is the apogee of the Paradigm of Balance, the integration of the fourth-dimensional Self, of the Human Soul. After that, the ***Spirit of Truth*** is sent: the fifth-dimensional Self. Whereas the Self is manifested in four dimensions as the **Soul**, in five dimensions the Self is expressed as ***Spirit.***

> In Gnostic typology ἄνθρωπος ψυχικός [ánthropos psychicós], 'psychic man', is inferior to the πνευματικός [pneumátikos], 'spiritual man', [...][162]

JUNG argues constantly that the unconscious is symbolized by the Ocean or mercury, liquid[163]. The nature of the psyche is aquatic. Therefore, the Soul, or the fourth-dimensional Self, the central Archetype and regulator of the psyche, exists in an aquatic dimension. John the Baptist, who prepares Christ's arrival, the Soul, baptises him with water. John the Baptist says:

> "In the course of his preaching he said, 'After me is coming someone who is more powerful than me, and I am not fit to kneel down and undo the strap of his sandals. I have baptised you with water, but he will baptise you with the Holy Spirit.'"[164].

John the Baptist says that after him there is someone higher, Christ, who will baptise with the Holy Spirit. As John 4:2 says that ""though in fact it was his disciples who baptised, not Jesus himself"[165], everything points to the fact that the baptism with the Holy Spirit performed by Christ means the arrival of the Spirit **after his departure**, according to his own words. Indeed, soon after his death and resurrection, the Spirit arrives:

> "When Pentecost day came round, they had all met together, when suddenly there came from heaven a sound as of a violent wind which filled the entire house in which they were sitting; and there appeared to them **tongues as of fire**; these separated and came to rest on the head of each of them. They were all filled with the Holy Spirit and began to speak different languages as the Spirit gave them power to express themselves."[166] [author's own highlights]

The spiritual entity Holy Spirit, the Spirit, differently from Christ and posterior to him, is manifested as fire. It is extremely significant that the Spirit is manifested in **tongues** of fire and that its first effect causes the apostles to speak in other **tongues**: the Spirit is the Self that rules *viśuddha*, the throat *cakra,* associated to mantra.

> "What **sounds from his mouth** is not the ordinary word, the *shabda*, of which speech is composed. It is *mantra,* **the compulsion to create a mental image**, power over that which IS, to be as it really is in its pure essence. Thus it is knowledge. It is the truth of being, beyond right and wrong; it is real being, beyond thinking and reflecting. It is knowledge pure and simple, knowledge of the Essential [...]"[167][author's own highlights]

Taken by the *Spirit*, the Apostles start to speak **words of power**, words that refer to **what is**, the ***Truth***, beyond good and evil, beyond the unconscious unity of the *cakra mulādhāra*, beyond the duality of the *cakras svādhiṣṭhāna* and *maṇipūra*, beyond the acknowledged duality of *anāhata*.

Synchronically, the Spirit descends over the Apostles on the days of **Pente**cost – πέντε (Greek), which means five, thereby opening the consciousness structure of the fifth *cakra*.

We are facing a manifestation of the Spirit.

Which type of psychological structure starts with the arrival of the Spirit? In the end, what is the Spirit?

In order to answer these questions, one must overcome a huge psychological resistance. The western psyche sees in the symbol of Christ the **final** goal of the psychological development. To imagine something beyond Christ, something more advanced, is a **crime** against the Paradigm of Balance, a crime against which the unconscious strongly reacts.

In alchemy, for example, the Christ appears as *lapis philosophorum*, the Philosopher's Stone. To imagine something beyond this point is extremely rare. In *Mysterium Coniunctionis*, "The third stage: the *unus mundus*", JUNG mentions:

> The production of the lapis was the goal of alchemy in general. Dorn was a **significant exception**, because for him this denoted only the completion of the second stage of conjunction [...] For him the third and highest degree of conjunction was the union of the whole man with the *unus mundus*.[168] [author's own highlights]

The alchemist DORNEUS senses the crime he is committing:

> You will see the heretofore spagyric [i.e., secret] heaven, which you can bedeck with the lower stars, as the upper heaven is bedecked with the upper stars. [...] Will now the unbelievers, who have imitated the Physicists, marvel that we handle in our hands the heaven and the stars? [...] For us, therefore, the lower stars are all individuals produced by nature in this lower world by their conjunction with heaven, like [the conjunction] of the higher with the lower elements. Now I hear the voice of many raging **against us**, and crying out, Avaunt! **Let those men be destroyed who say that heaven can conjoin itself to earth**.[169] [author's own highlights]

Nonetheless, it is necessary to commit this crime if we want the *Spirit* to descend upon us, if we want to enter the fifth dimension and experience the Paradigm of Sense. Let us carry on, therefore, as the alchemist DORNEUS who had this courage, towards the third *coniunctio*, the *Unus Mundus*.

The second *coniunctio* culminated in a consciousness that integrated the synthesis between the Sun and the Moon, the paradox between them: the construction of an ego with four dimensions is complete.

The third *coniunctio* starts: tongues of fire descend from the sky. The image is clear: the *Spirit* is manifested as **another Sun** whose tongues of fire descend from the sky. The paradox Sun-Moon generated by the second *coniunctio* must perform another synthesis with the Spiritual Sun that appears in the third *coniunctio* – DORNEUS evinces this by mentioning the correspondence between the inferior and superior stars. The third *coniunctio* will occur, therefore, through the relationship between the 5D ego just produced by Crucifixion, and the *Spirit.*

> Thus, he [DORNEUS] knew that even the wise man could not reconcile the opposites unless "a certain heavenly substance hidden in the human body" came to his help, namely the "balsam", the quintessence, the "philosophic wine", a "virtue and heavenly vigour" – in short, the "truth".170

The celestial substance needs to help. It comes: the *Spirit,* the **quintessence** descends from heaven in the **fifth** dimension. This is an extremely important fact. Nobody goes into this dimension because they want. No amount of techniques used can bring someone here. In order to reach the conscience structure of the **fifth** *cakra, viśuddha*, it is necessary to have experienced Crucifixion, and from there, it is necessary that the *Spirit* makes the move, coming to help the 5D ego.

So, what is the nature of the *Spirit?*

The nature of the *Spirit* is the maximum simplicity, or "simply the 'truth'"171. This is one of the main differences between the Soul and the *Spirit.* The Soul expresses itself through the Symbol, whereas the *Spirit* expresses itself through the *Truth.*

In the beginning of the Paradigm of Balance, the 4D ego is completely partial. Its journey to integrate the Soul (4D Self) is fundamentally a journey in the direction of **completeness**. JUNG affirms that the unconscious is **compensatory**, always compensating the ego's partiality, bringing to him what is missing[172].

The Symbol is always **transcendent** in relation to the psychological dualities whose halves are expressed in the ego and the compensatory unconscious content. The Symbol is always the paradox, therefore **unified**, of the psychological dualities. Partial, the 4D ego interacts with the Symbol, who points to a transcendent ulterior reality, in relation to the duality it presently finds itself. Evidencing a unified ulterior reality, the Symbol **acts** on the 4D ego, taking it beyond the dichotomy ego x unconscious. Being unified and transcendent, the Symbol is not directly accessible to the dualist understanding of the 4D ego. The Symbol needs to be **interpreted**.

The Crucifixion, however, drastically modifies this situation, since there, the 4D ego transcends duality, integrating the Soul, and has all the Archetypes around itself, consciously integrated, in Balance. The ego is complete. From thereon, there is no more duality. – Paradoxically, whereas the fifth dimension is lived, the ego continues eternally integrating more unconscious contents in the fourth dimension, it continues to become stronger in the third dimension, it continues to increase its social integration in the second dimension, and so on.

For the 5D ego, who has reached completeness, the *Spirit* is manifested through the *Truth.* The *Truth* does not require interpretation. The apostles, having received the Holy Spirit, **immediately** speak in different tongues and make prophecies. In face of the arrival of the *Spirit* the 5D ego immediately accesses self-evident realities.

The vision of Paul, in his way to Damascus, is illustrative:

> It happened that while he was travelling to Damascus and approaching the city, suddenly a light from heaven shone all round him. He fell to the ground, and then he heard a voice saying, "Saul, Saul, why are you persecuting me?" "Who are you, Lord?" he asked, and the answer came, "I am Jesus, whom you are persecuting. Get up and go into the city, and you will be told what you are to do".[173]

Then Paul[174] goes to Damascus and executes what his vision ordered him.

Clearly, the vision should, and must, be interpreted in four dimensions, as would any dream, since the fourth dimension is eternal. We could, as has been done by many, **interpret** this event as a Symbol for the conversion of Paul, the moral defeat of Paul by its Self. This interpretation would be correct in four dimensions.

However, if we look to the exact same experience in five dimensions, it will be perceived as the expression of *Truth.* That way, we see Paul as a 5D ego, someone who has received the *Spirit,* and this experience **does not require interpretation**, it is self-evident. Paul is indeed having an encounter with Christ, who gives him instructions about how to act.

JUNG often mentions dreams with the Voice. According to him, the dreams with the Voice are of a different nature to the symbolic dreams. He describes them as much "simpler" dreams, in which the Voice says things in a "simple" and clear way, albeit paradoxical. He also says that what is said by the Voice does not need to be interpreted and must be followed without questioning[175]. In my opinion, these dreams are irruptions of the fifth dimension in the middle of less complex structures of the fourth and third dimensions. If the *Spirit* manifests itself as **tongues of fire**, it is understandable that it expresses itself in dreams as a Voice. Paul's vison in his journey to Damascus fits perfectly in this concept: Paul **heard a Voice.**

Such is the nature of the *Spirit*: the expression of *Truth,* simple and direct.

Note that in Paul's experience, Christ acts directly on the material reality. It causes a symptom in Paul, blindness. It tells him exactly what to do. Paul follows the instructions, which prove to be physically realistic, producing material consequences in his life and that of others. For Paul, Christ's reality is exactly that of his soldiers and any other person in Paul's life: Christ does not manifest itself for Paul as a Symbol, but as a person, a concrete person, as a *Truth.*

Paul's experience shows us how a penta-dimensional reality works: **there is no separation between what is spiritual and what is physical**. Or even, the "spiritual world" coincides with the "physical world". In fact, it is only **one world**. It is this reality that DORNEUS refers to when he writes about *Unus Mundus*:

> Learn from within thyself to know all that is in heaven and on earth, and especially that ail was created for thy sake. Knowest thou not that heaven and the elements were formerly *one*, and were separated from one another by divine artifice, that they might bring forth thee and all things? If thou knowest this, the rest cannot escape thee. Therefore in all generation a separation of this kind is necessary [...] Thou wilt never make from others the One which thou seekest, except first there be made *one* thing of thyself [...][176]

Made **one** by Crucifixion, "the rest cannot escape" to the 5D ego.

For someone with less than five dimensions, Paul's experience is, at least, an irruption of the "psychological world" into the "physical world", something that must be interpreted and understood. For the 5D ego, the *Truth* is "simpler": Christ found Paulo in his journey to Damascus and gave him instructions on how to act. For the 5D ego, there is no longer a "psychological world" and a "physical world"; there is only the *Unus Mundus*.

The *Unus Mundus*, although potentially present since Crucifixion, is the final objective of the fifth dimension. So, if we are dealing with a third *coniunctio* here, which are the elements that are coming into conjunction during the experience of the Paradigm of Sense?

The 4D ego, which experiences Crucifixion, was until now busy with the synthesis of pairs of psychological energies. The synthesis occurred completely **intra-psychologically**. At this point we can still talk of a **psychological reality**, separate from a **physical reality**. It is true that, during the fourth dimension, the psychological reality is practiced within the physical reality. The person acts what they have learned intra-psychologically. The two realities are **correspondent**. However, the fact that psychological contents are put into practice does not in any way shortens the abyss that exists between the psychological and physical realities. Only in Crucifixion does the change from the Paradigm of Balance to Sense remove the separation that the dual consciousness of the ego used to impose on the *Truth*, separating it in psychological and physical realities. Henceforth, the 5D ego will have the opportunity of progressively experiencing the *Unus Mundus*. Therefore, the third *coniunctio* operates the integration of the **physical reality** (Sun of the fifth dimension) to the **integrated psychological reality** (Sun-Moon conjunction reached in the second *coniunctio* in fourth dimension).

Now it is possible to consider what JUNG says about the fifth *cakra*, *viśuddha*:

> So if one speaks of *viśuddha*, it is of course with a certain hesitation. We are stepping into the slippery future right away when we try to understand what that might mean. For in *viśuddha* we reach beyond our actual conception of the world. [...] *Viśuddha* means [...] a full recognition of the psychical essences or substances as the fundamental essences of the world, and by virtue not of speculation but of fact, namely as *experience*.[177]

To simplify it, JUNG is saying that in *viśuddha* one **experiences** a coincidence between the "psychical essences" and the "physical essences". The *Unus Mundus* is a paradox between the psychological and physical realities. The 5D ego experiences an event as being **paradoxically** spiritual **and** physical.

Speaking to a dualist audience, JUNG makes an effort to show them an unified reality:

> It is as if the elephant [symbol of *viśuddha*] were now making realities out of concepts. We admit that our concepts are nothing but our imagination, products of our feeling or of our intellect – abstractions or analogies, sustained by no physical phenomena. [...] Yet these are apparently the things sustained and pushed by the elephant, as if the elephant were making a reality of such concepts which are really the mere products of our mind. That is our prejudice – to *think* that those products are not also realities.[178]

There is, however, a huge difference between a material reality that has been **harmonised** with a psychological reality – a state where the 4D ego is in shortly before Crucifixion, where it makes an **effort** to act **according to** the psychological reality – and the penta-dimensional reality, where the physical and psychological realities **paradoxically coincide** and tend towards a total unification at the end of the third *coniunctio*, end of the Paradigm of Sense, in *Unus Mundus*:

> You begin to consider the game of the world as your game, the people that appear outside as exponents of your psychical condition. Whatever befalls you, whatever experience or adventure you have in the external world, is your own experience.[179]

The paradox here is **blunt**. On one hand, there is just the psychological experience itself. **Everything** that is experienced only exists in its own psychological perception, including all the "people", all "objects", all "situations", all "spaces", and all "times". On the other hand, people are really people, acting according to their "free-will", **independent**. The objects, situations, spaces and times are elements of the physical world, subject to physical laws, **independent**. Despite that, despite this apparent separation in "sides", **there is only one reality**: people, although exercising their untouched free-will, and the objects, situations, space and time, despite determined by physical law, will behave **exactly** as they do in their own psychological perception. It is not about two totally compatible realities: this is the dualist way of interpreting the fifth dimension. In fact, there is only one "person" in a single **spiritual** reality, in a single reality that henceforth, we will call ***Pneumatic* reality** (πνεῦμα, pneûma *gr.* = spirit). When the Paradigm of Sense is concluded, this reality will be the *Unus Mundus*.

For that reason, although I understand JUNG's situation when he had to explain these things to an audience with a dualist consciousness, whether this duality was acknowledged (4D) or not (2D and 3D), I cannot agree with his affirmation:

> If you have reached that stage, you begin to leave *anāhata*, because you have succeeded in dissolving the absolute union of material external facts with internal or psychical facts.[180]

I disagree with JUNG because this is a dualist concept, favourable to a psychological supremacy over matter. The fifth dimension is not in any shape or form a way out from the material world, nor is it a state where experience is totally psychological. A unity between material and psychological facts is also not existent before the fifth dimension. Reality is the opposite to JUNG's affirmation. Before the fifth dimension, the material reality was separate from the psychological reality and prevailed, at least insofar as the ego's perception. The fifth dimension, on the other hand, is such an absolute and paradoxical union between the "material facts" and the "psychical facts", that this distinction disappears. It does not, however, disappear in favour of a completely psychological existence. As JUNG himself teaches, when he writes about the transcendent function, when a tension between two opposites is transcendent, **both disappear, making space to a third entity. Therefore, the physical reality (that of the Body) disappears as a separate reality and the psychological reality (that of the Soul)** also **disappears as a separate reality, and in its place a *Pneumatic* reality (that of the *Spirit*) appears, which encompasses and transcends the realities of the *Body* and the Soul, now unified.**

* * * * *

All that remains is to find out what, then, happens to the Soul, at the appearance of the *Spirit.*

The Soul remains.

In the Paradigm of Balance, when the Soul ruled the whole process and there was no access to the *Spirit,* the 4D ego experienced it psychologically, through symbols. From a penta-dimensional perspective, however, looking backwards and simplifying it to facilitate understanding, we see that the *Truth* of the *Spirit* penetrated the Soul, and masking the *Truth*, the Soul generated Symbols; this was a completely unconscious phase. The symbols, in turn, refracted, in the fourth dimension, into energies that the ego associated to itself and others which remained unconscious.

The *Spirit* expresses the *Truth* and the Soul constellates Symbols. This marriage is fundamental.

The penta-dimensional experience of the *Spirit* reveals itself to be extremely clear, and for that very reason, extremely hard. The *Spirit* of *Truth* reveals all the Light and all the Darkness. The Light is extremely difficult to stand due to its grandiosity. The Darkness is extremely difficult to stand due to its grandiosity. Let us take the example of the Apostles, having received the *Holy Spirit*, certainly knew that their Destinies were martyrdom. However ready they felt to fulfil it – after all if they received the *Holy Spirit*, they would have already been Crucified and knew how to surrender – it is not a pleasant experience and it is not human to enjoy such Destiny.

It is, therefore, essential that the fresh and damp Night of the Soul-Moon covers the dry and scorching Day of the Spirit-Sun. Even with the direct and open access to the *Truth* of the fifth dimension, this has nothing to do with the Transcendent Omniscience. It is necessary to be unconscious about a few things. It is necessary to rest.

> By a symbol I do not mean an allegory or a sign, but an image that describes in the best possible way **the dimly discerned nature of the spirit**.[181] [own author's highlights]

The *Spirit* is transcendent, there is nothing individual about it. It is the "Soul of all Souls"[182].

The Soul is also transcendental, but it relates directly with the ego, creating space for the individual. In creating Symbols, from the *Truth* of the *Spirit*, the Soul attributes **individual meaning** to the experience. In being Moon, in relation to the Spirit-Sun, the Soul allows **reflection** about the spiritual experience, avoiding a complete depersonalization.

Finally, the Soul is the bridge between the *Spirit* and the *Body*.

---

[127] RAFF, J. (2000) *Jung and the alchemical imagination.* Chapter 1: "Jung as a spiritual tradition". "The self". JUNG Florida: Nicolas-Hays, Inc. (Kobo eBook version). Quoting Carl JUNG in *Mysterium coniunctionis.* CW XIV/1 §220.

[128] "[...] she (Luna) is also the principle of the feminine psyche, in the sense that Sol is the principle of a man's". JUNG, C. G. (1977) *Mysterium coniunctionis.* Translated by Hull, R. F. C. 2nd edition. CW XIV. Bollingen Series XX. Princeton University Press. §222.

[129] JUNG, C. G. (1985) *The practice of psychotherapy. Abreaction, dream analysis and transference.* Translated Hull, R. F. C. 2nd edition. CW XVI/2. Bollingen Series XX. Princeton University Press.

[130] JUNG, C. G. *Mysterium coniunctionis.* Op. Cit. §220.

[131] "Historically the sun has been associated with the Sky God, the *Pater Familias*, representing solar consciousness, the logos principle." HOLLIS, J. (1995) *Tracking the gods: The place of myth in modern life studies.* Canada: Inner City Books. p. 94.

[132] "Just as the physical sun lightens and warms the universe, so, in the human body, there is in the heart a sunlike arcanum from which life and warmth stream forth. "Therefore Sol," says Dorn, "is rightly named the first after God (*primus post Deum*), and the father and begetter of all, because in him the **seminal and formal virtue of all things whatsoever lies hid**". (*quorumvis siminaria virtus atque formatus delitescit*). JUNG, C. G. *Mysterium coniunctionis.* Op. Cit. § 113. [author's own highlights]

[133] "The heroes are like the wandering sun. [...] the myth of the hero is a solar myth". JUNG, C. G. (1976) *Symbols of transformation.* Translated by Hull, R. F. C. CW V. Bollingen Series XX. Princeton University Press. §299.

[134] "Logos is the active principle behind human thought and reason, often considered to be identical to the Word. It is the principle behind all human and cosmic order. Wisdom, justice, law and human consciousness are all manifestations of Logos." STEIN, R. (1973) *Incest and human love.* Dallas, TX: Spring Publications. p. 86.

[135] "Stevens says (1993: p. 120): *The Logos is the personification of the divine intelligence: it produces order in chaos and illuminates all creation with the consciousness light.*" LIMA FILHO, A. P. (2002) *O pai e a psique.* São Paulo: Editora Paulus. p. 228.

[136] "According to Jung, the Logos has a differentiating and cognitive character, besides implicating a reflective capacity. This means the thought or concept expressed and

articulated, that is, simultaneously a content and a product of consciousness. JUNG, C. G. (1979) *Aion – researches into the phenomenology of the self.* Translated by Hull, R. F. C. 2nd edition. CW IX, part 2. Bollingen Series XX. Princeton University Press. §293.

[137] The Father archetype (Logos) is responsible for those qualities which enable the individual to be stable, to withstand the disrupting storms and pressures of life, to be steadfast and committed to something beyond the immediate and personal. [...] It is inner strength, perseverance and stability to stand alone, to endure the tensions of living which are essential for psychological development." STEIN, R. (1973) *Incest and human love.* Dallas, TX: Spring Publications. p. 86.

[138] "The moon is the embodiment of the unconscious, maternal, waxing and waning in twenty-eight-day cycles, source of all, harbor of respite and siren call to regression." HOLLIS, J. (1995) *Tracking the gods: The place of myth in modern life studies.* Los Angeles: Inner City Books. p. 94.

[139] "For every stage and development that presses toward patriarchal consciousness – i.e., toward the sun – the moon-spirit becomes the spirit of regression, the spirit of the Terrible Mother and the Witch." NEUMANN, E. (1994) *The fear of the feminine: and other essays on feminine psychology.* Princeton University Press. p. 94.

[140] "Matriarchal consciousness experiences the mysteriously unknown process of the coming-into-being of an insight or of knowledge as an activity in which the Self as a whole is at work. This is a process running its course in the dark. The Self is dominant as the moon, but above and beyond it the Self rules as the Great Mother, as the unity of all things nocturnal and of the nocturnal realm." Ibid. p. 91.

[141] "When Eros is conceived as feminine, the principle of openness, receptivity and responsiveness is stressed. As a masculine Deity it becomes much more active, outgoing, penetrating, and, therefore, phallic principle. Eros is at once the *great opener* and *great receiver* – so that its true nature is hermaphroditic. Eros seems to function as a mediator between the Divine and the human." STEIN, R. (1973) *Incest and human love.* Dallas, TX: Spring Publications. p. 119.

[142] Katabasis: from the Greek κατὰ (downwards) + βαίνω (go): go downwards, descend.

[143] "Regarding κατάβασις (katabasis), the 'descent' of Heracles to Hades, it is known that it represents the supreme initiation rite: the katabasis, the symbolic death, is the indispensable condition for an *anabasis*, an 'ascent', a definitive hike in search of the ἀναγνώρισις (anagnorisis), of self-awareness, of the transformation of what is left of the old person into the new person. I this respect, Luc Benoist rightly wrote: 'The underground trip, during which the encounters with the mythical monsters represent the ordeals of an initiation process, was, in reality, a recognition of oneself, a rejection of the inhibiting psychological residues, a 'disposal of the metals', a 'dissolution of the shell', in consonance with the inscription recorded on the gates of Delphi temple: 'Know thyself'". BRANDÃO DE SOUZA, J. (1989) [Translated from the Portuguese: *Mitologia grega.* Petrópolis, RJ: Editora Vozes. p. 114.]

[144] "The *coniunctio oppositorum* in the guise of Sol and Luna, the royal brother-sister or mother-son pair, occupies such an important place in alchemy that sometimes the entire process takes the form of the *hierosgamos* and its mystic consequences". JUNG, C. G. (1985) *The Practice of psychotherapy. Abreaction, dream analysis and transference.* Translated by Hull, R. F. C. 2nd edition. CW XVI/2. Bollingen Series XX. Princeton University Press. §401.

145 "The sun is an aspect of consciousness, being a phenomenon partly linked with the ego and partly with the Self. One aspect of the sun is open to the unconscious, for the two rays imply a principle of consciousness capable of embracing the opposites, while the other sun is "a closed system" it is one-sided and therefore destructive. In *Mysterium Coniunctionis* Jung describes the sun as an image of the spiritual divinity, i.e., the *Self* on the one hand, and an aspect of the ego on the other". von FRANZ, M. L. (1980) *Alchemy: an introduction to the symbolism and the psychology.* – Canada: Inner City Books. p. 155.

146 "The moon with her antithetical nature is, in a sense, a prototype of individuation, a prefiguration of the self: she is the 'mother and spouse of the sun, who carries in the wind and the air the spagyric embryo conceived by the sun in her womb and belly.' [...] Just as the anima represents and personifies the collective unconscious, so Luna represents the six planets or spirits of the metals". JUNG, C. G. (1977) *Mysterium coniunctionis.* Translated by Hull, R. F. C. 2nd edition. CW XIV. Bollingen Series XX. Princeton University Press. §217.

147 "For Jung, the image of the soul belonged to the idea of unity. Not only did the soul **unite two people**, it also **functioned internally** as a kind of **psychic ligament that kept the dissimilar parts of our personality united within us**. So, Jung can speak of "the reconciler, the soul". For this reason, he says, we must have people in our lives who are in a meaningful relationship to us, for otherwise we cannot develop. A purely detached insight into ourselves lacks soul-vitality, and **a radical understanding of ourselves is impossible without a human partner** [...]". SANFORD, J. (1991) *Soul journey*: *A Jungian analyst looks at reincarnation.* Crossroads Publications. P.119. [author's own highlights]

148 JUNG, C. G. *The Practice of psychotherapy. Abreaction, dream analysis and transference.* Op. Cit. §504.

149 "Just as it is said of Christ that he sacrificed himself for the whole of humanity and for each single human being – even for the still unborn generations – in the same way we may say that the Buddha's Enlightenment (as that of any other realized being) included all living beings and will benefit them till the end of time". GOVINDA, A. (1975) *Foundations of Tibetan mysticism.* New York: Samuel Weiser. p. 235.

150 "The inner instability of Yahweh is the prime cause not only of the creation of the world, but also of the pleromatic drama for which mankind serves as a tragic chorus. **The encounter with the creature changes the creator**. [...] Job is the innocent sufferer, but Ezekiel witnesses the humanization and differentiation of Yahweh. By being addressed as "Son of Man", it is intimated to him that Yahweh's incarnation and quaternity are, so to speak, the pleromatic model for what is going to happen, through the **transformation and humanization of God**, not only to God's son as foreseen from all eternity, but to man as such". JUNG, C. G. (1975) *Psychology and religion: West and East. – Answer to Job.* Translated by Hull, R. F. C. 2nd edition. CW XI/2. Bollingen Series XX. Princeton University Press. §686. [author's own highlights]

151 "Job marks the climax of this unhappy development. He epitomizes a thought which had been maturing in mankind about that time – a dangerous thought that makes great demands on the wisdom of gods and men. Though conscious of these demands, Job obviously does not know enough about the Sophia who is coeternal with God. Because man feels himself at the mercy of Yahweh's capricious will, he is in need of wisdom; not so Yahweh, who up to now has had nothing to contend with except man's nothingness. With the Job drama, however, the **situation undergoes a radical change**. Here Yahweh

comes up against a man who stands firm, who clings to his rights until he is compelled to give way to brute force". Ibid. §623. [author's own highlights]

152 "Jesus, it is plain, **translated the existing tradition into his own personal reality, announcing the glad tidings**: "God has good pleasure in mankind. He is a loving father and loves you as I love you, and has sent me as his son to **ransom you from the old debt**." He offers himself as an expiatory sacrifice that shall effect the reconciliation with God. The more desirable a real relationship of trust between man and God, the more astonishing becomes Yahweh's vindictiveness and irreconcilability towards his creatures. From a God who is a loving father, who is actually Love itself, one would expect understanding and forgiveness. So it comes as a nasty shock when this supremely good God only allows the purchase of such an act of grace through a human sacrifice, and, what is worse, through the killing of his own son. Christ apparently overlooked this anticlimax; at any rate all succeeding centuries have accepted it without opposition. One should keep before one's eyes the strange fact that the God of goodness is so unforgiving that he can only be appeased by a human sacrifice! This is an insufferable incongruity which modern man can no longer swallow, for he must be blind if he does not see the glaring light it throws on the divine character, giving the lie to all talk about love and the 'Summum Bonum'. [...] **the focus of the divine drama shifts to the** mediating *God-man*. [...] Although it is generally assumed that Christ's unique sacrifice **broke the curse of original sin and finally placated God**, Christ nevertheless seems to have had certain misgivings in this respect. Ibid. §689-691. [author's own highlights]

153 According to the rather complicated teachings of Basilides, the "non-existent" God begot a threefold sonship (υἱοτῆς). The first "son," whose nature was the finest and most subtle, remained up above with the Father. The second son, having a grosser (παχυμερέστερα) nature, descended a bit lower, but received "some such wing as that with which Plato equips the soul in his *Phaedrus*." The third son, as his nature needed purifying (ἀποκαθάρσις), fell deepest into "formlessness." This third "sonship" is obviously the grossest and heaviest because of its impurity. In these three emanations or manifestations of the non-existent God it is not hard to see the trichotomy of **spirit, soul, and body** (πνευματικόν, ψυχικόν, σαρκικόν). Spirit is the finest and highest; **soul, as the *ligamentum spiritus et corporis***, is grosser than spirit, but has "the wings of an eagle," so that it may lift its heaviness up to the higher regions. Both are of a "subtle" nature and dwell, like the ether and the eagle, in or near the region of light, whereas the body, being heavy, dark, and impure, is deprived of the light but nevertheless contains the divine seed of the third sonship, though still *unconscious and formless*. This seed is as it were awakened by Jesus, purified and made capable of ascension (ἀναδρομή) [...]" JUNG, C. G. (1979) *Aion – researches into the phenomenology of the self*. Translated by Hull, R. F. C. 2nd edition. CW IX, part 2. Bollingen Series XX. Princeton University Press. §118. [author's own highlights]

154 "Though we do not possess a physics of the soul, and are not even able to observe it and judge it from some Archimedean point "outside" ourselves, and can therefore know nothing objective about it since all knowledge of the psyche is itself psychic, in spite of all this **the soul is the only experient of life and existence**. It is, in fact, the only immediate experience we can have and the *sine qua non* of the subjective reality of the world. **The symbols it creates are always grounded in the unconscious archetype, but their manifest forms are moulded by the ideas acquired by the conscious mind. The archetypes are the numinous, structural elements of the psyche and possess a certain autonomy and specific energy which enables them to attract, out of the conscious mind, those contents which are best suited to themselves. The symbols act as *transformers,* their function being to convert libido from a "lower" into a**
112

"higher" form." JUNG, C. G. (1976) *Symbols of transformation*. Translated by Hull, R. F. C. CW V. Bollingen Series XX. Princeton University Press. §344. [author's own highlights]

155 "As against this historical evolution of the idea of the soul, **analytical psychology opposes the view that the soul does not coincide with the totality of the psychic functions. We define the soul on the one hand as the relation to the unconscious, and on the other as a personification of unconscious contents. [...] If the "soul" is a personification of unconscious contents, then, according to our previous definition, God too is an unconscious content, a personification in so far as he is thought of as personal, and an image or expression of something in so far as he is thought of as dynamic. God and the soul are essentially the same when regarded as personifications of an unconscious content. [...] God, life at its most intense, then resides in the soul, in the unconscious.**" JUNG, C. G. (1976) *Psychological types*. Translated by Baynes, H. G. CW VI. Bollingen Series XX. Princeton: Princeton University Press. §§420 and 421. [author's own highlights]

156 Notes 153, 154 and 155 are different from the original in Portuguese.

Note 153: "The **unconscious** is part of the psyche." JUNG, C. G. (1975) *The structure and dynamics of the psyche. On the nature of the psyche*. Translated by Hull, R. F. C. CW VIII. Bollingen Series XX. Princeton University Press. §298. [author's own highlights]

Note 154: "It is in my view a great mistake to suppose that **the psyche** of a new-born child is a *tabula rasa* in the sense that there is absolutely nothing in it. In so far as the child is born with a differentiated brain that is predetermined by heredity and therefore individualized, it meets sensory stimuli coming from outside not with *any* aptitudes, but with *specific* ones, and this necessarily results in a particular, individual choice and pattern of apperception. [...] **They are the archetypes**, which direct all fantasy activity into its appointed paths and in this way produce, in the fantasy-images of children's dreams. [...] It is not, therefore, a question of inherited *ideas* but of inherited *possibilities* of ideas. Nor are they individual acquisitions but, in the main, common to all, as can be seen from the universal occurrence of the archetypes". JUNG, C. G. (1977) *The archetypes and the collective unconscious*. Translated by Hull, R. F. C. CW IX, part 1. Bollingen Series XX. Princeton University Press CW IX/1. §136. [author's own highlights]

Note 155: "For, as Jung says, the mandala communicates "the sensing of a enter of personality, **a kind of central point within the psyche**, to which everything is related, by which everything is arranged, and which is itself a source of energy." JACOBI, J. (1959) *Complex/Archetypes/Symbol in the Psychology of C. G. Jung*. Translated by Manheim, R. Bollingen Series LVII. Bollingen Foundation, Inc. p. 129. [author's own highlights]

157 Symbol: from the Greek σύν (with, together) + βαλλεῖν (throw): throw together. Literally, it is a symbol, a sign or a proof (in general a coin), where one half was compared to the other to verify authenticity. PEREIRA, I. (1990) [Translated from the Portuguese version: *Dicionário Grego-Português e Português-Grego*. São Paulo: Apostolado da Imprensa Martins Fontes.]

158 "[...] the unconscious produces *compensating symbols* which are meant to replace the broken bridges, but which can only do so with the active co-operation of consciousness. In other words, these symbols must, if they are to be effective, be "understood" by the conscious mind; they must be assimilated and integrated. A dream that is not understood remains a mere occurrence; **understood, it becomes a living experience**". JUNG, C. G. (1985) *The practice of psychotherapy* Translated by Hull, R. F. C. 2nd edition. CW XVI. Bollingen Series XX. Princeton University Press. §252. [author's own highlights]

[159] "The number of archetypes operative in man coincides with that of the "nodal points" of the collective unconscious and seems to be very great. But the number of symbols based on them must be conceived as infinitely greater, since individual states of mind also play a part in their formation; their variations are indeed unlimited. **Their specific content appears only in the course of the individual's (or group's) life when personal experience is taken up** in precisely these forms (i.e., the archetypes)." JACOBI, J. (1959) *Complex/Archetype/Symbol in the psychology of C. G. Jung.* Translated by Manheim, R. Bollingen Foundation, Inc. p. 116. [author's own highlights]

[160] *The New Jerusalem Bible.* John 16:5-13.

[161] Ibid. John 16:7.

[162] JUNG, C. G. (1977) *The archetypes and the collective unconscious.* Translated by Hull, R. F. C. CW IX, part 1. Bollingen Series XX. Princeton University Press. §55.

[163] Mercurius is also the "water" [...] Mercurius shares his "aquaeositas" with water, since on the one hand he is a metal and amalgamates himself in solid form with other metals, and on the other hand is liquid and evaporable. The deeper reason why he is so frequently compared with water is that he unites in himself all those numinous qualities which water possesses. Thus, as the central arcanum, the ὕδωρ θεῖον [hýdor theîon] or *aqua permanens* dominated alchemy from those remote times". JUNG, C. G. (1977) *Mysterium coniunctionis.* Translated by Hull, R. F. C. 2nd edition. CW XIV. Bollingen Series XX. Princeton University Press. §717.

[164] *The New Jerusalem Bible.* Op. Cit. Marc 1:7-8.

[165] *The New Jerusalem Bible.* John 4:2.

[166] *The New Jerusalem Bible.* Acts 2:1-4.

[167] GOVINDA, A. *Foundations of Tibetan mysticism.* Op. Cit. p.18.

[168] JUNG, C. G. *Mysterium Coniunctionis.* Op. Cit. §413.

[169] Ibid. §681.

[170] Ibid.

[171] Ibid.

[172] "I conceive it as functional adjustment in general, an inherent self-regulation of the psychic apparatus In this sense, I regard the activity of the unconscious as a balancing of the one-sidedness of the general attitude produced by the function of consciousness. Psychologists often compare consciousness to the eye: we speak of a visual field and a focal point of consciousness. The nature of consciousness is aptly characterized by this simile: only a limited number of contents can be held in the conscious field at the same time, and of these only a few can attain the highest grade of consciousness. The activity of consciousness is selective. Selection demands direction. But direction requires the exclusion of everything irrelevant. This is bound to make the conscious orientation (q.v.) one-sided. The contents that are excluded and inhibited by the chosen direction sink into the unconscious, where they form a counterweight to the conscious orientation. The strengthening of this counterposition keeps pace with the increase of conscious onesidedness until finally a noticeable tension is produced. This tension inhibits the activity of consciousness to a certain extent, and though at first the inhibition can be broken down by increased conscious effort, in the end the tension becomes so acute that the repressed unconscious contents breakthrough in the form of dreams and

spontaneous images. The more one-sided the conscious attitude, the more antagonistic are the contents arising from the unconscious, so that we may speak of a real opposition between the two. In this case the compensation appears in the form of a counter-function, but this case is extreme. As a rule, the unconscious compensation does not run counter to consciousness, but is rather a balancing or supplementing of the conscious orientation. In dreams, for instance, the unconscious supplies all those contents that are constellated by the conscious situation but are inhibited by conscious selection, although a knowledge of them would be indispensable for complete adaptation". JUNG, C. G. (1976) *Psychological types.* Translated by Baynes, H.G. CW VI. Bollingen Series XX. Princeton University Press. §694.

[173] *The New Jerusalem Bible.* Op. Cit. Acts 9:3-6.

[174] Saul changes his name to Paul. *The New Jerusalem Bible.* Acts 13:9.

[175] "The phenomenon of the "voice" in dreams always has for the dreamer the final and indisputable character of the αὐτός ἔφα, i.e., the voice expresses some **truth** or condition that is beyond all doubt". JUNG, C. G. (1980) *Psychology and alchemy.* Translated by Hull, R. F. C. 2nd edition. CW XII Bollingen Series XX. Princeton University Press. §115.

[176] JUNG, C. G. *Mysterium Coniunctionis.* Op. Cit. §685

[177] JUNG, C. G. (1996) *The psychology of Kundalini Yoga.* Bollingen Series XCIX. Princeton University Press. P. 47.

[178] Ibid., p. 55.

[179] Ibid., p. 49-50.

[180] Ibid., p. 49.

[181] JUNG, C. G. (1975) *The structure and dynamics of the psyche. On the nature of the psyche.* Translated by Hull, R. F. C. CW VIII. Bollingen Series XX. Princeton University Press. §644.

[182] "The thought Dorn expresses by the third degree of conjunction is universal: it is the relation or identity of the personal with the suprapersonal *atman*, and of the individual *tao* with the universal *Tao*". JUNG, C. G. *Mysterium coniunctionis.* Op. Cit. §762.

Paradigm of Sense

BODY

The present humanity is fanatic about the separation of body and mind. This separation, however, is merely circumstantial, and part of the present phase of psychological development of humanity, not at all close to "reality". In fact, reality is something that constantly changes.

The body precedes consciousness.

Before the existence of the ego, before someone can pronounce the word "me", and understand its meaning, even if negligibly, there is a psychological experience named **corporeal Self** by Eric NEUMANN[183,184]. According to the author, the first phase of one's life is uroboric, when there is no ego. The child lives in a paradisiac state, with no psychological tension, in a relationship with the mother. There is no distinction between the mother and the child, nor between the ego and the Self. The uroboric phase comprises of an intrauterine part, and another that spams from two months to one year of age, approximately. In this second part, the psyche organises itself around the corporeal Self. In a simplistic way we can say that, since the child does not yet have a formed ego, it experiences itself through the body, which, in turn, in this phase, coincides entirely with the Self. Since the Self is Wholeness, this means that any stimulation to the child's body will be understood as a stimulation to Wholeness. For that reason, if the child's body is satisfied, the child feels totally satisfied, not just their body. On the other hand, if the child's body is hurt, the child feels hurt, not just their body. This phase is marked by an immediatism, since all the child's needs are usually satisfied as immediately as possible. There is no lapse of time between a need and its satisfaction, in the same way as there is no psychological space for the birth of consciousness.

However, very quickly, the good mother becomes the bad mother. A delay begins to appear between the physical need of the child and its satisfaction by the mother. This delay slowly teaches the child that they continue to exist despite the physical discomfort. It is fundamental that this learning occurs, otherwise the child loses its natural sense of omnipotence (identification with the Self), will not form their ego and will be unable to live in society.

This understanding increases with the way the mother and other adults continue to treat the child as a separate being to the body. Despite the child's hunger, the mother says: "Lunch is not ready. Wait." Despite the child's agitation, the mother says: "It's time to sleep." Despite the child's bruise, the mother says: "You hurt **your** hand. You don't need to cry. Let's put a plaster on it." Taking the bruise as an example, reality is presented to the child as "the **hand** was bruised", **not** "the **child** was bruised". **The body has become an object owned by consciousness**.

In the face of the excesses of patriarchy, abstractionism, the destruction of the environment and the subjection of the body, it has been said that the separation between mind and body – albeit "mind" is a terrible substitute for "consciousness" – is a type of **cultural accident**. That is, a mistaken concept that has been perpetuated. Had this opinion been correct, Plato would have been greatly responsible for the accident, since he described reality through a rigid separation between the world of ideas – a potential and immaterial world where everything exists in perfection – and the world of appearances, the physical world in which we live, lacking reality and full of imperfections.

It is not an accident, but a phase of consciencial development. In *Incest and Human Love*[185], Robert STEIN shows that the Archetype of Incest has a particular way of functioning: **paradoxically**, it creates desire for incest between brother and sister **and** it also creates a strong taboo against the physical consummation of this incest. Unable to take place physically, the incest between brother and sister can only occur **imaginatively**. Through this mechanism, this Archetype is able to develop in the human being progressively higher levels of abstract consciousness, which is not restricted to the theme of incest, but applied to all spheres of human life[186]. Note that this Archetype causes the appearance of psychological instances that cannot be experienced in the body.

The phase change from the Nourishing Mother to the Terrible Mother and the mechanism of the Archetype of Incest are some of the evidences that a distinction, at least between consciousness and body, is absolutely essential, contributing to the development of consciousness and therefore a phase of development. The separation between consciousness and body is whole in the Paradigm of Self-Affirmation. The basic law of this paradigm is the development of the ego and its final objective is the construction of an ego capable of affirming itself more and more in relation to the unconsciousness, in relation to life. The ego wants to affirm itself. For that purpose, it transforms the body into something that it **owns** and can **control** as it sees fit, **using** it in its self-affirmations. Those who affirm themselves through force **have** a strong body, those who affirm themselves through beauty **have** a beautiful body, those who affirm themselves through disease **have** a sick body, and so on. As the third-dimensional ego is autocratic, everything else will be placed under its tyranny, including the body.

When the Self appears consciously to the ego and defeats it morally, opening the Paradigm of Balance, the psyche "appears" to the ego and brings the body with it. The body is no longer an object and becomes a **psychological perception**. Supporting this point of view, JUNG says:

> So when we say body, we really mean our psychic experience of the body. [...] The body, therefore, is also a psychological condition, a peculiar form of consciousness.[187]

Before anything else, a very important warning. The discovery of the psyche, the immensity of the psyche, the wonder of the psyche and even the meaning that the contact with the psyche attributes to aspects so far incomprehensible or unacceptable of reality, create a tendency to consider the abstract psyche as something superior or better than the body. The prejudices with the body, particularly established by PLATO (if we consider his writings as philosophy) and by Christianity, profess the **exit of this world**, leaving behind the body, considered inferior. Against this ignorant and distorted view of reality, JUNG takes a stand:

> All people who claim to be spiritual try to get away from the fact of the body; they want to destroy it in order to be something imaginary, but they never will be that, because the body denies them; the body says otherwise.[188]

The desire to leave the physical world is a hyperbole of the third-dimensional structure, in which the ego considers itself superior to the body because it professes, ultimately, that it can exist without the body. The desire to leave the physical world, besides being a demonstration of cowardice in the face of a reality deemed unbearable, reveals an ignorance about the structure of the psyche and of the fourth dimension.

> For what is the body? The body is merely the visibility of the soul, the psyche; and the soul is the psychological experience of the body. So it is really one and the same thing.[189]

The fourth-dimensional structure notices reality as an **acknowledged duality**. For that reason, it is necessary to concede that the psyche and the body will be seen as separate things, even if the Symbols that lead to the process of individuation continually show the unity Psyche-Body. Until a multi-paradoxical consciousness is reached at Crucifixion, the acknowledged duality will remain.

The body performs a crucial function in the process of individuation: it is its criteria of reality.

> Only if you return to the body, to your earth, can individuation take place, only then does the thing become true.[190]

> Whatever you experience outside of the body, in a dream for instance, is not experienced unless you take it into the body, because the body means the here and now.[191]

JUNG declares that the **individuation needs to be experienced in the body**. In practice, this means that the psychological processes are only valid if they modify the person's body directly, as well as its material reality. Individuation needs to cause concrete changes in the person's life because, if it is happening in the body, the individuation will affect the person's reality and cause a change of attitude. More than that, if the individuation is occurring in the body, changes in the organization of the unconsciousness (i.e. which complexes are there and how they are organised, and which Archetypes are constellated) will cause changes in the attitude that **life** has towards that person. This means that some events will stop occurring and new types of events will appear. Individuation has to show concrete results.

As it has been said before, it is normal that the present humanity experiences a dichotomy between psyche and body, since it is mainly third-dimensional. However, very unfortunately, this dichotomy is also present in many psychologists who consider themselves apt to work with Depth Psychology; and this is inadmissible. These psychologists **understand** the process of individuation and **explain** it to the patient. The patient **understands** their problem and **does nothing about it** because **understanding** is not a **concrete** change[192]. Understanding is an operation performed by the rational mind, which attributes a tiring monologue to the present perspective about the human consciousness. The rational mind is nowhere close to consciousness. The present teaching structure, which almost exclusively prefers the rational mind, contributes to this false sensation of knowing, created by understanding. Therefore, the fallacy of a "rational individuation" is validated.

Consciousness involves a small part known as rational mind, but goes way beyond it; it is also feeling, intuition, physical sensation, memory, and much more. The body is precisely the element that differentiates a fallacious understanding from an actual individuation. It is the same difference between reading about an experience, on a book in the comfort of your sofa, and having a corporeal experience. Reading about alpinism is not the same as climbing a steep peak. Only in the body the consciousness is capable of realizing the psychological processes necessary to individuation. How to de-identify, how to deal with a psychological projection, how to integrate a complex without living a concrete, corporeal experience? Even more, **to what purpose** would one carry out the process of individuation if not to live a life concretely different?

Consciousness is act.

The prejudices of Christianity (and PLATO) have led people to believe that the spiritual path is ascension – the more abstract, the **less corporeal**, the more spiritual. This is so false that the Gospel itself contradicts it:

> "In the beginning was the Word: the Word was with God and the Word was God. The Word was the real light that gives light to everyone; he was **coming into the world**. [...] **The Word became flesh**, he lived among us, and we saw his glory, the glory that he has from the Father as only Son of the Father, full of grace and truth."[193]

John makes it very clear: **the spiritual energy is descendant, not** ascendant. Its objective is to **incarnate, not** leave this wold. In the same way, in the *Kabbalah*, o *TzimTzum* is the energy that **descends** from *Keter* a *Malkhut*[194]. Finally, in the Tibetan Buddhism, the perfect (OM) wants to be realised in the more-than-perfect and the definition of more-than-perfect (HUM) is the perfection **realised in the *Body.***

There is a possible archetypal reason for the existence of the fallacy of ascension as a spiritual path. In order to understand it, we need to take a step back.

First, let us establish a clear difference between instinct and body.

> [...] This means – to employ once more the simile of the spectrum – that the instinctual image is to be located not at the red end but at the violet end of the colour band. **The dynamism of instinct is lodged as it were in the infrared part of the spectrum, whereas the instinctual image lies in the ultraviolet part...**[195] [author's own highlights]

The text has the advantage of defining instinct in a very schematic manner, using the metaphor of the spectrum of colours. JUNG outlines a fantastic relationship between instinct and Archetype, treating them, respectively, as **dynamism of the instinct** and **instinctual image** (Archetype). Yes, JUNG is saying that the Archetype is the **image** of an **instinct**. In putting things in those terms, JUNG affirms that the Archetype is, ultimately, an instinct: the instinct has a **dynamism** and an **image**, respectively the infrared and the ultraviolet ends of the spectrum. Bearing in mind that JUNG establishes a unique base – the **instinct** – for both, for the sake of didacticism, we will use the terms **Instinct** (dynamism of the instinct) and **Archetype** (image of the instinct).

If we take the visible colours as a symbol of consciousness, we notice something valuable about the instinct, something obvious but that does not normally stay in consciousness. If both the Instinct and the Archetype are in the invisible part of the spectrum, Instinct and Archetype are **transcendental**.

From this perception, it is easier to differentiate instinct and body. The instinct and the archetype are both **transcendental instances** which focus on the consciousness and the body.

Besides, if instinct and Archetype are transcendental, both should have the same spiritual value.

However, is does not work like that.

> The realization and assimilation of instinct never take place at the red end, i.e., by absorption into the instinctual sphere, but only through integration of the image which **signifies** and at the same

time **evokes** the instinct, although in a form quite different from the one we meet on the biological level.[196] [author's own highlights]

This occurs because, despite my previous affirmations about the spiritual energy being descendent, specifically in the fourth dimension there is a pronounced elevation of the energy in the direction of the abstract. By elevation of energy I mean the fact that the Paradigm of Balance prioritises the Archetype over the Instinct. This is fundamental because the objective of the paradigm is to integrate the Soul, the 4D Self, and this is only possible if there is an understanding of **meaning**. And this, only the archetypal image can generate, and the mere satisfaction of instinct will never do. **Paradoxically**, to integrate the Soul is to surrender to the Soul, to follow it in everything it determines. Once more, this is only possible if there is an understanding of the meaning brought by the archetypal image; the mere satisfaction of the instinct will never do.

For this reason, the *Rosarium Philosophorum* and many other alchemical documents show that, initially, it is fundamental that the Soul must leave the Body and ascend. Only **after** this process, it becomes fundamental that **the Soul returns to the Body, animating it**[197].

If anyone goes towards their own Crucifixion, it is necessary to overcome even the extremely powerful survival instinct, and that is only possible if the **meaning** is colossal, if the Archetype is enormous.

The instinct affects the body so greatly, especially in youth, that most people confuse the concepts of instinct and body. It is true that the immense psychological task of surrendering to the Soul through the archetypal meaning occurs, at least up to a certain point, in detriment of the body and instinct. This combination of ideas, unconscious to most people, can be the origin of the prejudices disseminated by Christianity.

In any case, this is the position of the Body in the Paradigm of Balance. **First**, with the exit of the Soul from the Body, the 4D ego prioritizes the Archetype, the meaning of the psychological experiences, following it in detriment of the Body and the Instinct. **Paradoxically**, to follow the Archetype – in spite of the Body and the Instinct – is part of the corporeal experience (of being able to restrict the instinct) needed for individuation to occur. Afterwards, **at the end of the process**, with the return of the Soul to the Body, the 4D ego needs to experience its individuated consciousness **in the Body**. After all, the consciousness is only individuated if it is in the Body.

When dealing with the Unconscious, nothing is so linear. The path to integration symbolized, for example, by the *Rosarium Philosophorum*, with many stages including the ascension of the Soul and the return to the Body, is travelled my times over. The alchemists say, for example, that "a thousand distillations" are necessary[198].

However, one of these times is particularly special. One of the ascensions of the Soul is the Crucifixion. In the Crucifixion, the ascension of the Soul is so high that it produces a definitive unification between the Soul and the *Spirit*. In this crucial moment, the Paradigm of Balance ends and the Paradigm of Sense starts. This time, the Soul returns to the *body* followed by the *Spirit*. After this ascension, the direction of the energy is inverted permanently: the spiritual energy becomes once again **descendent**.

The return of the Soul to the *Body* and the descent of the *Spirit* over the Soul and *Body* have as their primary effect the *Resurrection*, a **resurrected body**.

> After the Sabbath, and towards dawn on the first day of the week, Mary of Magdala and the other Mary went to visit the sepulchre. And suddenly there was a violent earthquake, for an angel of the Lord, descending from heaven, came and rolled away the stone and sat on it. His face was like lightning, his robe white as snow. The guards were so shaken by fear of him that they were like dead men. But the angel spoke; and he said to the women, 'There is no need for you to be afraid. I know you are looking for Jesus, who was crucified. He is not here, for he has risen, as he said he would.[199]

JUNG describes the phenomenon in alchemic language:

> The old philosophers knew of the coming of the end of the world and the resurrection of the dead. Then the soul will be united with its original body for ever and ever. The body will become wholly transfigured *[glorificatum]*, incorruptible, and almost unbelievably subtilized, and it will penetrate all solids. **Its nature will be as much spiritual as corporeal**. When the stone decomposes to a powder like a man in his grave, **God restores to it soul and spirit**, and takes away all imperfection; then is that substance (*ilia* res) strengthened and improved, as after the resurrection a man becomes stronger and younger than he was before.
>
> [...]

It is clear enough from this material what the ultimate aim of alchemy really was: it was trying to produce a *corpus subtile,* a **transfigured and resurrected body**, i.e., a **body that was at the same time spirit**.[200] [author's own highlights]

As mentioned in the chapter *"Spirit":* "[...] when a tension between two opposites is transcendent, both disappear, making space to a third entity. Therefore, the physical reality (that of the Body) disappears as a separate reality and the psychological reality (that of the Soul) also disappears as a separate reality, and in its place a ***Pneumatic* reality** appears (that of the *Spirit*), which encompasses and transcends the realities of the *Body* and the Soul, now unified." Being a reality of the *Spirit,* the *Pneumatic* reality is unified. Any distinction between a "reality of the *Spirit"*, and a "reality of the *Body"* is no longer possible; this would be completely artificial, unreal. As JUNG explains, in the resurrection of the dead, the *Body* is entirely transfigured, and its nature is **both spiritual and corporeal**.

Spirit IS *Body*[201,202].

With no access to the fifth dimension, without a fifth-dimensional ego, this reality is inapprehensible. It is unbelievable that the *Spirit,* seen in previous dimensions as something so elevated and subtle, is the *Body*. In fact, the *Spirit* is so much *Body* that it can be touched by anyone.

Thomas, called the Twin, who was one of the Twelve, was not with them when Jesus came. So the other disciples said to him, 'We have seen the Lord,' but he answered, 'Unless I can see the holes that the nails made in his hands and can put my finger into the holes they made, and unless I can put my hand into his side, I refuse to believe.' Eight days later the disciples were in the house again and Thomas was with them. The doors were closed, but Jesus came in and stood among them. 'Peace be with you,' he said. Then he spoke to Thomas, 'Put your finger here; look, here are my hands. Give me your hand; put it into my side. Do not be unbelieving any more but believe.' Thomas replied, 'My Lord and my God!' Jesus said to him: You believe because you can see me. Blessed are those who have not seen and yet believe.[203]

In the same way, **spiritual reality IS physical reality**. From this point on, any spiritual action is simultaneously physical, and every physical action is simultaneously spiritual. Even the expression of this, in terms of simultaneity, is artificial, because a 5D ego **does not** experience a Spirit-

Body simultaneity. It experiments a **Pneumatic unity** and, since we need some language to express it, experiences a **Pneumatic Body**.

Not just the corporeal reality has been left behind – since the 5D ego now experiences a *Pneumatic* body – but also what was experienced as a psychological reality has also been left behind, in favour of an **entirely Pneumatic reality**, where the images, before experienced as psychological images, are now experienced as **Pneumatic Bodies** of the same nature to the 5D ego.

Jeffrey RAFF is the author of a monumental work *Jung and the alchemical imagination*[204], one of the first books that I found which describes penta-dimensional experiences. In the chapter "Jung as a spiritual tradition", RAFF clearly demonstrates the difference between one psychological reality (4D) and a *Pneumatic* experience (5D). He starts by describing a psychological experience:

> Active imagination connects individuals with inner figures which, while very powerful, are clearly imaginal and **derived from the psyche**. These figures feel as if they were coming from within oneself. Typically one experiences them with eyes closed, and attention directed inward. These are the psyche figures that personify the forces of the unconscious.[205] [own author's highlights]

Following that, he describes what seems to be a **Pneumatic** experience:

> However, every so often, one may experience a figure that feels completely different. This figure feels as if it were coming from outside oneself, as if it existed in the external world, in the room in which one finds oneself, for example. One's eyes are open, and the felt sense is that one perceives **a figure that does not come from within**. The attention of the ego is focused outward, not inward. These are the experiences I refer to using the term 'psychoid'.[206] [own author's highlights]

The completely different figure "does not come from within". If the ego has "open eyes" with the attention "focused outward", what it is seeing is the **Pneumatic Body** of a figure. In the introduction of this work, the author defines what he means by psychoid:

"When body becomes spirit and spirit and spirit becomes body, we enter a new realm of experience that I call the *psychoid*".[207]

RAFF refers to the unity between Spirit and Body, making clear that it is about "a new realm of experience", which is **not** psychological, a realm that he calls **psychoid**.

JUNG also uses the term "psychoid". Paulo Ferreira BONFATTI cites JUNG about this terminology, in *The dynamics of the unconscious* (CW VIII), in the texts "Synchronicity: a principle of acausal connections" and "Theoretical considerations about the nature of the psyche":

> Although [the archetypes] are associated to causal processes [...], they are continuously overcoming their own limits, a procedure that I would call *transgression because the archetypes are not certainly or exclusively found in the psychological sphere, but could also occur in non-psychological circumstances* (equivalence of an external physical process with a psychological process)[208].
>
> [...]
>
> [About the] nature of the archetype. We must not mistake the archetypical representations that are transmitted by the unconscious with the *archetype itself*. These representations are widely varied structures that lead us to a basic unrepresentable form which is characterized by certain formal elements and certain fundamental meanings, which, however, can only be apprehended in an approximate manner. The archetype in itself is a psychoid factor that belongs, so to speak, to the invisible and ultraviolet part of the psychological spectrum. [...] it seems to me probable that the true nature of the archetype is incapable of becoming conscious, that is, is transcendent, reason why I call it psychoid.[209]

So, for JUNG, the terminology psychoid designates something such as the simultaneously psychological and non-psychological nature of the Archetype, in which case the Archetype would be an "external physical process".

Although there is some proximity between the meanings used by RAFF and JUNG to the term "psychoid", they are not the same. Both consider that "psychoid" refers to "non-psychological" figures. However, JUNG is saying that the Archetype is psychoid because it is "psychological and physical". RAFF says that the figure is psychoid because it is **not** "derived from the psyche".

Paradigm of Sense

The definition that JUNG gives to "psychoid" refers to themes that are very different to the ones of this work. The definition given by RAFF, on the other hand, is totally adherent. However, even using RAFF's definition, the term "psychoid" seems inadequate to me, because it simply means **similar to the psyche, similar to the Soul**. If we were to use this term, we would be dealing with fifth-dimensional themes in fourth-dimensional terms. Bearing in mind that there is an equivalence with the term "psychoid" as used by RAFF, I prefer to use the term ***Pneumatic***, that is, **regarding the *Spirit***. Therefore, the "new reign of experience" referred to by RAFF, a reign of unity between the *Spirit* and the *Body*, is a ***Pneumatic* reign**.

RAFF shows that this *Pneumatic* reality is beyond the psyche:

> "In ordinary active imagination, the experience is one of the psyche only, but in the psychoidal experience the image and the encounter with it take on a **reality the transcends the psyche**".[210] [author's own highlights]

After the dramatic difference between a **psychological reality** – fourth-dimensional –, and a ***Pneumatic* reality** – fifth-dimensional – is established, RAFF continues describing the figures and events that exist in this reality.

> Elaborating on these figures, [the Sufi mystic] Ibn' Arabi wrote that the "form is related to the spiritual being just as a light that shines from a lamp into the corners of a room is related to the lamp ... **the form is not other than the spiritual being itself**; on the contrary, it is identical with it, even if it is found in a thousand places, or in all places and is diverse in shape". In other words, the form that a psychoidal being takes in the psyche, **the inner figure into which it manifests, is identical to its psychoidal entity**. There is no difference between the spiritual being, itself, and the imaginal form in which one experiences it. Active imagination with such a figure therefore **relates one to the world beyond the psyche, to the spiritual domain and reality in which the divine resides**. Though it may never be possible to experience that reality in and of itself, one can experience it through the form that it assumes. Since that form is no different than the thing itself, the imaginal encounter with the form is the encounter with the divine entity from which it originates.[211] [author's own highlights]

To say that "the form that a psychoid being takes is identical to the psychoid entity" is equivalent to saying that **the *Pneumatic Body* is identical to the *Pneumatic* entity**; or, in a language that is closer to the fifth dimension, that **the *Pneumatic* entity IS the *Pneumatic Body*.** There is no sense in discriminating between the *Pneumatic* entity and the *Pneumatic Body* of the *Pneumatic* entity, because, in doing that, we would be taking the duality from the previous dimensions to the fifth dimension, which is a unified dimension.

According to RAFF, the contact with a *Pneumatic* entity "relates one to the world beyond the psyche, to the spiritual domain and reality in which the divine resides"[212]. It is true. However, it is necessary to say that, although "it may never be possible to experience that reality in and of itself"[213] for a 4D ego, for a 5D ego the spiritual reality is the daily reality. The 5D ego is a *Pneumatic Body* and constantly finds *Pneumatic* entities (who **are** *Pneumatic* bodies).

Since the spiritual reality is experienced the whole time, it is important to highlight that the 5D ego see all people – all entities – as *Pneumatic* beings, including those who are structured in previous dimensions, that is 4D and 3D egos. The unified spiritual vision of a 5D ego is not dependant on the psychological development of the other. The fact that a 4D ego is not able to consciously notice its "own" *Spirit* does not mean that the *Spirit* does not inhabit it. And as the *Spirit* is present in all people – all entities – the 5D ego sees all people as unified realities. Strictly speaking, animals, plants, inanimate objects and even spaces, situations, the time, and much more, are also part of the reality of the *Spirit*, of the *Pneumatic* reality, the unified reality, existing **paradoxically** in the perception of the 5D ego and as an "independent" reality.

It is necessary to clarify something: a dimension is a gigantic field of experiences. As JUNG said, "Each cakra is a whole world"[214]. This includes *viśuddha*, the fifth-dimensional *cakra*. Therefore, living through a dimension is a process, a **long** process. The Paradigm of Balance, for example, is an extremely long process that spans from the moral defeat of the ego until the Crucifixion. Besides having to build a strong third-dimensional ego (which is already long), capable of initiating the process and capable of being morally defeated by the Self, in order to fully live the Paradigm of Balance one must travel through the personal unconscious, dealing with various identifications and projections, travel through the collective unconscious, dealing with various archetypes, face the Self and be Crucified, undergoing effective modifications, even corporeal ones, at each step. In the beginning of the Paradigm of Balance, the miracle of the apparition of the Self prefigures the surrender of the ego to the Self, the complete harmonization between the ego and the Self. The harmony between ego-Self potentially exists since the first moment of the paradigm, and without that, the progress of the 4D ego in this paradigm would be impossible, because the ego cannot consciously connect to the 4D Self, to the Soul, on its own. It is necessary that the Self makes the first move, establishing a firm connection with the ego, although still strongly unconscious of it. It is only by living the extremely long process of the Paradigm of Balance that the 4D ego goes from a potential and unconscious connection to the Soul to a complete and conscious connection with the Soul and its integration. It is a Herculean amount of work.

In the same way, the Paradigm of Sense is a very long process which spans from Crucifixion until the opening of the Apocalypse. In Crucifixion, the *Soul Retreats*, and, in face of death, the *Spirit* descends upon the crucified, transfiguring its *Body* so that the *Spirit* will "fit". This connection is, nevertheless, potential. It is necessary that the 5D Self makes the first move. Once again:

> When the stone decomposes to a powder like a man in his grave, **God restores to it soul and spirit,** and takes away all imperfection [...]²¹⁵ [author's own highlights]

With the *Spirit* in the *Body*, the 5D ego can **start** its movement towards what is the final structure of the fifth dimension: the *Unus Mundus*. One of the aims of the present work is to illustrate various aspects of this process. One of these can already be analysed in this chapter.

Once again, this process needs to be experienced in the *Body*, in the *Pneumatic Body*, never just conceptually. Consciousness is action. For a 5D ego to realize fifth-dimensional actions, one of the central elements is the *Instinct*.

In the chapter "*Lilith*", we saw that up until the Crucifixion, the experience of the instinct can be guided by the Self. Let us remember JUNG's affirmation, mentioned above: "The realization and assimilation of instinct never take place at the red end, i.e., by absorption into the instinctual sphere, but only through integration of the image which **signifies** and at the same time **evokes** the instinct, although in a form quite different from the one we meet on the biological level."²¹⁶. The instinct can only be realized through archetypal images. Without that, there is a risk of a regression to the instinctual level, with serious losses to consciousness. For that reason, Lilith, the Instinct, lives her self-exile, away from Jehovah, the celestial god, the Archetype.

In Crucifixion, the maximum demand for adequacy to the 4D Self, the most ferocious of the instincts, that of survival, is "defeated". There is no longer the risk of a regression to the instinctual level. Through the immense elevation experienced by the 4D ego, the instinct is **spiritualized**.

With the opening of the Paradigm of Sense, the Gates to Eden are open and Michael allows Lilith to return to Paradise again:

> The Sufi alchemists understood that the matter on which they operated was not purely physical in nature, but belonged more to the world of Paradise.[217]

The self-exile of Lilith has ended. The instinct is no longer the regressive pole of the archetype to compose the *Pneumatic* unity. In the fourth dimension, the psychological development was ascendant: from the instinct to the archetype. In the fifth dimension, the *Pneumatic* development is **descendant**: from the archetype to the *Instinct*. As in the fourth dimension the Archetype is the direction to which the instinct must flow, in the fifth dimension the *Instinct* is the direction to which the Archetype must flow.

Spirit IS *Body*.

The *Instinct* is the **Pneumatic** energy capable of progressively unify *Spirit* and *Body*, producing the *Unus Mundus*.

The 5D ego will need to make choices alone, without the demands and guidance of the Self. The *Instinct* is a fundamental factor to its **choices**.

---

[183] "In the matriarchal period of development, given that the unconscious guidance predominates (primacy of the Corporeal Self) [...] With the differentiation of the I, an egoic entity emerges from the Corporeal Self, which becomes stage and support for the experience. Previously mistaken with the mother's, it is now defined as their own body."

LIMA FILHO, A. P. (2002) [Translated from the Portuguese: *O pai e a psique*. São Paulo: Editora Paulus. p. 64.]

[184] NEUMANN, E. (2002) *The origins and history of consciousness*, Vol I. Part I – "The Mythological Stages in the Evolution of Consciousness". "The Creation Myth". "Uroborus". Translated by Hull, R. F. C. London: Routledge. Kindle eBook. Available at: <https://www.amazon.com/Origins-History-Consciousness-International-Psychology-ebook/dp/B019P2PSDM>. Access: April 20th 2020.

[185] STEIN, R. (1973) *Incest and human love*. Dallas, TX: Spring Publications.

[186] "[...] Whenever an instinct is effectively inhibited from action, this stimulates the flow of internal images. [...] sexual inhibition is essential for the opening up of the imaginal world." STEIN, Robert. *Incest and Human Love*. 1993. Part II Incest. Chapter 3 "Incest and Wholeness". Spring Publications, Dallas, TX. pp. 37-38.

[187] JUNG, C. G. ETH Lecture 26 Jan 1940. p. 226.

[188] JUNG, C. G. (1998) *Seminar on Nietzsche's Zarathustra*. Abridged edition. Bollingen Series XCIX. Princeton University Press. p. 46.

[189] Ibid., p. 99.

[190] JUNG, C. G. (1998). *Visions: Notes on the Seminar Given in 1930-1934*. Routledge, p. 1314.

[191] Ibid., p. 1316.

[192] "Sometimes one is apparently quite aware of one's projections though one does not know their full extent. And that portion of which one is not aware remains unconscious and still appears as if belonging to the object. This often happens in practical analysis. You say, for instance: "Now, look here, you simply project the image of your father into that man, or into myself," and **you assume that this is a perfectly satisfactory explanation and quite sufficient to dissolve the projection. It is satisfactory to the doctor, perhaps, but not to the patient**. Because, if there is still something more in that projection, the patient will keep on projecting. **It does not depend upon his will**; it is simply a phenomenon that produces itself. Projection is an automatic, spontaneous fact. It is simply there; you do not know how it happens. You just find it there. And this rule, which holds good for projection in general, is also true of transference. Transference is something which is just there. If it exists at all, it is there *a priori*. **Projection is always an *unconscious* mechanism, therefore consciousness, or conscious realization, destroys it**". JUNG, C. G. (1980) *The symbolic life*. Translated by Hull, R. F. C. CW XVIII. Bollingen Series XX. Princeton University Press. §315. [author's own highlights]

[193] *The New Jerusalem Bible*. John 1:1,9 and 14.

[194] "The highest level of Keter is the ultimate cause, while the physical world is the ultimate effect". KAPLAN, A. (1997) *Sêfer Yetsirá – The book of creation – in theory and practice*. Revised edition. Boston: Weiser Books. Chapter 1, p. 63.

[195] HANNAH, B. (2006) *The archetypal symbolism in animals*, quoting JUNG in *The nature of the psyche*. Lectures Given at the C. G. Jung Institute, Zurich, 1954-1958., Wilmette, IL: Chiron. p. 16.

[196] Ibid.

197 JUNG, C. G. (1985) *The Practice of psychotherapy. Abreaction, dream analysis, transference.* Chapter 9 "The return of the soul". Translated by Hull, R. F. C. 2nd edition. CW XVI/2. Bollingen Series XX. Princeton University Press.

198 "The production of one from four is the result of a process of distillation and sublimation which takes the so-called "circular" form: the distillate is subjected to sundry distillations so that the "soul" or "spirit" shall be extracted in its purest state. The product is generally called the **'quintessence'**"... JUNG, C. G. (1980) *Psychology and alchemy.* Translated by Hull, R. F. C. 2nd edition CW XII Bollingen Series XX. Princeton University Press. §165. [author's own highlights]

199 *The New Jerusalem Bible.* Matthew 28:1-6.

200 JUNG, C. G. *Psychology and alchemy.* Op. Cit. §462 and §511.

201 The last drawings of the *Rosarium Philosophorum*, particularly IX and X, which correspond, respectively, to the resurrection and the resurrected body – given that, in the former, the soul returns to the body, and, in the latter, the body appears alive and paradoxical – constitute at the same time the climax of the Paradigm of Balance and the beginning of the Paradigm of Sense. Despite being in fundamentally different contexts, the climax of a Paradigm and the base of another share some important characteristics: "The alchemist's failure to distinguish between *corpus* and *spiritus* is in our case assisted by the assumption that, owing to the preceding *mortificatio* and *sublimatio,* the body has taken on "quintessential" or spiritual form and consequently, as a *corpus mundum* (pure substance), is not so very different from spirit. It may shelter spirit or even draw it down to itself". JUNG, C. G. *The Practice of psychotherapy. Abreaction, dream analysis, transference.* Op. Cit. §499.

202 "[...] the center of the individual was the *archeus,* an individual unit in which 'spirit and matter had been united to become inseparable and indistinguishable in a new being. This was neither matter nor spirit, but had something of both, namely a physical and a psychological aspect..." RAFF, J. (2000) *Jung and the alchemical imagination.* Chapter 2 "The alchemical imagination". Quoting Walter PAGEL, *Joan Baptista von Helmot: reformer of science and Medicine.* Florida: Nicolas-Hays, Inc (Kobo eBook version).

203 *The New Jerusalem Bible.* John 20:24-29.

204 RAFF, J. *Jung and the alchemical imagination.* Op. Cit.

205 Ibid. Chapter 1. "JUNG as a spiritual tradition".

206 Ibid.

207 Ibid. "Introduction".

208 JUNG, C. G. (1975) *The structure and dynamics of the psyche. On the nature of the psyche.* Translated by Hull, R. F. C. CW VIII. Bollingen Series XX. Princeton University Press. §954.

209 Ibid. §417.

210 RAFF, J. *Jung and the alchemical imagination.* Op. Cit. Chapter 1. "JUNG as a spiritual tradition". "Psyche and psychoid".

211 Ibid.

212 Ibid.

213 Ibid.

[214] JUNG, C. G. (1996) *The psychology of Kundalini Yoga.* Bollingen Series XCIX. Princeton University Press. p. 13.

[215] JUNG, C. G. (1980) *Psychology and alchemy.* Translated by Hull, R. F. C. 2nd edition CW XII Bollingen Series XX. Princeton University Press. §462.

[216] HANNAH, B. (2006) *The archetypal symbolism in animals,* quoting JUNG in *The nature of the psyche.* Lectures Given at the C. G. Jung Institute, Zurich, 1954-1958., Wilmette, IL: Chiron. p. 16.

[217] RAFF, J. *Jung and the alchemical imagination.* Op. Cit. "Introduction".

FREE-WILL

In our present third-dimensional society, composed by autocratic egos, the existence of free-will is largely admitted. If the ego is the main character, maybe the only one, in a person's life, then they are free to do whatever they want.

Considering this fact, people are directly responsible for all their acts. Initially, the responsibility of knowing the civil laws and moral rules of where they live – both interchangeable to a certain degree – is attributed to the people. Possessing this knowledge, people are then capable of opting to follow or break the laws and suffer the consequences. Note that the **moral** weight of this world view is huge and used by States and Religions to impose their moral systems.

Several issues constitute serious problems to these assertions.

For a start, there is no absolute free-will. One cannot, for example, choose to belong to another species that is not the human species. Even within the same species, it is not possible to choose to be born male or female or choose one's ethnicity. It is also not possible to choose the circumstances of one's birth, in which city or century. Such questions compose a group of circumstances which are beyond the human reach.

Even within the third dimension, the remaining free-will is still debatable. Social circumstances prevent people from making decisions that, had circumstances been different, would have been possible. For example, there are probably many people who would like to have been doctors, and have the talent for such, however, never will because they cannot finance their studies. People who have many less opportunities due to sexism, racism, homophobia or any other type of prejudice, are another example.

Still within the third dimension, even the very restricted free-will remaining is debatable. In less prejudiced societies, there is practically a consent about people not choosing their gender or sexual preference.

Being born male or female does not mean that the person will behave in that manner, and gender will be defined without the person making any choices. Equally, sexual orientation does not depend on being born male or female and will be defined without the person making any choices. The current understanding is that gender and sexual orientation are naturally manifested in a person; they have to recognize that tendency in themselves and express it in their behaviour, with varying levels of difficulty. Other themes could be compared to these, in the sense that they require an 'internal' recognition of a natural tendency, such as professional vocation: people need to recognise which profession they have a natural vocation for.

These last examples, however, open a dangerous discussion for the third dimension and its notion of free-will. After all, what are these things that are naturally manifested in people? What is a natural propensity?

The third-dimensional structure of consciousness is based on dividing aspects of reality into two groups: one is associated with the ego and the other is not, whether because the ego denies it – with more or less vigour – or because the ego has never made contact with it. We can say that the aspects of reality that are associated with the ego are **conscious** to it. The aspects of reality that are not associated with the ego – because they are denied – are **unconscious** to it, they were never experienced, however much the ego thinks it is conscious of them through other means: reading about it, hearing about it, knowing someone who has that aspect, etc.

A person cannot, obviously, make choices about themes that they ignore or circumstances they do not experience, being unconscious of them and remaining that way.

There are only two categories left: aspects that the person associates with their own ego and aspects that the person does not associate with their own ego because they are denied, even though this person has made contact with them. However, what makes a third-dimensional ego associate some aspects or characteristics of reality to themselves and not others?

Although some argue that people are simply born that way, and others argue that it is the interaction with society that defines one's personality (the nature vs nurture argument), or even a balance of both, **this question has no possible answer in three dimensions**.

Trying to answer this question in three dimensions is the equivalent of trying to understand why a boat rocks, accelerates, slows down or sinks, whilst completely ignoring the existence of the sea. The movements observed on a boat are almost entirely the consequence of the sea's movement. One cannot even say that these movements are due to the interaction between the boat and the sea, because as the sea is infinitely larger than the boat, the importance of the boat in determining its movements is almost nil.

More important than that is to note that most people are not interested in finding out **why** things are that way. The fact that they are that way is accepted *a priori*, as if there was no reason to explain it.

In the Paradigm of Self-Affirmation, there is no interest in finding out why the personality was formed in a certain way and certain characteristics are considered inadequate and denied. The main interest of people living this paradigm is to affirm the characteristics associated to themselves, and strongly differentiate themselves – to put it mildly – from those characteristics which are denied. For that reason, for example, third-dimensional conversations involve people focusing on affirming their point of view and differentiating it from the others, without even trying to understand the other's point of view.

I have made several experiments concerning this theme. Having witnessed heated discussions between two people, at times I have interrupted the argument and asked each of them if they had understood the other person's viewpoint. Invariably, they would say yes. However, when I asked them to repeat what the other person had said, they simply could not because they did not know. In the rare occasions when they could repeat it, I asked them to explain what they had understood and, again, they simply had not understood it. Most times, people disagree without knowing what they are disagreeing with, since they have not even understood each other's point of view.

A third-dimensional ego is not interested in knowing why their personality is a certain way because, in order to access that information, they would need to investigate their unconscious and this is only possible with a further psychological dimension. Therefore, this is not about not wanting to know how their personality was formed, but it is about **not being able** to know. An analysis of the unconscious, in four dimensions, would be **disastrous** for a third-dimensional ego because it would relativize the ego completely, destroying its capacity to self-affirm and damaging the healthy experience of the Paradigm of Self-Affirmation. It is necessary to wait.

In any case, knowing that the unconscious exists and creates the ego, associating certain characteristics to the ego and keeping others for itself, it is necessary to admit that **the ego is not making any choices**. Even its personality is **given**, as is everything it hates. The argument that a person is also influenced by the environment where they live is totally valid, since it is considered that the Self also has absolute power over the environment where the 3D ego lives, and uses this power to direct the ego.

Proof of this is that 3D egos do not change personality through their own initiative. Sometimes they try to do that, but the effort is redundant and will soon dissipate. It is the case of those people who try to contain their anger only to explode sometime later, or those who try to repress their sexuality only to commit an act of paedophilia sometime later.

When a 3D ego is able to make a significant and effective change of personality, this is generally due to experiencing intense situations, beneficial or otherwise, but always regardless of that ego's choice, never caused by it. These situations, apparently fortuitous, are brought about by Destiny; and we know exactly who has control over Destiny.

Finally, deep loving relationships are, sometimes, capable of leading the 3D ego to effectively change personality. Indeed, these relationships owe this ability to the fact that they are a third-dimensional situation closest to a fourth-dimensional relationship with the unconscious.

Once again, **all** the movements that the boat makes, including those which give the impression that they are free choices, are due to the sea movement, or its stillness.

That way, in the Paradigm of Self-Affirmation, the existence of 'choice' for the ego is determined by the directions from the Self to affirm its personality and deny its opposite – in other words, the choice is nil.

In this scenario, Spinoza compares the human belief in free-will to a stone thinking that it chooses the path travelled while it crosses the air until it falls. The philosopher says:

> [...] men believe themselves to be free, simply because they are conscious of their actions, and unconscious of the causes whereby those actions are determined.[218]

The Greek mythology is extremely clear in this respect. The Μοῖραι (*Moîras*), goddesses of Destiny, meticulously plot everyone's path. There are several examples of moments when even the gods are submitted to the *Moîras*.

A very enlightening mythological element which illustrates this is the Oracle. Knowing everyone's destiny, the Oracle enunciates it to the consulter, and it is impossible to avoid. The classic example is the myth of

Oedipus. After his parents, the king and queen of Thebes, consulted the Oracle and learned that Oedipus would kill his father and marry his mother, they abandoned him on a mountain. Oedipus survived and was taken to Corinth. He was raised there in the king's court, **unaware** that he was adopted. One day, having learned from a drunk man about his Destiny, as it had been defined by the Oracle, Oedipus decided to **avoid his destiny** by moving away from his 'parents' and left Corinth. **Completely unaware**, he chose to go to Thebes. On his way, **completely unaware**, he killed his father. Arriving in Thebes, **completely unaware**, he married his mother. A 3D ego will fulfil its Destiny no matter what, but it seems that avoiding it accelerates its fulfilment.

An even more dramatic mythological element is given by BRANDÃO DE SOUZA:

> [...] sometimes, Zeus is transformed into an executor of Moîra's decisions, as if confounded with herself.
>
> Still as an external factor which, following Zeus's wishes, acts upon mankind and troubles their mind, we find in Homer the word Áte, which could be translated as blindness of reason, "involuntary madness", whose consequences the hero later regrets.[219]

Even though the term 'involuntary madness' is a pleonasm, it is exactly what happens.

The **moral defeat**, the event that concludes the Paradigm of Self-Affirmation and starts the Paradigm of Balance, is perhaps the first time when the ego realises that **it has no free-will**. One way to define the moral defeat is to imagine a situation where there is a problem that the ego wants to resolve very much, needs to resolve, but the problem persists with no resolution, even after all attempts have been exhausted, and no doubt after the ego's power has been exhausted. It is in that moment that the Self appears, not without an element of cruelty. The impact of the moral defeat is not even the incapacity of resolving an unresolvable problem. This becomes relativized and small in view of the fact that the ego is not the centre of the psyche, and in the progressive realization of the autonomy of the psyche.

In the Paradigm of Balance, the 4D ego notices that its personality, so very protected by it, was based on a series of identifications with unconscious contents, and that its incessant criticisms of others, silent or otherwise, were based on a series of projections of unconscious contents. The most shocking fact is that most characteristics of its personality, if not all of them, considered **conscious** in a 3D perspective, are revealed to be identifications – therefore **unconscious** – in a 4D perspective. Even more shocking is that all of those hated traits found in others, as seen in 3D, are revealed to be contents which, sooner or later, will be integrated in consciousness, on a 4D process.

Suddenly, the 4D ego notices that the "huge knowledge" it possessed – after all, the Paradigm of Self-Affirmation ends with the construction of a **strong ego** – is, in fact, an infinitesimal part of its Being, since unconsciousness is infinite, and the Self transcends the ego and the unconscious. Returning to the discussion about free-will and stating the obvious – that one cannot make choices about unconscious themes and circumstances – the 4D ego realizes just how small is its free-will.

> [...] free will only exists within the limits of consciousness. Beyond those limits there is mere compulsion.[220]

However, the perception of the Self's **grandiosity** puts in perspective not only the ego's perception of its own free-will, but also its **desire** for free-will.

The first conscious encounter with the Self, the moral defeat, is extremely painful for the ego. It realizes then its own incapacity to solve its own problems, and finds out that it does not command the psyche. The ego notices that the Self is very different from the image of the good grandfather: the Self can be **evil**. After this shock, however terrible are the future tasks imposed by the Self, there remains a constant psychological sensation, a certainty that 'the Self is what I am deep down, even though I am not yet able to manifest it consciously in my behaviour'. However much one fights with the Self during a fourth-dimensional journey, however much these fights are necessary to remain healthy and non-identified with the Self, the arrogance and defiance of the 3D ego are progressively replaced by a desire to surrender to the Self. One perseveres in this path, even in moments of anger, because the 4D ego knows that the Self is, ultimately, itself. Divorcing the Self would be to divorce itself. In this scenario, JUNG teaches:

> Free will is doing gladly and freely that which one must do.[221]

As the contact with the Self allows for the integration of unconscious complexes and Archetypes, consciousness grows. JUNG says that free-will exists within the limits of consciousness[222,223]. So, the progress in the Paradigm of Balance promotes a progressive increase of the free-will. **Paradoxically, the desire** of the 4D ego to have free-will decreases. Once again: the perception that surrendering to the Self is the equivalent of becoming what one is, makes the free-will not so interesting anymore. It is noted that when free-will is exercised contrary to the Self, the only thing happening is the ego distancing itself from its deep individuality.

In Crucifixion, the desire for free-will is totally extinguished:

> Father, if you are willing, take this cup away from me. Nevertheless, let your will be done, not mine.[224]

Note that the ego is conscious of its free-will but sacrifices it.

In Crucifixion, at the precise moment when the desire for free-will disappears and the surrender of the 4D ego to the Soul is total, **paradoxically, the *Soul Retreats*,** and there is no more possible surrender.

> My God, why have you forsaken me?[225]

The Paradigm of Sense begins.

The *Soul* has *Retreated* There is no imposition from the Soul. There is no guidance from the Soul.

The ego, only recently fifth-dimensional, is very used to not exercising *Free-will*, surrendering to the Soul in order to connect to its deep individuality and become what it is. The ego waits for symbolic guidance. But there is only a psychological silence. The ego would prefer that something was imposed by the Self. But the psychological silence remains.

Suddenly, the *Free-will* is total.

This is not about an illusory three-dimensional free-will, where the 3D ego ignores the huge quantity of unconscious psychological energy that governs it. **Despite not being omniscient, the 5D ego is a synthesis of the consciousness and the unconscious. Therefore, it is paradoxically conscious of the existence of the unconscious and used to dealing with it.**

This is not about the sacrifice of a growing capacity to exercise the fourth-dimensional free-will in favour of meeting the Self, and ultimately meeting its deep individuality. The 5D ego has already sacrificed free-will completely, it has already surrendered its life to the Soul, it has already turned its life into "a story of the self-realization of the unconscious".[226]

Suddenly, the *Free-will* is total because the power that could eradicate it, the *Soul*, has been integrated and *Retreated.*

Suddenly, the colossal weight of the *free-will* is total. The third-dimensional morality, with its good and evil, has been overcome. **There is no** more right or wrong. The fourth-dimensional ethics[227], with its positive (ethical) and negative (non-ethical), has been overcome. **There is definitely no** more right or wrong. Now that the choice **must** be made, the criteria to follow is unknown.

The 5D ego will need to make choices alone, without the demands and guidance of the Self. The 5D ego is **paradoxically** obliged to make free choices, now.

---

[218] SPINOSA, B. (2009) *Ethics* Translated from Latin by ELWES, R. H. M. Project Gutemberg eBook. Available at: http://www.gutenberg.org/files/3800/3800-h/3800-h.htm. Access: May 1st 2020. Book III, Proposition 2, note.

[219] BRANDÃO DE SOUZA, J. (1989) *Mitologia grega,* Vol. I. Petrópolis, RJ: Editora Vozes. p. 142.

[220] JUNG, C. G. (1973) *Letters*, Vol. I. Edited and translated by Hull, R. F. C. Bollingen Series XCV. Princeton University Press. p. 227.

[221] "Free will is doing gladly and freely that which one must do." JUNG, C., JUNG, E. and WOLF, T. (January 11, 2020) *A collection of remembrances.* [online: weblog]. Available at: <https://carljungdepthpsychologysite.blog/2020/01/11/carl-jung-on-free-will-anthology/#.Xoc-kP1Khdg> Access: January 22nd 2020

[222] "The ego is, by definition, subordinate to the self and is related to it like a part to the whole. Inside the field of consciousness it has, as we say, free will. By this I do not mean anything philosophical, only the

well-known psychological fact of "free choice," or rather the subjective feeling of freedom. But, just as our free will clashes with necessity in the outside world, so also it finds its limits outside the field of consciousness in the subjective inner world, where it comes into conflict with the facts of the self. And just as circumstances or outside events 'happen' to us and limit our freedom, so the self acts upon the ego like an *objective occurrence* which free will can do very little to alter. It is, indeed, well known that the ego not only can do nothing against the self, but is sometimes actually assimilated by unconscious components of the personality that are in the process of development and is greatly altered by them". JUNG, C. G. (1979) *Aion – researches into the phenomenology of the self.* Translated by Hull, R. F. C. 2nd edition. CW IX, part 2. Bollingen Series XX. Princeton University Press. §9.

223 "The question will certainly be asked whether for some people their own free will may not be the ruling principle, so that every attitude is intentionally chosen by themselves. I do not believe that anyone reaches or has ever reached this godlike state, but I know that there are many who strive after this ideal because they are possessed by the heroic idea of absolute freedom. In one way or another all men are dependent; all are in

some way limited, since none are gods". JUNG, C. G. (1975) *The structure and dynamics of the psyche. On the nature of the psyche.* Translated by Hull, R. F. C. CW VIII/2. Bollingen Series XX. Princeton University Press. §636.

224 *The New Jerusalem Bible.* Luke 22:42

225 *The New Jerusalem Bible.* Matthew 27:46

226 JUNG, C. G. *Memories, dreams and reflexions.* Prologue. Translated by Winston, R. and C. Revised Edition. Vintage Books. (eBook) Available at: <http://www.venerabilisopus.org/en/books-samael-aun-weor-gnostic-sacred-esoteric-spiritual/pdf/200/265_jung-carl-memories-dreams-reflections.pdf> Access: April 28th 2020. p. 16.

227 See chapter 9, Part I, "Creation".

CREATION I

When I approach any Psychological, Philosophical or Spiritual system, including religions, the first point I analyse is how they deal with the **existence of evil**. If this problem is not adequately dealt with, I will not waste my time in deeper analysis. Therefore, if I want to be taken seriously, I need to deal with this question immediately.

Given that each paradigm has a basic law and a specific type of consciousness structure, the existence of evil needs to be dealt with in each paradigm.

Let us start with the paradigm in which the vast majority of humanity currently lives: the Paradigm of Self-Affirmation. The basic law that rules this paradigm is the development of the ego, and its final aim is the construction of a strong ego, capable of progressively affirm itself in relation to the unconscious, in relation to life.

The mechanism used by the psyche to reach this aim is the construction of a **dualist consciousness**. The characteristics that the ego perceives as its own, which it attributes to itself and uses to describe itself are defined as "**me**". The characteristics that the ego perceives as incompatible, contrasting or opposed to its own are defined as "**not-me**".

This psychological organization is then transported to a **moral system**. There are many options of moral systems: the constitution of the State, the sacred book of a Religion, the thesis of a Philosophical system, the house rules, the rules of a marriage, etc. However, whatever the moral system adopted, its basic characteristic is always the division of the various aspects of life and people in two categories: **good and evil**. A possible example of this division is the idea that being faithful is good and cheating is evil.

Another characteristic of moral systems is the fact that the categories of good and evil are considered **valid to all**. When the State enacts a constitution, a civil law, a criminal code, etc., it expects everyone to follow it, and establishes clear punishment for those who do not follow it, alleging preservation of social well-being. Religion is even more severe: its objective is moral superiority. Therefore, across different degrees of radicalism, it considers the non-followers inferior beings (sometimes to the point of persecuting them) and teach missionaries to convert people (sometimes believing this will save them).

Finally, moral systems tend to behave as **unchangeable**, functioning as though it has always existed and will last forever. Christianity, for example, despite being based on the temporal event of Christ's birth and the Apostles journeys, still functions as if its moral system has existed since Creation. Adam and Eve would have been the first betrayers of this moral system, establishing the original sin, only redeemed by Christ himself. From a Christian perspective, various prophets had predicted the birth of Christ.

An interesting point about this dimension is that, **as the 3D ego considers itself to be always right, it also considers itself as always good.**

That is why, in general, there is a strong tendency for the 3D ego to align itself alongside the **good side** in the moral system within which it lives. In order to self-affirm, besides its personal strength, the ego needs other people to boast to, to compare itself or to oppose. For that reason, the ego wants to be seen as popular, always staying on the good side – it is easier to be popular.

Besides this structural reason, it is important to consider that the first people who the 3D ego wanted to impress were the parents. Parents are more or less settled into the existing moral system and therefore moralize their children. Noticing that their parents are aligned with the good side of the moral system, children will want to impress them, aligning themselves on the same side. They construct their ego in that way, and having associated those characteristics to themselves, remain with those later on. Both due to the relationship with the parents, and in relation to the State and Religion (whether they practice it or not), any divergence with the good side is considered a deviation of conduct and will cause guilt. To avoid **guilt**, the 3D ego remains aligned with the good side.

Finally, it is easier to follow the moral system already defined by the society one lives in. The moral rules are already defined, are seen as unchangeable and understood as valid for everyone. Not needing to redefine, modify or evaluate it every time and for each person avoids spending a huge amount of psychological energy for the 3D ego. By following the moral system, **the expenditure of psychological energy is low**.

It is important to remember though, that in a third-dimensional society, not everybody aligns themselves with the good side. Some will align themselves with the **evil side**, and others will occupy some middle-ground level. This might seem to contradict other points already established, but it does not. Although there are certain moral codes covering a large number of people, which create moral macro-environments, such as the constitution of a State or the commandments of a Religion, there are also moral micro-environments. The most obvious one is the family. The education given by the parents, good or bad, will deeply impact the personality of a given person, who will tend to follow it (the unruliness will be a way of secretly following it), even if this makes them distance themselves from the moral macro-environment. If someone, for example, grows up in an environment where crime is commonly practiced, it is possible that the practice of crime will be well-regarded and attractive for the 3D ego. Independently of the ego following the good or evil path – including all the possibilities in between – it will succeed in the third dimension and self-affirm in whichever path it chooses.

Finally, it is necessary to say that morals are fundamental in the Paradigm of Self-Affirmation, because the 3D ego will not be able to define itself without it.

The moral system is the criteria for the Paradigm of Self-Affirmation.

TABLE OF MORAL RULES

Forbidden Actions	Permitted Actions
Evil	Good

The 3D Self **imposes** morals over the 3D ego. This is clear in various mythologies. Jehovah gives the 10 Commandments to Moses, at Mount Sinai. In the Hammurabi Code, we read:

> When Anu the Sublime, King of the Anunaki, and Bel, the lord of Heaven and earth, who decreed the fate of the land, assigned to Marduk, the over-ruling son of Ea, God of righteousness, dominion over earthly man, and made him great among the Igigi, they called Babylon by his illustrious name, made it great on earth, and founded an everlasting kingdom in it, whose foundations are laid so solidly as those of heaven and earth; then Anu and Bel called by name me, Hammurabi, the exalted prince, who **feared God**, to bring about the rule of righteousness in the land, to destroy the wicked and the evil-doers; so that the strong should not harm the weak; so that I should rule over the black-headed people like Shamash, and enlighten the land, to further the well-being of mankind.[228] [author's own highlights]

These mythical themes are expressed in the formation of the human consciousness through the Archetype of the Father. The human representative of this archetype, the father, presents the child with the principle of νόμος (*nómos*), the law. He takes the child away from the anomia phase – the total absence of rules observed in babies – and puts them in the heteronomy phase, that is, the capacity to follow rules imposed by the father and, later, by society[229]. Without the imposition of rules, the child will not be able to integrate into society and the father will have failed.

For this reason, **the child must be moralized**. This needs to happen even if the child's parents have 4D or 5D egos, because all the psychological phases need to be experienced, for the sake of psychological health. It is necessary to have some morals, so that later they can be overcome: ethics can never be reached unless one has been through morals.

As a person's morality increases, the Paradigm of Self-Affirmation progresses and reaches its objective, because the ego is then able to affirm itself more and more. At some point, the morality reaches its maximum, the ego is strong, and has reached rectitude by following the rules, integrating the 3D Self. At this point, precisely at this point, the 4D Self appears and destroys the moral system that has been guiding the 3D ego, throwing that ego into the fourth dimension. It is not by chance that JUNG called this moment a **moral defeat**.

> His faithful servant Job is now to be exposed to a rigorous moral test, quite gratuitously and to no purpose, although Yahweh is convinced of Job's faithfulness and constancy, and could moreover have assured himself beyond all doubt on this point had he taken counsel with his own omniscience.[230]

Job is a moral exponent. It is not about a human assessment: it is **Yahweh** who is "convinced of his faithfulness and constancy" and "could have assured himself beyond all doubt". Having reached the moral excellence, Job is **not** rewarded by God, but instead, contrary to what is taught in the third dimension, is exposed to **God's evil**.

> It is indeed no edifying spectacle to see how quickly Yahweh abandons his faithful servant to the evil spirit and lets him fall without compunction or pity into the abyss of physical and moral suffering. From the human point of view Yahweh's behaviour is so revolting that one has to ask oneself whether there is not a deeper motive hidden behind it. Has Yahweh some secret resistance against Job? That would explain his yielding to Satan.[231]

Before we continue, it is important to clarify something even more scandalous from the moral perspective of the third dimension. The moral excellence does not necessarily need to occur through good, **it can perfectly be reached through evil**. The objective of the Paradigm of Self-Affirmation is not to produce a **good ego**, it is to produce a **strong ego**. If the ego becomes strong by reaching the moral excellence through evil, the moral defeat brought about by the 4D Self will still happen in the same way, because the formation of the ego is viable in the same way, and because there is a moral coherence of the ego in relation to the evil it practices. Although JUNG has not defended anywhere that moral excellence can be reached through evil, he repeatedly states in many texts that the psyche tends towards completeness, towards the integration of good and evil (and everything else). It makes no difference that the initial partiality of the ego is about being partial towards goodness or evil. Both are **partialities** and both need their complement. Believing that one should start with good is just another third-dimensional moral belief. An excellent example is Paul of Tarsus:

> Saul approved of the killing. That day a bitter persecution started against the church in Jerusalem, and everyone except the apostles

scattered to the country districts of Judaea and Samaria. There were some devout people, however, who buried Stephen and made great mourning for him. **Saul then began doing great harm to the church; he went from house to house arresting both men and women and sending them to prison.**[232] [author's own highlights]

Meanwhile Saul was still breathing threats to slaughter the Lord's disciples. He went to the high priest and asked for letters addressed to the synagogues in Damascus, that would authorize him to arrest and take to Jerusalem any followers of the Way, men or women, that he might find. It happened that while he was travelling to Damascus and approaching the city, suddenly a light from heaven shone all round him. He fell to the ground, and then he heard a voice saying, 'Saul, Saul, why are you persecuting me?' 'Who are you, Lord?' he asked, and the answer came, 'I am Jesus, whom you are persecuting.'[233] [author's own highlights]

Paul persecutes men and women, persecutes disciples of the Lord, breaks into people's homes, **arrests** people, locks them up, threatens and kills. He is a torturer and a murderer. Nevertheless, he has a beatific view of the Lord he follows. At no point we sense a critical tone in Jesus' treatment of him; and, let us be honest, Jesus knew how to be critical. Paul is not even punished, apart from a temporary blindness for a few days. Despite all his crimes, even against saints, he is chosen to be Christ's Apostle (I will not even discuss which paradigm Paul was in, but the moral astonishment is beyond that).

It is curious that Job, who had reached the moral excellence through goodness, had faced such a demoniac Jehovah, whereas Paul, who reached the moral excellence through evil, had faced such a forgiving Christ. Although this is only a supposition, this seems more like another evidence of the compensatory character of the unconscious.

In any case, the Paradigm of Balance was open, and its first event, the moral defeat, had already destroyed the moral. We cannot even speak of moral relativization, because God showed that He is not loyal. The third-dimensional image of God, of complete rectitude, as the law-making Jehovah who appeared to Moses, was cruelly replaced, with no warning, by a fourth-dimensional image of God, of complete maliciousness and betrayal, as the Jehovah who allows Satan to **play** with Job, a fair man, or Christ who does not care about Paul's cruelty. If not even God is concerned with morality, why should human beings?

> Good cannot exist without evil, and if one accepts the notion of God then, on the other hand, one must postulate a devil likewise. This is balance. This duality is my life.[234]

At this point, the psyche has enough dimensions to notice that the Christian dogma has fundamental ambiguities. One of them is the impossibility of conciliating the notions of an omnipotent god and of a purely good god. To say that God is purely good is the equivalent of saying that God **cannot** practice evil. If not, he is not omnipotent. If he is omnipotent, he needs to be able to practice evil. Both the mythologies and the Bible clearly show which option is real.

Crazier still is the doctrine of *summum bonun*, from St. Augustine. God commits atrocities from Genesis to the Apocalypse and is purely good? God incites human beings to be evil, suggesting, for example, lynching and murdering, including of their own family, and he is purely good? Incidentally, God does this with his own Son.

> *Summum Bonum* or supreme good. A conception of divinity stemming from Platonism and adopted by the Church fathers who sought to establish the moral perfection of the Christian deity. The belief that God is the omnipotent *Summum Bonum* makes it logically necessary to reduce evil to *privatio boni*. Jung condemned the doctrine of *summum bonum* as a projection of inflated, hyper-trophied ego upon the *imago dei*. For Jung God is the *Summum Coincidentia Oppositorom* that encompasses everything and its opposite in a single interde- pendent reality and strives not for one-sided goodness but for plenary consciousness. Jung blamed the *summum bonum* doctrine for setting impossible standards of perfection that induce guilt and despair and thereby incapacitate us for dealing with real evils. The doctrine lies behind the popular and deleterious expression, "*omne bonum a Deo, omne malum ab nomine*" (all good is from God, all evil is from man). Therein God gets credit for everything good, and man, with no good of his own, takes the blame for all evil. Jung's rejection of the *summum bonum* doctrine decidedly places him outside orthodoxy and aligns him with the Gnostic tradition.[235]

In summary: **God is both evil and good.**

Before such God, it is no longer possible to follow morals. More than that, morals become a **danger**, because where there is a moral limit, there will be an incapacity to recognize the nature of the Soul and of the psyche, and there will be naivety and risk.

> Let us give voice to this *new demand*: we need a *critique* of moral values, *the value of these values should itself, for once, be examined* [...] we have neither had this knowledge up till now nor even desired it. People have taken the *value* of these 'values' as given, as factual, as beyond all questioning; up till now, nobody has had the remotest doubt or hesitation in placing higher value on 'the good man' than on 'the evil', higher value in the sense of advancement, benefit and prosperity for *man in general* (and this includes man's future). What if the opposite were true? What if **a regressive trait lurked in 'the good man', likewise a danger,** an enticement, a poison, a narcotic, so that the present lived at the *expense of the future*? Perhaps in more comfort and less danger, but also in a smaller-minded, meaner manner? [...] So that morality itself were to blame if man, as species, never reached his *highest potential power and splendour*? So that morality itself was the danger of dangers?[236] [author's own highlights]

The shock of the moral defeat is only the first moment of a dismantling reality that the 4D ego will experience. But several people who experience the moral defeat and are able to admit a new and shocking fact about reality or themselves – and, by doing that, can solve their problem in four dimensions – believe that, from that point, they can return to live as before. That will never happen.

The Paradigm of Balance is an immense sequence of confrontations with incomprehensible problems that the ego cannot resolve within its restrictive limits. Slowly, the 4D ego realizes that it feels inadequate in practically all areas of its life. It is not happy with its personality, with its marriage, with its job, with its financial life. All that seemed stable and pleasant is put into question.

The unconscious disturbs the 4D ego constantly.

In the Paradigm of Balance, the confrontation with the unconscious is inevitable; the confrontation is the very nature of the paradigm. The confrontation with the unconscious will result in the progressive destruction of morals. In the third dimension, the moral system was based on good and evil values, and the 3D ego built its personality by associating it with characteristics considered as part of "me", denying and projecting onto others characteristics considered "not-me". In fourth dimension, the confrontation with the unconscious will **force** the person to become complete, integrating the divided, unconscious, parts of the being. In a simplified way, we can say that the 4D ego will keep the personality traits it already had, associated with itself and considered "me", but it will also have to include the personality traits it denied and projected onto others, calling them "not-me". The 4D ego is a sum of "me" and "not me". The fact that the "**not-me**" needs to be part of its personality constitutes a **continuous moral defeat**, particularly because the unconscious is infinitely larger than the ego, therefore the "**not-me**" is infinitely larger than the "**me**".

Slowly, however, the moral defeats stops being the problem, because a bigger problem appears on the horizon: the collapse of the moral system opens a distressing relativism. The moral system was **defined**, **unchangeable**, **valid for all**. It was a clear system, which could be easily applicable. For example, if it was part of the person's moral system to not be aggressive, it was enough for them not to be aggressive, independently of the situation. When the moral system is destroyed and it is not forbidden to be aggressive anymore, various situations where before the automatic response restrained the aggression, now cause doubt: should I be aggressive? This is just a small example: aggressiveness. But the human being has a myriad of emotions that are manifested in a myriad of situations... The complexity has grown exponentially.

> All that exists is just and unjust and is equally justified in both respects.[237]

Even more impressive is that the relativity is exclusively associated to the **criteria of choice**, not the **value** of good and evil, whatever the characteristic they express themselves through. What I mean is that the moral system used to be an absolute criterion of choice – certain things are allowed (good) and other are forbidden (evil). Now, each situation is presented differently, and **evil is as permitted as good is**; more than that, **evil can constitute a psychological demand**. The choice criterion was totally relativized. However, good has not stopped being good: if someone helps another person in an extreme situation of need, this tends to be considered good, regardless of the choice criterion used. Likewise, evil has not stopped being evil: if someone takes revenge on someone else, this tends to be considered evil, regardless of the choice criterion used. The weight of good and evil is much heavier in the fourth dimension because the 4D ego is being called upon to have actions that, more than being considered evil, are **effectively** evil.

> The relativity of "good" and "evil" by no means signifies that these categories are invalid, or do not exist. Moral judgment is always present and carries with it characteristic psychological consequences. [...] Only the contents of judgment are subject to the differing conditions of time and place and, therefore, take correspondingly different forms. For moral evaluation is always founded upon the apparent certitudes of a moral code which pretends to know precisely what is good and what evil. But once we know how **uncertain** the foundation is, **ethical decision becomes a subjective, creative act**. We can convince ourselves of its validity only *Deo concedente* (with God's grace) that is, there must be a spontaneous and decisive impulse on the part of the unconscious. Ethics itself, the decision between good and evil, is not affected by this impulse, only made more difficult for us. Nothing can spare us the torment of ethical decision.[238] [author's own highlights]

If the moral choice between good and evil is no longer the criterion, what is? With the relativity growing exponentially, it is imperative that another criterion of choice appears.

The Soul has disturbed the third-dimensional moral system because it has generated a problem that the 3D ego was not able to solve using its "me" characteristics, which it had associated to goodness. With that, the Soul confronts the ego with its "not-me" characteristics, now known as unconscious characteristics, associated by the ego to evil. The 4D ego realises that there are certain situations that need evil to be resolved or experienced. At this point it is important to abandon childishness, the **risk** of childishness:

> Only an infantile person can **pretend** that evil is not at work everywhere, and the more unconscious he is, the more the devil drives him. [...] Only ruthless self-knowledge on the widest scale, which sees good and evil in correct perspective and can weigh up the motives of human action, offers some guarantee that the end-result will not turn out too badly.[239] [author's own highlights]

More than that, for the despair of moralists and childish spiritualists who sell the utopic image of a purely good God, of a purely good world, of a purely good human being – which always leaves me baffled -, the Soul **forces the ego to acknowledge and practice evil**, as well as to acknowledge and practice goodness. This acknowledgement and practice of both sides demonstrates that the problem is no longer, in the fourth dimension, the opposition between good and evil, but instead the journey towards **totality**, towards the **individual**. Having been in the third dimension, the ego interprets what comes from the Soul as good or evil. However, the Soul is simply completing the 4D ego, leading it towards a consciousness of all aspects of its being, and making it available for action.

While it progresses through the fourth dimension, the 4D ego realises that nothing is right or wrong *a priori*, there is no standard recipe for how to do things – this is part of the third dimension. In the fourth dimension, **each situation is unique**, because its causes have changed, its factors have changed, its consequences have changed, the people involved have changed, etc. Even if an identical situation to one in the past was to occur (which I have never seen), the 4D ego has changed and is still changing. **The contact with the Soul prevents the stability of personality**. The Soul constantly changes the interior state of the being, at each instant its interior disposition is different. The 3D ego had a stable personality, whose strength increased as its characteristics – the "**me**" characteristics – were intensely affirmed. That is what 3D egos are complimented for, their coherence and reliability. The 4D ego does not have a stable personality, because it constantly experiences an internal storm caused by the Soul, forcing it to acknowledge new information from its interior and exterior realities. Unknown emotions appear, identifications and projections are noticed, disturbing dreams are constant. Because they constantly see new aspects of reality, 4D egos cannot keep a stable personality, and they need to adapt to the Soul at each instant. They will be inevitably criticised by appearing incoherent, unpredictable, for "not keeping their word", for "having no character", for being **evil**.

It is important to not escape the structure of the fourth dimension, to not pretend. It is not that the 3D egos have a wrong view of 4D egos. It is not that, because they are guided by morals, 3D egos see the actions of 4D egos "as if they were" evil. Let us not forget: what was relativized was the choice of criterion, but good is still good and evil is still evil. Some of the actions of 4D egos are good, **but others are effectively evil**. This is not about a point of view, it is about facts. In contact with its own Soul, the ego learns that, in certain internal and external circumstances, the best thing to do is to practice evil.

> [...] because I take an empirical attitude it does not mean that I relativize good and evil as such. I see very clearly: this is evil, but the paradox is just that for this particular person in this particular situation at this particular stage of development it may be good.

> Contrariwise, good at the wrong moment in the wrong place may be the worst thing possible. If it were not like this everything would be so simple – too simple.[240]

Slowly, the 4D ego completely overcomes, not without pain, the moral system, and realises that, regardless of good and evil, its action must observe the interior reality that is presented by the Soul. This is the fourth-dimensional criterion: to observe the interior reality that is presented by the Soul. Differentiating it from moral, JUNG calls this **ethics**:

> [...] when seen in a psychological light, two different factors: on the one hand a recollection of, and admonition by, the mores; on the other, a conflict of duty and its solution through the creation of a third standpoint. The first is the moral, and the second the ethical, aspect of conscience.[241]

Mores is the Latin word for customs. Although it can also refer to customs, ἦθος (*êthos*), the Greek term for **character, deep disposition**. According to the Merriam-Webster Dictionary, "*moral implies conformity to established sanctioned codes or accepted notions of right and wrong [and] ethical may suggest the involvement of **more difficult or subtle questions** of rightness, fairness, or equity*" [bold highlights added by the author]. The difference is evident: whereas the moral is guided by social costumes – the moral codes – ethics is guided by deep disposition, by the Soul.

But we are in the fourth dimension. Things are not that simple.

The third-dimensional belief in a purely good God leads to the conclusion that, if you get in touch with God, he will tell you what is best to do, and this will always be good. A very common mistake made by those who enter the fourth dimension is to bring over this third-dimensional belief in the divine, good and infallible advice to the fourth dimension. When in contact with the Self, the risk is to start believing that what the Self brings through dreams should be immediately and literally put into practice, as if "God" had ordered it. Nothing could be further from the truth. This concept ignores some of the fundamental concepts of Analytic Psychology, as, for instance, the symbolic nature of dreams, the fact that dreams represent the psyche of the dreamer and the compensatory character of the unconscious.

That way, if I dream that my teacher is a very evil person, who plots against me, the **worst** interpretation is to understand this as a concrete fact, and act on it by immediately destroying my relationship with him or her. The very least one must understand is that the dream is symbolic, representing my own interior world, and that due to the compensatory nature of the unconscious, it is very likely that the dream is a criticism of my unilaterally good behaviour.

Besides that, we are human beings. We cannot ignore the fact that we are in a world where most people are in the moralized third dimension, they do not know about ethics and will be hurt by evil actions. In fact, people from any dimension would be hurt by evil actions, because evil is evil, although, perhaps, people with at least four dimensions can understand it better. It is important to consider people's feelings; after all, a genuine psychological development is very human and not brutal.

Therefore, to literally follow what is brought by the Self, ignoring the humanity in people, and ultimately in ourselves, is the path to disaster. This is **not** ethics. Ethics is the perception that the Self – and with it the whole interior world – **collides** with its own 4D ego, and then with the reality around it, including other people. The demands of the Self make the life of a 4D ego very difficult, because the Self is always leading that ego towards perceptions and actions which do not belong to the status quo. That way, every appearance of the Self is a huge conflict for the ego, a huge **ethical conflict**. Human beings **are** not ethical. Human beings experience **ethical conflicts**, constantly.

The ethical conflict is the criteria of the Paradigm of Balance.

> Here (in face of the conflict of obligation), only the creating force of *ethos*, which represents the whole person, can make the final decision. As it happens with all of mankind creative faculties, *ethos* also emanates from two sources: consciousness, on one hand, and unconsciousness, on the other. *Ethos* is a special instance of what we call "transcendent function", that is, an understanding and cooperation between conscious and unconscious factors, expressed in the religious language as reason and grace."[242]

It is important to remember that the Paradigm of Balance is a long process. Things present themselves differently in the beginning and at the end of the paradigm.

In the beginning of the paradigm, the ego finds a series of energetic dualities: male and female, body and spirit, etc. In view of any energetic duality, the 4D ego tends to be more conscious of one side and deny the other. The correct behaviour is to **not** give way to the unconscious energy, as if it came from "God", but to maintain the conscious position, preventing a leak[243] from the unconscious energy[244]. There will then be an increase of the psychological energy[245] and, at some point, the transcendent function will act[246]. **The conscious position disappears. The unconscious position disappears. And a third term appears, which synthetizes and transcends the duality.**

In the same way as any energetic duality, good and evil are separate when one enters the fourth dimension. However, as the ego keeps its more conscious position of one side, avoiding the leak from the other side, the psychological tension will occur and, at some point, the transcendent function will act, synthetizing and transcending the duality good and evil. The 4D ego, at the end of the Paradigm, will be capable of unified actions that **transcend good and evil**. These actions, when affecting other people, are felt as good and evil at the same time, therefore impossible to be classified, which could cause a feeling of confusion. Indeed, this is true for any duality.

> For all things are baptized at the font of eternity, and beyond good and evil; good and evil themselves, however, are but fugitive shadows and damp afflictions and passing clouds.[247]

The fact that the end of the Paradigm of Balance tends to overcome the duality between good and evil does not extinguish them, once all previous dimensions continue to exist. Undoubtedly, however, good and evil are no longer criteria of choice. Good and evil will always be elements strongly considered during the reflexions of the fourth-dimensional ego, but no longer criteria of choice. At the end of the Paradigm of Balance the attention of the ego will be directed towards the alignment of the ego's will with the Soul's will. "'Father,' he said, 'if you are willing, take this cup away from me. Nevertheless, let your will be done, not mine.'"[248] If good and evil have been transcended and are no longer criteria of choice, the criterion now is the alignment between the ego's and the Soul's will. We will name this alignment **positive**. In opposition, we will call the misalignment between the ego's and the Soul's will, **negative**.

> The formulation of ethical rules is not only difficult but actually impossible because one can hardly think of a single rule that would not have to be reversed under certain conditions. Even the simple proposition "Conscious realization is good" is only of limited validity, since we not infrequently meet with situations in which conscious

realization would have the worst possible consequences. I have therefore made it a rule to take the "old ethic" as binding only so long as there is no evidence of its injurious effects. But if dangerous consequences threaten, one is then faced with a problem of the first order, the solution of which challenges the personality to the limit and demands the maximum of attention, patience and time. The solution, in my experience, is **always individual and is only subjectively valid**.[249] [author's own highlights]

"Ethical rules" is something of an oxymoron. Norms are moral. JUNG shows that the "old ethic", the moral, can have detrimental effects and dangerous consequences. The "solution [...] is always individual and **is** only subjectively valid" because it is in alignment with the Soul. What JUNG is calling "solution" in the context of an ethical conflict is what I call **positive**.

The ethical conflict leads to a reorientation of the ego's decisions, because it swaps the decision criteria from a choice between **good and evil** to a choice between **positive and negative.** As the access to a new dimension does not eliminate the previous dimensions, the appearance of an ethical conflict as a criterion of choice, with its positive and negative poles, does not extinguish the existence of good and evil, nor does it relativize them as forces, but as criteria of choice. So, four types of actions are now possible:

- Beneficial positive actions
- Maleficent positive actions
- Beneficial negative actions
- Maleficent negative actions

TABLE OF ETHICAL CONFLICTS

	Evil	Good
Actions permitted: Positive	Positive evil	Positive good
Actions forbidden: Negative	Negative evil	Negative good

According to the fourth-dimensional criteria of choice, in the Paradigm of Balance the 4D ego progressively learns to acknowledge the Soul's will and starts to align itself with it, **only putting into practice** the beneficial positive actions and the maleficent positive actions, **avoiding** the beneficial negative actions and the maleficent negative actions.

To experience the ethical conflict as a fourth-dimensional criteria of choice is infinitely harder than to follow morals, the third-dimensional criteria. The moral system was destroyed "because one can hardly think of a single rule that would not have to be reversed under certain conditions"[250]. JUNG is radical in affirming that even the therapeutic action of consciousness itself is questioned.

The impossibility to formulate "ethical rules"[251] leads to the extremely hard situation of having to evaluate each case at a time, never repeating previous solutions and, above all, seriously consulting the Soul's will. An attitude that requires "the maximum **of** attention, patience and time"[252]. Only at this level of dedication it is possible to lead the 4D ego to get to know the Soul and align its will with the Soul's will.

Adding to this difficulty, is the reaction of other people. In saying that "The solution is always individual and is only subjectively valid."[253], JUNG is saying that the solution is aligned with the Soul's will. However, this means that other people may not acknowledge this solution as such, since it is "individual and is only subjectively valid"[254]. In fact, the present third-dimensional humanity, which can only understand the actions of any other person within their binary system of good and evil, will both hate the practice of positive maleficent actions as it will demand the practice of negative beneficial actions. The present third-dimensional humanity criminalizes fourth dimensional people because their ethics leads them to practice moral and **immoral** actions – I will not use the euphemism **amoral**.

> They began their accusation by saying, 'We found this man inciting our people to revolt'[255]

Pilatus, Roman, with a different cultural matrix from the Jewish – therefore, with **another moral system** – does not see immorality in Christ.

> Pilate came outside again and said to them, 'Look, I am going to bring him out to you to let you see that I find no case against him.'[256]

The fourth-dimensional consciousness causes a disorientation in the third-dimensional consciousnesses because these consider ethics as immoral.

However, behind this disorientation, hides the real reason why the 3D egos hate the 4D egos: the coincidence between ego and Soul, the presence of the Divine in the Human.

> The Jews replied, 'We have a Law, and according to that Law he ought to be put to death, because he has claimed to be Son of God.'[257]

It does not matter in which paradigm a certain group is. **The maximum crime is always having someone who is one paradigm ahead.**

[228] *The Hammurabi Code. (2011)* Translated by L. W. King. (online) Available at: <http://www.general-intelligence.com/library/hr.pdf> Access: April 25th 2020. p. 3. [author's own highlights]

[229] "The father is a mediator of a relationship; [he] determines the basis, to what extent, within which scope or limits, the rules, the quality of input or distancing, the methods, regularity, objective, responsibility and objectives the various relationships of the child with the world, the other and themselves will be established. The father discriminates the world in categories, making it comprehensible and therefore usable; [...]". LIMA FILHO, A. P. (2002) *O pai e a psique.* São Paulo: Editora Paulus. p. 69.

[230] JUNG, C. G. (1975) *Psychology and religion: West and East. – Answer to Job.* Translated by Hull, R. F. C. 2nd edition. CW XI. Bollingen Series XX. Princeton University Press. §579.

[231] Ibid.

[232] *The New Jerusalem Bible.* Acts 8:1-3.

[233] *The New Jerusalem Bible.* Acts 9:1-5.

[234] Bruno ERNST citing ESCHER. *The magic mirror of M. C. Escher.* 1976. Ballantine Books. New York. Available at: <https://www.articons.co.uk/escher.htm> Access: April 25th 2020. Page not found.

[235] DRISCOLL, J. P. (1992). *The unfolding God of JUNG and Milton.* Glossary. University Press of Kentucky. p. 194.

[236] NIETZSCHE, F. (2006) *On the genealogy of morality.* Preface. Translated by Diethe, C. Cambridge University Press. Aphorism 6.

[237] NIETZSCHE, F., (2016) *The birth of tragedy.* (Quoting *Faust,* verse 409, by GOETHE), J. W. Translated by Haussmann, W. A. Project Gutenberg eBook. Available at: <https://www.gutenberg.org/files/51356/51356-h/51356-h.htm> Access: December 10th 2019. p. 80.

[238] JUNG, C. G. *Memories, dreams and reflexions.* "Late Thoughts". Translated by Winston, R. and C. Revised Edition. Vintage Books. (ebook) Available at: <http://www.venerabilisopus.org/en/books-samael-aun-weor-gnostic-sacred-esoteric-spiritual/pdf/200/265_jung-carl-memories-dreams-reflections.pdf> Access: April 28th 2020. p. 395.

[239] JUNG, C. G. (1979) *Aion – researches into the phenomenology of the self.* Translated by Hull, R. F. C. 2nd edition. CW IX, part 2. Bollingen Series XX. Princeton University Press. §255.

[240] JUNG, C. G. (1978) *Civilization in transition.* Translated by Hull, R. F. C. CW X. Bollingen Series XX. Princeton University Press. §866.

[241] Ibid. §857.

[242] *GORRESIO, Z. A ética da individuação: um estudo sobre a ética do ponto de vista da psicologia jungiana.* etext, Available at: <http://www.hypnos.org.br/revista/index.php/hypnos/article/view/284/301>.

[243]A leak is the expression of some form of unconscious psychological energy – whether originated from unconscious complexes, Archetypes or 5D Images – on the ego's behaviour, in the way the ego sees other people or in situations in the ego's life, **without**

the ego being conscious, desiring or choosing such expression. Unconscious complexes, Archetypes and 5D Images exist whether or not the ego is aware, whichever dimension the ego is in. When constellated (activated by the Self), unconscious complexes, Archetypes and 5D Images are expressed in the ego's life, without it noticing, choosing or act from them. That is how the ego expresses behaviours and treads paths without noticing or choosing (identifications); only later, in hindsight, it becomes aware of it. that is how the ego projects in other people various unconscious contents, seeing in other things which are very different from what they are. That is how repetitive situations dominate the life of the ego, without it comprehending its causes. Although leaking seems to be a problem, it is extremely useful to the development of consciousness. Leaks are generated by the Self, **not** the ego – for that very reason, the ego cannot be blamed for the leaks. Through the leaks that take place in identifications, projections and repetitive situations, the ego enters into direct contact – without intermediaries – with psychological energies so far unconscious to it. That way, the ego learns directly with the Self. It is down to the ego to continuously and eternally recognize the leaks generated by the Self, stopping the leak to continue (what I call "damming"), with the aim to generate psychological tension and allow constellation, by the Self, in a posterior moment, of the transcendent function (See note 18, in this chapter).

244"The counter-position in the unconscious is not dangerous, the counter-tendency breaks through into consciousness, usually just at the moment when it is most important to maintain the conscious direction. [...]This moment is critical because it possesses a high energy tension which, when the unconscious is already charged, may easily "spark" and release the unconscious content". JUNG, C. G. (1975) *The structure and dynamics of the psyche. On the nature of the psyche.* Translated by Hull, R. F. C. CW VIII/2. Bollingen Series XX. Princeton University Press. §138.

245 "The third transcendent that emerges from any relationship, whether it is an image from dreams, a romance or an encounter with gods, serves to embody opposites; it points in both directions and exerts a certain influence until it can be transformed into experience. A genuine relationship, in any sphere, is a mystery: an encounter between oneself and the other, whether internal or external. [...] the relationship will demand growth and not regression, complexity and not simplicity, and will involve negotiation towards an agreement with **the tension of the opposites that each part involves**." HOLLIS, J. *On this journey we call our life.* [Translated from the Portuguese version: (2004) *Nesta jornada que chamamos vida.* São Paulo: Paulus. p.112] [author's own highlights]

246 "[...] such a procedure can legitimately take place only when there is a sufficient motive for it. Equally, the lead can be left to the unconscious only if it already contains the will to lead. This naturally happens only when the conscious mind finds itself in a critical situation. Once the unconscious content has been given form and the meaning of the formulation is understood, the question arises as to how the ego will relate to this position, and how the ego and the unconscious are to come to terms. This is the second and more important stage of the procedure, the bringing together of opposites for the production of **a third: the transcendent function**. At this stage it is no longer the unconscious that takes the lead, but the ego". JUNG, C. G. *The structure and dynamics of the psyche. On the nature of the psyche.* Op. Cit. §181. [author's own highlights]

247 NIETZSCHE, F. (1999) *Thus spoke Zarathustra.* Chapter XLVIII "Before sunrise". Translated by Common, T. Project Gutenberg eText. Available at:

<http://www.dominiopublico.gov.br/download/texto/gu001998.pdf>

Access: February 28th 2020.

[248] *The New Jerusalem Bible.* Luke 22:42

[249] JUNG, C. G. (1980) *The Symbolic life.* Translated by Hull, R. F. C. CW XVIII. Bollingen Series XX. Princeton University Press. §1413.

[250] Ibid.

[251] Ibid.

[252] Ibid.

[253] Ibid.

[254] Ibid.

[255] *The New Jerusalem Bible.* Luke 23:2

[256] *The New Jerusalem Bible.* John 19:4

[257] *The New Jerusalem Bible.* John 19:7

SENSE

During the Paradigm of Self-Affirmation, the 3D ego affirmed the characteristics that define it, the '**me characteristics**', denying all others, the '**not-me**' characteristics. Through this process, an ego with a defined personality was built, authentic in its characteristics, whichever they were. Maintaining a coherence with its characteristics, the ego reached a moral excellence, regardless of its definition of moral. Hence, a **strong ego** appeared. Self-Affirmation has been reached.

The Soul appears and morally defeats the ego.

During the Paradigm of Balance, the 4D ego was dedicated to the integration of several unconscious complexes. Then, several Archetypes were constellated in various combinations and intensities, and the ego established tensions with them until, one by one, they were integrated into consciousness. Having honoured all gods and goddesses, there are no resentments or demands from them. The ego has now synthetized the **not-me** characteristics into its **me** characteristics. The moral system proves to be a very narrow and relative group of social norms, which prevents the ego from reaching its deep individuality. Therefore, it was relegated to the background, to be observed only when its interior dispositions allow, if the ego wants to. **The ego has transcended morals.**

In Crucifixion, the Soul – the Archetype of the Self in four dimensions – was also integrated. A synthesis between consciousness and unconsciousness took place[258,259]. Being infinite, the integration of the unconscious will never end, but **paradoxically**, the integration of the unconscious was concluded – the 4D ego is willing to continue the infinite series of integrations. The disposition to follow the Soul is total, and the ego has reached an **ethical excellence**, and acquired the courage and expertise to live through the powerful and terrible ethical conflicts that the psyche exposes it to and will continue to do so. The psychological reality is now **multi-paradoxical**. The Balance has been reached.

"My God, why have you forsaken me?"[260]

In Crucifixion, the *Soul Retreats*, becoming silent.

The fourth-dimensional ego dies.

The fifth-dimensional ego resurrects.

The *Soul Retreated*: **there is no psychological guidance** whatsoever. The Soul will always produce symbols; however, it no longer has a guiding character. Ethics appear as a system through which the regulatory Archetype of the psyche has brought the ego closer to its various unconscious instances, completing the consciousness through deep individuality, and making it multi-paradoxical. In the absence of psychological guidance, these ethics are relegated to the background, to be observed only when the choices of the ego coincide with them. **The ego has transcended ethics.**

The 5D ego is not determined nor defined by any characteristic, neither by its opposite or by the simultaneity of these opposites, not even by the transcendence of these opposites; it is, therefore, beyond morals and ethics.

The 5D ego perceives other people and reality in the same way that it perceives itself: not defined by any characteristics, neither by their opposites or by the simultaneity of these opposites, not even by the transcendence of these opposites; therefore, devoid of morals and ethics.

Entering the Paradigm of Balance has shown the ego that its free-will was not real, it was simply a false impression allowed and stimulated by the 3D Self. In this phase, the 3D ego notices that it does not have free-will because the unconscious puts pressure on it, irresistibly, every time the ego is unconscious; this is **extremely** common. In the fourth dimension, however, the free-will increases as complexes and archetypes are integrated into consciousness. **Paradoxically**, the will to exercise this free-will decreases, because the 4D ego realises that following the Soul is not like obeying another person, but itself, surrendering not to slavery, but to deep individuality. When the ego finally gives up on its own desires – "Father, if you are willing, take this cup away from me. Nevertheless, let your will be done, not mine."[261] – the *Soul Retreats*. Having experienced the Paradigm of Balance, the 5D ego is perfectly used to waiting for the guidance of the Soul and following it. The 5D ego waits and desires directions. In this phase of psychological development, it is much easier to follow the psychological guidance of the Soul. But it never comes. In Crucifixion, the *Soul Retreats*, becoming silent.

Free-will **is total.**

Free-will is total, not because the 5D ego denies morals or ethics. It has simply transcended them. It is not about, either, denying the unconscious. On the contrary, the 5D ego is a synthesis between consciousness and unconsciousness, and has the archetypes in Balance, integrated. It is clear that no one can resist an unconscious pressure indefinitely. But, in Crucifixion, the surrender to the soul was total and the resistance to the unconscious ceased, although, **paradoxically**, there is no identification with the unconscious.

Free-will is total because the 5D Self **no longer wants** to rule the process, it no longer puts pressure on the ego. After Crucifixion and *Resurrection*, it is notable how the Father becomes an **idle god**, leaving the way free for the Resurrected Christ.

The 5D ego realises that it can **freely choose** whatever it wants to experience or do.

It is completely alone and should choose alone.

At precisely this moment, the colossal weight of freedom falls over it.

Having nothing else to guide its actions, the free choice will be made based solely on what **makes *Sense* for the 5D ego.** The perception of *Sense*[262] is **strictly *Personal***[263]. The free fifth-dimensional choice will be made based strictly on the *Personal Sense*.

The ego is in the centre of the *maṇḍala*, in total harmony with the integrated Soul, with the archetypes around it, in Balance. All this power is integrated and available to the 5D ego. The free fifth-dimensional choice will mobilize all this power. The free fifth-dimensional choice will be made based strictly on a *Personal Sense*.

It is essential to understand that *Sense* is **not** meaning. Meaning is brought about by the Symbol[264]. The Symbol is constellated by the Soul, it is fourth-dimensional, therefore meaning is fourth-dimensional[265]. The fourth-dimensional experience depends entirely on the Symbol and on its meaning in order to bring the unconscious material into consciousness[266,267].

Being an experience inherent to the fifth-dimensional consciousness, *Sense* is perceived as an **effect of the paradoxical coincidence between consciousness and the unconscious**.

On the one hand, the *Sense* of free choice is derived from the unconscious, integrated into consciousness. In Balance, the unconscious extends infinitely in all symbolic fourth-dimensional directions, i.e., the archetypes. Infinite influences and information, more or less defined, flow from the archetypes and are brought into consciousness. Amidst the infinite nature of the unconscious, some of these influences and information deal with the 5D ego itself and its reality, showing ease and difficulty. Other influences and information deal with other people, of any dimension, and with their realities, showing the 5D ego the ease and difficulty that will happen to them. The infinite extent of the unconscious in all symbolic fourth-dimensional directions gives the 5D ego the opportunity to contemplate a huge complexity, a vast number of realities and possibilities of evolution in each of these realities. All this reaches the 5D ego through the integrated unconscious and can be accounted for and used.

On the other hand, the *Sense* of free choice is derived from the consciousness, integrated into the unconscious, which in turn prefers to invest its energy in one thing instead of another and can clearly formulate what makes *Sense* for itself.

In the Paradigm of Balance, a more or less complex archetypal constellation would determine a **precise direction** of psychological development, to which the 4D ego could only temporarily and painfully resist. Through the force of the archetype, this precise direction would become a **highly significative purpose** to the 4D ego. In the Paradigm of Sense, all archetypes are integrated into consciousness, therefore **all directions constitute integrated purposes** available to the 5D ego. So, in the paradoxical coincidence between consciousness and unconsciousness, typical of the fifth dimension, *Sense* **is the self-determination of an integrated purpose.**

Sense **is the strictly individual perception that a certain reality is preferred in relation to all others.**

Reality is normally understood as single, unequivocal and immutable. This understanding of the third dimension depends on reality being taken as something "exterior", formed by "concrete facts".

A fourth-dimensional consciousness, however, perceives reality as an "interior" reality, as a **psychological reality**. In this case, reality is no longer perceived as unequivocal, because it becomes clear that what is called reality is, in fact, a group of entirely personal perceptions and interpretations. Therefore, each person inhabits a specific, personal reality – a personal universe. Reality is, likewise, no longer perceived as immutable, because psychological alterations will necessarily reflect proportional material alterations.

In the Paradigm of Sense, **reality is *Pneumatic*** (= spiritual), and no longer perceived as single. A fifth-dimensional consciousness perceives the reality in which it is living, but also perceives several other possible realities. The 5D ego has access to various *Pneumatic Images*, each being the mould of a specific reality[268]. A certain *Pneumatic Image* manifests a certain reality, whereas another *Pneumatic Image* manifests another reality[269]. Therefore, each *Pneumatic Image* that the 5D ego chooses to manifest will unfold a series of different events which will, ultimately, take the ego to entirely new realities[270]. For that reason, in the fifth dimension, the ego progressively learns to move within the various perceived realities, and will, **paradoxically**, need to **choose** and prioritize which *Pneumatic Image* it **wants** to manifest, as this will, in turn, involve choosing which reality it wants to **live**. This **choice** will be made exclusively based on the *Personal Sense.*

From this point onwards, the fifth-dimensional ego goes into **action**. It starts a process through which the *Pneumatic* images will be manifested in a reality of life that is **complete,** with all its imaginable components.

It is very important to highlight that the realities of life created by the 5D ego are fifth-dimensional structures, and that, given the scenario of total unity of the fifth dimension, they are entirely contained in the fifth-dimensional ego. However, the fifth-dimensional ego includes the Soul and the unconscious – with which it is in coincidence –, it includes the archetypes in Balance 'around it' and it includes other people and the reality 'exterior to it', which are totally free to act according to their degree of *Free-will*, and, **paradoxically**, are exact reflections of the fifth-dimensional psyche. The fact that this reflection exists in fact increases the weight of freedom. Therefore, what makes SENSE to the 5D ego will culminate in the *Creation* of a ***Pneumatic* reality of life,** which will determine everything that happens in its own psyche and that of others, as well as what happens in its own physical reality and that of other people – which, is, ultimately, the same thing.

The ***Creation***[271] is the basic law of the Paradigm of Sense, its very criterion. Every fifth-dimensional process is only legitimate if it is *Creative*; otherwise, the process will be repetitive and will imprison the fifth-dimensional consciousness in the Shadow of the fifth dimension[272].

Given the complexity inherent to the fifth dimension, and the fact that the fifth-dimensional ego is a human being, it is evident that ***Sense* does not give any guarantee to the action**. The fact that the 5D ego, from a fifth-dimensional context, sees *Sense* in making this free choice and not another one, in acting in this way and not in that way, does not guarantee the action to be right. Strictly speaking, having transcended morals, it no longer makes sense to think in terms of right and wrong. Strictly speaking, having transcended ethics, it no longer makes sense to even think in terms of positive and negative – the "right" and the "wrong" in the realm of ethics. Either way, there is no right or wrong. We can, however, define the notion of **mistake** in five dimensions as something with consequences that are different from those that the 5D ego expected, and are, possibly, unpleasant in its view. In that sense, it is more about things 'working out' or 'not working out', regardless of whether they satisfy the 5D ego's expectations, than it being about morally or ethically 'right' or 'wrong'. Therefore, *Sense* does not guarantee that the action will **work out**, as it can, very well, **go wrong**.

To fantasize that a fifth-dimensional psyche is never wrong would be making many mistakes at the same time. From the start, it would mean assuming an omniscience that does not exist in five dimensions: the multi-paradoxical coincidence between consciousness and the unconscious is in no way a synonym of omniscience. Besides that, omniscience presupposes perfection – and perfection means "entirely done" [273]. If omniscience is perfect and complete, it necessarily needs to include the mistake, which implies that the omniscience, **paradoxically**, makes mistakes. Finally, to never err would be dependent on the assumption of an omniscience that never errs (an impossible idea that would break the all-encompassing unity of the multi-paradox that constitutes the base of the fifth dimension), and that always guides the 5D ego in the 'right' direction. Besides the fact that there is no longer something that can be called 'right', this structure, an ego guided by a transcendent instance, is fourth-dimensional, and does not exist in the fifth dimension. The 5D ego makes many mistakes. More than that, the 5D ego needs its mistakes[274].

The fact that the 5D ego errs, instead of putting its multi-paradoxical consciousness into question, affirms its freedom of choice and increases the weight derived from it. For that reason, the apprehension of *Sense* is so fundamental in five dimensions. The impact of the action of a 5D ego is immense: it directly interferes in its own psyche, it directly interferes in the psyche of other people, it directly interferes in the sequence of events that will unfold in their own life and in other people's lives. Ultimately, its action culminates in a new reality for everyone, and there is **no** guarantee of success whatsoever...

The *Sense* is apparently miniscule: it is about a strictly individual perception, one which establishes a strictly individual preference and is liable to being completely wrong. However, this perception and this preference will create whole new realities which will involve many people. **It is disturbing that something so small and so individual can be so important amidst the colossal and overwhelming spiritual reality of the *Universe*.** But this is precisely the final aim of the Paradigm of Sense: **the development of a *Personal Sense*.** In face of that, the importance of the *Human Being*, of what they see *Sense* in, and their choices, appears inexpressible.

Such is the Paradigm of *Sense*. At some point, the process of psychological development works, and a level of consciousness is reached so that the individual will need to learn to **make choices for oneself, and *Act with no Guarantees.*** This is only possible if the individual learns to guide themselves by what makes Sense to them.

At some point, it is necessary to reach **freedom**.

---

258 "[...] **the union of the conscious mind or ego personality with the unconscious** personified as anima **produces a new personality compounded of both**—"ut duo qui fuerant, unum quasi corpore fiant." Not that the new personality is a third thing midway between conscious and unconscious, it is both together. Since it transcends consciousness it can no longer be called "ego" but must be given the name of "self." JUNG, C. G. (1985) *The Practice of psychotherapy. Ab-reaction, dream analysis, transference.* Translated by Hull, R. F. C. 2nd edition. CW XVI. Bollingen Series XX. Princeton University Press. §474. [author's own highlights]

259 "The process of differentiating the ego from the unconscious, then, has its equivalent in the *mundificatio*, and, just as this is the necessary condition for the return of the soul to the body, so the body is necessary if the unconscious is not to have destructive effects on the ego-consciousness, for it is the body that gives bounds to the personality. The unconscious can be integrated *only if the ego holds its ground*. Consequently, the alchemist's **endeavour to unite the *corpus mundum*, the purified body, with the soul is also the endeavour of the psychologist** once he has succeeded in freeing the ego consciousness from contamination with the unconscious." JUNG, C. G. *Ab-reaction, dream analysis, transference.* Translated by Hull, R. F. C. 2nd edition CW XVI. Bollingen Series XX. Princeton University Press. §503 [author's own highlights]. In this comment, about an illustration with which we can undoubtedly establish a parallel with the Resurrection, a *Pneumatic Image* clearly related to the Paradigm of Sense, it becomes impossible to ignore that JUNG is clearly saying that a synthesis between consciousness and unconsciousness "is possible", if the ego can take it. [author's own highlights]

260 *The New Jerusalem Bible.* Matthew 27:46.

261 *The New Jerusalem Bible.* Luke 22:42.

262 Jolande JABOBI offers a definition of "sense". Although her definition is in an entirely fourth-dimensional context, it works as a fourth-dimensional proto-definition for the

fifth-dimensional term Sense, whose amplitude is immensely higher, and the context is completely different:

"[...] but it is mostly aptly expressed by the German word for symbol, *Sinnbild*, the two words of which is composed disclose the two spheres that the symbol combines into a whole: **Sinn (sense, meaning), the integrating component of the cognitive and formative consciousness**, and *Bild (image)*, the content, the raw material of the creative, primordial womb of the collective unconscious, which takes on meaning and shape through its union with the first component." JACOBI, J. (1959) *Complex/Archetypes/Symbol in the psychology of C. G. Jung.* Translated by Manheim, R. Bollingen Series LVII. Bollingen Foundation, Inc. p.95. [author's own highlights]

[263] "Without the reflective consciousness of mankind, the world would be totally devoid of sense, since humans, according to our experience, are the only beings who can verify the fact of "sense". JUNG, C. G. *Memories, dreams and reflexions.* [Non existent in the English version. Translated from the Portuguese version: (1981) *Memórias, Sonhos e Reflexões.* Rio de Janeiro: Editora Nova Fronteira. p.323.]

[264] "A symbol is alive only as it is "pregnant with meaning", only as long as the opposites "form" and the "raw material of imagery" (thesis and antithesis) combine in it to make a whole (synthesis) so that its relation to the unconscious remains effective and meaningful." JACOBI, J. *Complex/Archetypes/Symbol in the psychology of C. G. Jung.* Op. Cit. p. 95.

[265] "The psyche is in fact the only immediate experience we can have and the *sine qua non* of the reality of the world. The symbols it creates are always grounded in the unconscious archetype, but their manifest forms are moulded by the energy which enables them to attract, out of the conscious mind, those contents which are best suited to themselves." Ibid. p. 74.

[266] "Thus the symbol is a kind of mediator between the incompatibles of consciousness and the unconscious, between the hidden and the manifest. [...] Ibid. pp. 97-98

[267] "The symbol, as a visible expression of the accumulated energy charge of a "nucleus of meaning" within the psychoid collective unconscious, is able on the one hand, to relieve the tension, and on the other hand, through its deeper meaning, to make a new impression on the psychic process, i.e., to open up a new path and hence produce a new concentration of energy. Thus, advancing from synthesis to synthesis, it unceasingly redistributes the libido and converts it to meaningful activity. Ibid. p. 100.

[268] See Chapter "Macroimage".

[269] See Chapter "Manifestation".

[270] See Chapter "Manifestation", Part "Multidimensionality".

[271] See Chapter "Creation", Part II.

[272] See Chapter "Demon".

[273] "The way of individuation which Christ teaches and exemplifies requires the **total** efforts and resources of the personality. Nothing may be held back. The parable of the rich young man illustrates this: "Jesus said to him, 'If you would be perfect (teleios = complete, fullgrown) go, sell what you possess and give to the poor, and you will have treasure in heaven; and come follow me." (Matt. 19:21). EDINGER, E. F. (1992) *Ego and archetype.* Boston: Shambhala. pp. 144-145.

[274] ANDRADE, O. *Manifesto da poesia pau-Brasil. "A contribuição milionária de todos os erros. Como falamos. Como somos."* [Not published in English)] (eBlog). Available at: <https://www.passeiweb.com/estudos/livros/manifesto_pau_brasil> Access: April 15th 2020.

CREATION II

In the Paradigm of Balance, morals are overcome, and with them, the concepts of right and wrong. In its place, the ethical conflict guides the psychological development, where good and evil continue to exist and have their painful and joyful effects, however no longer as the criteria used to make choices. In the ethical conflict, the ego is urged on one side by its conscious dispositions, and on the other side by the dispositions to practice the good and the evil emanated by the Soul. The ego's choices are progressively directed towards the dispositions emanated by the Soul, and this is a movement that, ultimately, leads to the integration of the Soul. When "The Father and I are one"[275], the ego is behaving in alignment with the Soul (ethical, positive) and totally eliminating behaviours which are out of alignment with the Soul (unethical, negative).

In the Paradigm of Sense, ethics is outdated. In Crucifixion, the *Soul Retreats*. On the way to the third *coniunctio*, the *Unus Mundus*, the Soul maintains the role of reflecting the *Truth* of the *Spirit* onto the Symbol. The Soul continues to produce Symbols, which reflect the *Truth* of the *Spirit*. However, the Symbol no longer has a guiding character.

Nothing takes up the guiding role of the Symbol. The Soul guiding the ego – or any other type of guidance of the ego by a transcendent instance – is a fourth-dimensional psychological structure. Not even the guidance or protection given to the ego by the Guardian Angel survives[276]. The fifth-dimensional structure is completely different: the *Spirit* does **not** take up the role of guiding the ego, nor does any other transcendental dimension.

Since the Soul continues to produce Symbols, it is still possible to establish an ethical conflict. Actions in consonance with the Symbol constellated by the Soul in its reflection of the *Truth* of the *Spirit* are in alignment with the Soul and are positive. Actions which are not in consonance are not aligned with the Soul and are negative. However, the Symbol no longer has a guiding character.

The ethical conflict, fourth-dimensional, stops being the criterion of choice. Ethics has been **overcome**.

Which is the fifth-dimensional criteria of choice?

Choice is a complex term in the Paradigm of Sense because it is its gravitational centre.

Strictly speaking, having overcome morals and ethics, ending the unconscious determination over the ego, the 5D ego experiences for the first time the *Free-will*, freedom, the **freedom of choice**. Having no exterior criteria to base its choices on – at this point, there is nothing else that can be called "exterior" – the ego chooses according to what makes *Sense* to itself, according to its *Personal Sense*.

Until the fourth dimension, the ego's referential was always something external to it. For example, in two dimensions the referential is to be a god projected in the social organization. In three dimensions, the referential is a law-making god incorporated in some sort of religious or secular moral. In four dimensions, the referential is the Soul, an interior god, external to the ego. In five dimensions, **the ego has integrated the referential**: the *Sense* is *Personal*.

This does not mean, however, that there is no criterion.

Freedom is only possible in a scenario of total harmony with the Wholeness, with the *Universe*.

The 5D ego does not experience the freedom as libertinage, as a raw instinctual discharge. Libertinage is just unconsciousness. The development of consciousness was based on an experience of the instinct guided by the Symbol, fulfilled with meaning. There is no going back. Conscious people who opt for libertinage only express their cynicism in relation to life and themselves; ultimately, it is a disappointment they cannot overcome.

The 5D ego does not experience freedom as rebelliousness, as an act of opposition to some central and directing principle. The rebel is never at the centre. With no central authority, one cannot be a rebel. If the central authority was to disappear, the rebel would not know what to do. To see freedom as the possibility to do whatever comes to mind, to do 'whatever I want to', is a third-dimensional perspective.

The 5D ego does not experience freedom as an act of opposition to something external because there is nothing "external". The 5D ego is not determined nor can it be defined by any characteristics or its opposites, neither by the simultaneity of these opposites, and not even by the transcendence of these opposites. Therefore, those elements that were seen as "external" laws to be followed or rejected were internally acknowledged as parts of the being, as its own mechanisms to be exercised.

The 5D ego exercises its freedom in total harmony with the *Spirit*.

Analytical Psychology has a huge difficulty in defining what is *Spirit*, constantly returning to the Soul as the centre of the psyche, describing the Soul as the paradox between *Spirit* and *Body*.

> I must confess that I know as little what "spirit" may be, [...] I must first speak, instead of "spirit", of psychic factors.[277]

However, Marie-Louise von Franz defines an element which is central to the nature of the Spirit:

> One of the main ways in which we use the word spirit is in speaking of the inspiring, vivifying aspect of the unconscious [...]
>
> That is a **dynamic manifestation** of the unconscious, where the unconscious energetically does something on its own, **it moves and creates on its own**, and that is what JUNG defines as spirit.[278] [author's own highlights]

The *Spirit* is presented as dynamic and ***Creative***.

The idea that the *Spirit* is *Creative* can conflict with the idea that the *Spirit* is Wholeness itself, and therefore, perfect. Following this rationale, if the *Spirit* is the Whole and is perfect, it is complete, and if it is complete, nothing else needs to create. The idea of perfection as something finalized is what appears in Genesis:

> Thus heaven and earth **were completed** with all their array. On the seventh day God had completed the work he had been doing. He rested on the seventh day after all the work he had been doing. God blessed the seventh day and made it holy, because on that day he rested after all his work of creating.[279] [author's own highlights]

However, if, as we know, perfect means complete, perfection **needs** to include all elements, among them, the creation. Indeed, this exert is only the second chapter of the Genesis, and there is still a whole Bible ahead. Once even God changes, the space for creation is infinite.

Insofar as the *Spirit* is bigger than the unconscious and includes it, it is not possible, in a fifth-dimensional scenario, to affirm that *Spirit* is a "manifestation of the unconscious"[280]. Actually, it is the unconscious which is a manifestation of the *Spirit*: the Moon reflects the Light of the Sun.

von FRANZ is correct in saying that the *Spirit* is dynamic, it moves and *Creates* on its own accord. Hence, the *Spirit* already has all the elements and, **paradoxically**, *Creates* new elements all the time. The *Spirit* is, therefore, a *Creative Wholeness*. In fact, in being infinite, the *Spirit* is so *Creative* that its elements are **never** repeated, and each instant is entirely new and original.

In order to exercise its freedom in total harmony with the *Spirit*, the 5D ego needs to be *Creative*.

The *Creative Process* is the criterion for the Paradigm of *Sense*.

The 5D ego exercises its freedom of choice, based on what makes *Sense* to it. Having chosen, it moves to action. But its action is a *Creative Action*, as the 5D ego wants to be in harmony with the *Spirit* – whole only at the climax of the Paradigm of Sense – whose nature is a *Creative Wholeness*.

In the chapter "Lilith", we saw that, with the opening of the Paradigm of Sense, Lilith's self-exile ends, and with it, the 5D ego experiences the resurgence of the *Instinct*, as a spiritualized energy[281]. Indeed, JUNG cites the existence of a *Creative Instinct*.

> Although, in general, instinct is a system of stably organized tracts and consequently tends towards unlimited repetition, man nevertheless has the distinctive power of creating something new in the real sense of the word, just as nature, in the course of long periods of time, succeeds in creating new forms. Though we cannot classify it with a high degree of accuracy, the creative instinct is something that deserves special mention. I do not know if "instinct" is the correct word. We use the term **creative instinct** because this factor behaves at least **dynamically**, like an instinct. Like instinct it is compulsive, but it is not common, and it is not a fixed and invariably inherited organization. Therefore I prefer to designate the creative impulse as a psychic factor similar in nature to instinct.[282] [own author's highlights]

In my opinion, at least in five dimensions, *Instinct* is indeed the correct word. Once again, we see an affirmation that *creation*, now presented as instinctual (which, in five dimensions is the same as spiritual), is dynamic. JUNG affirms that this dynamic *Creation* is "compulsive", that is, it wants to *Create* all the time. Although JUNG describes it as physical factor, I believe that its description is truly **Pneumatic**. The 5D ego, *Pneumatic*, wants to continually satisfy its *Creative Instinct*.

The consequences of these conclusions are, however, devastating for the present parameters. They are also devastating for the 5D ego, new to the Paradigm of Sense.

The 5D ego makes free choices according to what makes *Sense* **to it**, and acts *Creatively*, observing the *Creative* process as a criterion for the Paradigm of Sense. This structure originates eight basic types of actions:

- Beneficial positive *Creative Actions*
- Maleficent positive *Creative Actions*
- Beneficial negative *Creative Actions*
- Maleficent negative *Creative Actions*
- Beneficial positive repetitive actions
- Maleficent positive repetitive actions
- Beneficial negative repetitive actions
- Maleficent negative repetitive actions

TABLE OF CREATIVE PROCESSES

	Evil	Evil	Good	Good
	Negative Evil	Positive Evil	Negative Good	Positive Good
Allowed actions: *Creative*	*Creative* Negative Evil	*Creative* Positive Evil	*Creative* Negative Good	*Creative* Positive Good
Forbidden actions: Repetitive	Repetitive Negative Evil	Repetitive Positive Evil	Repetitive Negative Good	Repetitive Positive Good

According to the criterion of the Paradigm of Sense – the *Creative* process – only the first four types of actions (the *Creative Actions*) should be practiced. The last four types of actions (the repetitive actions) should not be practiced, because they are in contradiction with the *Creative* nature of the *Spirit*, therefore being a *Perversion* of the *Spirit*.

Nevertheless, two of those elements can appear shocking at first sight. Knowing that positive actions refer to those actions that observe the **ethical conflict**, a fourth-dimensional criterion, beneficial positive repetitive actions and maleficent positive repetitive actions **should not be practiced** because they are not *Creative*, they are not in harmony with the nature of the *Spirit* and therefore do not observe the fifth-dimensional criterion. Although the **actions are ethical**, they are not adequate to the Paradigm of Sense.

Even more impressive is the fact that the beneficial negative *Creative Actions* and the maleficent negative *Creative Actions* **can be practiced** because they are *Creative Actions* and as such in harmony with the nature of the *Spirit*, observing the fifth-dimensional criterion. Although **unethical**, they are adequate to the Paradigm of Sense. So, as long as they make *Personal Sense* to the 5D ego and are *Creative*, **unethical actions** can be practiced in the Paradigm of Sense.

The *Truth* of the *Spirit* is so abrasive that we would rather protect against it.

Reality is much darker than we would like.

We would prefer the spiritual reality to be more beneficial than the psychological reality. Indeed, many present spiritual schools of thought which deal with the fifth dimension romanticize it as a non-dualist universe, but not as a *Universe* where good and evil, ethics and the lack of ethics are integrated in one unity. They believe in a fifth dimension that has lost its dual character because it excludes evil and the unethical behaviours. They romanticize it because, evidently, no exclusion can exist in unity.

Reality is much darker than we would like it to be because **any element excluded from this reality, however terrible, prevents access to unity.** Whether or not we like, evil and unethical behaviour will be part of reality.

> Just as the archetype is partly a spiritual factor, and partly like a hidden meaning immanent in the instincts, **so the spirit, as I have shown, is two-faced and paradoxical: a great help and an equally great danger**. It seems as if man were destined to play a **decisive role** in solving this uncertainty, and to solve it moreover by virtue of his consciousness, which once started up like a light in the **murk** of the primeval world.[283] [own author's highlights]

Even though he was not thinking through a fifth-dimensional perspective, JUNG affirms that the *Spirit* is "a great help and an equally great danger". Defining the role of mankind in face of the *Spirit*, he must also shed some light over this "murk of the primeval world".

All this seems indeed very terrible. And it is. But, at some point, we must face this reality.

> [...] "civilized" man reacts to new ideas [...] erecting psychological barriers to protect himself from the shock of facing something new.[284]

> Everyone who has hitherto overthrown a law of established morality has always at first been considered as a *wicked man*: but when it was

afterwards found impossible to re-establish the law, and people gradually became accustomed to the change, the epithet was changed by slow degrees. History deals almost exclusively with these *wicked men*, who later on came to be recognized as *good men*.[285]

In relation to the third-dimensional reality of two thousand years ago, Christ was a bad man, who dared be the Son of God and said other people were too: he was not the only one. He destroyed the existing moral system – that the Messiah should remain confined to the prophecies, never materializing – and this crime was considered worse than the murders committed by Barabbas. Nowadays, Christ is considered by many the best of all men. Even then, with humanity clinging to the third dimension, if anyone was to appear today declaring to be the Son of God, they would be, for lack of a cross, at least ostracized.

Finally, the affirmation of JUNG forces the reflection:

> Without stopping to discuss the question of whether this exacerbation of the opposites, much as it increases suffering, may not after all correspond to a higher degree of truth, I should like merely to express the hope that the present world situation may be looked upon in the light of the psychological rule alluded to above. Today humanity, as never before, is split into two apparently irreconcilable halves. The psychological rule says that when an inner situation is not made conscious, it happens outside, as fate. That is to say, when the individual remains undivided and does not become conscious of his inner opposite, the world must perforce act out the conflict and be torn into opposing halves.[286]

Therefore, we can either face the internal existence of evil and lack of ethics, or we see it as an external factor, as a fate. Indeed, it is extremely common to hear complaints from people about the huge quantity of evil and lack of ethics in the world today, about how much **other people** are evil and unethical. This criticism is made particularly to those who are in positions of power.

We ought to, then, ask ourselves, us the psychologically developed, us the spiritually advanced, why are we not practicing the evil actions, the unethical actions? Why are we not taking the positions of power to ourselves? Why do we let these actions to the **others**, and then complain about them? We would answer that we do not want these positions of power because we want no involvement with evil and the lack of ethics that rule the power spheres. But if we want to appropriate this answer, we need to accept that power will always be exercised by the scum of society.

Would it not be better, then, to **overcome duality**, overcome morals and ethics and practice actions which are **multi-paradoxically** good-evil-ethical-unethical, *Creative* Actions that make *Personal Sense*? If someone will practice evil and unethical behaviours anyway, would it not be better if those who are psychologically developed and spiritually advanced, made use of these energies in their multi-paradoxical *Creative Actions*, in a way that they made *Sense*? So as the old adage goes, if you want something done well, do it yourself.

> When the Christian Crusaders in the East fell upon that invincible order of Assassins, the order of free spirits *par excellence*, the lowest rank of whom lived a life of obedience the like of which no monastic order has ever achieved, somehow or other they received an inkling of that symbol and watchword that was reserved for the highest ranks alone as their *secretum*: "nothing is true, everything is permitted"... Certainly that was **freedom of the mind [des Geistes]**, with that the termination of the belief in truth was announced...[287]

Being the *Spirit* dynamic and *Creative*, its *Truth* will also be dynamic and *Creative*, changing at each instant. Having the *Spirit* also "a great help and an equally great danger"[288], its *Truth* will also have dangerous and terrible aspects. In order to reach the *Truth* of the *Spirit*, it is necessary to stop believing in any impervious truth, taught by some system or other. In order to reach the *Truth* of the *Spirit*, it is necessary to be a **free spirit**[289] and have the courage to admit that **everything is allowed**.

---

[275] *The New Jerusalem Bible*. John 10:30.

[276] There is what is called in Christian Hermeticism the "freeing of the guardian Angel". The guardian Angel is freed – often in order to be able to acquit new missions – when the

soul has acquired the disposition of its part of "likeness" in order to experience the Divine more intimately and more immediately, which corresponds to another hierarchical degree. Then it is an Archangel who replaces the freed guardian Angel. Human beings whose guardian is an Archangel have not only new experiences of the Divine in their inner life, but also, through this very fact, receive a new and objective vocation. They become representative, of a human group – a nation or a human karmic community (see Chapter 19 – "Collective ego and symbolic ego") – which means to say that from this time onwards their actions will no longer be purely personal but will at the same time have significance and value for those of the human community that they represent. It was so for Daniel, who in praying the following, was acting not only in his name but also – and above all – in the name of the people of Israel:

"...we have sinned and done wrong and acted wickedly and rebelled, turning aside from thy commandments and ordinances... Now, therefore, O our God, hearken to the prayer of thy servant and to his supplications, and for the love of the Lord, cause thy face to shine upon thy sanctuary, which is desolate. O my God, incline thy ear and hear! Open thy eyes and behold our desolations, and the city which is called by thy name..." (Daniel 9: 5, 17-18) And it was the Archangel Gabriel who "came to him in swift flight at the time of the evening sacrifice... he came to give him wisdom and understanding" (Daniel 9: 21-22). *Meditations on the Tarot.* (Author unknown) (1980) Chapter XIV, "Temperance". Massachussets: Element. (online) Available at: <http://tarothermeneutics.com/tarotliterature/MOTT/Meditations-on-the-Tarot.pdf> Access April 20th 2020. p. 379.

[277] JUNG, C. G. (1975) *The structure and dynamics of the psyche. On the nature of the psyche.* Translated by Hull, R. F. C. CW VIII. Bollingen Series XX. Princeton University Press. §604.

[278] von FRANZ, M. L. (1980) *On divination and synchronicity.* Inner City Books. p. 20.

[279] *The New Jerusalem Bible.* Genesis 2: 1-3.

[280] von FRANZ, M. L. *On divination and synchronicity.* Op. Cit.

[281] "Lilith's approach, however, changed since FREUD and JUNG. She is no longer seen as an exclusively archaic and chthonic deity; Lilith is analysed as an archetypical meaning of the split soul, internally reconducted to the original archetype of the bivalent ouroboric Great Mother, who reflects the partial repression of the instincts and the censorship of the sexual impulses. It deepens the Anima-Animus structure of polarity into the corpus of study from JUNG, NEUMANN and HILLMAN, after the pioneers of psychoanalysis – Jones, Silbere, Abraham – paved the way to the analysis of myths. It is the start of a whole mythology of the female as witness to a tireless battle between mankind and the instinctive, and consequently its repression. These are contemporary issues: is it perhaps the history of a trauma in mankind's childhood? Is it just a moral transgression to the patriarchal culture followed by the dethronement of the Mothers, or is it an ontogenetic catastrophe? Additionally, there is a constant repetition of the 'no' to joy, to the pulsing pleasure. Creativity flows back. The object of desire, the act of desiring and being desired are damaged by censorship and repression, and, in order to achieve this result – on the eve of great discoveries about the unconscious – the most unpleasant or destructive attributes, qualities and forms are attributed to the several personifications of the anima, in order to achieve the repulsiveness and the rejection of the experience." SICUTERI, R. *Lilith, la luna nera* [not published in English. Translated from the Portuguese version: (1985) *Lilith, a lua negra.* 3ª edição São Paulo: Editora Paz e Terra]

[282] JUNG, C. G. *The structure and dynamics of the psyche. On the nature of the psyche.* Op. Cit. §245.

[283] Ibid. §427.

[284] JUNG, C. G. (1964) *Man and his symbols.* New York: Anchor Press Doubleday. p. 31.

[285] NIETZSCHE, F. (2012) *The dawn of day.* Translated by Kennedy, J. F. Project Gutenberg eBook. Available at: <http://www.gutenberg.org/files/39955/39955-pdf.pdf> Access: October 21st 2019. Book 1. Aphorism 20.

[286] JUNG, C. G. (1979) *Aion – researches into the phenomenology of the self.* Translated by Hull, R. F. C. 2nd edition. CW IX, part 2. Bollingen Series XX. Princeton University Press. §126.

[287] NIETZSCHE, F. (2006) *On the genealogy of morality.* Translated by Diethe, C. Cambridge University Press. Aphorism 24.

[288] JUNG, C. G. *The structure and dynamics of the psyche. On the nature of the psyche.* Op. Cit. §427.

[289] Let us not underestimate this fact: that *we ourselves*, we free spirits, are already a "transvaluation of all values," a *visualized* declaration of war and victory against all the old concepts of "true" and "not true." NIETZSCHE, F. (2006) *The antichrist.* Translated by Mencken, H.L. Project Gutenberg ebook. Available at: <https://www.gutenberg.org/files/19322/19322-h/19322-h.htm> Access: February 28th 2020. Aphorism 13.

WORD

The relationship between the Transcendence and the *Word* is glaring in the whole of the spiritual tradition.

It is established since the beginning, when Jehovah creates heaven and earth:

> In the beginning **God created** heaven and earth. Now the earth was a formless void, there was darkness over the deep, with a **divine wind** sweeping over the waters. God **said**, "Let there be light," and there was light. God saw that light was good, and God divided light from darkness. God **called** light "day", and darkness he **called** "night".[290] [author's own highlights]

It is also established since the beginning, at Christ's incarnation:

> In the beginning was the **Word**: the **Word** was with God and the **Word was God**. He was with God in the beginning. **Through him all things came into being**, not one thing came into being except through him. What has come into being in him was life, life that was the light of men; and light shines in darkness, and darkness could not overpower it. The **Word** became flesh, he lived among us, and we saw his glory, the glory that he has from the Father as only Son of the Father, full of grace and truth.[291] [author's own highlights]

The parallel is huge. In the words above, both God the Father and God the Son are the word or say the word and create light, separating it from darkness. **The *Spirit* is the *Creative Word*.**

Further on, the third part of the Trinity goes along the same lines:

> When Pentecost day came round, they had all met together, when suddenly there came from heaven a **sound** as of a violent wind which filled the entire house in which they were sitting; and there appeared to them **tongues as of fire**; these separated and came to rest on the head of each of them. They were all filled with the **Holy Spirit** and began to **speak different languages** as the Spirit gave them power to **express** themselves.[292] [author's own highlights]

The *Holy Spirit* manifests itself as **sound** and **tongues** of fire. In contact with the *Holy Spirit*, people **speak** in other **languages**. However, much more personal in its *Manifestation*, the *Holy Spirit* grants the *Creative* gift of sound to **people**.

It is precisely this what happens in the fifth dimension. The unity is the norm in this dimension. *Spirit* is *Body*. The *Spirit* fulfils individuals, who, henceforth, **speak** other languages, emit *Creative* sounds.

The *Spirit* access to the human consciousness occurs in the psychological structure of the fifth *cakra*, *viśuddha*, located in the throat, where the vocal apparatus of the human being is found. It is, therefore, only natural that the *Spirit* should express itself as sound, as *Word*. The *Word* **Creates** because *Spirit* is *Body*, and as the *Spirit* is manifested as *Word*, the *Word* is necessarily *Body*. Any formulation that differs from that allows for duality, which does not occur in five dimensions.

The Tibetan Buddhism is a spiritual tradition strongly based on the *Creating Word*, the *mantra*, rooted precisely in *viśuddha*:

> What sounds from his mouth, is not the ordinary word, the *shabda*, of which speech is composed. It is mantra, the compulsion to create a mental image, power over which IS, to be as it really is in its pure essence. Thus it is knowledge. It is **the truth of being, beyond right and wrong**; it is real being beyond thinking and reflecting.
>
> [...] **With its sound [the *mantra*] calls forth its content into a state of immediate reality**. *Mantra* is power, not merely speech which the mind can contradict or evade. What the *mantra* expresses by its sound, exists, comes to pass. Here, if anywhere, **words are deeds**, acting immediately. It is the peculiarity of the true poet that **his word creates actuality, calls forth** and unveils something real. His word does not talk – it acts![293] [author's own highlights]

In the Paradigm of Sense, whose fundamental nature is unity, the 5D ego is a *Pneumatic Body*. In the 5D ego, the Word turns to Flesh. The *Spirit* is in unity with the ego in its consciousness, in its *Word*, in its acts. Being with the ego, the *Spirit* grants power to it.

> "And now, Lord, take note of their threats and help your servants **to proclaim your message with all fearlessness,** by stretching out your hand to heal and to **work** miracles and marvels through the name of your holy servant Jesus. As they prayed, the house where they were assembled rocked. From this time **they were all filled with the Holy Spirit and began to proclaim the word of God fearlessly**.[294] [author's own highlights]

Filled with the *Holy Spirit*, they are able to proclaim **fearlessly** the *Word* of God. Being from **God**, from the *Holy Spirit* **of God**, the *Word*, this *Word*, **acts**. That way, the association between the *Spirit* and the 5D ego is clear, giving that ego a ***Creative Word***, which **acts**.

> These are the signs that will be associated with believers: in my name they will cast out devils; they will have the gift of tongues; they will pick up snakes in their hands and be unharmed should they drink deadly poison; they will lay their hands on the sick, who will recover. And so the Lord Jesus, after he had spoken to them, was taken up into heaven; there at the right hand of God he took his place, while they, going out, preached everywhere, **the Lord working with them and confirming the word by the signs that accompanied it**.[295] [author's own highlights]

The *Word* is confirmed with signs, events, facts. Through the *Word*, the disciples perform prodigious tasks. We will return to this in due course. Now, it is striking that it is **the Lord who cooperates with the disciples, and not** the disciples serving the Lord. The Lord **co-operates**, with the *Creating Word*, so that the sign come to reality with the proffered *Word* – signs that include benefits to people, such as exorcisms and cures.

The *Spirit* cooperates with the fifth-dimensional ego with its *Creative* power, so that the **actions** of the 5D ego are ***Pneumatic***, through which the spiritual reality is immediately a physical reality.

But the dimension of action of the *Word* is even more surprising. After his *Resurrection*, therefore already having a 5D ego, Christ leads the *Holy Spirit* to its disciples:

> After saying this he breathed on them and said: Receive the Holy Spirit. If you forgive anyone's sins, they are forgiven; if you retain anyone's sins, they are retained.[296]

The disciples of Christ, filled with the *Holy Spirit*, **have the spiritual power** of forgiving **or not** the sins of **other** people. Now, the *Holy Spirit* is collaborating with the disciples when their actions are **maleficent to others**, such as when the disciples do **not** forgive the sins of others. Note how much this fact arises strong suspicions about the ethics of the *Holy Spirit*, of Christ and of the disciples. If the idea that there are human beings with such a level of consciousness development that the *Holy Spirit* is associated with them, granting them **spiritual power over other human beings** – a direct affront to the idea of equality – was not enough, there is also the concept that the *Holy Spirit* collaborates with **maleficent actions against other people**.

It is not about suspicion: the *Holy Spirit* does not have ethical honesty. It is important to bear in mind that we are dealing with the Paradigm of Sense, fifth-dimensional. The criterion of this paradigm is not ethics, a fourth-dimensional criterion. The fifth-dimensional criterion is the *Creation*, adequate to the *Creative* nature of the *Spirit*, to the *Creative Word*. The 5D ego has ethical actions, but it also has unethical ones. Beyond ethics and the lack of it, what guides the ***Pneumatic*** action of the 5D ego is only what makes *Sense* to it, *Creatively* guided. Indeed, the choice is **truly** granted to the 5D ego:

> So I now say to you: You are Peter and on this rock I will build my community. And the gates of the underworld can never overpower it. **I will give you the keys of the kingdom of Heaven**: whatever you bind on earth will be bound in heaven; whatever you loose on earth will be loosed in heaven.[297] [author's own highlights]

Note that the parallel between the actions of Peter and the actions of the heavens is **total**. According to the grammatical structure of the sentence, Peter's action even has **priority**, since whatever is bound in heaven will have as a **parameter** whatever Peter binds on earth. As Peter also has, with the same degree of freedom, the right to loosen things up on earth, causing heaven to also loosen up, it is evident that Peter has a free choice to make. It is obvious that if Christ is saying that the choice is **Peter's**, Peter will have to choose according to what makes *Sense* to **himself**.

The Paradigm of Sense is frightening to the third-dimensional reality of humanity now because there, the *Spirit* is the *Pneumatic Body* of an individual, and grants it the power to realize both good and evil, ethical and unethical actions, supporting its actions according to an exclusively personal criterion. It sounds absurd. From a 3D perspective it really is absurd.

It becomes even more absurd when it is considered that the 5D ego also errs. Since neither the Soul nor the *Spirit* are telling the ego what to do, there is no omniscience, the ego will fatally make mistakes sometimes. This means that whether someone is forgiven or not, cured or not, exorcised or not, by a fifth-dimensional person, is subjected to a potentially mistaken evaluation. Whatever the case, whether this evaluation is correct or not, the *Spirit* will support the action of the 5D ego.

How can such absurdity be true?

What gives the sensation that this reality is absurd is the fact that a transcendental power is in the hands of a human being, a 5D ego. A power so great that not even ethics needs to be observed. It is no use trying to attenuate the situation: the power is indeed high.

I have witnessed situations where fourth-dimensional people would hear about the fifth-dimensional reality and tried to understand. Frequently, the reactions are very negative, and the emotional load involved is one of envy regarding such power. With one dimension missing, fourth-dimensional people tend to interpret the power of a fifth-dimensional person in a third-dimensional way, which is what is closer in their view. According to this interpretation, the fifth-dimensional situation of making a free choice, based solely on a *Personal Sense*, *Creatively* guided, is understood as "doing whatever he/she wants", "whatever comes to mind", as it happens in the third dimension. It does not occur that, whatever the consequences of this free choice, they are **entirely** the responsibility of the 5D ego. In the same way as children are not entirely responsible for what they do, since their parents guide them and need to take the responsibility, an unconscious ego is not entirely responsible for what it does, since the Soul allows this unconsciousness (3D) or guides it (4D). When we become adults, however, the power is entirely ours, and we can make choices; but we are also **entirely** responsible for our acts and suffer the consequences whether we want it or not. In a way, going into the fifth dimension is like reaching a psychological legal age.

> And so I tell you, every human sin and blasphemy will be forgiven, but blasphemy against the Spirit will not be forgiven. And anyone who says a word against the Son of man will be forgiven; but **no one who speaks against the Holy Spirit will be forgiven either** in this world or in the next.[298] [author's own highlights]

Matthew says that the sins against the *Holy Spirit* are not forgiven. He adds two huge weights to the severity of this sin. One is to say that "every human sin and blasphemy will be forgiven", except that against the *Spirit*. The list of possible sins is immense. But they will all be forgiven, **except** that committed against the *Spirit*. Another weight is to say that even the sin against the Christ, the Son of the Man, will be forgiven. Well, the parameter is impressive: the Christ, the Son. Given the spiritual evolution of the Christ, a sin against him is scandalous. The Crucifixion is an atrocity. But even **this** sin is forgiven.

The sin against the *Holy Spirit*, however, will **not** be forgiven, particularly "one who **speaks** against the Holy Spirit". Why is this such a serious sin? Because in the fifth dimension, the structure of the 5D ego derives from a coincidence between consciousness and the unconscious. For that reason, the 5D ego is able to know what is necessary for it to not have actions which do not observe the rules of its paradigm, that extrapolate its power. If the ego **is able to know**, it cannot, under no pretext, claim unconsciousness, under no circumstance. This is not to say that the 5D ego is omniscient, but if it is able to know and does not, it will still be made responsible.

> As for those **people who were once brought into the light**, and tasted the gift from heaven, and **received a share of the Holy Spirit**, and tasted the goodness of God's **message** and the **powers** of the world to come **and yet in spite of this have fallen away** – it is impossible for them to be brought to the freshness of repentance a second time, since they are crucifying the Son of God again for themselves, and making a public exhibition of him.[299] [author's own highlights]

> If, **after we have been given knowledge of the truth**, we should deliberately commit any sins, then there is no longer any sacrifice for them [...][300][author's own highlights]

A fifth-dimensional action is not guided by any transcendent instance, has no guarantee of success, nor can the responsibility derived from it be attributed to any instance. A fifth-dimensional action can result in a mistake, including the sin against the *Spirit*, err whilst knowing, which will not be forgiven.

As we can see, there is no power without limits.

Precisely at this moment, a healthy limitation appears: the *Demon*.

---

[290] *The New Jerusalem Bible.* Genesis 1:1-5.

[291] Ibid. John 1: 1-5,14.

[292] Ibid. Acts 2:1-4.

[293]GOVINDA, A. (1975) *Foundations of Tibetan mysticism.* (Quoting ZIMMER, H.) New York: Samuel Weiser. pp 18-19.

[294] *The New Jerusalem Bible* Acts 4:29-31.

[295] Ibid. Mark 16:17-20.

[296] Ibid. John 20:22-23.

[297] Ibid. Matthew 16:18-19.

[298] Ibid. Matthew 12:31-32.

[299] Ibid. Hebrews 6:4-6.

[300] Ibid. Hebrews 10:26.

DEMON

(DYNAMIC FORCE)

Yahweh is both just and unjust, kindly and cruel, truthful and deceitful.[301]

"Hell is other people."[302] In the Paradigm of Self-Affirmation, there is no better sentence to define evil than Sartre's words, even though the philosopher used it in his own context. In the radically dualist and logical-rational third-dimensional structure of *manipūra*, there is no space within the human psyche of a single person for the conscious coexistence between good and evil. For that reason, everyone considers themselves right, regardless of whether their points of view are logical or absurd, of whether they are in harmony or in conflict with other people. For a 3D ego, the definition of 'good' and 'right' is always who they are and what they believe in.

This is logical, to a certain degree. By logic, if someone is a certain way and acts a certain way, it is because they believe that this is the best way. If they did not, they would not act in that way. So much so that, when someone changes their behaviour, for whatever reason, it happens because they started to believe in different definitions of 'good' and 'right'.

If the 3D ego believes to be good and right, as its own characteristics are good and right, all other characteristics are immediately considered bad and wrong. The discourse that the other characteristics are 'only different', instead of bad and wrong, is a socially necessary lie that allows conviviality. One can even **accept** others. But those most honest must admit that, internally, there is a constant criticism of the other due to their difference: accepting does not mean approving or liking. There is nothing wrong with that, since this is indeed the structure of the third dimension.

An interesting fact is that the definition of 'good' and 'right' is not always the most popular in society. In the chapter *Creation* I, we saw, for example, that there are people who establish evil and criminality as their definitions of 'good' and 'right'. In the same way, it is perfectly possible to develop characteristics considered bad, such as disease and incapacity, as definitions of 'good' and 'right'. Although this seems strange at first sight, we only need to notice how people who have these definitions praise their own suffering, how **serious** is their disease and incapacity, how they must be heroes in order to bear such a hugely **hard** life.

Given that the definitions of 'good' and 'right' are always characteristics of one's own personality and life, **hell is other people**.

All this changes radically in the Paradigm of Balance. The moral defeat is precisely the moment when the presence of the Soul **demonstrates** to the forming 4D ego that its moral elevation, whatever it is, is hypocritical, and that it has the same characteristics it criticised in others, or even worse ones – the hypocrisy is structural in the third dimension. From then on, a long sequence of confrontations with the 'bad' and the 'wrong' starts, where the ego will realize that its definitions of 'good' and 'right' are totally relative. There is no problem in that, as whereas the Self-Affirmation pulls in the direction of the 'good' and 'right', the Balance pulls in the direction of the Totality, a paradox between good and evil, right and wrong.

The confrontation between the various pairs of psychological opposites starts with the Shadow[303], although it continues later in the confrontation with the *Anima* and *Animus*, possibly with other archetypes, and finally with the Self[304,305]. According to Analytical Psychology, at the beginning of individuation, "the shadow is simply a 'mythological' name for all that within me about which I cannot directly know"[306] and, as individuation occurs, the outlines of the archetype of the Shadow become more defined and discernible in relation to the other archetypes[307]. This happens because the Shadow is **not** the **evil**[308]. The Shadow is the sum of all the characteristics which did not find space to be expressed through consciousness[309]. Therefore, if the ego is good, the Shadow will be evil. But if the ego is evil, the Shadow will be good. If the ego is calm, the Shadow will be aggressive. But if the ego is aggressive, the Shadow will be calm. A 3D ego, moral by nature, will perhaps be shocked by the fact that the Soul is **not interested** if the ego started its development through being good or evil. What really matters is that its development culminates in the Totality, in a paradox between good and evil.

Eternally tending towards Totality, the process of individuation can establish a paradox between good and evil, because in the Paradigm of Balance, duality is **acknowledged** and evil is no longer **denied**, as it happens in the third dimension; evil is **internalized**. The individual perceives the evil **within** themselves. The hell is **no longer** in the others: **the hell is in me**. That way, we must recognise at least some honesty, some decency, in our consciousness.

In the Paradigm of Balance, the Shadow is the archetype responsible for showing the ego its moral unilaterality. Although this is commonly the first archetype to be confronted during a process of individuation[310], it is fundamental to remember that every archetype is a god, therefore eternal. The process of relativizing morals through ethics is the centre of every ethical conflict, criterion for the whole psychological process in the fourth dimension. However, in being eternal, the process of relativization of morals, the demoralization, will continue through the future dimensions.

In the culmination of the Paradigm of Balance, the Crucifixion, good and evil are completely and paradoxically in balance: Christ is crucified between the Good Criminal and the Evil Criminal. Whereas Good and Evil are in perfect balance, they are also crucified, completely overcome by the immense transcendent function constellated by the huge tension of the Crucifixion. Their highly relativized existence is evidenced by the fact that Good and Evil are **criminals**, that is, **illegitimate**. Neither good nor evil are criteria of *Truth*, but only the one Crucified between them.

If the Shadow and the Evil were integrated in the fourth dimension, one could ask whether there is darkness in the fifth dimension. Bearing in mind that the fifth dimension is **unified**, **non-dual**, one could question whether it is possible to have darkness without **separation**. Nonetheless, the fifth dimension includes darkness, a much deeper darkness than that found in the fourth dimension: the **Demon**[311] himself.

* * * * *

The *Spirit* is the Totality of the *Universe*, including all things, including the deepest darkness imaginable. There is no way to "save" the *Spirit*. We either admit that all the filth in the *Universe* is totally included in the *Spirit*, together with dimensions of ineffable luminosity, or we will create a dualist perspective, which does not happen in five dimensions.

> Just as the archetype is partly a spiritual factor, and partly like a hidden meaning immanent in the instincts, **so the spirit, as I have shown, is two-faced and paradoxical: a great help and an equally great danger**. It seems as if man were destined to play a decisive role in solving this uncertainty, and to solve it moreover by virtue of **his consciousness, which once started up like a light in the murk of the primeval world**.[312] [author's own highlights]

The Crucifixion opens the Paradigm of Sense, and with it the access to the *Spirit*. According to JUNG, the encounter with the *Spirit* means meeting with one's dimensions of Ineffable Light as well as the Murk of the primeval world. Having discussed the luminous dimension in previous chapters, we now need to ask ourselves what the nature of this abyss is.

The Abyss exists since the creation of heaven and earth and is in very close relationship to the *Spirit* of God.

> In the beginning God created heaven and earth. Now the earth was a formless void, **there was darkness over the deep, with a divine wind sweeping over the waters**. God said, 'Let there be light,' and there was light. God saw that light was good, and God divided light from darkness. God called light 'day', and darkness he called 'night'. Evening came and morning came: the first day.[313] [author's own highlights]

In creating light and determining that it was good, God decides to keep the existence of darkness, only separating the two. The coexistence of light and darkness is a constant in all books of the bible, from the Genesis to the Apocalypse, only changing the way in which they behave and interact. The complete analysis of the relationships between light and darkness goes beyond the aims of this book, once JUNG and other Jungian authors have already done admirably so. However, if we want to understand the darkness of the fifth dimension, there is one element that is of huge interest: the **Demon**.

Although we already know that Lilith was created before Eve, and that she is directly related to the *Demon*, let us skip this part of the myth temporarily in order to contemplate the huge importance of the *Demon* for the Cosmos. This can be understood by contemplating the Tree of Knowledge of Good and Evil, or, as I prefer to call it, the Tree of Consciousness.

We already know that the *Spirit* of God, before the Creation, moved over the darkness that existed over the Abyss. We also know that God opts for keeping the Darkness of the Abyss in the Creation. However, omniscient, God **purposely** keeps the Tree of the Knowledge of Good and Evil, as well as the Serpent, in the Paradise of Eden.

> Then Yahweh God gave the man this command, 'You are free to eat of all the trees in the garden. But of the tree of the knowledge of good and evil you are not to eat; for, the day you eat of that, you are doomed to die.'[314]
>
> [...]
>
> Now, the snake was the most subtle of all the wild animals that Yahweh God had made. It asked the woman, 'Did God really say you were not to eat from any of the trees in the garden?'
>
> The woman answered the snake, 'We may eat the fruit of the trees in the garden. But of the fruit of the tree in the middle of the garden God said, 'You must not eat it, nor touch it, under pain of death.'
>
> Then the snake said to the woman, 'No! **You will not die! God knows in fact that the day you eat it your eyes will be opened and you will be like gods, knowing good from evil**.'
>
> The woman saw that the tree was good to eat and pleasing to the eye and that **it was enticing for the wisdom that it could give**. So she took some of its fruit and ate it. She also gave some to her husband who was with her, and he ate it.
>
> **Then the eyes of both of them were opened** and they realized that they were naked. So they sewed fig-leaves together to make themselves loin-cloths. The man and his wife heard the sound of Yahweh God walking in the garden in the cool of the day, and they hid from Yahweh God among the trees of the garden.[315] [author's own highlights]

The Tree of Knowledge of Good and Evil is the great landmark of the History of the Universe: it is the Tree of Consciousness. Before eating from the Tree, Adam and Eve **did not know** that they were naked. After eating from the Tree, Adam and Even **knew** that they were naked. It is not just about the conscious experience of nudity, but also about the conscious experience of evil and a myriad of others. The text is crystal clear: the Tree is "enticing for the wisdom it could give" and eating from the Tree has the effect of opening the eyes, that is, allowing things to be seen.

A free analysis of the current religious dogmas allows us to immediately notice that the values are inverted in this scenario from the Genesis. God, who purports to be the Absolute Good, defends the unconsciousness. The Serpent – Lucifer – normally seen as the Absolute Evil, offers consciousness[316]. Would the "understanding" be wrong?

Let us not forget: **consciousness is a crime**[317]. Which is the crime committed by consciousness?

Eating from the Tree of Knowledge of Good and Evil implicates on being immediately expelled from the Paradise, as punishment for the crime committed. Let us take these events as landmarks for both states: being in Paradise versus being expelled from Paradise. Comparing both states, we can see exactly what happened there.

Being in Paradise is:

- Being unconscious, as the eyes are closed and there is no understanding;
- Being in unity, as nothing has been eaten from the Tree of Knowledge of Good and Evil;
- To not feel shame, as they were naked and did not know.

To be expelled from Paradise is:

- To be conscious, as the eyes were opened;
- To be in duality, as they ate from the Tree of Knowledge of Good and Evil;
- To feel shame, as they hid.

It is immediately obvious that being in unity implies unconsciousness, and that consciousness is born with duality. Erich NEUMANN studies this passage meticulously in *The Great Mother*[318,319]. Inspired in this great work, we will make a simple analysis. A basic conscious formulation is: this is "x" not "y". For example, this is a pencil, not a pen. Or even, this is good not bad. Consciousness works by discriminating things, establishing **differences**. The importance of this goes way beyond the ability to differentiate things, since the very existence of one's consciousness of oneself is based on establishing a separation between consciousness and the Unconscious, without which the existence of the ego is impossible[320]. The very long process experienced in the first three dimensions is entirely based on a **progressive separation** between the ego's consciousness and the Unconscious. In the effort to differentiate from the Unconscious, the ego strives to clearly define which are its own characteristics[321]. The infinite characteristics relegated to the Unconscious are projected onto others[322,323], the "bad ones", or at least the "different".

Therefore, for the ego to exist, **for the consciousness to exist**, it is absolutely fundamental to break the unity in two, inaugurating the duality through the forked tongue of the Serpent. It is for that reason that the Tree of Knowledge of Good and Evil gives "understanding" and "opens the eye". So, eating from the Tree of Consciousness is unavoidable – even to decide whether one wants to be conscious or not, it is necessary to have consciousness. It does not matter if eating is a sin or not. In putting the Tree in the Paradise, God admitted its unavoidability.

This is the terrible crime committed by consciousness: **breaking the unity**.

There is, however, one consequence of the existence of duality that we cannot ignore.

When one is in unity, a fundamental characteristic of the Paradise, there is only **one** way of living, **one** way of doing things. **There is no** alternative because alternative presupposes duality. Since one is completely unconscious, there is only **one** way of acting: through **instinctual satisfaction**. In unity, when an instinct point to a necessity, the **only** possible reaction is to satisfy it. That is why Adam is so interested in the animals. We saw in the chapter "Lilith", that Adam's reality is fundamentally libidinous. In this state of unconscious unity, the **free-will is zero**[324].

The mere possibility of free-will only exists if there is a **real** possibility of **disobedience**. The free-will depends on disobeying the instinct. The free-will depends on breaking the unity. The free-will **depends on the Serpent**.

God gives an order. The Serpent offers a choice.

Both the Serpent and Lilith conceive **alternatives**, different realities to those that God created and imposed. In the same way that the Serpent offers a **choice** to Eve, Lilith **opts** for the exile even before the seven days of creation are over. With that, the unconsciousness is overcome through disobedience and the free-will is engendered (I use the term "engendered" because, as we have seen, the overwhelming pressure of the unconscious only starts to ease in the fourth dimension and the actual free-will is only possible in five dimensions). God created the Wholeness – he even created Lucifer – but Lucifer created the free-will.

Note that consciousness is considered a crime, and free-will, which enables the choice among alternatives, is associated with the evil.

Let us move forward a little.

Surprisingly, God defends the continuity of the unconscious and the libidinal reality, whereas the Serpent defends the advance towards the consciousness and humanization. However, when Eve and Adam eat from the Tree of Consciousness and are expelled from Paradise, entering duality, immediately God and the Serpent change position. God **arises**, becoming **celestial**. God becomes highly **symbolic**. The Serpent, before **perched up** on the Tree of Knowledge, **is thrown down** from it, and must **crawl on the ground**. The Serpent is relegated to the libidinal, instinctual dimension. Although I have no proof, it seems probable that this first human act marks the passage from the first to the second *cakra*, from the first to the second dimension, from unity to duality. As it happens with all changes of dimension, this event is synchronic with a change in God's behaviour.

For a celestial god to receive opposition from a chthonic god, is a common element in other mythologies. In the Egyptian mythology, for example, the god Shu, the air, opens a space between Nut, the goddess of the starry sky, and Geb, the chthonic god. In Greek mythology, Κρόνος (Krónos) cuts the phallus of Ούρανός (Ouranós), god of the starry sky, literally sectioning its connection with Γαῖα (Gaîa), the goddess of the earth. The sickle of Κρόνος ends a period of the Universe when everything is only conceptual, since Ούρανός conceives but does not allow the birth into form. The sickle opens space in the Universe, allowing for the discernment between high and low, so that there can be consciousness. In a way, Κρόνος creates the visible Universe (form) and enables the emergence of transcendental love, ἀγάπη, once the castration of Ούρανός also results in the birth of Ἀφροδίτη (Aphrodíte).

> Let us return to Uranus. Mutilated and impotent, the god of heaven has fallen into *otiositas*, into idleness, which is, according to Mircea Eliade, a tendency of the creating gods. After concluding their cosmogonic work, they retire to heaven and become *di otiosi*, idle gods.[325]

Despite the huge differences between the Greek mythology and Christianity, certain elements show an amazing similarity, as the separation caused by the Serpent will finally lead to the incarnation of Christ, the transcendental love. At least this is what the dogma of *culpa felix* shows[326,327].

Returning to the Genesis, biting the apple was a **human** act of cosmic proportions. The emergence of the human consciousness led God to change his behaviour. In expelling both mankind and the Serpent from Paradise, God becomes celestial and inaccessible – Michael blocks the entry with his flaming sword. At the same time, the Serpent takes the role that used to belong to God: the libido. The inversion that takes place with the expulsion from Paradise can be understood when one pays attention to the fact that, in arising as a **Symbolic God**, God remains as the path to the synthesis, to **unity**. The Serpent, now fundamentally libidinal, symbol of the dangerous instincts that threaten the human psychological development, is **opposed** to God, safeguarding the **duality**.

In the many phases of the myth, one element remains stable: the Serpent is always opposed to God. So much so that, later, it will be called Satan, the Opposer. The overwhelming tension between the easy and shameful instinctual satisfaction and the extremely hard and honourable path towards the Symbol will be the unbearable rule that will regulate the age-old human development, from the unconsciousness until the Crucifixion, which ends the duality.

* * * * *

Let us return to Lilith.

In the chapter Lilith, we saw that she is created by God at the same time as Adam. However, SICUTERI shows that her creation is closely linked to the *Demon*:

> Lilith is covered in blood and saliva, symbol of desire. **"The moment the woman was created, Satan was also created with her"**. This demon is also woman. The one who disturbed Adam's sleep all night. The Scriptures say: "he was wholly disturbed", and the erotic dream that emerges from the unconscious presents to Adam the whole power of the vital energy. It is Lilith who produces the dream.[328] [author's own highlights]

> But when is Lilith born? And what is her nature? Yalqut Reubeni's source textually says: "From the union of Adam and Eve with this demon (meaning, Lilith) and with another called Naamah, sister of Tubal Cain, were born Asmodeo and numerous demons who still trouble humanity." **Lilith is then appointed not as woman, but as demon**, since the start of the relationship with Adam.[329] [author's own highlights]

Both extracts show the clear intention of God to create a universe where light and darkness coexist. We already know the outcome of Adam and Lilith's story: Lilith chooses the exile and to live with the demon. Despite the altercation of cosmic proportions that takes place between Jehovah and Lilith, Jehovah insists in keeping the darkness within the creation, making the wheel go around again, through the Tree of Knowledge of Good and Evil and the Serpent, which has access to Paradise. To these events, there will inevitably follow the Fall of Men. We must admit that Jehovah's action is purposeful, at the cost of removing his omniscience.

Considering this information, we can only conclude that Jehovah not only allows the existence of the Abyss and Darkness, but also that these components are intrinsic parts of its nature. After all, "In the beginning [...] there was darkness over the deep, with a divine wind sweeping over the waters."[330] It is with this verse that the Bible **starts**.

Jehovah expresses, maybe for the first time, the demoniac dimension of its nature by creating Lilith, pure instinct. In creating her as demoniac, Jehovah proves that his demoniac dimension is instinctive, or, more specifically, the submission to the instinctual discharges and to its own satisfaction devoid of meaning. Let us come back to this.

> In spite or perhaps because of its **affinity with instinct, the archetype represents the authentic element of spirit**, but a spirit which is not to be identified with the human intellect, since it is the latter's *spiritus rector* [ruling spirit]. The essential content of all mythologies and all religions and all isms is archetypal. The archetype is spirit or anti-spirit: what it ultimately proves to be depends on the attitude of the human mind. Archetype and instinct are the most polar opposites imaginable, as can easily be seen when one compares a man who is ruled by his instinctual drives with a man who is seized by the spirit. But, just as between all opposites there obtains so close a bond that **no position can be established or even thought of without its corresponding negation**, so in this case also *"les extremes se touchent."* They belong together as correspondences, which is not to say that the one is derivable from the other, but that they subsist side by side as reflections in our own minds of the opposition that underlies all psychic energy. **Man finds himself simultaneously driven to act and free to reflect**. This contrariety in his nature has no moral significance, for instinct is not in itself bad any more than spirit is good. Both can be both. Negative electricity is as good as positive electricity: first and foremost it is electricity. The psychological opposites, too, must be regarded from a scientific standpoint.[331] [own author's highlights]

JUNG shows an organization where the spirit and the instinct occupy opposite and complementary positions in the psyche. In the chapter "*Body*", we saw that, until the Paradigm of Balance is completed, the spirit is presented as being "above" and the instinct "below" – God arising to heaven and becoming symbolic, throwing the Serpent, now libidinal, on the ground is the archetypal model for this. In this scenario, the "direction" of the psychological process is to arise more and more through the Soul, experiencing instinctual discharges **only** as and when guided by the Soul, therefore filled with meaning. That is why, throughout the whole psychological development that extends until the Crucifixion, **the instinct is strongly demonized**.

Let us take a closer look at the demoniac force.

Although we are focusing our appreciation of the demoniac force within the space of the conscience and in the exercise of the free-will, it is fundamental to observe the scenario in which consciousness is born: God is creating the universe. An important detail: the images of the Genesis emphasize that God is creating **matter** and the **body**.

> Then, Yahweh God made the man fall into a deep sleep. And, while he was asleep, he took one of his ribs and **closed the flesh up** again forthwith. Yahweh God fashioned the rib he had taken from the man into a woman, and brought her to the man.[332] [author's own highlights]

Indeed, **the carnal body precedes the Soul**. God blows (Greek. *psyché* = blow, Soul) onto men.

> Yahweh God shaped man from the soil of the ground and **blew the breath** of life into his nostrils, and man became a living being.[333] [author's own highlights]

We know that the *Spirit* is **descendant**. The *Spirit* of God creates the **world**, the **matter** and the **body** – the flow is from the abstract to the concrete. In the Gospel of John, we learn that **the Word became flesh**[334]. The Word is a reference to Christ, against who Lucifer is the great antithesis. According to the dogma of *homoousía*[335,336], Christ is God, and therefore **God becomes flesh**.

SICUTERI shows an important information about the demon:

> Here is the answer, in Beresit-Rabba: *And God made the wild animals of earth* (Genesis 1:25) [...] Says the Rabi Hamah b. Oshajjh. Living beings nominate four, but when they were created there were three: domestic animals according to its species; wild animals according to its species and all the reptiles of earth according to its species. The Rabi said: The fourth (being) refers to the **demons**, of which the Lord, bless Him, created the soul, but **when he was going to create the body, Saturday was about to begin, so he was not created**, to teach the good manners to the demons [...] As soon as spoken, and the world existed, the focus turned to creating the universe, **the demons' soul was created, but when their bodies was going to be created, Saturday came and he did not create them**.337 [author's own highlights]

The *Demon* has no *Body*.

This information has a huge cosmological impact – Christ has *Body*; Lucifer, the opposer, does not. This is the reason for the opposition.

It is necessary to go back a few steps.

Once again, let us return to the fact that the Serpent was in the Tree of Knowledge of Good and Evil. In disobeying God, the Serpent is **thrown down**, to drag itself on **the ground**. Therefore, the Serpent is atop and only by force (attention to this term: force), goes **down**.

When we look at the biblical references regarding Lucifer, its proud personality and preference for the **top** are evident. For example, in Isaiah, a terrible reprimand is made to the "king of Babylon". The Babylon, from the Genesis to the Apocalypse, is the place of iniquity. Its "king", therefore, is Lucifer.

> How did you come to **fall** from the heavens, Daystar, son of Dawn? How did you come to be thrown to the ground, conqueror of nations? You who used to think to yourself: I shall **scale** the heavens; **higher** than the stars of God I shall set my throne. I shall sit on the Mount of Assembly far away to the north. I shall **climb high above** the clouds, I shall rival the Most High." Now you have been flung down to Sheol, into the **depths of the abyss**!338 [author's own highlights]

In Ezekiel, once again, God reprimands Lucifer in the role of a "king". Now is the "king of Tyre" who is reprimanded. Note that this king has very little resemblance to humans, as it is called a **cherub** and it is said that he was in the **Eden**.

> "'[...] The Lord Yahweh says this: You used to be a model of perfection, full of wisdom, perfect in beauty; you were in Eden, in the garden of God. All kinds of gem formed your mantle: sard, topaz, diamond, chrysolite, onyx, jasper, sapphire, garnet, emerald, and your ear-pendants and spangles were made of gold; all was ready on the day you were created. I made you a living creature with outstretched wings, as guardian, you were on the holy **mountain** of God; you walked amid red-hot coals. Your behavior was exemplary from the day you were created until guilt first appeared in you, because your busy trading has filled you with violence and sin. I have **thrown you down** from the **mountain** of God and destroyed you, guardian winged creature, amid the coals. Your **heart has grown** proud because of your beauty, your wisdom has been corrupted by your splendour. I have **thrown you to the ground**; I have made you a spectacle for kings.[339] [author's own highlights]

In the Koran, we find a very interesting reference to Lucifer's resistance to **bow** to man, the being who has a **body**.

> Your Lord said to the angels, 'I am creating a human being from clay. When I have formed him, and breathed into him of My spirit, **fall prostrate** before him.'[340] [author's own highlights]

The movement made by Lucifer is to place its throne **higher than the stars**[341] of the **Most High**[342]. Now we know that this happens because Lucifer has no body, he does not want to descend to matter.

Then, there is the Fall[343].

> If thou beest he – but O how fallen! how changed
> From him who, in the happy realms of light
> Clothed with transcendent brightness, didst outshine
> Myriads, though bright! – If he whom mutual league,
> United thoughts and counsels, equal hope
> And hazard in the glorious enterprise
> Joined with me once, now misery hath joined

> In equal ruin; into what pit thou seest
> From what height fallen: so much the stronger proved![344]

God throws Lucifer by force "in the depths of the abyss". It is about a super-compensation: resistant to descending, Lucifer is thrown to the lowest level possible, **hell** (in Latin, the word for hell is *infernus* = inferior regions). In the infernal abyss, Lucifer lives in the "lake of fire and sulphur"[345]. JUNG deals with the symbol of the infernal fire and sulphur as symbols of instinctual passions out of control[346,347]. According to Christianity, the deadly sins – pride, gluttony, envy, lust, wrath, sloth and greed – which lead to hell, are evidently instinctual lack of control[348]. Therefore, the relationship between the Serpent and the libidinal instance of the being is affirmed several times. However, to avoid misunderstandings, it is important to highlight once again: Lilith, who is created with the Demon, who gives birth to the Demon or who goes to live with the Demon after leaving Eden, is the archetype of the **instinct**, not of the **body**.

Spirit is *Body*. *Demon* is *Instinct* with no *Body*.

For that reason, the *Spirit Creates* the world and the *Body*, whereas **the Demon resists Creation** – it is Satan, the Opposer – and prefers elevation, abstraction, to the body.

The expulsion from Paradise, the Fall of Lucifer, changes the Evil. From a beautiful and perfect cherub, Lucifer becomes a crawling Serpent. Let us return to what SICUTERI tells us in the myth of Lilith: "But Lilith's nature changed the moment she blasphemed against God, and there is no more obedience."[349] Which changes have we noted on the Demon?

The resistance to the Incarnation of the *Spirit*, to the *Embodiment* of the *Spirit*, is a negative action of *Demon*, because it is resisting the psychological development in the body. In the chapter "*Body*", we saw that the psychological development is only possible, spiritual, if it is experienced in the body. Let us remember JUNG's words: "Only if you first return to the body, to your earth, can individuation take place, only then does the thing become true."[350] Without the body, any development is unreal, because **consciousness is act**.

> Bad imagination was **'phantasia' which was responsible for the fall of Lucifer, and in the human being it created illusions and false desires that led one away from God**. By turning away fantasy rather than the true imagination, the soul became lost in illusion and far removed from the presence of God. True imagination, on the

other hand, is the embodiment of divine wisdom in the soul, and could lead to redemption and union with God.[351] [author's own highlights]

In the Fall, **the *Demon* creates unrealities**.

Why does this happen?

Lucifer in Paradise is completely different from the Demon Falling because the nature of Paradise is unity and the nature of the Fall is duality. In unity, Lucifer is the carrier of Light[352], therefore the biggest developer of consciousness, enthroned over the Tree of Knowledge of Good and Evil, the Tree of Consciousness. The Serpent is the creator of duality, of opposition, of separation.

The myth of Lucifer shows us that the **luminous** quality of consciousness, the **imagery** quality of consciousness is broken by the Fall – by breaking the quality of **imagery**, the real **imagination** becomes *phantasia*. When its imagery and luminous qualities are lost, which quality does the consciousness acquire? It is the Serpent's own nature that answers this question:

> Now, the snake was the most subtle of all the wild animals that Yahweh God had made.[353]

Shrewdness is a characteristic typical of the **rational mind**. Indeed, the Serpent was on the Tree of **Knowledge**, something immediately associated to the rational mind. We have seen that the proposal made by the Serpent is an alternative (Latin: *alter* = other). Adam and Eve were in Paradise following the divine law. Using its shrewdness, the Serpent proposed **another reality**. And it is **this** movement that breaks the duality in two, inaugurating consciousness, at the same time inaugurating duality. For that reason, although consciousness and all its instances are entirely dual, since its origin until Crucifixion, **the epicentre of duality is the rational mind**. Indeed, in circumstances where the rational mind strongly preponderates, evil flourishes much more easily[354]. This happens because the rational mind, besides allowing itself to fantasize about other realities, is strongly based on logic, distancing itself from its complementary function – the feeling – which is constantly performing ethical evaluations.

So far, we have seen that, when in Fall the demon is fundamentally *Instinct* that, **without a *Body*** in which to manifest, expresses itself through the **rational mind**.

> By means of "active imagination" we are put in a position of advantage, for we can then make the discovery of the archetype without sinking back into the instinctual sphere, which would only lead to blank unconsciousness **or, worse still, to some kind of intellectual substitute for instinct**.[355] [author's own highlights]

"Intellectual substitute for instinct" is an excellent description for the *Demon*. **The combination of the *Instinct* with the rational mind is extremely dangerous**. Note that JUNG considers the "intellectual substitutes for instinct" as "worse still" than total unconsciousness. In effect, **the *Demoniac* action deviates the strength from the *Instincts* of the *Body* to the fundamental duality of the rational mind**. Why is this so dangerous, so *Demoniac*?

Instinct is **dynamism**[356], therefore pure **energy**, an **immeasurable source of energy**. Psychoanalysis makes sure that the crucial role of the *Instinct* in the psyche is very clear, both when it uses the term instinct (*instinkt*) and when it uses the term pulse (*trieb*)[357]. So, however much JUNG's theory of libido is very different from FREUD's[358], the importance of instinct in Analytical Psychology is not any smaller. Only under the influence of powerful archetypes and at great cost, consciousness can uproot itself from the instinct and engage in a process of spiritualization[359]. Therefore, the fact that *Demon* has access to this amplitude of energy is extremely worrying.

Nevertheless, it is not just the huge quantity of energy possessed by the *Demon* that makes it dangerous, but its ability to **deviate** it. In a healthy psychological structure, *Instinct* is a type of energy (transcendent, independent from the ego) that strongly influences the psyche, directly on the instance that we call **body**. However, the *Demon* is the **libidinal** instance of the *Spirit* that **has no *Body***, and, resisting the descent, **prefers the abstraction of the rational mind**. Therefore, when the *Demon* prevails over the *Spirit*, instead of flowing towards the *Body* (*Spirit*), the *Instinct* flows towards the rational mind (*Demon*).

This type of composition can be observed in the third-dimensional psychological structure of *maṇipūra*. It is extremely curious that *maṇipūra* is a term that designates "fullness of jewels"[360], that its symbolic representation is the fire, that JUNG defines it as the hell of all passion[361] and, even so, precisely in this *cakra*, the conscience is so devastatingly dual, so terribly **rational** (no other dimension is so rational as the third). It seems incompatible.

We must remember that the 3D Self is expressed through its own concealment, allowing the ego to **not** notice it, allowing the ego to **be the "Self"**, the centre of its own life, aiming at developing the ego as much as possible. Therefore, in the third dimension, the ego fantasizes that it is entirely in control, that it rules its own reality through rational logic, and finds no other successful opposing external psychological force – this will only occur with the moral defeat that the 4D Self imposes to the ego at the start of the fourth dimension. Indeed, if in this *cakra* the separation between the ego and the Self is the largest of all, precisely here is the **realm of the *Demon***. Precisely in *maṇipūra*, the ego is more subjected to identification with unconscious contents, including the Self, having super-human behaviours – **fantasizing that one is God** is an activity typical of the *Demon*.

Although this is totally inaccessible to the understanding of a 3D ego, a fifth dimensional perspective about the third *cakra* is absurdly paradoxical. On the one hand, *maṇipūra* is the centre of **energy**, of **libido**. On the other, **paradoxically**, the third dimension is the one where the ego can disassociate entirely from the rest of the psyche. On yet another hand, precisely here, and precisely because the ego disassociates from the psyche, it is in the third dimension that the most possible identification with the Self happens[362] (considered the classic definition of identification, according to which, it is an unconscious process). Therefore, in the Paradigm of Self-Affirmation, the 3D ego experiences a dimension whose basic characteristic is a huge quantity of available libido (the fire of *maṇipūra*), but as the goal of this paradigm is the construction of a **strong ego**, the 3D ego does **not** give in to an activity merely libidinal, considered regressive. However much there is a colossal quantity of energy available, the ego does not perceive it as something that could or should be used; on the contrary, the ego perceives it as something to which **it must resist** and **protect itself from**, through **morals**. The 3D ego, strong, only experiences the "fire of passions" **when it wants**, establishing **control** over them. In the Paradigm of Self-Affirmation, an ego is considered stronger, more advanced and more **elegant** if it has control over its energy, over the libido, without giving in to it.

This is why the 3D Self remains concealed in this dimension: so that it is possible to **not** do what the libido wants, what the unconscious wants, **what the Self wants**. If, in this dimension, the Self is teaching the ego to **not** follow it – and to not follow the Self is extremely similar, if not identical, to not following God – **it is in this dimension that the *Demon* has more free movement**. In the human plan, the ego is living a whole dimension distant in relation to the Self. However, in the metaphysical plan, this is the dimension of the retreat in relation to God, when it is allowed to not experience the energies in the body. Dual consciousness – based on the epicentre of duality, the rational mind – establishes **control** over the experience of energies in the body, determining **whether** and **how** they will be experienced, instead of just experiencing them spontaneously. The metaphysical name of this mechanism is Demon. Therefore, it can be said that the 'natural' (structural) mechanism of *manipūra* is **usurped**; **the energy is usurped by the rational mind.**[363]

The control that the ego has over the fire that is constantly occurring in *manipūra* can fail at any point. This frequently happens: people give way to the libido in its crude form and give in to the instinctual lack of control: to gluttony, wrath, lust, etc. These are the moments when the Demon starts its action, since what was initially just an instinctual lack of control can transform into the whole psychological experience of that person – it is what we call **addiction**. To consume a large quantity of drugs – be it sugar or heroin – can be a single instinctual lack of control; but if this becomes the only experience the ego desires, the only thing it "thinks" about, day after day, it is locked in a third-dimensional demoniac dimension, the addiction. Note that, although it seems that the rationality was overcome by the libidinal instance, actually the instinctual dimension has been hypertrophied and now occupies the whole "mental screen" of that person. The satisfaction of that instinct is the only thing that "goes through the mind" of that person.

It is true that, as *manipūra* is the epicentre of duality, this dimension tends to create the highest levels of dissociation, **dangerous levels of dissociation**. For that reason, this is the dimension of free movement for the Demon. Even so, it is **not** in this dimension that the demoniac activity is most dangerous. The free transit of the Demon is compensated by the fact that the 3D Self causes a very rigid separation between consciousness and the Unconscious, allowing the ego to protect itself from the shadow – and dynamic – aspect of the Unconscious through morals and religion[364]. The third-dimensional structure is too small even to allow big damages, and normally, the worst that can happen is to succumb to an addiction, however sad that might be.

However, everything becomes more dangerous in the Paradigm of Balance. Here, the rigid separation between consciousness and the Unconscious no longer exists. On the contrary, the Unconscious puts pressure on the ego with its existence, makes the ego see it. The confrontation with the Shadow opens the "gates of the underwold"[365] and the ego can give in to the practice of Evil, the unconscious, therefore inhuman, practice of Evil. There are various fairy tales, for example, where Evil "swallows" people entirely[366]. SANDFORD, analysing Jekyll & Hyde, by Robert STEVENSON, affirms that "there is an intrinsic or archetypal evil, since the further Hyde's personality absorbed Jekyll's the more sheer destructiveness was manifested."[367] Even so, **there is a form of protection in the fourth dimension**: the Self is ahead of the process. If the ego is paying attention to the direction established by the Self, the chances of not succumbing to Evil are very high. The confrontation with the Shadow will still occur, and it is strictly necessary that it does, but if it is experienced in the wider context of Wholeness and Meaning offered by the Self, the **regulating** archetype of the psyche, the ego will manage to integrate the Shadow.

In the Paradigm of Sense, there is no protection whatsoever: the ego is directly exposed to the *Spirit*, and therefore, directly exposed to the *Demon*.

The fifth dimension, differently from the second, the third and the fourth, is a **unified** dimension, therefore every *Pneumatic Image* that is manifested, it is so in the *Spirit* and in the *Body* (since they are the same thing), it is so "internally" and "externally" (since they are the same thing). For that reason, when the *Spirit* is manifested, it is all its *Truth* that is manifested in the *Body*; and the *Instinct*, completely spiritualized in the fifth dimension, is manifested in the *Body* [368]. This is how the *Spirit* is manifested in the *Universe*.

A healthy 5D ego is no longer driven by duality, and therefore, experiences *maṇipūra* in a completely different way. For this ego, the third dimension is no longer usurped: in the fifth-dimension, the energy does not have its free flow blocked by the duality of the rational mind. For this ego, Lilith's self-exile has ended. A 5D ego is unified and **is entirely comfortable with its *Instinct***. It does not need to limit itself by morals or ethics, it does not need to follow any Symbol or psychological direction; the 5D ego experiences **freedom** in relation to its *Instinct*. Therefore, for the 5D ego, *maṇipūra* is the **fullness of jewels**[369] and its fire can spread without loss of energy. The **energy** is free.

However, in the fifth dimension, when the *Demon* preponderates over the *Spirit*, the *Instinct* does **not** flow towards the **unified** reality of the *Body*, but to the **dual** reality of the rational mind, giving it full power. The **unified** *Pneumatic Image* **cannot** remain like so in the **dual** reality of the rational mind, and is "broken", with only one **part** of it being expressed in the rational mind. Therefore, the ego goes into a reality in which a **lie** (=

"partial truth", "broken" *Image*) preponderates over the whole *Truth*. Receiving a **huge injection of libidinal energy** from the *Demon*, the specular nature of the mind (the mind **reflects**) starts to replicate infinitely (repeat) the broken image, the partial truth created by the DEMON, and in a very short time this **lie** becomes **a whole reality, the only reality that exists, the only reality that the 5D ego can perceive**. That way, the *Demon* deviates energy from the *Instinct* towards the creation of alternative realities – alternative in relation to the *Universe* of the *Spirit* – *Demoniac* realities. This is how the *Demon* is expressed in the *Verse*, a reality that divorced from the *Truth* of the *Universe*[370]. Such is the nature of a *Demoniac* prison. Jeffrey RAFF proves this danger by showing that the *phantasia* creates "in the human being [...] illusions and false desires that led one away from God."[371]

That way, the Serpent offers resistance to the *Incarnation* of the *Spirit*, proposing an **alternative** that originates duality, consciousness and free-will – very dear to the human being – and, **paradoxically**, originates an alternative reality: **hell**.

* * * * *

Crucifixion is a cosmic event of extreme importance, impacting directly on the relationship between *Spirit* and *Demon*.

We have seen that being in the Paradise of Eden is to be in unity. Leaving the Paradise (Lilith) or being expelled from Paradise (Adam and Eve) is to enter duality. Whichever the myth, the passage from unity to duality causes a change in the behaviour of God, from libidinal to symbolic. Simultaneously, the Serpent, Lucifer, leaves its place of developer of consciousness to occupy the place that belonged to God: the instinct. The whole cosmic history that goes from leaving/expulsion from Paradise until Crucifixion observes the same structure: a symbolic God above, a libidinal Lucifer below. The human being must always aim above, searching the symbol, which can promote a gradual expansion of consciousness through the integration of unconscious contents. The lower instincts can still be experienced, as long as they are entirely absorbed in the archetypical scenario, in the Symbol, so that the consciousness does not crumble in the unconsciousness that existed in the Eden.

Crucifixion changes this structure completely. The path above was entirely travelled, the elevation is at its maximum and the Symbol was followed until its wholeness – the multi-paradoxical reality of the Soul, the *complexio oppositorum*. In this singular place, the surrender to the Soul is maximum. Not even the extremely powerful survival instinct disturbs the Crucified, and in face of the demoniac temptation – "Then save yourself if you are God's son and come down from the cross!"[372] – he remains on the Cross. **From this point**, it is possible to get closer to the *Instinct* without the risk of losing itself in a merely sensual instinctual discharge. In the peak of the Paradigm of Balance, the multi-paradoxical reality of the Soul is integrated, and duality is transcended in favour of unity. God's behaviour and his relationship with the Demon will have to change.

In the Paradigm of Sense, the 5D ego is again in unity. "The extremes touch"[373], *Spirit* **and** *Instinct* **coincide**: the dimensions of Jehovah are again seen and experienced in unity. We already know that to enter unity is to **enter Paradise**. It is important, therefore, to understand that the nature of the Paradise of Eden **includes Lilith and the Serpent**. To not admit to this would implicate in regressing to a dualist view. Therefore, **the arrival of the *Spirit* necessarily implicates in the arrival of the Demon**.

Let us see how this works in practice.

In Crucifixion, the 4D ego has completely surrendered to the Soul, and paradoxically, integrated the Soul. The multi-paradoxical reality of the Soul necessarily entails ending the denial of any of its dimensions, however luminous or dark. In conjunction with the Self, the 4D ego reaches Balance: all the Archetypes are figuratively around it, in balance. This image ends the Paradigm of Balance.

This beautiful image contains a serious problem: it is very final. Reaching Balance, having a conjunction with the Self and a balance with all archetypes, it seems that there is nothing else to do. Apparently, many alchemists have had this sensation, and stopped their work at the second *coniunctio*.

But DORNEUS continues in the direction of the *Unus Mundus*, the third *coniunctio*. We have already seen how the *Unus Mundus* is the perfect unity between the psychological and the material, a **Pneumatic reality** that we call *Spirit*. However, how does the 5D ego proceed in this reality? Which types of **psychological mechanisms** are there in the structure of this reality?

In face of the *Retreat of the Soul* in Crucifixion, we know that the main conscious activity of a fifth-dimensional ego is to determine, in the experience it is having, the *Personal Sense* – consulting both conscious and unconscious (transcendent) instances, now in conjunction. Thereafter, knowing what makes *Sense* to it, the 5D ego will make free choices, always *Creatively* guided.

However, it is necessary to notice how the *Sense* and free choices interact with the Balance. The answer is simple – through the *Imbalance*.

If the 5D ego is in conjunction with the Soul in the *Pneumatic* reality, having around and in equidistance from it the archetypes, it is in a **static** position. Any movement will break the Balance, creating an *Imbalance*, because any choice will implicate in the preponderance of one archetypal energy over the others. This is the primordial point from which a *Creative* fifth-dimensional action starts: having access to any archetypal energy, at this point integrated to its consciousness, and being able to act *Creatively*, the choice of the 5D ego for this or that archetypal energy starts a **Creative process**.

We cannot, and should not, be naive to the point of using the **Creative process** as an euphemism for **Imbalance**. We cannot deny the fact that a fifth-dimensional *Creative* process is an *Imbalance* of the cosmic order reached in Crucifixion and will **demand repair**. No *Imbalance* can be purposely *Created* in the Cosmos without having to re-establish Balance – posterior dimensions do not cancel out previous dimensions. Therefore, a fifth-dimension *Pneumatic* action supported by the *Spirit* is a purposely caused *Imbalance*, which immediately causes a reaction from *Demon*, contrary to this action, a *Demoniac* attack. If the *Spirit* is "a great help and an equally great danger", *Spirit* and *Demon* are always together, since, ultimately, they are aspects of the same thing. On its path through the fifth dimension, the 5D ego will find sequential *Demoniac* reactions, which it will have to face and **Educate**.

What exactly is a *Demoniac* uprising?

From the myths of Lucifer, the Serpent over the Tree of Knowledge of Good and Evil, and Lilith, we have every condition to answer.

However, not having a *Body*, the *Demon* resists to the Incarnation of the *Spirit*, to *Creation*.

In the Paradigm of Balance, the ego has no direct access to the *Spirit*, so it has also no direct access to the *Demon*. Therefore, in the fourth dimension, the confrontation with the devil is described as the confrontation with the Shadow, an archetype that must also be in Balance.

In the Paradigm of Sense, however, the entry in the unity of the Paradise of Eden means that both the *Spirit* and the *Demon* will act directly over the ego. Since the 5D ego has the *Spirit* in the *Body*, its actions are eminently **Creative**. The *Demon* resists *Creation*, therefore resisting the *Creative* actions of the fifth-dimensional ego. The *Demon*, a type of fifth-dimensional Shadow, is precisely the *Pneumatic* force that resists the *Embodiment*, the materialization of the *Creative* processes of the fifth-dimensional ego. The *Demoniac* action shows the 5D ego which of its parts still resist to the *Manifestation* of the *Spirit.*[374]

To achieve these results, the *Demon* operates through temptation, lies and accusation.

The **temptation** is so insidious on the human being that the protection against it is asked for in the Lord's prayer: "And do not put us to the test, but save us from the Evil One"[375]. The fundamental characteristic of the *Demon* is to be *Instinct*, which puts pressure on needs to be satisfied. Until the fourth dimension, the instinct was regulated by the Symbol. In the fifth dimension, the self-exile of Lilith ended, and the incidence of the *Instinct* is total. The fifth-dimensional ego is *Instinctual*. The Paradigm of Sense is a process of development through which the *Instinct*, forgotten for eras, is legitimated and reinserted into the spiritual structure. As any psychological content that is relegated, the *Instinct* reappears wild and the 5D ego must be capable of applying it as a manifestation force of the *Spirit* – the *Demon* finds ways to resist this.

We have seen that the structure of the 5D ego is in conjunction with the Soul, consciousness coinciding with the unconscious. This is the reality of the *Spirit*. The 5D ego is strongly conscious, and **paradoxically**, strongly receptive to the Transcendence, with what it is in harmony. The determination of the *Personal Sense*, a fundamental element of the Paradigm of Sense, occurs precisely through the coincidence between consciousness and Transcendence[376]. At any moment that the 5D ego is not capable of apprehending the Wholeness of the *Truth* of the *Spirit* – yes, the 5D ego is not omniscient – there will be space for a *Demoniac* attack. It is about an *Instinct* out of control, not limited, since it is unconscious, a *Perversion*. These are the "false desires that led one away from God"[377], mentioned by Jeffrey RAFF. The *Demon* wants to throw the 5D ego in the **Perversion**.

The *Demon* also operates through **lies**.

> You are from your father, the devil, and you prefer to do what your father wants. He was a murderer from the start; he was never grounded in the truth; there is no truth in him at all. **When he lies he is speaking true to his nature, because he is a liar, and the father of lies**.[378]

Therefore, the *Demon* lies in the sense of creating **alternative realities**, realities which are distant from the *Truth* of the *Spirit*, of the *Creation*. In the human consciousness, the *Demoniac* alternative realities are manifested as prisons in "illusions [...] that led one away from God"[379], also mentioned by RAFF. Astutely, the *Demon* creates illusions by magnifying real **parts** of the fifth-dimensional consciousness – or, more precisely, of the *Pneumatic* reality. Whereas the *Spirit* is All, the *Demon* is the Part. So, the *Demon* tries to make the Part seem like All. An extremely simple example: if the 5D ego hurt its partner, the *Demon* can magnify this fact to the point of it seeming like this is All – suddenly, the 5D ego has fallen for the illusion that they are someone who hurts everyone in the world in a very cruel way. It is important to remember that, although this example was given as the magnification of an unpleasant circumstance, the *Demon* can perfectly magnify a circumstance that is pleasant to the ego, and often this works better for the *Demon*.

Finally, the *Demon* has a strong predilection for **accusation**. This characteristic is reflected even in the term "devil", sometimes translated from the Greek *diábolos* as **accuser**. Through the accusation, the *Demon* has a regressive action on the 5D ego, since the accusation makes moral and ethical demands, totally transcended by the fifth dimension.

Resisting *Creation*, the *Demon* is incapable of uniting with the Divine, is incapable of lowering. Therefore, its only possible end is to reach **power**.

> Better to rule in Hell than serve in Heaven.[380]

This is the alternative reality of **hell**.

* * * * *

The discussion about whether the Demon is something internal or external to the human being is absolutely irrelevant, since in five dimensions, internal and external are undiscernible.

301 JUNG, C. G. (1978) *Civilization in transition*. Translated by Hull, R. F. C. CW X. Bollingen Series XX. Princeton University Press. §845.

302 SARTRE, J. P. (2011) *No Exit* (online) Available at: <https://archive.org/stream/NoExit/NoExit_djvu.txt> Access: February 28th 2020

303 "The meeting with oneself is, at first, the meeting with one's own shadow. The shadow is a tight passage, a narrow door, whose painful constriction no one is spared who goes down to the deep well. But one must learn to know oneself in order to know who one is. For what comes after the door is, surprisingly enough, a boundless expanse full of unprecedented uncertainty, with apparently no inside and no outside, no above and no below, no here and no there, no mine and no thine, no good and no bad. It is the world of water, [...] where I am indivisibly this *and* that; where I experience the other in myself and the other-than-myself experiences me". JUNG, C. G. (1977) *The archetypes and the collective unconscious.* Translated by Hull, R. F. C. CW IX, part 1. Bollingen Series XX. Princeton University Press. §45.

304 "So in the first stage of approach to the unconscious, the shadow is simply a "mythological" name for all that within me about which I cannot directly know. [...] But then this person will discover that there is in this unknown areas still another cluster of reactions called the anima (or the animus), which represents feelings, moods, ideas, etc.; and we also speak of the concept of the Self. For practical purposes, Jung has not found it necessary to go beyond **these three steps**. von FRANZ, M. L. (1995) *Shadow and evil in fairy tales*. Boston: Shambhala Publications. p. 10. [author's own highlights]

305 In *Science of the Soul: A Jungian Perspective*, Page 22, Edward EDINGER (2002, Inner City Books) shows a diagram that evidences the phases of deepening the psychological process: Shadows, Anima/Animus and Self.

306 von FRANZ, M. L. *Shadow and evil in fairy tales*. Op. Cit. p. 3.

307 "Only when we start to dig into this shadow sphere of the personality and to investigate the different aspects, does there, after a time, appear in the dreams a personification of the unconscious, of the same sex of the dreamer". Ibid. p. 10.

308 "The shadow behaves compensatorily to consciousness; hence its effects can be **positive as well as negative**. [...] If it has been believed hitherto that the human shadow was the source of all evil, it can now be ascertained on closer investigation that the unconscious man, that is, his shadow, does not consist only of morally reprehensible tendencies, but also displays a number of good qualities, such as normal instincts, appropriate reactions, realistic insights, creative impulses, etc". JUNG, C. G. *Memories, dreams and reflexions*. Glossary; "Shadow". Translated by Winston, R. and C. Revised Edition. Vintage Books. (ebook) Available at: <http://www.venerabilisopus.org/en/books-samael-aun-weor-gnostic-sacred-esoteric-spiritual/pdf/200/265_jung-carl-memories-dreams-reflections.pdf> Access: April 27th 2020. p. 481. [author's own highlights]

309 "[the shadow is the] sum of all personal and collective psychic elements which, because of their incompatibility with the chosen conscious attitude, are denied expression in life and therefore coalesce into a relatively autonomous "splinter personality" with contrary tendencies in the unconscious." Ibid.

310 "The most accessible of these, and the easiest to experience, is the shadow, for its nature can in large measure be inferred from the contents of the personal unconscious."

JUNG, C. G. (1979) *Aion – researches into the phenomenology of the self.* Translated by Hull, R. F. C. 2nd edition. CW IX, part 2. Bollingen Series XX. Princeton: Princeton University Press. §13.

[311] JUNG uses both "devil" and "demon" to refer to the dark dimension of the psyche. In *Symbols of Transformation,* (1976. CW V. §581, reference 155) JUNG compares the term "devil" and "demon": "Etymologically, 'devil' and 'divinity' are both related to Skr. *deva,* 'demon'. – Translated." In *Psychology and religion: West and East,* (1975. CW XI, §32, reference 12) JUNG uses both terms in the same sentence: The power and cunning of the demon, i.e., of a heathen god or the Christian devil."

Nevertheless, JUNG seems to use slightly more often the term "devil" to refer to the "fourth Person, opposed to the Trinity", as in *Psychology and religion: West and East – A psychological approach to the Dogma of Trinity* (Op. Cit. §249 e §250). As the adversary of Christ, he would have to take up an equivalent counterposition and be, like him, a "son of God." But that would lead straight back to certain Gnostic views according to which the devil, as Satanael, is God's first son, Christ being the second. A further logical inference would be the abolition of the Trinity formula and its replacement by a *quaternity.* The idea of a quaternity of divine principles was violently attacked by the Church Fathers when an attempt was made to add a fourth – God's "essence" – to the Three Persons of the Trinity. This resistance to the quaternity is very odd, considering that the central Christian symbol, the Cross, is unmistakably a quaternity. The Cross, however, symbolizes God's suffering in his immediate encounter with the world. The "prince of this world", the devil (John 12:31, 14:30), vanquishes the Godman at this point, although by so doing he is presumably preparing his own defeat and digging his own grave. According to an old view, Christ is the "bait on the hook" (the Cross), with which he catches "Leviathan" (the devil). It is therefore significant that the Cross, set up midway between heaven and hell as a symbol of Christ's struggle with the devil, corresponds to the quaternity.

JUNG seems to also use slightly more frequently the term "demon" to refer to "unconscious complexes" and "possessions", as in *Psychological Types,* (1976. CW VI, §175): "Indeed, from the psychological point of view demons are nothing other than intruders from the unconscious, spontaneous irruptions of unconscious complexes into the continuity of the conscious process. Complexes are comparable to demons which fitfully harass our thoughts and actions; hence in antiquity and the Middle Ages acute neurotic disturbances were conceived as possession. Thus, when the individual consistently takes his stand on one side, the unconscious ranges itself on the other and rebels – which is naturally what struck the Neoplatonic and Christian philosophers most, since they represented the standpoint of exclusive spirituality. Particularly valuable is Synesius' reference to the imaginary nature of demons. It is, as I have already pointed out, precisely the fantastic element that becomes associated in the unconscious with the repressed functions. Hence, if the individuality (as we might call the "individual nucleus" for short) fails to differentiate itself from the opposites, it becomes identical with them and is inwardly torn asunder, so that a state of agonizing disunion arises. Synesius expresses this as follows: Thus this animal spirit, which devout men have also called the spiritual soul, becomes both idol and god and demon of many shapes. In this also does the soul exhibit her torment. By participating in the instinctive forces the spirit becomes a "god and demon of many shapes."

Although he uses both terms, JUNG seems to use the term "devil" slightly more often than "demon". Besides that, he uses "devil" to designate the **fourth** person, in relation to the **three** people of the Trinity. During the formulation of the Paradigm of Sense, I had to choose between the "devil" and "demon" to create a 5D term that would refer to the 5D Shadow. Taking into consideration JUNG's preference for the term "devil" to refer to the shadow of the psyche – which, in my system, is fourth-dimensional – I opted for choosing the term "demon" to refer to the 5D Shadow.

My choice also observes the etymology of the terms.

According to the *Merriam Webster Dictionary*, the etymology of "**devil**" is: "Middle English *devel*, from Old English *dēofol*, from Late Latin *diabolus*, from Greek *diabolos*, literally, slanderer, from *diaballein* to throw across, slander, from *dia-* + *ballein* to throw."

It is worth noting that, etymologically, "**devil**" is the opposite to "**symbol**". According to the same *Merriam Webster Dictionary*, the etymology of "**symbol**" is: "from Latin *symbolum* token, sign, symbol, from Greek *symbolon*, literally, token of identity verified by comparing its other half, from *symballein* to throw together, compare, from *syn-* + *ballein* to throw." Thus, we can say that the devil "throws separate" (*dia-* + *ballein*), whereas the symbol "throws together" (*syn-* + *ballein*). Given that the symbol is structurally and dynamically 4D, the devil, its opposite, is structurally and dynamically 4D.

In *Mitologia Grega*, Vol. I, chapter IX, "*A primeira fase do universo: do Caos a Pontos*", note 135, Junito BRANDÃO DE SOUZA (1989) shows the Greek origin of the term "**demon**": *Demon*, in Greek δαιμόνιον (daimónion), means god, goddess, deity, god of inferior category, as often appears in Homer; tutelary genius, intermediary between the gods and the mortals, as the soul of mankind from the Age of Gold; internal voice that speaks to mankind, guides them, advises them, as the demon who inspired Socrates. In principle, therefore, demon has no derogatory connotation, as "devil" does. The demon is not documented in the Old Testament as Satan, or devil. It seems that, with the current sense that it is attributed to it, the "demon" has emerged from the Septuagint (III and II centuries A.D.), being later generalized in the New Testament.

The meaning of "obstruction" present in the etymology of the term "devil" is valid in a fifth-dimensional structure, since the behaviour of the *Demon* is to resist, opposing the creation of the *Spirit* and the 5D ego. However, I chose to prioritize the meaning of "spiritual guide" present in the etymology of the term "demon" to emphasize the unity of the fifth dimension: *Spirit* and *Demon* as the *Imagetic* and dynamic-*Instinctual* aspects of one single thing, the *Spirit*.

Besides that, as it is developed, the 5D ego understands that the resistance to the *Demon*, the *demoniac* attacks are desirable. When the 5D ego is performing a *Creation*, a *demoniac* attack shows that part of the 5D ego resists to creation, or that, in part, the 5D ego has given in to repetition. In any case, the *Demon* functions as a guide, since it clearly shows that part of the Whole needs to be included for the *Creation* to realize.

Finally, the process of *Educating* the *Demon* creatively integrates the *Demon* to the *Spirit*, revealing the character of *Dynamic Force* of the *Demon*, capable of dynamizing the process of *Creation* and lead it much faster and integrally to realization.

In both cases, if the 5D ego observes the unity of the fifth dimension, it will prefer the occurrence of *demoniac* attacks which evidence where the repetitions are occurring, so that they can be *Educated* in order to dynamize the process of *Creation*. Thus, the *Demon* works more as a spiritual guide than as an opposing force. Carl JUNG mentions this in *The archetypes of the collective unconscious*. (1977. CW IX/1. §154): "[...] but the more the magical note predominates, the easier it is to make the distinction, and it is not without relevance in so far as the demon can also have a very positive aspect as the 'wise old man'."

For a deeper understanding of this note, see chapters "Force" and "Evolution".

[312] JUNG, C. G. (1975) *The structure and dynamics of the psyche*. Translated by Hull, R. F. C. CW VIII. Bollingen Series XX. Princeton: Princeton University Press. §427.

[313] *The New Jerusalem Bible*. Genesis 1: 1-5

[314] Ibid. Genesis 2: 16-17

[315] Ibid. Genesis 3:1-8

[316] "The Ophites, a Gnostic sect, worshiped the serpent. They had essentially the same view as modern psychology. To them the serpent represented the spiritual principle symbolizing redemption from bondage to the demiurge that created the Garden of Eden and would keep man in ignorance. The serpent was considered good and Yahweh bad. Psychologically the serpent is the principle of *gnosis*, knowledge or emerging consciousness. The serpent's temptation represents the urge to self-realization in man and symbolizes the principle of individualization. Some Gnostic sects even identified the serpent in the Garden of Eden with Christ." EDINGER, E. F. (1992) *Ego and archetype*. Boston: Shambhala Publications. p. 18.

[317] "The myth depicts the birth of consciousness as a crime which alienates man from God and from his original preconscious wholeness". Ibid.

[318] "Here as everywhere the Great Mother encompasses and "is" heaven and earth, and water as night sky. **Only later, with the separation of the primordial parents**, are light, sun, and consciousness born, and with them, differentiation. Now, but only now, there is an upper and a lower heaven [...]." NEUMANN, E. (1963) *The great mother – an analysis of the archetype*. Translated by Manheim, R. Bollingen series XLVII. Princeton University Press. p. 223. [author's own highlights].

[319] "Moreover, because the patriarchal world strives to deny its dark and "lowly" lineage, its origin in this primordial world, it does everything in its power to conceal its own descent from the Dark Mother and–both rightly and wrongly at once–considers it necessary to forge a "higher genealogy," tracing its descent from heaven, the god of heaven, and the luminous aspect. But nearly all the early and primitive documents trace the **origin of the world and of man to the darkness**, the Great Round, the goddess. Whether, as in countless myths, the source of all life is the primordial ocean or whether it is earth or heaven, these sources have one thing in common: *darkness*. It is this primordial darkness which bears the light as moon, stars, and sun, and almost everywhere these luminaries are looked upon as the offspring of the Nocturnal Mother. It is this common factor, the darkness of the primordial night as the symbol of the unconscious, which accounts for the identity of night sky, earth, underworld, and the primeval water that preceded the light. **For the unconscious is the mother of all things**, and all things that stand in the light of consciousness are childlike in relation to the darkness-as is consciousness, which is also a child of these primordial depths." Ibid. p. 212. [author's own highlights].

[320] "Consciousness = deliverance: that is the watchword inscribed above all man's efforts to deliver himself from the embrace of the primordial uroboric dragon. Once the ego sets itself up as center and establishes itself in its own right as ego consciousness, the original situation is forcibly broken down. We can see what this self-identification of the waking human personality with the ego really means only when we remember the contrasted

state of *participation mystique* ruled by uroboric unconsciousness. Trite as it seems to us, the logical statement of identity – "I am I" – the fundamental statement of consciousness, is in reality a tremendous achievement. This act, whereby an ego is posited and the personality identified with that ego – however fallacious that identification may later prove to be – alone creates the possibility of a self-orienting consciousness." NEUMANN, E. (2002) *The origins and history of consciousness,* Vol I. Part I "The Mythological Stages in the Evolution of Consciousness", "The Creation Myth". Chapter 3 "The Separation of the World Parents: The Principle of Opposites". Translated by Hull, R. F. C. London: Routledge. Kindle eBook. Available at: <https://www.amazon.com/Origins-History-Consciousness-International-Psychology-ebook/dp/B019P2PSDM>. Access: April 26th 2020.

321 "The more unconscious a man is, the more he will conform to the general canon of psychic behavior. But the more conscious he becomes of his individuality, the more pronounced will be his difference from other subjects and the less he will come up to common expectations. Further, his reactions are much less predictable. This is due to the fact that an individual consciousness is always more highly differentiated and more extensive." JUNG, C. G. (1975) *The structure and dynamics of the psyche. On the nature of the psyche.* Translated by Hull, R. F. C. CW VIII. Bollingen Series XX. Princeton University Press. §344.

322 "**The subject gets rid of painful, incompatible contents by projecting them**, as also of positive values which, for one reason or another – self-depreciation, for instance – are inaccessible to him". JUNG, C. G. (1976) *Psychological types.* Translated by Baynes, H. G. CW VI. Bollingen Series XX. Princeton University Press. §783. [author's own highlights]

323 "With insight and good will, the shadow can to some extent be assimilated into the conscious personality, experience shows that there are certain features which offer the most obstinate **resistance** to moral control and prove almost impossible to influence. These resistances are usually bound up with *projections,* which are not recognized as such, and their recognition is a moral achievement beyond the ordinary. While some traits peculiar to the shadow can be recognized without too much difficulty as one's own personal qualities, in this case both insight and good will are unavailing because the cause of the emotion appears to lie, beyond all possibility of doubt, in the **other person**". JUNG, C. G. (1979) *Aion – researches into the phenomenology of the self.* Translated by Hull, R. F. C. 2nd edition. CW IX, part 2. Bollingen Series XX. Princeton University Press. §16. [author's own highlights]

324 "Through the intervention of the Holy Ghost, however, man is included in the divine process, and this means that the principle of separateness and autonomy over against God – which is personified in Lucifer as the God-opposing will – is included in it too. But for this will there would have been no creation and no work of salvation either. The shadow and the opposing will are the necessary conditions for all actualization. An object that has no will of its own, capable, if need be, of opposing its creator, and with no qualities other than its creator's, such an object has no independent existence and is incapable of ethical decision. At best it is just a piece of clockwork which the Creator has to wind up to make it function.

Therefore Lucifer was perhaps the one who best understood the divine will struggling to create a world and who carried out that will most faithfully. For, by rebelling against God, he became the active principle of a creation which opposed to God a counter-will of its own. Because God willed this, we are told in Genesis 3 that he gave man the power to will otherwise. Had he not done so, he would have created nothing but a machine, and then the incarnation and the redemption would never have come about. Nor would there have been any revelation of the Trinity, because everything would have remained One for ever". JUNG, C. G. (1975) *Psychology and religion: West and East.* Translated by Hull, R. F. C. 2nd edition. CW XI. Bollingen Series XX. Princeton University Press. §290.

325 BRANDÃO DE SOUZA, J. (1989) *Mitologia grega*, Vol. I Petrópolis, RJ: Editora Vozes. p. 200.

326 "The Church, however, knows of this paradox when she speaks of the *felix culpa* of our first parents (in the Liturgy for Easter Eve). If they had not sinned there would have been no *felix culpa* to bring after it the still greater miracle of the redemption. Nevertheless, evil remains evil. There is nothing for it but to accustom ourselves to thinking in paradoxes." JUNG, C. G. (1978) *Civilization in transition.* Translated by Hull, R. F. C. CW X. Bollingen Series XX. Princeton University Press. §868.

327 "Knowledge is either poisonous or healing, it is one or the other, and that is why some myths say that knowledge brings about the corruption of the world and others that knowledge is healing, and then we have the biblical idea which says that it is first corruption, but later turns, thank God, into healing. In the Old Testament it meant corruption, but Christ, who made something out of it, turned it into healing, so one has to have a double attitude about it, the teaching of the *felix culpa*". von FRANZ, M. L. (1980) *Alchemy: an introduction to the symbolism and the psychology.* Inner City Books. p. 55.

328 SICUTERI, R. *Lilith, la luna nera* [not published in English. Translated from the Portuguese version: (1985) *Lilith, a lua negra.* 3ª edição São Paulo: Editora Paz e Terra p. 17.]

329 Ibid. p. 15.

330 *The New Jerusalem Bible.* Genesis 1:1-2

331 JUNG, C. G. (1975) *The structure and dynamics of the psyche. On the nature of the psyche.* Translated by Hull, R. F. C. CW VIII. Bollingen Series XX. Princeton University Press. §406

332 *The New Jerusalem Bible.* Genesis 2:21-22

333 Ibid. Genesis 2:7

334 Ibid. John 1:14

335 "I shall only emphasize that Egyptian theology asserts, first and foremost, the essential unity (homoousia) of God as father and son [..]" JUNG, C. G. (1975) *Psychology and religion: West and East. – A psychological approach to the dogma of the Trinity* Translated by Hull, R. F. C. 2nd edition. CW XI. Bollingen Series XX. Princeton: Princeton University Press. §177.

336 "[...] the differentiation of Yahweh's consciousness. This differentation is evidenced by the complete *separatio* that Yahweh undergoes with the advent of Christ. His two sides represented by his good son, Christ, and his evil son, Satan, are totally separated, indeed dissociated, from each other. Christ becomes identical with Yahweh through the doctrine of the *homoousia*, while Satan is cast out of heaven and thus condemned to live the life of a dissociated, autonomous complex". EDINGER, E. F. (1984) *The creation of consciousness.* Canada: Inner City Books. p. 82.

[337] SICUTERI, R. *Lilith, la luna nera* [not published in English. Translated from the Portuguese version: (1985) *Lilith, a lua negra.* 3ª edição São Paulo: Editora Paz e Terra p.15]

[338] *The New Jerusalem Bible.* Isaiah 14:12-15.

[339] Ibid. Ezekiel 28: 12-17.

[340] *Koran* 38:71-7.

[341] *The New Jerusalem Bible.* Isaiah 14: 12-15 .

[342] *Septuagint Bible.* Luke 1:32. The evangelist uses the term ὑψίστου *(hypsístou)*, i.e., Most High.

[343] The Fall is the metaphysical event where Lucifer, sometimes joined by other Angels and Archangels, falls from the celestial to the infernal dimensions. JUNG mentions the fall in *Psychology of religion: West and East. – A psychological approach to the dogma of the Trinity.* (1975. CW XI, §255): Inasmuch as the devil was an angel created by God and "fell like lightning from heaven," he too is a divine "procession" that became Lord of this world.

The dark and dynamic – infernal – aspect of Divinity exists *a priori*, once, since before Creation, "there was darkness over the deep, with a divine wind sweeping over the waters" (Genesis 1:2). "[...] there is a view which holds that the devil, though created, *is autonomous and eternal.*" (JUNG, C. 1975. *Psychology of religion: West and East. – A psychological approach to the dogma of the Trinity.* CW XI, §248) But the occurrence of the Fall immediately evidences this dark and dynamic aspect in the cosmic drama. The psychological importance of this event is huge, since, in the context of Analytical Psychology, God and Demon are symbols of the Self and its Shadow dimension.

The impact of the Fall is spread throughout all dimensions. The Fall has already occurred in the first dimension, since it exists *a priori*. It is expressed at its maximum and most dramatic, however, in the passage from the first to the second dimension, with Lucifer on top of the Tree of Knowledge of Good and Evil, offering access to consciousness and duality. To accept Lucifer's offer and opt for Consciousness immediately means Expelling from Paradise.

In the second and third dimensions, the Fall is expressed as a progressive increase of duality, which remains unconscious. In these phases, all psychological characteristics which compose Totality but cannot be assimilated by the ego's consciousness – the not-me characteristics – are projected in others. In the third dimension, the 3D Self allows the Luciferian aspect to be even more striking: the 3D Self remains occult and allows the ego to not recognize it and believe to be the centre of the being.

In the passage from the third to the fourth dimension, the Fall is expressed in a new confrontation between the human being and the abysmal dimension of God. The moral defeat, as presented by JUNG, is the moment where the moral excellence of the human being does not attract a benign reward from the Self, but instead, attracts a maleficent action, in the shape of an insoluble problem except through the transcendental power. This reveals not only the dark side of divinity, but its aspect of Wholeness, which transcends good and evil.

In the fourth dimension, the Fall becomes conscious. Duality still exists, but the conscious relationship with the Self reveals that the duality is internal, ending the possibility of projecting onto others the not-me characteristics, the evil.

At the end of the fourth dimension, Crucifixion structurally changes the Fall through Rendition. God and Demon are no longer experienced as fundamentally opposing forces, but as paradoxes instead. Crucifixion produces a multi-paradoxical consciousness, which transcends duality and opens access to unity.

In the fifth dimension, the Fall is experienced in the all-encompassing context of unity. The Doors of Paradise, closed at the exit from the first dimension, are re-opened. In Paradise, Lucifer stays on the Tree of Knowledge of Good and Evil. But now, there is access to the Tree of Life. The *Spirit* in its *Imagetic* aspect (God) and the *Spirit* in its *Instinctual* and dynamic aspect (*Demon*) are both seen as *Spirit* and structurally united. The 5D Ego is able to experience the *Image* and the dynamic character of the *Instinct* in unity, even if the latter opposes the 5D creations, as is its nature to do so.

[344] MILTON, J. *Paradise lost.* Book I. Edited by Armstrong, E. (online) Available at: <https://www.yorku.ca/earmstro/text/ParadiseLostBk1.pdf> Access: April 29th 2020. Line 85.

[345] *The New Jerusalem Bible.* Revelation 20:10.

[346] "As long as you are in *maṇipūra* you are in the terrible heat of the center of the earth [...] There is only **the fire of passion, of wishes, of illusions**. It is the fire of which Buddha speaks in his sermon in Benares where he says, The whole world is in flames, your ears, your eyes, everywhere you pour out the fire of desire, and that is the fire of illusion because you desire things which are futile. Yet there is the great treasure of the released emotional energy". JUNG, C. G. (1996) *The psychology of Kundalini Yoga.* Bollingen Series XCIX. Princeton University Press. p. 35. [author's own highlights]

[347] "sulphur represents the active substance of the sun or, in psychological language, the *motive factor in consciousness:* on the one hand the will, ... and on the other hand compulsion, an involuntary motivation or impulse ranging from mere interest to possession proper." (JUNG, C. G. (1977) *Mysterium coniunctionis.* Translated by Hull, R. F. C. 2nd edition CW XIV. Bollingen Series XX. Princeton University Press. §151.) [...] I would say that sulphur is desire. It is the fire of libido, vital energy itself. [...] But the alchemical writings tell us that there are two kinds of sulphur: a raw and vulgar sulphur and a real sulphur. [...] Psychologically, this referred to the ego-centered desire in contrast with the Self-centered desire. The ego-centered desire is of infantile nature, unconscious, which demands to have whatever it wants, when it wants it, whereas the desire centered on the Self is a transformed or regenerated desire, which the ego serves as a religious obligation. [...] A non-regenerated desire is evil, and this evil nature can be very easily demonstrated. All you have to do, when confronted with the raw sulphur, the non-regenerated desire, whether in yourself or in others, is to frustrate it, deny it, and you will immediately see that it becomes depraved. It becomes tyrannical, driven by power." EDINGER, E. F. *The mystery of the coniunctio.* [Translated from the Portuguese version: (2008) *O Mistério da coniunctio.* São Paulo: Editora Paulus pp. 26-27].

[348] Defined by the Pope Gregory the Great and cited by St Thomas of Aquinas in *Summa Theologica.*

[349] SICUTERI, R. *Lilith, la luna nera* [not published in English. Translated from the Portuguese version: (1985) *Lilith, a lua negra.* 3ª edição São Paulo: Editora Paz e Terra p. 21.]

[350] JUNG, C. G. (1998*) Visions: Notes on the Seminar Given in 1930-1934.* Routledge. p. 1314.

351 RAFF, J. (2000) *Jung and the alchemical imagination.* Chapter 2 "The alchemical imagination". "Fantasy and imagination". Florida: Nicolas-Hays, Inc. (Kobo eBook version).

352 "Quomodo cecidisti de coelo, Lucifer, qui mane oriebaris?" [How did you come to fall from the heavens, Daystar, son of Dawn?] JUNG, C. G. (1979) *Aion – researches into the phenomenology of the self.* Translated by Hull, R. F. C. 2nd edition. CW IX, part 2. Bollingen Series XX. Princeton University Press. §157. Note 18.

353 *The New Jerusalem Bible.* Genesis 3:1.

354 "The problem of our duality can never be resolved on the level of the ego; it permits no rational solution.

But where there is consciousness of a problem, the self, the *Imago Dei* within us can operate and bring about an irrational synthesis of the personality. [...] This irrational healing process, which finds a way around seemingly insurmountable obstacles, has a particularly feminine quality to it. It is the **rational, logical** masculine mind that declares that opposites like ego and Shadow, light and dark, **can never be united**. However, the feminine spirit is capable of finding a synthesis where **logic says non can be found**." SANFORD, J. A. (1998) Evil: *The shadow side of reality.* The Crossroad Publishing Co. pp.105-106. [author's own highlights]

355 JUNG, C. G. (1975) *The structure and dynamics of the psyche. On the nature of the psyche.* Translated by Hull, R. F. C. CW VIII. Bollingen Series XX. Princeton University Press. §406.

356 As we will see in the chapter "*Force*", the "*Demon*" is a "*Dynamic Force*".

357 LAPLANCHE, J. and PONTALIS, JB. (2018) *The language of psychoanalysis.* Routledge.

358 "I have suggested calling the energy concept used in analytical psychology by the name "libido". The choice of this term may not be ideal in some respects, yet it seemed to me that this concept merited the name libido if only for reasons of historical justice. [...] Together with "libido" Freud used the expressions "drive" or "instinct" (e.g., "ego instincts") and "psychic energy". Since Freud confines himself almost exclusively to sexuality and its manifold ramifications in the psyche, the sexual definition of energy as a specific driving force is quite sufficient for his purpose. In a general psychological theory, however, it is impossible to use purely sexual energy, that is, one specific drive, as an explanatory concept, since psychic energy transformation is not merely a matter of sexual dynamics. Sexual dynamics is only one particular instance in the total field of the psyche. This is not to deny its existence, but merely to put it in its proper place." JUNG, C. G. (1975) *The structure and dynamics of the psyche. On psychic energy.* Translated by Hull, R. F. C. CW VIII. Bollingen Series XX. Princeton University Press. §54.

359 See chapter "Lilith".

360 "So it is just that – you get into the world of fire, where things become red-hot. After baptism you get right into hell – that is the enantiodromia. And now comes the paradox of the East: it is also the fullness of jewels. **But what is passion, what are emotions? There is the source of fire, there is the fullness of energy**. A man who is not on fire is nothing: he is ridiculous, he is two-dimensional. [...] A flame must burn somewhere, otherwise no light shines; there is no warmth, nothing. It is terribly awkward, sure enough; it is painful, full of conflict, apparently a mere waste of time – at all events, it is against reason. But that accursed Kundalini says, "It is the fullness of jewels; there is the source of energy." As Heraclitus aptly said: war is the father of all things". JUNG, C. G.

(1996) *The psychology of Kundalini Yoga.* Bollingen Series XCIX. Princeton University Press. pp. 33-34. [author's own highlights]

361 Ibid.

362 "So *manipūra* is the center of the identification with the god, where one becomes part of the divine substance, having an immortal soul". Ibid. p. 31.

363 "It is far less easy to understand *manipūra* from a psychological point of view. [...] It is very difficult to explain in psychological terms what will follow when you have made your acquaintance with the unconscious. [...] Mind you, this question is not easy to answer, because **you will be inclined to give an abstract answer,** for a psychological reason. [...] Yes, desire, passions, the whole emotional world breaks loose. Sex, power, and every devil in our nature gets loose when we become acquainted with the unconscious. Then you will suddenly see a new picture of yourself. That is why people are afraid and say there is no unconscious, [...] you must admit that there are such powers. **Then you make an abstraction, you make marvelous abstract signs of it** [...] Ibid. p. 32. [author's own highlights]

364 "The Shadow cannot be denied but must be dealt with in the light of a higher authority. The religions of the world have recognized this and instructed mankind in the art of living in the consciousness of God. However, for many persons today the traditional ways of mediating the consciousness go God are no longer efficacious, and some persons now turn to psychology in order to relate directly to the God within, which psychology call the self." SANFORD, J. A. (1998) Evil: *The shadow side of reality.* The Crossroad Publishing Co. pp.109-110.

365 *The New Jerusalem Bible.* Matthew 16:18.

366 "In this case it was not only that her demon was eating everything she was given so that one couldn't get anything into her, neither human feeling nor psychological food. It was much worse, for one saw how the animus was working everywhere against life. If she got life energy from Jung, she tried to hurt the other medical doctor by making mischief out of what Jung had supposedly said against him. She was working for destruction, for what I would call a psychological death atmosphere." von FRANZ, M. L. (1995) *Shadow and evil in fairy tales.* Boston: Shambhala Publications. p. 209.

367 SANFORD, J. A. *Evil: The shadow side of reality.* Op. Cit. p. 128.

368 See chapter *"Manifestation".*

369 JUNG, C. G. *The psychology of Kundalini Yoga.* Op. Cit. p.30

370 See chapter *"Manifestation".*

371 RAFF, J. (2000) *Jung and the alchemical imagination.* Chapter 2: "The alchemical imaginations". "Fantasy and imagination". Florida: Nicolas-Hays, Inc. (Kobo eBook version).

372 *The New Jerusalem Bible.* Matthew 27:40.

373 JUNG, C. G. (1975) *The structure and dynamics of the psyche. On the nature of the psyche.* Translated by Hull, R. F. C. CW VIII. Bollingen Series XX. Princeton University Press §406.

374 See chapters *"Macroimage", "Draw"* and *"Manifestation".*

375 *The New Jerusalem Bible.* Matthew 6:13.

376 See chapter *"Macroimage".*

[377] RAFF, J. *Jung and the alchemical imagination.* Chapter 2: "The alchemical imaginations". Fantasy and imagination". Op. Cit.

[378] *The New Jerusalem Bible.* John 8:44.

[379] RAFF, J. *Jung and the alchemical imagination.* Chapter 2: "The alchemical imaginations". Fantasy and imagination". Op. Cit.

[380] MILTON, J. *Paradise lost.* edited by Armstrong, E. (online) Available at: <https://www.yorku.ca/earmstro/text/ParadiseLostBk1.pdf> Access: April 29th 2020. Line 263.

MACROIMAGE

Jung describes the "religious attitude" as careful and scrupulous observation of [...] a dynamic agency or effect not caused by an arbitrary act of will".[381] [...] This was the tradition passed on to me in Zurich, and one I have followed for the last thirty years. This simple formulation conveys the heart and soul of Jung's spiritual model. Though many today would deny him any significance as a spiritual teacher, there was no doubt to those of us studying in Zurich with Marie-Louise von Franz and Arnold Mindelll that Jungian work was a spiritual process. We did not confine our work with the unconscious to our analytical sessions. But made it the very fabric of our lives.

Today, however, more and more Jungians are redefining Jungian work and concepts with a decidedly non-spiritual emphasis. [...] originally and essentially, Jungian work was a system aimed at promoting profound transformational experience. Analytic work with individuals that does not foster such transformational experiences should only loosely be termed Jungian.[382]

I will take the opportunity in this chapter to establish position.

The effects of Christianity for humanity were disastrous. From Civilizations – such as the Greek and Roman – humanity retroceded to the Dark Ages, where spiritual crime, cultural superstition and lack of hygiene reigned. The robust **clarity of consciousness** in Greece and Rome submerged in the medieval ignorance, and freedom of thought and commitment with reality gradually became crimes subjected to punishment by fire.

The Enlightenment was a true exorcism. Its Lights saved humanity, bringing back a degree of reasonability. Then it was possible to breathe, **think** and **discuss**. We had room for science again.

As with every good medication, however, the secret is in the dosage. **Reason is not consciousness**, but only one of its parts, one of its "organs"; JUNG demonstrates this brilliantly in *Psychological types*[383]. The confusion between the concepts of **reason** and **consciousness** has caused great distortions in the world. Coupled with the trauma caused by the Age of Darkness, the present hegemony of reason is obstructing the development of consciousness, exaggerating its healthy characteristic of inhibiting superstition to a type of witch-hunt, ridiculing the exploration of themes that cannot be scientifically demonstrated. The absolutism of reason is so circumstantial as the scholasticism, and if we want to write timeless books, we cannot be imprisoned to circumstances by their own temporary nature.

JUNG is a transcendence from both models. Centred in an actual conscience, JUNG uses reason with mastery, putting his immeasurable **culture** to the service of **proving** his **analysis**. But he is not restricted to reason, equally using his other psychological faculties to apprehend sensorial, intuitive and even paradoxical realities. JUNG placed himself in a relationship with the Symbol and the Soul, therefore being able to experience the Transcendence. However, his **scientific rigour**, his empiricism, his huge data collection, his experimentation, later successfully repeated by many people with the same results predicted by him, are evident. This is science.

JUNG's behaviour is extremely important because it is rational, conscious and transcendental all at the same time, and in balance. His history **shows** that the human being is much more intelligent than the narrow boundaries allowed by the rational mind. To stay confined there is just an example of lacking reach and development.

> Reason sets the boundaries far too narrowly for us, and would have us accept only the known and that too with limitations and live in a known framework, just as if we were sure how far life actually extends. As a matter of fact, day after day we live far beyond the bounds of our consciousness; without our knowledge, the life of the unconscious is also going on within us. The more the critical reason dominates, the more impoverished life becomes; but the more of the unconscious, and the more of myth we are capable of making conscious, the more of life we integrate. Overvalued reason has this in common with political absolutism: under its dominion the individual is pauperized.[384]

In the extract above, Jeffrey RAFF shows that Analytical Psychology faces a tendency towards rationalization, regressing and distorting itself, therefore losing its live centre, the Transcendence. I greatly admire this author for remaining authentic, publicly expressing his experience and maintaining it despite the absolutism of reason, risking being ridiculed. Without his monumental work *Jung and the alchemical imagination*[385], the present book would be impossible.

* * * * *

Each dimension is a whole universe and entails an immense complexity. The second dimension, for example, entails the creation of whole civilizations. The third dimension entails the creation of a strong ego, which in turn entails the acquisition of various realms of knowledge, such as etiquette, formal education, professional experience, relationship with the family of origin and the family they form, and many others.

As in any dimension, the fourth one also entails the existence of a whole unique complexity. It is **necessary** to get into contact with the unconscious and, ultimately, with the Self, and for such, develop a huge culture about Symbols, Archetypes, Mythologies, etc. It is necessary to learn to interpret one's own dreams, for example. One of the wonders of Analytical Psychology is the mapping of the Unconscious and the development of techniques to relate to it. Many times, when I showed someone what the fourth dimension is, I had outraged responses such as: "So you are saying that I need to know all that to experience the fourth dimension!" Yes, I am. It is necessary to know all this to experience the fourth dimension, in the same way that much knowledge is necessary to develop a strong ego in the third dimension: people even go to college to do that. How can someone know the **universe** that is a certain dimension, without going through an enormous learning? The fourth dimension **is** the unconscious and the relationship with it. Therefore, the experience of the fourth dimension entails the understanding of the unconscious.

The fourth dimension has a fundamental characteristic: the **conscious relationship with the Transcendence**. In the fourth dimension, the Transcendence manifests itself as the Soul, as the 4D Self. In this relationship, as in any relationship, there are (at least) two instances: the ego and the Soul. In this relationship, as in any relationship, there is a rule that guarantees the health of the relationship: each one must exist independently, without fusion of personalities, so that love and mutual influence can be experienced. We are extremely familiarized with the personality of the ego and its psychological speech, because in a sense, we are the ego, we are the consciousness. But the nature of the Soul and its psychological speech are much less accessible because they are **unconscious** and **transcendent**. The fact that something is unconscious is simultaneously a difficulty, since obviously we do not know what exists there, but also a wonderful thing, since it allows the consciousness to expand infinitely. It is precisely this **infinite** that becomes evident in the fourth dimension that is the Transcendence – the fact that something **in ourselves** makes us **transcend** infinitely, no matter how much we grow. The fact that we infinitely and eternally transcend ourselves is probably the most beautiful **progressive paradox** there is.

If the unconscious is unconscious – rest assured, this is not as obvious as it seems – how can we hear its voice, establish a relationship, a dialogue, at the same time maintaining a distance, an independence, without fusion? JUNG shows various mechanisms through which this can happen, but perhaps the most important is the **dream**. One of the advantages of the dream is that it occurs while the ego sleeps, while the consciousness is off or is very dim, preventing the ego from interfering in the image of the dream, thereby deforming it. This is an important point, as dismissing the "mechanisms of defense of the ego"[386], admitting that dreams show images produced directly from the unconscious with no alteration from the ego[387] – since Nature "[does] not lie"[388,389], – was one of the points that lead to the disagreement between FREUD and JUNG. Dreams allow the Soul to express its point of view directly, without the interference of the ego.

In order to establish a dialogue, however, the ego needs to understand what the Soul is saying through the dream and be able to answer. The comprehension of a dream depends on the understanding that the nature of the dream is **symbolic**[390]. The images of the dream are Symbols that carry **meaning** and **act** on the conscience and life of the dreamer[391]. Hence the need to dedicate to the learning of the huge range of knowledge necessary to the complete experience of the relationship with the Soul and of the fourth dimension. Since humanity has obviously not collectively reached this level, this process has frequently been experienced in therapy, with the help of a professional who often acts as a spiritual master, tribe sorcerer, shaman, etc. (however unpleasant these images might be for those who experience the present obsession with reason). But it is likely that this will be common-place in the centuries to come.

The progression through the fourth dimension occurs by a symbolic progression that tends to culminate in symbols of *coniunctio*, the union of opposites, usually in multiples of four[392]. An important example is the *mandala*, a disc with an axis, split in multiples of four[393]. The peak of this symbolic progression has been expressed in the West by the Symbol of Crucifixion, through which the Soul is integrated and from where it *Retreats*.

The Paradigm of Sense opens with the *Retreat of the Soul*, and shortly after we see the arrival of the *Spirit*, in Pentecost, 50 days after *Resurrection*, a multiple of **five**. This paradigm will be marked by the relationship of the whole integrated ego-Soul and *Spirit*. This relationship, as in any relationship, also needs to guarantee its health: they must each exist independently, without fusion.

However, this "independence" is infinitely more complex in five dimensions, because in 5D there is no duality, therefore, strictly speaking, it is impossible to talk of independence. For example, how can consciousness exist separately from the Unconscious, if we have always seen that, in the second *coniunctio*, peak of the fourth dimension, a coincidence between consciousness and the Unconscious has been reached? This question is in itself a dualist one, and with the fifth dimension missing from it, can only entail one answer: it does not exist, it is not possible. But, in the same way as the division of 4 by 3 does not have an answer in the scope of the natural numbers – but does in the scope of rational numbers – the dualist question above does not have an answer in three or four dimensions but does in five dimensions. In integration with the Soul, the 5D ego no longer experiences the existence of the unconscious as something beyond comprehension, that must be denied, that opposes to it or even as something separate. The unconscious is experienced as something **comprehensible**, because the 5D ego has spent a whole dimension (the fourth) learning its language and has achieved it. The unconscious is experienced as something **acceptable**, even more, **desirable**, since it is a whole potentiality of consciousness expansion, of infinite transcendence of itself. The unconscious is experienced as something **harmonious** with the ego, since they cooperate. The ego supports the consciousness, marks its position, integrates unconscious contents and **realises** the unconscious, while the unconscious is constantly seen by the ego, is in constant relationship with the ego, and can bring any content that it seeks in the far-flung places of its **infinite**. Besides this **relationship**, learned in the fourth dimension, the various available possibilities in the fifth dimension – autonomy, growing consciousness of *Macroimage*, mobilization of archetypes, *Interference*, *Strength*, *Manifestation* and others – allow the 5D ego to **be, paradoxically**, the unconscious itself. In five dimensions, ego and unconscious are indeed distinct things, but they are not separate things. The relationship can exist without fusion and without separation.

Nonetheless, in the Paradigm of Sense, the axis of the relationship is no longer between the 4D ego and the Soul, but between the 5D ego (a conjunction between the 4D ego and the Soul) and the *Spirit*. Therefore, the question now is: how does the *Spirit Manifest* itself?

Part of this answer has already been given in the chapter "*Body*". **Spirit is Body**. In a fifth-dimensional reality, there is no duality of any kind, since the physical *Body* of the individual is a direct expression of the *Spirit* that inhabits it – even this sentence only serves a didactic purpose, because ultimately, the *Body* **is not the expression** of the *Spirit*, but **the physical Body is the Spirit**. Besides that, by "*Body*" I do not refer simply to the physical *Body* of the individual, limited by its skin. Since there is no duality, there is no "inside" and "outside". That way, the individual's bed, house, car, as well as the city, country and planet they live in are also part of their "physical *Body*" and are also *Spirit*, since *Body* is *Spirit*. Moreover, it is important to remember that other people are actually other people, independent, but **paradoxically** they are part of the 5D ego; therefore, the physical *Body* of other people are also part of the "physical *Body*" of the individual and are also *Spirit*, since *Body* is *Spirit*. This totally **paradoxical** reality, where duality is null, where **paradoxically** *Spirit* is *Body*, where "inside" and "outside" **paradoxically** coincide, where "I" and "the other" **paradoxically** coincide – this reality is the **Pneumatic reality**. The *Manifestation* of the *Spirit* is the *Pneumatic* reality.

> When **body becomes spirit and spirit becomes body**, we enter a new realm of experience that I call the *psychoid*.[394] [author's own highlights]

(I remind the reader that in this work, where RAFF uses the term **psychoid**, we use the term **Pneumatic**.)

The fifth dimension is the process of psychological development that arises from the complete realisation of the second *coniunctio* and culminates with the complete realisation of the third *coniunctio*, the *Unus Mundus*. Although the integration of the Soul, the 4D Self, in the Paradigm of Balance, can give the impression that there is no longer Transcendence, this is a false conclusion. On the contrary, the relationship with the Transcendence in the fifth dimension is even bigger, more **intimate** and more **mature**. There, the *Spirit* is the 5D Self and is the transcendent centre that regulates the fifth-dimensional development process.

"The first stage unites the conscious and the unconscious; the second makes this union permanent; the third unites the self already created with a center that transcends the human psyche, a center that one might call Divine. [...] The first two centers are psychic, but **the last is psychoidal in that it creates a center that is in part transpsychic**.[395] [author's own highlights]

According to RAFF, the third centre (5D Self) is psychoidal (= *Pneumatic*). His affirmation that it is transpsychic is astounding. This term implies the concept that yes it involves the human psyche, but also **transcends the psyche**, it is larger than that and includes the physical world, or even that it **is *Spirit* AND physical world**. After all, this is the essence of the *Unus Mundus*, towards which the *Pneumatic* reality of the fifth dimension progressively aims for. Having a third centre, a fifth-dimensional Self, how does this centre manifests its own transcendence?

The *Spirit* is manifested through *Images*. In fact, **Spirit is *Image***, *Image* in movement.

Jung wrestled with the problem of the meaning of spirit. He came to the conclusion that there were three major attributes. The first is spontaneous movement and activity. The spirit is free to do and create as it will, and is free of the control of the ego, the conscious part of the personality. The ego can experience the spirit, but not dictate to it. **The second attribute of spirit is the capacity to spontaneously produce images independently, and the third attribute is the "sovereign manipulation of these images"**.[396]

Experientially, every human being encounters the spirit in his or her dreams, for the images that populate dreams derive from the spirit. Not only the images themselves, but all that they do in the dreams are a **reflection of spirit**. In this sense, the ego does not make up dreams; rather, it experiences them as they unfold through the spontaneous manifestation of the spirit. Jung felt that the archetype od spirit appeared in dreams as the wise old man.[397] [author's own highlights]

In the fourth dimension, the *Manifestation* of the *Spirit* is not direct. The *Spirit* reflects its *Images* in the Soul, in the same way that the Sun reflects its light in the Moon. The *Truth* of the *Spirit* is **reflected** in the Symbol of the Soul. *Spirit* and Soul produce **the dream, symbolic**. The 4D ego, however, at this point, does not see the *Spirit* and its *Truth* (5D); it only sees the Soul and its Symbols (4D).

There are, however, two exceptions.

JUNG mentions at certain points in his work, dreams with the Voice. According to him, the structure of this type of dream is different. A disembodied voice, whose origin is not identifiable in the dream since it does not come from any of the characters, but it is clearly audible. It is the Voice of the dream. It says very simple, yet paradoxical sentences, which do not need to be interpreted because they do not have a classically symbolic nature. On the contrary, its character is of a **"irrefutable truth"** and is highly recommended that whatever this Voice says, is followed[398]. The characteristics pointed out by JUNG are incredibly similar to the characteristics of the *Spirit* that I have been pointing out: it's a Voice that speaks paradoxically, but that does not need interpretation.

Besides that, JUNG highlights another type of dream that differs from the rest. He describes it as a symbolic dream which simultaneously seems **to be actually happening**, as if the dreamer was experiencing a physical, concrete situation, even though it is happening in the psyche. The dream can be seen as symbolic and be interpreted. However, it can simultaneously be understood as the experiencing of a concrete experience, a fact, and from this perspective, it does not need to be interpreted. Let us see two examples of this type: one experience that JUNG had whilst awake and a dream he had.

> One night I lay awake thinking of the sudden death of a friend whose funeral had taken place the day before. I was deeply concerned. Suddenly I felt that he was in the room. It seemed to me that he stood at the foot of my bed and was asking me to go with him. I did not have the feeling of an apparition; rather, it was an inner visual image of him, which I explained to myself as a fantasy. But in all honesty I had to ask myself, "Do I have any proof that this is a fantasy? Suppose it is not a fantasy, suppose my friend is really here and I decided he was only a fantasy would that not be abominable of me?" Yet I had equally little proof that he stood before me as an apparition. Then I said to myself, "Proof is neither here nor there! Instead of explaining him away as a fantasy, I might just as well give him the benefit of the doubt and for experiment's sake credit him with reality." The moment I had that thought, he went to the door and beckoned me to follow him. So I was going to have to play along with him! That was something I hadn't bargained for. I had to repeat my argument to myself once more. Only then did I follow him in my imagination. He led me out of the house, into the garden, out to the road, and finally

to his house, (In reality it was several hundred yards away from mine.) I went in, and he conducted me into his study. He climbed on a stool and showed me the second of five books with red bindings which stood on the second shelf from the top. Then the vision broke off. I was not acquainted with his library and did not know what books he owned. Certainly I could never have made out from below the titles of the books he had pointed out to me on the second shelf from the top. This experience seemed to me so curious that next morning I went to his widow and asked whether I could look up something in my friend's library. Sure enough, there was a stool standing under the bookcase I had seen in my vision, and even before I came closer I could see the five books with red bindings. I stepped up on the stool so as to be able to read the titles. They were translations of the novels of Emile Zola. The title of the second volume read: "The Legacy of the Dead." The contents seemed to me of no interest. Only the title was extremely significant in connection with this experience.

[...]

Equally important to me were the dream-experiences I had before my mother's death. News of her death came to me while I was staying in the Tessin. I was deeply shaken, for it had come with unexpected suddenness. The night before her death I had a frightening dream. I was in a dense, gloomy forest; fantastic, gigantic boulders lay about among huge jungle-like trees. It was a heroic, primeval landscape. Suddenly I heard a piercing whistle that seemed to resound through the whole universe. My knees shook. Then there were crashings in the underbrush, and a gigantic wolfhound with a fearful, gaping maw burst forth. At the sight of it, the blood froze in my veins. It tore past me, and I suddenly knew: the Wild Huntsman had commanded it to carry away a human soul. I awoke in deadly terror, and the next morning I received the news of my mother's passing.[399]

Both dreams mentioned by JUNG are exceptions in four dimensions but are common-place in five dimensions. We can consider these, therefore, as irruptions of the fifth dimension within the fourth dimension, instants when the *Spirit* is manifested directly in the reality of the Soul.

The "dreams" in 5D are *Images Created* by the 5D Self, the *Spirit*, now directly accessible in its *Truth*.

> Because the spirit [...] manifests in dreams, visions and active imagination, **one can maintain relationship with the self by engaging those images**.[400] [author's own highlights]

In the Paradigm of Sense, reality starts to have five dimensions, because the Self that regulates it has five dimensions. The nature of the 5D Self *Creates* the whole *Pneumatic* reality of the fifth dimension.

> The self manifests when opposites are unified to form a new state of consciousness and being. **The new center so formed is a union of opposites. Since the self includes the inner and outer dimensions of realities, it would then transcend both psychic and physical realities, and live in the world beyond both, though one that also includes both**. [...] it is possible to say that a sequential union of opposites creates a self that is at one moment psychic and the next physical in its manifestations. Considered from the perspective of the simultaneous union, however, **the self is both physical and psychic at *the same time***. Thus, the self belongs to neither reality completely, but to a third that unites them. It is in this sense that the manifest self does not exist in the outer world alone, or in the psychic world, but in the world of subtle bodies, wherein physical and psychic are united. Just as Ruland defined imagination as a subtle body, the self to which it belongs is also a **subtle body**.[401] [author's own highlights]

Transcending duality completely, the 5D Self gives rise to the fifth-dimensional ***Pneumatic* reality**. For that reason, in 5D, a "dream" is a **transpsychic** occurrence (using RAFF's language): it is a psychological and a physical reality at the same time. There is no difference between the events experienced by a 5D ego whilst awake, in their day-to-day life, and the events experienced by a 5D ego that sleeps and "dreams". The "dream" in 5D is a **physical event** that is part of a sequence of events **equally physical** that take place in the daily life of the awake 5D ego. 5D "dreams" and physical events whilst awake intersperse as scenes of the same story.

> Active imagination connects individuals with inner figures which, while very powerful, are clearly imaginal and derived from the psyche. These figures feel as if they were coming from within oneself. Typically one experiences them with eyes closed, and attention directed inward. These are the psychic figures that personify the forces of the unconscious. However, every so often, one may

experience a figure that feels completely different. This figure feels as if **it were coming from outside oneself, as if it existed in the external world**, in the room in which one finds oneself, for example. **One's eyes are open**, and the felt sense is that one perceives **a figure that does not come from within. The attention of the ego is focused outward, not inward**. These are the experiences I refer to using the term "psychoid".

There are other attributes of psychoidal experiences as well. They are more likely to be coupled with **synchronistic experiences**, and their effects are often **physical as well as psychological**. The quality of the experience is **less "imaginal" and more "real"**, though the reality in which one is engaging is not that of the ordinary world.[402] [author's own highlights]

In the ***Pneumatic* reality** of the fifth dimension, the relationship with the *Spirit* occurs through *Images*, which, during the day, are manifested as daily physical events, and at night as 5D "dreams". Even during the day, when the 5D ego experiences seemingly banal realities, the *Pneumatic* reality is the common-place: the *Spirit* can manifest itself directly as visions and imaginary processes that happen with "open eyes". More than that, the "banal" daily events are perceived as full of spiritual value.

[...] active imagination becomes a state of being. [...] Living in the world of active imagination does not imply that we are in an altered state of consciousness constantly, having visions day and night. It means that our attention is never far from the center, and we can access the self very easily at any moment. Moreover, **the world is alive and vital, filled with magical possibilities and a numinous background that takes very little to activate**. Individuals in such a state of being are present in the moment, and participate consciously in every situation. At the same time, however, the world of the unconscious is also present, and imaginal encounters close at hand.[403] [author's own highlights]

In a dualist perspective, the *Spirit* can only be reached through fantastic and mysterious experiences, spiritual events are extremely rare and for the rest of the time we live a banal reality, destitute of *Spirit*. This can be true until the third dimension, and perhaps, somewhat, in the fourth dimension. But in the fifth dimension the **banal events progressively disappear**, whilst one walks towards the *Unus Mundus*. Cleaning the house, buying bread and going to bed are both spiritual and transcendental experiences. The *Pneumatic* reality is totally spiritual.

Even the **timing** of the *Pneumatic* reality is spiritual. JUNG coined the term "synchronicity" to define a certain type of experience where physical events have **no causal relationship** among them, but a **meaningful relationship**. Since there is no causal relationship between these events, people tend to be surprised and call it coincidence. Indeed, JUNG also calls synchronicity a "meaningful coincidence". It can be said that, when the physical reality presents events which are directly related with the psychological reality, both realities are **synchronic**, and a **synchronicity** occurs[404]. A unified expression of two opposed realities, synchronicity is, therefore, part of a **third, larger reality**, that involves the first two[405]. This reality belongs to the *Spirit*.

Once again, something that is infrequent in four dimensions, is common-place in five dimensions. The fact that the *Spirit* is continuously manifested in ordinary daily events, both in transcendental experiences and in 5D "dreams", grants a **numinous** quality to "ordinary" daily events, full of **meaning** (4D). Furthermore, it makes these "ordinary" daily events the very expression of the *Truth* of the *Spirit*. Therefore, the **time** in the Paradigm of Sense is a **continuous synchronicity**, where all events, however small, are perceived as simultaneously physical and psychological, full of Meaning, full of *Truth*.

Having considered these points, it can certainly be said that the ***Pneumatic* reality is imaginary**, a reality of ***Images***.

> "We have to conceive of these processes not as the immaterial phantoms we readily take fantasy-pictures to be, but as something corporeal, a "subtle body," semi-spiritual in nature… **The *imaginatio*, or the act of imaging, was thus a physical activity** that could be fitted into the cycle of material changes, that brought these about and was brought about by them in turn. […] The singular expression astrum (star) is a Paracelsian term, which in this context means something like **quintessense**. Imagination is therefore a concentrated extract of the life forces, **both physical and psychic**.[406] [author's own highlights]

Note that, both to JUNG and to RAFF, the imaginary reality is a **reality**, a **physical reality**. It is not at all a fantasy reality – to see the imaginary reality as fantasy is a third-dimensional interpretation of a fifth-dimensional reality that cannot be understood. **Quintessence**, the fifth-dimensional reality, is simultaneously physical and psychological: it is imaginary.

Summing it all up, it is possible to see that the structure of a fifth-dimensional "dream" is completely different from that of a fourth-dimensional dream. For that reason, from this point forward the fifth-dimensional "dream" will be designated as *Pneûma*[407]. The structure of *Pneûma* is **physical**, and it is not possible to distinguish a *Pneumatic Image* from a physical event. Indeed, **the 5D ego is conscious** inside *Pneûma*, as it would be in "any" other physical event, since *Pneûma* **IS** a physical event.

> "[...] **the form is not other than the spiritual being itself**; on the contrary, **it is identical with it**, even if it is found in a thousand places, or in all places and is diverse in shape." In other words, **the form that a psychoidal being assumes in the psyche, the inner figure in which it manifests, is identical with the psychoidal entity**. There is no difference between the spiritual being, itself, and the imaginal form in which one experiences it. Active imagination with such a figure therefore relates one to the world beyond the psyche, to the spiritual domain and reality in which the divine resides. Though it may never be possible to experience that reality in and of itself, one can experience it through the form that it assumes. Since that form is no different than the thing itself, the imaginal encounter with the form is the encounter with the divine entity from which it originates.[408] [author's own highlights]

The consciousness of the 5D ego within a *Pneûma* is so clear that it knows itself to be inside the *Pneûma*. Sometimes, the 5D ego says to itself inside the *Pneûma* that it must remember to tell someone about it when it is "awake". Other times, the *Spirit*, which is manifested through *Images*, in this case a *Pneûma*, creates problems for the ego to solve, then **the 5D ego must make choices** inside the *Pneûma*, and without it the *Pneûma* cannot advance and stops. In this type of situation, one characteristic of the Paradigm of Sense becomes very clear: in face of the *Retreat of the Soul*, with no transcendental guidance, the 5D ego must make free choices, which will receive support from the *Spirit*, whether they are right or wrong – although, strictly speaking, any choice in five dimensions is simultaneously right and wrong, since it transcends morals and ethics.

Indeed, the relationship between the *Spirit* and the 5D ego is not one of guidance, but of **interaction between the Transcendental and the Consciousness**. The *Spirit* manifests itself by autonomously *Creating* the

Images that compose the *Pneûma*. These *Images* include self-evident information; the dreamers refer to this by saying that "in the dream I **just knew** that such and such was true". The *Spirit* is also manifested through the Voice (*Word*), which clearly expresses the *Truth*. Whatever the *Manifestation* of the *Spirit*, it is expected that the 5D ego **will make free choices and have actions, *Pneumatic* actions**.

The **time** of *Pneûma* is a **continuous synchronicity** where all its physical events are full of psychological meaning. But, more than a continuous synchronicity, the time of *Pneûma* is the ***All-the-times***, which will be described later in the Chapter "*Manifestation*".

Examples of clinical cases transcend the scope of the first edition of this work, but will be mentioned in the second edition. For now, let us have an example cited by RAFF, the dream of an alchemist called George STARKEY:

> In this dream he was working in his laboratory when **a spiritual being suddenly materialized**. Recovering from his shock and assuring himself that the apparition was not evil, Starkey asked it a question about the nature of the alchemical *Alchahest*, or original material. The spiritual entity revealed to him its nature, and though Starkey could not understand what he had heard intellectually, he knew it for truth. The revelation of the recipe for the magical substances is a common thing in alchemical writings; alchemists frequently warned that success in the work could only come through revelation from God.[409] [author's own highlights]

Evidently, we can interpret the dream symbolically, extracting its **meaning** (4D). However, in the *Pneumatic* reality, fifth-dimensional, the *Pneûma* shows a **physical event**. It is evident that this physical event is full of meaning, in fact, as every physical event is. But beyond the meaning, the event is a *Pneumatic* reality. Indeed, STARKEY tells that **a spiritual being materialized**, causing him surprise. The *Pneumatic* reality probably surprised him because a spiritual being was suddenly in his laboratory, **physically**. Inside the *Pneûma*, STARKEY is also **physically** in his laboratory.

The **time** of the dream is synchronic, once the spiritual being appears in order to give him the recipe at a time when STARKEY is in the lab.

But what is more striking is the number of choices given to STARKEY. He **makes the decision** to make sure that the "apparition was not evil", instead of simply accepting the apparition. STARKEY also **chooses** to ask a question about the *Alchahest*, a question of **personal interest**. So, even though the apparition of a spiritual being carries an enormous quantity of *numen*, the **action** of the *Pneûma* comes solely from STARKEY.

Finally, in the dream, STARKEY does not rationally understand, but **knows it to be true**. Before the *Pneûma*, STARKEY does not have the alchemical recipe, but after the *Pneûma*, after this physical fact, STARKEY possesses the recipe.

RAFF also gives a personal example of a *Pneûma:*

> [...] I found myself on top of a mountain, almost at the very peak. The slope was very steep, and my fear of heights made me drop to the ground and grab hold for fear I might fall at any moment. At the same time, I was fully aware of being at home in bed. I was cognizant of both realities simultaneously, and at the time it did not feel particularly strange. **I was not asleep, but fully awake, and the mountain scene was completely real**. I could feel the cold and smell the ground. My fear was sharp and clear. As I lay there, a hooded figure appeared directly above me and said, "Do you not trust me even here?" Encouraged by his words, I stood up and looked him in the face. Or rather I looked him in the eyes, for within the hood there was a skeleton with bright, shining red eyes. Rather than being afraid, I was filled with a deep sense of love and of being loved. He reached out his hand and touched me on the chest, and I found myself off the mountain and in bed, but in a state of ecstasy that lasted five or six hours. Typical of psychoidal encounters were the reality of the mountain scene, he complete aliveness of the hooded figure, the profound impact of his touch, and the state of ecstasy.[410]
> [author's own highlights]

Evidently, the *Pneûma* has a meaning (4D). Once again, however, the *Pneûma* has various 5D characteristics – to be awake inside the *Pneûma*, the coincidence between the psychological and the physical to the point of feeling a **physical touch**, in an absolutely real scene.

At this point, considering particularly the fact that the *Pneumatic* reality is an absolute coincidence between the psychological and the physical realities, it becomes possible to understand that the **whole *Universe* is built with *Images***.

In the Paradigm of Self-Affirmation, the ego tends to experience the unconscious only through projections and identifications, "noticing" the energies from the unconscious only through others and itself. Any phenomena that occur outside what is called "normality" are issues of religion, paranormal, inexplicable, considered unreal or laughable.

Only in the Paradigm of Balance the perception of *images* appears, initially through the Symbols produced by the Soul, **reflecting** the *Truth* of the *Spirit* – the *Truth* remains, therefore, revealed[411]. The Symbols produced by the Soul seem to be closely related to the physical reality, even if separate from it. For example, the Symbol of a certain unconscious complex or Archetype can show the relationship between that unconscious complex or Archetype and a certain physical symptom[412]. A Symbol can show how a certain unconscious complex or Archetype can directly determine the behaviour of the ego, leading to explosions of rage or obsessive-compulsive disorders. A Symbol can show how a certain unconscious complex or Archetype can directly determine the type of person the ego will invariable attract for dating, causing declarations such as "All men are the same, they only change addresses". A Symbol can show how a certain unconscious complex or Archetype can directly determine a type of situation recurrently experienced by the ego, such as always being cheated on, always being in second place or never being able to commit to anyone. In any case, the Symbols always show **how the psychological images determine physical events**. Anyone who undergoes a successful and good quality Jungian therapeutic process will inevitably notice this.

If this is not enough evidence, there is a stronger one. Jungian therapy includes procedures that allow the work to focus on a particular unconscious complex, modifying it, or on a particular archetype, and in both cases the aim is to integrate them. Well, this complex or archetype, before the therapeutic intervention, would determine a certain reality. With the therapeutic intervention the complex is modified, or the complex and the archetype are integrated, altering the psychological reality. It is astonishing to realise that the modification of the complex or the integration of the complex or the archetype are **synchronic** with the **modification of the physical reality that they used to determine, that is, of the same quality and intensity**. Again, anyone who successfully undergoes a respectable Jungian therapeutic process will inevitably notice that. So, there is no doubt: **the psychological images directly determine the physical reality**, for better or for worse.

The Paradigm of Sense goes way beyond this reality. Since there is no longer a **reflection** of the *Image* of the *Spirit* in the Symbol of the Soul, the situation where **a psychological image would directly determine the physical reality** is replaced by the situation where **the *Image* of the *Spirit* IS the physical reality**, since *Spirit* IS *Body*.

This observation has a bombastic consequence: the ***Macroimage***.

People of any dimension will know some parts of the physical world, and a limited number of people who will enter and leave their lives, momentarily or forever. However, those who live in the *Pneumatic* reality of the Paradigm of Sense experience a coincidence between the spiritual and the physical realities. Therefore, the parts of the physical world and the physical people that the 5D ego knows are identical to the parts of the spiritual world and the spiritual people that the 5D ego knows. But just as the fact that the 5D ego, for example, knows Brazil and some Brazilians and does not know Italy and some Italians does not mean that Italy and Italians do not exist – the 5D ego has simply not yet accessed the reality of Italy and Italians – so the fact that the 5D ego does know certain parts of the *Pneumatic* reality and not others does not mean that these others do not exist.

Let us take RAFF as an example. RAFF had a *Pneumatic* experience and saw a *Pneumatic* region that he called the "on top of a mountain" and a *Pneumatic* being who he called an "a skeleton with bright, shining red eyes". His experience had a beginning ("I found myself on top of a mountain") and an end ("He reached out his hand and touched me on the chest"). But, attention: both the mountain and the skeleton are *Pneumatic* realities possessed of ***Body***. Evidently, if they are possessed of ***Body***, the mountain and the skeleton did not start to exist just because RAFF needed the experience and stopped existing the minute it ended. On the contrary, the mountain and the skeleton exist in a *Pneumatic* reality, continuous, stable, which RAFF accessed momentarily through an irruption of the fifth dimension in his consciousness. The *Pneumatic* being evidences that by saying: "Do you not trust me even here?". This sentence proves that there had been other contacts, in other moments and places, where the skeleton and RAFF met, and RAFF did not trust the skeleton. It is also evident that RAFF was unconscious of that, to the point of not recognizing the skeleton and fear it. But the skeleton, in turn, was conscious of this, and showed its love to RAFF.

For these reasons, it would be sheer arrogance to imagine that the *Pneumatic* reality, as vast as the infinite *Draw*, and the numerous *Pneumatic* beings exist simply so that people can have *Pneumatic* experiences. This would place people at the centre of the universe – something that GALILEO, DARWIN, FREUD, JUNG, RAFF and so many others have been demonstrating to be a stupidity. **The *Pneumatic* reality exists by itself**. Eventually, we will develop enough consciousness to access it.

In the Paradigm of Sense, this consciousness is developed, and we do access the *Pneumatic* reality. But to be born into this reality is like being born in the physical reality. When we are born, we meet a mother and a home, we meet other people and other places throughout life. When we are born into a *Pneumatic* reality, we meet a *Pneumatic* being and a *Pneumatic* region, meeting other *Pneumatic* beings and regions throughout life. I do not know if this meeting with the skeleton was RAFF's first *Pneumatic* experience. But supposing it was, those were the first *Pneumatic* being and region he met, and there would certainly be others afterwards.

In the *Pneûma* that RAFF meets the skeleton and the mountain, he sees two spiritual *Images*, two *Images* produced autonomously by the *Spirit* – the skeleton and the mountain – and to see the *Image* is something absolutely real, it is to live that experience. In a later experience, RAFF will see more *Images*, meet more *Pneumatic* beings and regions, which exist before this experience and will continue to exist after it. In the same way that someone meets more and more people and places throughout life, never being able to meet all people nor the whole universe, RAFF will continue to meet *Pneumatic* beings and regions, never being able to meet them all. In the same way that the number of people and places that can be known does not equate to the total number of people there are and the to whole universe – but the total number of people and places still exist regardless – the number of *Pneumatic* beings and regions that can be known by RAFF does not equate to the total *Pneumatic* beings there are or to the whole *Pneumatic Universe*, but the total number of *Pneumatic* beings and regions still continue to exist, regardless of RAFF knowing them or not. Bearing in mind that each *Pneumatic* being, each *Pneumatic* region, each *Pneumatic* event and every smallest *Pneumatic* detail exists due to an **Image of the Spirit, and that your Body is an Image of the Spirit**, the infinite totality of *Images* of the *Spirit* is called **Macroimage**. A *Pneûma* is, therefore, a miniscule piece of the *Macroimage*, a fifth-dimensional access to a miniscule piece of the *Macroimage*.

Although, from the perspective of the first to the fourth dimensions, both the fifth dimension and the experience of the *Spirit* and the *Macroimage* are non-existent – or, to be more precise, are only accessible through transcendental experiences –, from the perspective of the fifth dimension, **the *Truth* is the *Macroimage***, a sum of all the elements of the *Pneumatic* reality and **it is the *Macroimage* that determines the visible reality**, regardless of whether people are conscious of this or not. RAFF may not be conscious of the skeleton, but the skeleton is conscious of RAFF.

Inner figures that embody psychoidal entities come from the dimension in which the opposites of physical and psychic have been united, they have far greater power and impact, and **are able to effect physical changes**.[413] [author's own highlights]

To perceive the *Universe* through the perspective of the *Macroimage* is an impacting experience, since the perspective is totally different. In the Paradigm of Self Affirmation, the psychological reality does not even exist; there is only the ego, which considers that everything else is just an extension of itself and can be controlled by it. In the Paradigm of Balance, the psychological reality is discovered and experienced, and the ego learns that there is a direct relationship between the psychological reality and the physical reality. However, in the Paradigm of Sense, there is no separation between the psychological and physical realities, but **one single reality**, a *Pneumatic* reality that **determines** everything that people in other dimensions call "psychological reality" and "physical reality".

This happens because **the *Universe* is entirely built by *Images*** and that which we call "physical reality" is in fact a group of *Images* of the *Spirit* (the white elephant of *viśuddha*), reflected in the physical reality (the grey elephant of *mūlādhāra*), through the great mirror of the Soul. Even the ego, this region of the psyche which we like so much, which we are so proud of being (rightly so), is an *Image* of the *Spirit*.

There is a need for the ego to know itself well, and to be able to sustain its **self-image** and perspective in the face of strong pressure from inner forces.[414] [author's own highlights]

Even more important to realise is the fact that, if the physical reality is a reflex of the *Images* of the *Spirit*, changes in that *Image* will reflect **directly and immediately** in the "physical reality". For that reason, the "physical reality" cannot exist independently of the *Image* of the *Spirit*, since it is not an objective reality by itself. If the *Image* of the *Spirit* changes, the "physical reality" changes immediately. If an *Image* of the *Spirit* were to suddenly stop existing, the part of the "physical reality" that used to reflect this *Image* would also disappear.

Let us make a digression about a fact of extreme importance. For a consciousness with less than five dimensions, it is extremely easy to mistake the fifth dimension with the third, arguing that in both dimensions, "the ego can do whatever it wants". Such conclusion is, however, the same as mistaking a surfboard with a transatlantic cruise ship.

In the Paradigm of Self-Affirmation, the ego has no idea about what the unconscious is, and the Soul only exists as a way of making the ego happy according to its own concepts. Childish concepts appear, such as "you are with your Soul when you are happy" – as if any sadness, evil, disappointment or adversity could not have come from the Soul. Or even still, the idea that the ego can ask things to the Soul, such as houses, cars, jobs, victory for your football team.

In the Paradigm of Sense, the ego has gone through a moral defeat, being defeated by the Soul, who showed the ego clearly that, if it wants houses, cars, jobs or anything similar, it must work for it instead of trying to manipulate the psyche with psychological exercises of questionable ethics. The ego has experienced other moral defeats, moving through various regions of its own unconscious, learning about everything that it had relegated to its personal unconsciousness, learning about the divine grandiosity of the Archetypes. The ego has experienced the Crucifixion, the total surrender to the Soul, even though it had been abandoned by it. In the Crucifixion, the ego is in **conjunction with the Soul** – after all, this is what *coniunctio* means – and sees all the Archetypes in Balance around it. In the Paradigm of Sense, the ego has concluded the Paradigm of Balance. There is no comparison between a fifth-dimensional psychological structure and a third-dimensional one.

One idea that could lead to a false parity between the fifth and the third dimensions is the possibility that the ego can make decisions without the interference of the Self or the unconscious. Indeed, the similarity ends there. In the third dimension, the ego can make decisions without the interference of the Self or the unconscious whilst **being completely unconscious of the existence of the unconscious or the Self** – the ego only considers itself, its own desires, which exist within its miniscule reality. In the fifth dimension, the ego can make decisions without the interference of the Self or the unconscious, whilst **being completely conscious of the existence of the unconscious and the Self** – it does consider itself, its own egoistic desires, above all it considers the *Personal Sense*, but also considers the **transcendent reality of the Soul**, the whole archetypal reality, the whole reality of the Self, the whole **transcendent reality of the *Spirit***, as far as it can see. It is not possible to compare a third-dimensional reality with a fifth-dimensional one. A surfboard is not a transatlantic cruise ship.

The 3D ego chooses **regardless of the Transcendence**, which is totally unknown to it, which it does not experience. The 5D ego does not choose only through the reality of its ego because this would return it immediately to a **dualist reality**.

In the ***Pneumatic* reality**, there is a profound relationship between the Transcendence and the 5D ego: the **visionary state**. The visionary state is the capacity of the 5D ego to see the *Images* of the *Macroimage*, both in the physical reality that it sees while awake and the physical reality it sees in its *Pneúmata* while it sleeps. That way, the 5D ego continually considers the infinite Transcendence that is the *Spirit*, since the *Macroimage* is the sum of the *Images* that the *Spirit* "spontaneously produces and supremely manipulates"[415].

On the one hand, the 5D ego sees and considers the maximum number of *Images* from the *Macroimage* that it can capture, and in that way, strongly connects with the Transcendence. However, it is important to remember that, in the fifth dimension, there is a conjunction between consciousness and Transcendence, therefore the 5D ego also needs to be seen and considered by itself. On the other hand, the 5D ego chooses, among the *Images* of the *Macroimage*, the one it wants to work with.

Since the *Soul Retreated* and no longer offers guidance, the 5D ego makes its choice from the *Images* of the *Macroimage* without any transcendental guidance. Its choice is completely free, in the way the *Spirit* wants. However, it is essential that the ego makes a choice that has *Personal Sense*, as this factor strongly decreases the impersonality of the choice and in turn decreases the risk of both the fifth-dimensional consciousness structure and its contact with the *Spirit* being used without legitimacy, that is, without humanity.

Note that, given that there is no transcendental guidance as to which *Image* should be chosen, and given that the *Image* of the *Macroimage* are all available to be chosen, the images are in **balance**. This is what the Paradigm of Balance has produced – a state where the denial of the various archetypal contents of the unconscious has ceased, therefore the pressure of the unconscious to bring those denied archetypal contents has also ceased. A state of **balance** where the ego can deal with any archetypal energy. After choosing one of the many *Images* in **balance** from the *Macroimage*, that makes *Personal Sense*, the 5D ego **Unbalances** this *Image*. To *Unbalance* an *Image* means that the 5D ego will start a **Creative process** so that the *Image* that it sees in the *Macroimage* is also **manifested** in Symbols and in people's unconscious (fourth dimension), to the egoic consciousness of people (third dimension), in society (second dimension), and in acts and facts (first dimension).

The process that starts with the perception of the *Macroimage* and the choice of an *Image* (fifth dimension), until its *Manifestation* in acts and facts (first dimension), passing through all dimensions in between, is called *Draw* and the state in which this process occurs is the visionary state. Therefore, like the water drawer, astrological symbol of Aquarius, the 5D ego *Draws Spirit* (see) in Matter (have). In other words, the 5D ego contributes **Creatively** to the process of reflection of the white elephant, symbol of *viśuddha*, on the grey elephant, symbol of *mūlādhāra*.

Draw is an entirely transcendental process, since the fifth-dimensional *Image* is seen in the *Macroimage*, which is the *Spirit* itself in movement. **Paradoxically**, *Draw* is an entirely conscious process, since the fifth-dimensional *Image* is freely **chosen** by the 5D ego, observing the *Personal Sense*. The only criteria of the fifth dimension, besides the *Sense*, is that the process must be **Creative**, never repetitive. Being in unity, *Spirit* and 5D ego need to work together towards the characteristics they have in common: the *Creation*. We have learned with JUNG that the *Spirit* is *Creative*, "producing *Images* in a spontaneous way"[416]. But the 5D ego also needs to be *Creative*, not only making choices through the *Sense*, but also **compulsory modifying the *Pneumatic Image* that it chose in the *Macroimage*, applying to it its personal style and aesthetic, so that, at the end of the *Creative* process, a *Pneumatic Image* produced by the *Spirit* is manifested with the style and the aesthetic of the 5D ego.**

After the *Macroimage* has been observed and an *Image* has been chosen, in accordance to the *Sense*, the *Spirit* and the fifth-dimensional ego are working together and *Creatively*. **These** actions are supported by the *Spirit*, whether they are right or wrong: "**I will give you the keys of the kingdom of Heaven**: whatever you bind on earth will be bound in heaven; whatever you loose on earth will be loosed in heaven."[417] However, manifesting a *Pneumatic Image* literally, or more than once in the same way is not *Creative*, therefore does not follow the criteria of the fifth dimension, and becomes **Demoniac**.

It is extremely important to note that the free choices made by the 5D ego **must necessarily** stem from the *Macroimage*. It is this observation that characterizes the ***imaginatio***, the real imagination, because only in these circumstances we can say that the *Spirit* and the 5D ego are operating together, *Creatively*. It is this that prevents the 5D ego to embark on a demoniac path of **fantasy**, instead of the *Pneumatic* path of **imagination**.

> Bad imagination was "phantasia" which was responsible for the fall of Lucifer, and in the human being it created illusions and false desires that led one away from God. By turning toward fantasy

rather than true imagination, the soul became lost in illusion and far removed from the presence of God. True imagination, on the other hand, is the embodiment of divine wisdom in the soul, and could lead to redemption and union with God.[418]

Indeed, whereas **imagination** leads to a progressively more intimate relationship with the Transcendence, the *Spirit* itself, **fantasy** leads to a progressively intimate relationship with the *Demon*, with illusion.

> While imagination opens the door to profound experiences of the self, and makes the formation of the self possible, fantasy leads to inflation, illusion, and stagnation.[419]

> While imagination contains information about the other parts of the psyche and discloses the path to be followed, fantasy is about the ego's needs, desires, and quest for aggrandizement.[420]

As it can be seen, the fifth dimension is **not** a paradisiac state in the popular sense of the term: a state with no error, no pain, no evil, no darkness. The popular understanding of paradise is an illusion only possible when the evil is thrown on the other, when the universe is divided in two. The dualist ego believes that it will obviously go to heaven, and its enemies will go to hell, whatever their definition of heaven and hell, whatever their definition of God.

Curiously, there are various best-sellers that, in the past decades have attempted to describe the fifth dimension, but they are essentially dualist. They describe the use of psychological techniques **apparently** similar to those described in the present work: the visualization of images in order to materialize them. They call this "law of attraction". The same confusion made between the third and the fifth dimension occur between *DRAW* and the so-called "law of attraction". Clearly third-dimensional, they attempt to describe the fifth dimension without having even entered the fourth. These authors and their followers cannot distinguish between ego and Soul, since they do not know it, a common circumstance of the third dimension. So due to this lack of knowledge, I cannot criticize them. That way, the choice of images that will be materialized evidently comes from the ego, completely ignoring the existence of the Soul. What we see are people choosing mansions and luxury cars from magazines and sticking pages on the wall so that they can have it "through visualization". At most they seek physical cures, which is, to some extent, honourable. Commonly in the third dimension, people do not realise that not having a mansion or a luxury car could actually be a richer psychological experience than having those things, nor do they realise that the disease could be the experience that leads them to the psychological advance[421]. They do not know that "a neurosis is truly removed when only when it has removed the false attitude of the ego [...] we do not cure it – it cures us".[422] More importantly, they do not know that the Soul is good and evil at the same time, and as such, can perfectly go against our desires, defeating them: they believe that if the ego is happy with their mansions, their luxury cars, and their perfect bodies, the Soul will be approving. – As I have mentioned, a "spiritual" system that is not capable of solving the problem of evil cannot go beyond the third-dimension and therefore cannot be taken seriously. – **The practice of the "law of attraction" is the practice of phantasia**. As RAFF says, the *phantasia* "fantasy is about the ego's needs, desires, and quest for aggrandizement" and "fantasy leads to inflation, illusion, and stagnation."[423] By **only** observing the desires of the ego, it completely ignores the *Spirit* and the *Macroimage*, and this is the quickest way to the *Demoniac*. Such is the price of ignorance and the irresponsible manipulation of the spiritual laws by those inapt to do so. Thankfully, except for unfortunate exceptions, the psychological power of the third-dimensional ego is very low, and its spiritual power is null, which, in a way, protects it.

The fifth dimension is indeed a paradisiac estate – its Symbol is the Paradise of Eden. But as we have seen extensively, Lucifer has complete access to Paradise. Not only are the Shadow and the evil (4D) completely included, but also the *Demoniac* (5D). The observation of the *Macroimage*, the choice of images that make *Sense* and the *Creative* work in harmony with the *Spirit* are practices of ***imaginatio*** and allow the 5D ego to draw images of the *Spirit*; such practices avoid ***phantasia***, avoid *Drawing Demoniac* images and avoid the *Demon*'s access to the consciousness, with all the damaging effects described in the chapter "*Demon*".

However, if it is said that the *Demon* is included in the fifth dimension, its presence is not conditioned to the practice of *phantasia*. **Even in the strict observation of *imaginatio*, the *Demon* is present.** Let us never forget that the *Spirit* is the Light AND the Abyss. The *Spirit* is the Whole, the *Demon* is part of it. The *Spirit* is the *Image* and the Wisdom, the *Demon* is the *Dynamic Force*. So, when one is in the visionary state contemplating the *Macroimage*, when an *Image* is chosen, and which will be *Unbalanced* and materialized in a *Creative* process supported by the *Spirit* – when one *Draws* – there is a *Demoniac* upheaval. This occurs because any fifth dimensional *Creative* process **strongly *Unbalances*** the energy and every

Unbalance violently demands that the Balance is re-established. Christ is Balance, *Demon* is *Unbalance*. Therefore, although a correct and thorough realisation of the *Draw* process should avoid the *Drawing* of a demoniac *phantasia*, it does **not** avoid a *Demoniac* upheaval; on the contrary, it **causes it**.

When facing the *Demon*, *Force* is necessary.

---

[381] JUNG, C. G. (1975) *Psychology and religion: West and East.* Translated by Hull, R. F. C. 2nd edition. CW XI. Bollingen Series XX. Princeton University Press. §6.

[382] RAFF, J. (2000) *Jung and the alchemical imagination.* Florida: Nicolas-Hays, Inc. (Kobo eBook version).

[383] JUNG, C. G. (1976) *Psychological types.* Translated by Baynes, H. G. CW VI. Bollingen Series XX. Princeton University Press.

[384] JUNG, C. G. *Memories, dreams and reflexions.* Chapter XI "On life after death". Translated by Winston, R. and C. Revised Edition. Vintage Books. (ebook) Available at: <http://www.venerabilisopus.org/en/books-samael-aun-weor-gnostic-sacred-esoteric-spiritual/pdf/200/265_jung-carl-memories-dreams-reflections.pdf> Access April 29th 2020. p. 363.

[385] RAFF, J. (2000) *Jung and the alchemical imagination.* Chapter 1 "Jung as a spiritual tradition". "The self" Florida: Nicolas-Hays, Inc. (Kobo eBook version).

[386] FREUD, A. (1993) *The ego and the mechanisms of defense.* London: Karnac Books.

[387] "For Jung, the lack of clarity in a dream is not a disguise, but exactly the representation of its essence, i.e., a spontaneous expression of psychic depth that lacks rational transparency due to its autonomy and lack of contact with consciousness. Thus, the memory of a dream is not a facade, nor the product of deformation. The manifest image of the dream embodies its entire meaning and represents interior reality as it is. For this reason, the dream is defined as "the spontaneous self representation of the present situation of the unconscious in a symbolic form". GALLBACH, M. R. (2006) *Learning from dreams.* Published by Daimon Verlag. p. 28.

[388] "Dreams are neither deliberate nor arbitrary fabrications; they are natural phenomena which are nothing other than what they pretend to be. They do not deceive, they do not lie, they do not distort or disguise, [...] they are invariably seeking to express something that the ego does not know and does not understand." JUNG, C. G. (1981) *The Development of personality.* Translated by Hull, R. F. C. CW XVII. Bollingen Series XX. Princeton University Press. §189.

389 "Here, once more, there is a great difference in the points of view of Freud and Jung. They agreed that dreams are the regal pathway to the unconscious, however they disagreed as to where that path would lead. Freud believed that it would take us to the discovery of unconscious desires, and that the symbolic nature of dreams could be explained by postulating some kind of censorship. Jung did not accept this idea whatsoever; he considered the dream a product of nature. Nature does not deceive, it only speaks its own language, and it is down to us to learn that language and come to an understanding of it." EDINGER, E. *Science of the Soul: A Jungian perspective*. [Translated from the Portuguese version: (2004) *A ciência da alma*. São Paulo: Editora Paulus p. 17.]

390 "Dreams, indeed, speak a symbolic language, which we must acquire the ability to understand" Ibid.

391 "Ever since man has possessed self-knowledge, dreams, those messengers from the nocturnal half of life, have been carriers of the intrapsychic process, in which past, present and future can take form with an inimitable richness of imagery and meaning. Hence, the realm of dream is the psychic area where we most encounter archetypal themes. Here they appear in strangely impressive images, symbols, events and sequences. Often they put the conscious mind in a state of rapture that it cannot resist; for it is at the mercy of the numinous action of the archetypal images." J JACOBI, J. (1959) *Complex/Archetypes/Symbol in the Psychology of C. G. Jung.* Translated by Manheim, R. Bollingen Series LVII. Bollingen Foundation, Inc. pp.126-127

392 "As experience shows, symbols of a reconciling and unitive nature do in fact turn up in dreams, the most frequent being the motif of the child-hero and the squaring of the circle, signifying the union of opposites. Those who have no access to these specifically medical experiences can derive practical instruction from fairy tales, and particularly from alchemy. The real subject of Hermetic philosophy is the *coniunctio oppositorum*". JUNG, C. G. (1975) *Psychology and religion: West and East. – Answer to Job.* Translated by Hull, R. F. C. 2nd edition. CW XI. Bollingen Series XX. Princeton University Press. §738.

393 "We shall now pass on to individual mandalas [...] a rearranging of the personality is involved, a kind of new centring.[...] They then have the purpose of reducing the confusion to order, though this is never the conscious intention. At all events they express order, balance, and wholeness. [...] I must preface the pictures that now follow with a few remarks on the formal elements of mandala symbolism [...] 1. *Circular, spherical,* or *egg-shaped* formation. 2. The circle is elaborated into a *flower* (rose, lotus) or a *wheel*. 3. A centre expressed by a *sun, star,* or *cross,* usually with four, eight, or twelve rays". JUNG, C. G. (1977) *The archetypes and the collective unconscious.* Translated by Hull, R. F. C. CW IX, part 2. Bollingen Series XX. Princeton University Press. §645.

394 RAFF, J. (2000) *Jung and the alchemical imagination.* Introduction. Florida: Nicolas-Hays, Inc. (Kobo eBook version).

395 Ibid.

396 JUNG, C. G. *The archetypes and the collective unconscious.* Op. Cit. §393.

397 RAFF, J. *Jung and the alchemical imagination.* Op. Cit. Chapter 1 "Jung as a spiritual tradition". "The self". [own author's highlights]

398 "[..] The only ritual that actually takes place seems to be a concentration or meditation, leading up to the ecstatic phenomenon of the voice [...] It is nearly always a final statement, usually coming toward the end of a dream, and it is, as a rule, so clear and convincing that the dreamer finds no argument against it. It has, indeed, so much the

character of indisputable truth that it can hardly be understood as anything except a final and trenchant summing up of a long process of unconscious deliberation and weighing of arguments. [...] Sometimes, as in this case, there is simply a voice coming apparently from nowhere. [...] Thus the voice revealed itself as an important and even decisive spokesman of the unconscious [...] phenomenon of the voice in dreams and in other peculiar states of consciousness, I am forced to admit that the unconscious is capable at times of manifesting an intelligence and purposiveness superior to the actual conscious insight". JUNG, C. G. (1975) *Psychology and religion: West and East.* Translated by Hull, R. F. C. 2nd edition. CW XI. Bollingen Series XX. Princeton University Press. §63.

[399] JUNG, C. G. *Memories, dreams and reflexions.* Chapter XI "On life after death". Translated by Winston, R. and C. Revised Edition. Vintage Books. (ebook) Available at: <http://www.venerabilisopus.org/en/books-samael-aun-weor-gnostic-sacred-esoteric-spiritual/pdf/200/265_jung-carl-memories-dreams-reflections.pdf> Access April 29th 2020. pp. 375 – 376.

[400] RAFF, J. *Jung and the alchemical imagination.* Op. Cit. Chapter 1 "Jung as a spiritual tradition". "The self".

[401] Ibid. Chapter 2 "The alchemical imagination". "Alchemy and imagination".

[402] Ibid. Chapter 1 "Jung as a spiritual tradition". "Psyche and psychoid".

[403] Ibid. Chapter 1 "Jung as a spiritual tradition". "Active imagination".

[404] "I would like to call attention to a possible misunderstanding which may be occasioned by the term "synchronicity." I chose this term because the simultaneous occurrence of two meaningfully but not causally connected events seemed to me an essential criterion. I am therefore using the general concept of synchronicity in the special sense of a coincidence in time of two or more causally unrelated events which have the same or a similar meaning, in contrast to "synchronism," which simply means the simultaneous occurrence of two events". JUNG, C. G. (1975) *Psychology and religion: West and East. Synchronicity.* Translated by Hull, R. F. C. 2nd edition. CW XI. Bollingen Series XX. Princeton University Press. §849.

[405] "Jung (1974) recognizes the spirit as a principle in equal standing to matter and states that instinct and archetype are identical structures **belonging to the same world**, which can appear to us either as spiritual or material. As mentioned earlier, we may be dealing with a single factor. The synchronicity phenomena point to this meaning when the non-psychic behaves as psychic and vice-versa." GALLBACH, M. R. (2006) *Learning from dreams.* Published by Daimon Verlag. p.28 [author's own highlights]

[406] RAFF, J. *Jung and the alchemical imagination.* Op. Cit. Chapter 2 "The alchemical imagination". "Alchemy and imagination".

[407] Pneûma, from the Greek. πνεῦμα, plural πνεύματα = blow; *fig.* wind; breath; exhale, odour; spirit; *t. gram.* aspiration. PEREIRA, I. (1990) [Translated from the Portuguese: *Dicionário grego-português e português-grego.* São Paulo: Apostolado da Imprensa Martins Fontes. Unpublished in English.]

[408] RAFF, J. *Jung and the alchemical imagination.* Op. Cit. Chapter 1 "Jung as a spiritual tradition". "Psyche and psychoid".

[409] Ibid. Introduction. "The beginnings of alchemy".

[410] Ibid. Chapter 1 "Jung as a spiritual tradition". "Psyche and psychoid".

[411] The *Merriam Webster Dictionary* gives the following etymology for "reveal": middle English *revelen*, from Anglo-French *reveler*, from Latin *revelare* to uncover, reveal, from *re-* + *velare* to cover, veil, from *velum* veil.

[412] "As an imagery of experience, a complex is a translation, an embodiment of the invisible. Only when the invisible is manifest as an image can we discern it and track it. The body is a path to incarnation, and a portion of it collapses when a complex is activated." HOLLIS, J. *On this journey we call our life.* [translated from the Portuguese version: (2004) *Nesta jornada que chamamos vida.* São Paulo: Paulus. p. 34.]

[413] RAFF, J. *Jung and the alchemical imagination.* Op. Cit. Chapter 2 "The alchemical imagination". "Imagination and the psychoid".

[414] Ibid. Chapter 1 "Jung as a spiritual tradition". "Active imagination".

[415] JUNG, C. G. (1977) *The archetypes and the collective unconscious.* Translated by Hull, R. F. C. CW IX, part 1. Bollingen Series XX. Princeton University Press. §393.

[416] RAFF, J. *Jung and the alchemical imagination.* Op. Cit. Chapter 1, "Jung as a spiritual tradition".

[417] *The New Jerusalem Bible.* Matthew 16:19.

[418] RAFF, J. *Jung and the alchemical imagination.* Op. Cit. Chapter 2 "The alchemical imagination". "Fantasy and imagination".

[419] Loc. cit.

[420] Loc. cit.

[421] ROTHENBERG, R. E. (2004) *A joia na ferida.* São Paulo: Editora Paulus

[422] JUNG, C. G. (1978) *Civilization in transition.* Translated by Hull, R. F. C. CW X. Bollingen Series XX. Princeton University Press. §361.

[423] RAFF, J. *Jung and the alchemical imagination.* Op. Cit. Chapter 2 "The alchemical imagination". "Fantasy and imagination".

FORCE

[...] the fire does not just belong to the manifest Self. The
references to the fire of God and to the higher powers being
hidden in the lower, suggest that the process is being fuelled, not
only by the Self, but also by **the divinity that exists beyond the
self**. The process by which the third coniunctio comes into being
aims at a new union of opposites – the union of the human and
the divine. As Dorn explained it, this level of union **binds the
individual to the unus mundus, the world of the pure spirit
and divine unity**. The motivating force for this merger comes not
only from the individual Self, but from God itself, as the two
entities are pulled together in the highest of all marriages. The
fire is the spiritual force creating a final transformation in the Self,
through which **the divine is incarnated in the human
psyche**.[424]

The very long path that goes from Eden to Golgotha is the path of
consciousness development.

Up until the third dimension, all the huge effort made was aimed at
building a strong, conscious, self-centred, defined and capable ego: the
consciousness is a type of super-specialized **energy** in which the Self has
made a huge investment to create.

The entry into the fourth dimension starts with the moral defeat, which
removes the ego from the psychological prevalence and makes the
unconscious prominent. A careless outlook, even from those who have
entered this dimension, might interpret this as a diminishing of the ego,
especially of the ego's power, which would mean a decrease in
consciousness. This is a mistake. It is true that the ego loses power when

it is made to submit to the infinite power of the Soul. But the ego only becomes smaller when compared to the Soul itself. In relation to society, to other people – whether or not from its circle of personal relationships –, and even in relation to what the ego was in the third dimension; the fourth-dimensional ego is much bigger. It is important to notice that the fourth-dimensional ego is much deeper than the third-dimensional, since it has met the Shadow; it is much more relativized, since it constantly experiences the ethical conflict; it forgives much more, since it has found morals to be void; and it experiences a much higher degree of anguish, since it must face the abysses of existence. However, darkness, relativization, conflict, forgiveness and anguish have a level of complexity – and therefore a level of development – which is much higher than the effort the third-dimensional ego makes to self-affirm and to remain in the leading position. The ego believes this position to be one of perpetual stability, given that it has indeed achieved this. In fact, this position is granted to the ego by the Soul, in an extremely temporary nature, until the moral defeat occurs. The fourth-dimensional ego knows that its power is relative, in relation to the Soul, and this relativity is due to its own consciousness about the complexity of life, a complexity that can easily defeat the ego. The third-dimensional ego believes that its power is absolute, only to see it collapse successively until it is forced to give it up completely, at the moral defeat. The fourth dimensional ego is higher than the third dimensional ego in the same way that an adult who is aware of reality and responsible is more mature than a teenager who believes that they will conquer the world. That way, when the differences between the Paradigms are correctly understood, something very controversial is noticed: **in the path to the consciousness development, the ego always grows and there is no "death of the ego"**, at least not a definitive death.

The growth of the ego in the fourth dimension is exponential in comparison to the third. Whereas a third-dimensional ego tends to identify itself with the psychological energy arising from a single archetype, which strongly dominates, the fourth-dimensional ego progressively learns to not identify itself with any of them, earning freedom with all of them. If we take the Twelve Olympian Gods as a metaphor for the Totality in the fourth dimension, a very adequate metaphor, we can say that the fourth-dimensional ego is metaphorically twelve times larger than the third-dimensional ego. To those who consider this metaphor artificial, I suggest they reflect about this in terms of the restricted capacity that the third-dimensional ego has to deal with archetypes, when compared to the fourth-dimensional ego.

The fourth dimension is a space of exponential development of consciousness. Although the risk of dissolution of the consciousness is always present, particularly in face of the intensity and savagery with which the unconscious sometimes manifests itself, it is necessary to acknowledge that the third dimension has managed to establish a strong ego, capable of, in the fourth dimension, confront divine forces, the archetypes, and finally, the Soul. The successive confrontations with these forces developed it exponentially. The ego, previously a continuous affirmation of a single way of life, has gradually become conscious and capable of managing a multi-paradoxical reality. This extremely complex path of an unquantifiable beauty was accurately described by Analytical Psychology, which more than describe it, made it possible as a practical process where anyone who has been through the moral defeat can experience.

The climax of the Paradigm of Balance, the huge multi-paradoxical consciousness, is reached in Crucifixion. It is a **death ritual**. This death occurs in a very significant place: the Golgotha. This is an Aramaic word which means **skull**. For that reason, the term was translated to Greek as κρανίου τόπος (kraníou tópos), **place of the skull**.

> They brought Jesus to the place called Golgotha, which means the place of the skull.[425]

Considering the huge distance between the Christian Symbol and the Buddhist Symbol, the most dramatic scene of Christianity finds a striking mythic parallel in the Tibetan Buddhism, in the image of *Ḍākinī*. Lama Anagarika GOVINDA reports to the Siddha literature where the *Ḍākinī* symbol appears:

> "She dwelt [...] in a sandal-wood garden, in the midst of a cemetery, in a palace of **human skulls**. When *Padmasambhava* arrived at the door of the palace, he found it closed. Thereupon a servant-woman appeared, carrying water into the Palace; and Padma sat in meditation so that her water-carrying was halted by his yogic power.
>
> Thereupon, producing a knife of crystal, she cut open her breast, and exhibited in the upper portion of it the forty-two Peaceful and in the lower portion of it the fifty-eight Wrathful Deities. Addressing Padma, she said: "I observe that thou art a wonderful mendicant, possessed of great power. But look at me; hast thou not faith in me?" Padma bowed down before her, made apology, and requested the

teachings he sought. She replied: "I am only a maidservant. Come inside".

Upon entering the palace, Padma beheld the *Ḍākinī* enthroned on a **sun and moon throne**, holding in her hands a double drum and **human-skull cup**, and surrounded by thirty-two *Ḍākinīs* making sacrificial offerings, and begged her to teach him both esoterically and exoterically. The one hundred **Peaceful and Wrathful Deities then appeared** overhead. "Behold", said the *Ḍākinī*, "the deities. Now take initiation". And Padma responded, "Inasmuch as all the Buddhas throughout the aeons have had gurus, accept me as thy disciple."

Then the *Ḍākinī* absorbed all the deities into her body. She transformed Padma into the **syllable HŪṀ**. The HŪṀ rested on her lips, and she conferred upon it the *Buddha Amithāba* blessing. Then she swallowed the HŪṀ, and inside her stomach Padma received the *Avalokiteśvara* initiation. When the HŪṀ reached the region of the Root Centre, she conferred upon him the initiation of Body, Speech and Mind.[426] [author's own highlights]

The environment where *Ḍākinī* lives is strongly indicative of her nature. The second *coniunctio* (Crucifixion) appears here as the *complexio oppositorum* that it is: *Ḍākinī* is enthroned over the Sun and the Moon. However, it is not only on this symbol that the multi-paradoxical reality of this moment is expressed: *Ḍākinī* congregates in herself the Peaceful and the Wrathful Deities, therefore it has integrated both good and evil.

But the human **skull** is the centre of the *Ḍākinī* symbolism. Lama GOVINDA teaches that, before becoming "genii of meditation", and "spiritual helpers"[427] in the Tibetan Buddhism, the *Ḍākinīs* in the classic Sanskrit were "demoniacal beings hostile to humans and haunting cremation grounds and similar lonely and uncanny places, where unknown dangers lurked"[428]. The similarity of this image with that of Lilith is huge; we will return to it later. For now, let us concentrate on its definition as deities drinking blood in human skulls and dwelling in cemeteries.

The Symbol of the skull, although extremely vast, immediately remits to death, disseminated both in the Crucifixion and in the *Ḍākinī* palace. This specific type of death means exactly what?

I categorically said above that there is **no** such a thing as the "death of the ego". And indeed, there is no **definitive** death of the ego, because such death would mean the elimination of consciousness, which would be a nihilist waste. However, the **temporary** death of the ego not only exists, but is also common – there are even archetypes for this: Διόνυσος (Dionysius), Ἅιδης (Hades), Περσεφόνεια (Persephone) and others. The moral defeat is an example of the ego's death. Nevertheless, there is no bigger death than Crucifixion. In this moment, the ego is butchered by the Self – it was not the Jews who butchered Christ, but God. This specific type of death means exactly what?

We know that the psychological structure of this moment is the multi-paradoxical reality. Such reality is characterized by a simultaneity of opposed psychological characteristics – JUNG's *complexio oppositorum*. Just as *Ḍākinī*, who has in herself both the Peaceful Deities and the Irate Deities, the Crucified 4D ego has in itself various pairs of opposed conscious and integrated energies, such as selfishness and altruism, good and evil, male and female, spiritual and corporeal, just to mention a few of the most common pairs. Each of these pairs consists of a paradox, and it is already clear that a paradox is not a compromise (nothing could be further from a paradox than a compromise); a paradox is the coexistence of two valid and opposed truths. (4D). Considering that both truths are valid and opposed, imagine the tension that a paradox creates. Now imagine the escalatory tension that the multi-paradoxical reality creates. It is **that** tension that butchers the ego.

The ego spent three dimensions striving to maintain a defined personality, one that **excluded** other possibilities. Even in the fourth dimension, the integrations took place because of the ego's sustainment of **its** position, whereas the unconscious sustained **its own**. However, in the multi-paradoxical reality, the ego is suddenly no longer able to maintain any position, and its structure is shattered.

What does that mean, in practice? It means that the ego can no longer sustain a defined personality (however much it has its preferences), therefore it can no longer say "I am this and not that": **it can no longer exclude**. The limitation that the ego imposed upon itself in order to exist disappears: the ego is this **and also** that, the ego is selfish and simultaneously altruist, it is good and simultaneously evil, it is masculine and simultaneously feminine, it is spiritual and simultaneously corporeal, etc. Therefore, the structure of limitation that defined the ego for many eras, from Eden to Golgotha, is destroyed, and with it, the ego itself.

Christ does not love all because he forces himself to accept them all, even if begrudgingly, as do the passive-aggressive spiritualists of various denominations. Christ loves all because he has no interior limitations and found in himself all the characteristics, so he is not shocked with the existence of these characteristics in others. Christ does not love the whore because she is a human being despite being a whore; this is an arrogant stance, because it establishes a supposed superiority of Christ in relation to the whore. Christ loves the whore because he has discovered that he is himself a whore, he has the same desires as the whore and acts upon them. Being himself a whore, why would he not love whores? More than that, why would he not have sex with the whores? The same rationale is applied to any other "enemy" with which Christ has reconciled: the "tax collectors", Pharisees, centurions, thieves, Caesars and other criminals. Christ, besides all virtues considered good, which are classically attributed to him, was simultaneously a whore, an ambitious man, a liar, aggressive, thief, powerful and all else that one can imagine of good and evil. **This** is the multi-paradoxical reality that shatters the Crucified ego: no longer being capable of **defining** (ending), **restricting** (impose limits), **sustaining** itself as before, the structure of the ego becomes too unstable and **dies**.

It is precisely at this point that the access to the *Truth* is opened, the *Truth* of the *Spirit*, which reigns in the Paradigm of Sense. ***Truth* kills**. The *Truth* kills because the ego realises that everything it believed itself to be, everything it was proud to be, everything it passionately defended, everything it believed in was but a means for the ego to constitute itself, so that the consciousness could be formed and established. Nothing else. All this was strictly necessary, indispensable, since without all that there would be no consciousness. Nothing else. That in which the ego believed was just one of the many paths that lead to God, equal to many others. Nothing else. There was nothing special about that way of being. When the ego finishes its formation and consciousness is established, the limited personality of the ego and its beliefs have fulfilled their role until the end and become useless, disposable. From the perspective of the egos in formation, of the egos that run across the path from Eden to Golgotha, this is a huge disappointment, a stabbing pain; it is death on the cross. **The *Truth* kills because, paradoxically, "nothing is true, everything is permitted"**[429].

* * * * *

A moment before dying on the Cross, consciousness is at its peak. The ego does not die in chaos. On the contrary, it dies in the totally defined psychological organization of the **four** arms of the Cross, a classic Jungian Symbol. In the same way, before entering the palace of death of *Ḍākinī*, Padma **meditated** and saw the servant cut herself with a **crystal knife**. Remember that, up until Crucifixion the human consciousness is dualist, so it depends on duality to develop and differentiate one thing from the other; the knife is an excellent Symbol for differentiation. It is a crystal knife, however, since this consciousness is clear, crystalline. The very long path that goes from Eden to Golgotha is a path of consciousness development. A moment before dying on the Cross, consciousness is at its peak.

On the Cross, **consciousness expires**. Until Golgotha, the structure of consciousness is dualist. The multi-paradoxical reality tenses the consciousness until its limits explode, and with that, duality explodes. Without the dualism which supported its fundamental stone, consciousness is no longer sustained and expires. **This** is the ego's death. After death on the Cross, the **ego** will *Resurrect*. The consciousness that appears after *Resurrection* is of a completely different nature – no longer based on duality, for the first time, the fundamental stone of consciousness is unity. Consciousness in the Paradigm of Sense is unified. To expire on the Cross is the lapse of eternity necessary to replace the fundamental stone, from dual to unified, for the *Spirit* to manifest in the *Body*.

Let us contemplate the Symbol of *Ḍākinī* more in depth. Lama GOVINDA teaches that the notion of *Ḍākinī* was reinterpreted when translated from Sanskrit to Tibetan Buddhism.

> This change in the conception [...] is reflected in the Tibetan rendering of the word '*Ḍākinī*' as '*Khadoma*' (*mkhaḥ-ḥgro-ma*): 'mkhah' means 'space' as well as 'ether' (Skt.: *ākāśa*), the **fifth element**, according to the Buddhist definition; in other words, that which makes movement possible (Symbol: '**Wind**', Tib.: *rluṅ*) and makes forms appear (Tib.: *snaṅ-ba*), without being itself movement or appearance.[430] [author's own highlights]

It is very meaningful that *Ḍākinī*, as *Khadoma*, is symbolised by the Wind, the western Symbol for *Spirit*, and that it represents the **fifth** element. Considering that the Paradigm of Sense is the conscience structure of the *cakra viśuddha*, the *cakra* of the larynx, and that the *Spirit* is *Manifested* through the *Word*, the fact that a **mantric syllable** appears associated with *Ḍākinī* – the HŪṀ – becomes extremely important. In order to reach a minimum understanding of HŪṀ, however, it is necessary to have a minimum understanding of OṀ, another mantric syllable. Let us see what Tibetan Buddhism teaches about HŪṀ.

In the experience of OṀ, man opens himself, goes beyond himself, **liberates himself, by breaking through the narrow confines of egohood or self-imposed limitation, and thus he becomes one with the All, with the Infinite**. If he would remain in this state, there would be an end to his existence as an individual, as a living, thinking and experiencing being. He would have attained perfect self-annihilation, perfect quietude, but also perfect immobility, passivity, emotionlessness, and insensibility with regard to all differentiation and individuality not only within, but also outside himself, i.e., with regard to all living and suffering beings.431 [author's own highlights]

Contemplating the idea translated from OṀ, we see that it is close to the notion of Crucifixion: in both Symbols, the egoic limits are completely overcome and there is a union with the Whole, the Infinite. However, in the same way that DORNEUS says that the second *coniunctio* is **not** the end of the alchemic process, insisting on the third *coniunctio*, the *Unus Mundus*, the Tibetan Buddhism does not see OṀ as the end of the consciousness development, since ending the union with the Whole would mean the end of existence for the individual, a depersonalisation, a dehumanisation. It is precisely to go beyond OṀ that HŪṀ appears.

It is the *human* element in the character of the Buddha, which softens the brightness of his perfection and relieves it of the apparent distance and aloofness from ordinary human life; for his compassion is as great as his wisdom, his **humanity** and warmth of feeling as all-embracing as his mind.

He **has returned from the experience of universality** – from the sacred all-consuming and purifying flame of OṀ – to the human plane, without losing the consciousness of completeness, the knowledge of the unity of man and cosmos. And thus in the depth of his heart the primordial sound of Reality is transferred into the sound of the cosmic-human mystery (purified through suffering and compassion) which reverberates through all the scriptures of the Mahāyānā and Vajrayāna, and in the sacred seed-syllable HŪṀ.

OṀ is the ascent towards universality, **HŪṀ the descent** of the state of universality into the depth of the human heart. HŪṀ cannot be without OṀ. But HŪṀ is more than OṀ: it is the Middle Way which neither gets lost in the finite nor in the infinite, which is neither attached to the one or the other extreme.

[...]

OṀ, in its dynamic aspect, is the breaking through of the individual into the super-individual consciousness, the breaking through towards the 'absolute', the liberation from egohood, from the illusion of 'I'. To dwell in the 'absolute' is as impossible for a living being as floating in a vacuum, because life and consciousness are possible only where there are relations. The experience of OṀ must be sheltered and brought to maturity in that of HŪṀ. **OṀ is like the sun, but HŪṀ is like the soil**, into which the sun's rays must **descend** in order to awaken the dormant life.

OṀ is the infinite, but HŪṀ is the infinite in the finite, the eternal in the temporal, the timeless in the moment, the unconditioned in the conditioned, the formless as basis of all form, the transcendental in the ephemeral: it is the Wisdom of the Great Mirror, which reflects the Void (*śūnyatā*) as much as the objects, and reveals the 'emptiness' in the things as much as the things in the 'emptiness'.[432] [author's own highlights]

The parallel between saying that [after being] "purified through suffering and compassion", [Buddha] **"has returned from the experience of universality [...] to the human plane"** and saying that Christ, after suffering on the Cross, returned from the experience of union with God, resuscitating amongst mankind.[433] is astounding. It is also astounding to notice the parallel between the Wisdom of the Great Mirror, which reflects the Emptiness in the objects and vice-versa, and the *Unus Mundus*, which reflects the *Spirit* in the Matter and vice-versa.

However astounding these parallels are, we aim to understand – even if minimally – the HŪṀ. From what has been seen – after an experience of universality (OṀ), that is, after an experience of stable union with the Whole – it is fundamental to return to the human level, in order to realise the Whole in the human life and in the material world[434] (HŪṀ). For that reason, "HŪṀ is more than OṀ", since even bigger than to be united to the Whole is to realise the Whole in the human life and material world. **This** was the initiation that *Ḍākinī* gave to Padma – HŪṀ – the realisation of the Whole in the human life, in the BODY and in the material world.

Let us look at the path as a whole. The long path of consciousness formation has as its first objective reaching the OṀ: the shattering of duality and the limits of the egoic personality, to reach universality, the union with the Whole. This process leads to *Ḍākinī*. *Ḍākinī* then grants the initiation of the HŪṀ. From this point, the objective is to reach HŪṀ: return from the union with the Whole to the human life, realising the Whole in the human life and in the material world. In the Tibetan Buddhism we also see the image of ascend and descend: "OṀ is the ascent towards universality, HŪṀ the descent of the state of universality into the depth of the human heart." Or: "OṀ is like the sun, but HŪṀ is like the soil, into which the sun's rays must descend in order to awaken the dormant life." The ascend to OṀ leads to *Ḍākinī*, whose symbol is the skull, from which point the initiation to HŪṀ is granted and the descend starts. In the Symbol of *Ḍākinī*, the HŪṀ descends from its lips until *mulādhāra*, the root *cakra*, in the hips. The image is undeniable: the process of uniting with the Whole is a process of consciousness development through duality, which ascends to the skull, where death occurs, and from this point, the direction of energy is inverted and starts to descend.

The same movement occurs in the Symbol of Christ. The long path of consciousness development is an ascend that starts at Eden and culminates at Golgotha, the skull. Immediately, the direction of the energy is inverted, and it starts to descend. The death of Christ, in the skull, causes an immediate effect **below**:

> But Jesus, again crying out in a loud voice, yielded up his spirit. [...] **the tombs opened** and the bodies of many holy people rose from the dead, and these, after his resurrection, came out of the tombs, entered the holy city and appeared to a number of people.[435] [author's own highlights]

Christ himself, after its Crucifixion in the skull, is taken by Joseph of Arimathea to the grave.

> He then took it **down**, wrapped it in a shroud and put it in a **tomb which was hewn in stone** and which had never held a body.[436] [author's own highlights]

The *Symbolum Apostolicum*, the Apostolic Creed[437], in its fourth and fifth articles, also mentions the descend of Christ:

> 4. Suffered under Pontius Pilate, was crucified, died and was buried;
>
> 5. **he descended into hell**; [author's own highlights]

Even though, following that, the *Symbolum Apostolicum* mentions the ascend of Christ, we have seen that this ascension is aimed at the arrival of Παράκλητος (Paraclete), sent by him; and the *Holy Spirit* **descends from heaven**.

The inversion of the energy direction that occurs when OṀ is reached, the inversion of the energy direction that occurs in Crucifixion, is the inversion of energy that occurs in the passage from the Paradigm of Balance to the Paradigm of Sense. In the Paradigm of Sense, the energy is descending: the *Spirit* descends from heaven.

In practice, however, what does the inversion of energy direction mean? The nature of the ascendant energy must be different from the nature of the descendant energy.

> So John declared before them all, "I baptise you with **water**, but someone is coming, who is more powerful than me, and I am not fit to undo the strap of his sandals; he will baptise you **with the Holy Spirit and fire**."[438] [author's own highlights]

We know that the path that goes from Eden to Golgotha is the path of consciousness development: the ascendant energy is the energy named **consciousness**. We now need to understand the descendant energy of the Paradigm of Sense.

The end product of ascension is the ground zero of the descent: unity. Let us bear this in mind, whilst we study the descendant energy. This is how the *Ḍākinī* (= *Khadoma*) is described:

> *Khadomas*, like all female embodiments of *vidyā*, or knowledge, have the property of intensifying, concentrating, and integrating the **forces** of which they make use, until they are focused in one **incandescent** point and **ignite** the **holy flame of inspiration**, which leads to perfect enlightenment. The *Khadomas*, who appear as visions or as consciously produced inner images in the course of meditation, are therefore represented with an aura of **flames** and called up with the seed-syllable HŪṀ, the mantric symbol of integration. They are the embodiment of the 'Inner **Fire**', which in Milarepa's biography has been called 'the **warming breath** of *Khadomas*', which surrounds and protects the saint like a 'pure, soft mantle'.[439] [author's own highlights]

Both the *Holy Spirit* and *Khadoma* are igneous descendant energy. The first element that is related to this interior fire is *Inspiration*. As we have seen several times, both "spirit" and "inspire" have the same etymologic root. According to the *Merriam-Webster Dictionary*, both "spirit" and "inspire" come from the Latin *spirare*, to breathe. All these terms refer to the Greek notion that Spirit is *pneûma*, that is, wind. That way, *Holy Spirit* and *Inspiration* are the same thing – the *Spirit* inspires. The *Merriam-Webster Dictionary* defines *inspire*: "*to influence, move, or guide by divine or supernatural* **inspiration**".

Unfortunately, nowadays, there is no ample knowledge of what *Inspiration* is. I suspect that the poorly elaborated notion that is currently used is that inspiration is something soft, tenuous, vague, almost inapprehensible, something like a thought or an idea that, for example, artists choose to create this or that way. Inspiration is treated as a rationally chosen definition, for example, the artist can choose if they want to carry out their work this or that way. This vague notion is based on the strong tendency for rationality, typical of our times.

Nothing could be further from the truth. *Inspiration* is **overwhelming**, takes one with violence and suddenly. Peter tells us: "'One day, when I was in the town of Jaffa', he began, 'I fell into **a trance** as I was praying and had a vision'"[440]. Note that this is not about a thought that passes through consciousness, but about **being swept** from one consciousness state to another.

Has anyone at the end of the nineteenth century any distinct notion of what poets of a stronger age understood by the word inspiration? If not, I will describe it. If one had the smallest vestige of superstition left in one, it would hardly be possible completely to set aside the idea that one is the mere incarnation, mouthpiece, or *medium* of an **almighty power**. The idea of revelation, in the sense that something which profoundly convulses and upsets one becomes suddenly visible and audible with indescribable certainty and accuracy – describes the simple fact. One hears – one does not seek; one takes – one does not ask who gives: a thought suddenly flashes up like lightning, it comes with necessity, without faltering – **I have never had any choice** in the matter. There is an ecstasy so great that the immense strain of it is sometimes relaxed by a flood of tears, during which one's steps now involuntarily rush and anon involuntarily lag. There is the feeling that **one is utterly out of hand**, with the very distinct consciousness of an endless number of fine thrills and titillations descending to one's very toes; – there is a depth of happiness in which the most painful and gloomy parts do not act as antitheses to the rest, but are produced and required as necessary shades of colour in such an overflow of light. There is an instinct for rhythmic relations which embraces a whole world of forms (length, the need of a wide-embracing rhythm, is almost the measure of the force of an inspiration, a sort of counterpart to its pressure and tension). **Everything happens quite involuntarily, as if in a tempestuous outburst of freedom, of absoluteness, of power and divinity. The involuntary nature of the figures and similes is the most remarkable thing; one loses all perception of what is imagery and metaphor**; everything seems to present itself as the readiest, the truest, and simplest means of expression. It actually seems, to use one of Zarathustra's own phrases, as if all things came to one, and offered themselves as similes. ("Here do all things come caressingly to thy discourse and flatter thee, for they would fain ride upon thy back. On every simile thou ridest here unto every truth. Here fly open unto thee all the speech and word shrines of the world, here would all existence become speech, here would all Becoming learn of thee how to speak.") This is my experience of inspiration. I do not doubt but that I should have to go back thousands of years before I could find another who could say to me: "It is mine also![441] [author's own highlights]

Inspiration is not rational and cannot be chosen by the ego – "one does not seek". NIETZSCHE shows the **transcendental** character of *Inspiration*, highlighting its involuntary and sudden character. The inspired individual experiences being "utterly out of hand" and "never [having] any choice".

Inspiration is "involuntary". Being *Spirit*, *Inspiration* is manifested as "involuntary nature of the figures and similes is the most remarkable thing; one loses all perception of what is **imagery and metaphor**". Being *Spirit*, *Inspiration* is manifested paradoxically as *Body*, as something that "becomes suddenly visible and audible", "an ecstasy so great that the immense strain of it is sometimes relaxed by a flood of tears [...] with the very distinct consciousness of an endless number of fine thrills and titillations descending to one's very toes". *Inspiration* is *Image* AND it is *Body*.

Being *Spirit*, *Inspiration* is manifested both as something **luminous**, as a "overflow of light", and as something **dark**, "painful and gloomy", nonetheless "required" – *Inspiration* is not dual.

Inspiration is involuntary, and makes the individual learn things that it did not know before, makes it "speak different languages"[442]. We saw that *Spirit* is the *Creating Word* and cooperates with the fifth-dimensional ego in *Creative Pneumatic Acts*. In NIETZSCHE's text, we realize the creating power of *Inspiration*, as "things came to one, and offered themselves as similes": "here do all things come caressingly to thy discourse and flatter thee, for they would fain ride upon thy back. On every simile thou ridest here unto every truth. Here fly open unto thee all the speech and word shrines of the world, here would all existence become speech, here would all Becoming learn of thee how to speak". *Inspiration* leads the individual to *Create*; "with necessity", the individual **needs** to *Create.*

In a very similar way, the Tibetan Buddhism describes the dimension of Buddha's "body", which they call *Sambhogakāya*, Body of Bliss:

> [...] that which constitutes the spiritual or ideal character of a Buddha, the **creative** expression or formulation of this universal principle in the realm of inner vision: the *Sambhogakāya*, the 'Body of Bliss' (rapture or spiritual enjoyment), from which **all true inspiration is born**; [...]

> In the *Dharmakāya*, the universal principle of all consciousness, the totality of becoming and being is potentially contained – comparable to the infinity of space, which embraces all things and is the *condition sine qua non* of all that exists. Yet we can neither say that space is identical with things, nor that it is different from them. As little as we can become conscious of space without its opposite pole, i.e., form, so the *Dharmakāya* cannot become reality for us without **descending** into forms.

> This happens in two ways: in the realm of pure form, or pure mental perception, i.e., in the realm of ideas – and in the realm of action, of individuality, of materialization or embodiment. In states of rapture, trance and highest intuition, as characterized by the stages of deep absorption in meditation (*dhyāna*), we experience the *Dharmakāya* as the luminous forms of purely spiritual perception – as pure, eternal principles of form, freed from all accidentals – or as the exalted visions of a higher reality. In them the *Sambhogakāya*, 'the Body of Bliss [= Inspiration]' is realized. From it flow all immortal art, all deep wisdom, all profound truths (*dharma*, in the sense of formulated or proclaimed truth). Its enjoyment is of two kinds, like that of every great work of art: the rapture of the creative act and the enjoyment of those who contemplate the completed work by retrospectively experiencing and reliving the act of creation.[443] [author's own highlights]

What we find in common in the descriptions of NIETZSCHE and Lama GOVINDA about the *Inspiration* is the states of **ecstasy** and **trance**. There are many ways of reaching these states. NIETZSCHE describes it as entirely autonomous. Lama GOVINDA admits this possibility and adds the access through deep meditative states. It is worth noting that one of the ways to reach such states is through rituals that use psychoactive substances. In Ancient Greece, there were the Dionysian rites, which used both wine and other psychoactive substances to reach ecstasy and trance[444]. In South America, particularly in Brazil, various indigenous cultures used the *ayahuasca* plant, which opens a powerful trance. One of the most widespread traditions is the *Daime*, a syncretism between the indigenous culture and Christianity. The participants refer to a powerful state of ecstasy and trance, of Divine *Inspiration*, triggered by *ayahuasca* as "being in the force".

So, *Inspiration* has nothing of vague, tenuous or rational.

Being *Spirit*, **the *Inspiration* must be understood as *Powerful Force***. Therefore, *Spirit*, *Inspiration*, the descendant energy (5D) of the Paradigm of Sense is **not** consciousness, although it originates from a multi-paradoxical climax of consciousness, in Crucifixion, in the skull (4D). *Spirit*, *Inspiration*, the descendant energy (5D) of the Paradigm of Sense is *Force*. Whether it is autonomously triggered by deep meditative states, or by the ritual use of psychoactive substances, the *Force* as an *Inspiration* is *Pneumatic* – simultaneously *Image* and *Body*. On the one hand, it is *Macroimage*. The path that the ego has tread in the direction of the Symbol (*Image*), in detriment of the *Instinct*, was much longer and, initially, the experience of the *Force* is closer to the *Pneumatic Image* in its **visual** aspect. On the other hand, the descendant nature of the *Force* tends to grow the *Instinctive* experience of the *Pneumatic Image* in the *Body*, until the **instinctive** aspect of the *Force* is as evident in its experience as it is in its **visual** aspect.

Since the beginning, the *Force* is *Instinctive* (**libidinal**). Being fifth-dimensional, the ego is already capable, on the first day in the Paradigm of Sense, of having strongly *Instinctual* experiences, as an integral dimension of the *Pneumatic* experience – Lilith's self-exile has ended. However, in its descent, the *Force* gathers even more *Instinctual* power to the *Pneumatic* experience, because the *Force Educates Demons* (= *Dynamic Forces*).

* * * * *

The *Force* arises from the climax of an ascendant consciousness. The climax bursts the limits of duality, projecting itself in the infinite. Henceforth, the fifth-dimensional "consciousness", beyond the multi-paradoxical reality (4D), becomes a *Pneumatic Truth*, is unified, is *Inspiration*, is *Force*.

Now that we know its origin, we turn to look at its destiny.

Returning to the metaphor JUNG used for the psyche, where he compared consciousness to the spectrum of colour, with the visual archetypal dimension at the ultraviolet end, and the instinctual archetypal dimension at the infrared end, we see that the *Force* goes from the ultraviolet to the infrared. Therefore, **the *Force* moves from the *Image* towards the *Instinct*.** In other words, the consciousness developed through the contact with the multi-paradoxical reality of the infinite is now focused on the *Instinct*. Indeed, in the Paradigm of Sense, the archetype of Lilith ends its self-exile, entering Paradise again. This means that, in the fifth-dimensional ego, the *Instinct* is no longer in second place, subordinate to the archetype, but instead moves to the first place and is priority. The objective is no longer to reach the conscience of the paradoxical Balance among the archetypes, but to **realise** the *Pneumatic Truth*, in the *Body* and matter. With this as an end to be reached, one can no longer ignore the *Instinct*.

The *Instinct* is, however, at this point, extremely dangerous, since any element kept outside consciousness for too long reveals its raw and inferior state when finally reached[445]. The *Instinct* was kept outside the consciousness since the origin of consciousness itself. Imagine its state when it finally finds its way back to consciousness: it is in a totally raw state, it is *Demoniac*.

To avoid this danger and make the development of consciousness and self-consciousness viable, Lilith remained in self-exile from Eden to Golgotha, and the ego kept following the archetypal dimension in detriment of the instinctual dimension. As an exiled instinctual force, Lilith is the *Demon*, whose character is essentially libidinal, instinctual.

But Lilith's self-exile cannot persist forever, and her return to the Paradise of Eden is one of the milestones for opening the Paradigm of Sense. The reality of this paradigm is the *Spirit*, whose structure is completely different from that of the Soul. *Spirit* is unity, "a great help and an equally great danger."[446]. The *Spirit* is the Whole, encompassing everything there is – the *Universe*. This is the sky-high reality reached in Crucifixion. However, if the *Spirit* encompasses **everything**, it also encompasses the *Demon*, the Part – the *Reverse*.

Said in that way, though, everything becomes very abstract. We saw that the *Spirit* is manifested in practice as *Force*. Now, we must ask how does the *Demon* manifest in practice.

William Blake gives an important clue when he shows that Hell takes care of Energy and Action:

> Good is the passive that obeys reason; Evil is **the active springing from Energy**. Good is heaven. Evil is hell.[447] [author's own highlights]

JUNG, in turn, points in the same direction, showing that the **energy** and the **dynamism** of the psyche are identical to the instinctual arena.

> In all ordinary cases the unconscious is unfavourable or dangerous only because we are not at one with it and therefore in opposition to it. A negative attitude to the unconscious, or its splitting off, is detrimental in so far as **the dynamics of the unconscious *are identical with instinctual energy***. Disalliance with the unconscious is synonymous with loss of instinct and rootlessness.[448] [author's own highlights]

Or still:

> Whatever man's wholeness, or the self, may mean per se, empirically it is **an image of the goal of life** spontaneously produced by the unconscious, irrespective of the wishes and fears of the conscious mind. It stands for the goal of the total man, for the realization of his wholeness and individuality with or without the consent of his will. **The dynamic [force] of this process is instinct**, which ensures that everything which belongs to an individual's life shall enter into it, whether he consents or not, or is conscious of what is happening or not.[449] [author's own highlights]

In this extract, JUNG is even clearer. The meaning of Self for mankind is empirically an **image** of life's purpose, whereas the *dynamis* **[force]** of this process is the **instinct**. Image and instinct appear as complementary poles and instinct is called δύναμις (*dýnamis*) [force] of this process. It follows that the image and the purpose that the Self is and provides to the ego only **happen to human life** when the instinct comes into play, as it is the *dýnamis* [force] of this process. For that reason, the instinct has the important role of making sure that whatever is transcendent is integrated to the "individual's life".

In the Paradigm of Sense, all this moves to first place.

The *Pneumatic Image* is the construction of the *Universe* itself, is reality itself, therefore it is everything that we are, what we see and what we live. For that reason, it is also the space of *Creation* and *Inspiration* itself. Nonetheless, if we contemplate only the imagistic aspect of the cosmos, we would be in awe, but would not **act**. Everything would be extremely beautiful – the cosmos is extremely beautiful – but nothing would **happen**. The cosmos would be static. It is, therefore, necessary that some sort of energy **moves** this infinitude of *Images*. The *Instinct* is precisely this aspect: it is the **dynamism**, the **energy** necessary for the *Image* to **incarnate. To integrate the *Instinct* to *Image* is to make the *Image* happen in the *Body***. Therefore, the objective of the Paradigm of Sense is to consciously integrate the *Demon* to the *Spirit*, to progressively and wholly integrate the *Instinctual* dynamism to the *Pneumatic Image*, paving the way until the *Unus Mundus*. In the *Pneumatic* reality, *Image* and *Instinct* are both absolutely indispensable.

The relationship between the *Spirit* and the *Demon* reveals even more intimate. Given that the *Spirit* understands the *Totality* of *Images*[450] (*Macroimage*) and that from it comes *Inspiration*, it manifests itself as *Force*. A part of the *Spirit*, the *Demon*, is *Instinct* [451], is Energy, is the **dynamic** part of the *Force*, and for that reason named *Dynamic Force*.

The Paradigm of Sense treads precisely this path: it goes from the *Pneumatic Image* in direction of the *Instinct*, which, as we have seen, is initially *Demoniac*. This is an extreme danger – the *Spirit* is dangerous – since the *Demon* is temptation, lies and accusation. The *Demon* is **power**, natural power. At this point, one must fatally face the **temptation of power**. How to deal with this terrible aspect, so absolutely necessary?

Once again, the image of *Ḍākinī* contributes to understanding. Contemplating *Ḍākinī*, we saw that the *Force* goes from OṀ to HŪṀ, which is in the heart. However, from there, the *Force* descends until the hips, until the *cakra mulādhāra*. In this *cakra*, resides the force known as *Kuṇḍalinī*.

> United with the *Śakti* (~*Kuṇḍalinī*) be full of **power**. [...] From the union of *Śiva* and *Śakti* the world is created.[452] [author's own highlights]

Therefore, we can say that *Śakti* [~*Kuṇḍalinī*] is **power**. However, Lama Govinda teaches that this power is illusionary.

To the Buddhist *śakti* is *māyā*, the very **power that creates illusion** [...]. It is therefore not the aim of the Buddhist to acquire power, or to join himself to the powers of the universe, either to become their instrument or to become their master.[453] [author's own highlights]

Knowing that the nature of *Śakti* or of *Kuṇḍalinī* is instinctive, and that the union with her leads to power, an illusionary power, power to "create the world", one sees that the notion of *Kuṇḍalinī* is close to the notion of *Demon*.

The latent energy of this centre is depicted as the dormant force of the goddess *Kuṇḍalinī* – who as the *śakti* of *Brahma* embodies **the potentiality of nature**, whose effects may be either divine or **demoniacal**. The wise, who control these forces, may reach through them the highest spiritual power and perfection, while **those who ignorantly release them, will be destroyed by them**.

Just as the primordial forces, locked up in the atom, can be utilized for the benefit as well as for the destruction of humanity, so the forces, which dwell in the human body, may lead to liberation as well as to bondage towards the light as well as **into utter darkness**.[454] [author's own highlights]

In the same way that to abandon the *imaginatio* of the *Images* of the *Spirit* because of the *phantasia* of the *Demon* is not the objective of the Paradigm of Sense, *Śakti* is not the objective of the Tibetan Buddhism, which in its turn, contemplates the Image of *Ḍākinī*.

In place of *Kuṇḍalinī Śakti* the opposite principle occupies the centre of the meditation, namely that of the *Ḍākinī* [...] This does not mean that the Buddhist Tantrics denied or underrated the importance or the reality of the forces connected with the *Kuṇḍalinī*, but only that their methods were different, and that the use they made of these forces was different. They did not use them in their natural state, but through the influence of another medium.

Water-power, which in a waterfall appears in its crude, untamed form, can be tamed, directed, distributed and utilized on different levels. In a similar way in the Buddhist *Tantra Yoga* concentration is not directed upon the *Kuṇḍalinī* or the Root Centre [=*mūlādhāra*], but on the channels, the main power-currents whose tension (or 'gravitational' force) is regulated through a temporal damming-up and modification of the energy-content in the upper Centres.

> Instead of the **natural power** of the Kundalini, the **inspirational impulse** of consciousness (*prajñā*) in form of *Khadoma* and her mantric equivalents is made the **leading principle** [...].[455][author's own highlights]

> [HŪṀ] is this power of supreme sacrifice [returning from Totality and realizing it in life], which vanquishes the Evil One (Māra) and drives away his **hosts of demons**.[456] [author's own highlights]

The *Force* as an impulse of *Inspiration*, is erected as a guiding principle of the *Demon* (= *Dynamic Force*).

Entering the Paradigm of Sense involves access to the *Spirit*, simultaneously *Pneumatic Image* and *Demoniac* Abyss. *Spirit* is movement, therefore, *Creative*. However, the *Demon*, being a dimension of the *Spirit*, resists *Creation*, the new, proposing *Repetition*. This difference causes friction, in other words, **energy**. Aligned with the *Force*, impulse of *Inspiration* of the *Spirit*, the fifth-dimensional ego observes the *Pneumatic Image* and creates from it (*imaginatio*), performing fifth-dimensional acts. But *Creation* causes a *Demoniac* uprising, in resistance to it, proposing *Repetition*. The 5D ego, existing in a totally unified reality, needs to acknowledge that the *Demon's* resistance to *Creation* is its own resistance to *Create*, i.e., of making the energy descend. In order to overcome this resistance, it will need to use *Force* and *Create*.

One cannot underestimate the importance of the *Demoniac Forces*, because although the *Spirit* is *Image* and *Inspiration*, the *Demon* is power. However much a non-integrated power creates illusion (*phantasia*), without power nothing can be done. It is essential that the *Force* directs the *Demon* towards the realization of the *Pneumatic Image* in the *Body* and matter through fifth-dimensional acts. It is the role of the 5D ego to associate itself to the *Force* and *Educate* the *Demon*.

> Man is the central seat of all created things. Through the force of his imagination (this being the focal point of everything), all things in the world must obey him, as before the Fall.[457]

That way, the fifth-dimensional ego acquires a legitimate fifth-dimensional power to realize the *Pneumatic Image* in the *Body* and matter through fifth-dimensional acts.

That way, the *Unus Mundus* is realized.

* * * * *

Let us return to the practical experience of the *Force*.

Before anything else, it is important to affirm that, while the Paradigm of Sense is already open, the previous dimensions do not discontinue their movement. So, the third dimension continues to strengthen the ego, now supported by mechanisms that come from two dimensions above (fourth and fifth), and the fourth dimension continues to produce a consciousness climax, integrating more and more symbolic contents, reflected by the Soul through the *Truth* of the SPIRIT that moves in the fifth dimension.

Such consciousness climax continually discharges influxes of *Force*, which descend. The fifth-dimensional ego continually contemplates the *Macroimage*, and from it makes choices that make *Sense* to it. This ego continually follows the *Force*, which means that it is constantly *Inspired*. "The *Force* acts. [...] pulls the spiritual consciousness until its *Manifestation*."[458] Therefore, the 5D ego is in continuous action in order to *Draw* images of the *Spirit, Creating*.

However, we cannot forget that, when the 5D ego chooses a certain *Image* in the *Macroimage*, it causes a cosmic *Unbalance* – since one *Image* will receive more investment of energy than the others – resulting in the appearance of the *Demon*. The *Unbalance* and the appearance of the *Demon* are in no way undesirable or result of a mistake of the 5D ego, but instead something totally natural in the fifth dimension, and therefore expected, even desired. For that reason, the *Demon, Dynamic Force* of the *Spirit* will always resist the *Creation* of the *Spirit*. That way, a *Demoniac* uprising is opposed to the fifth-dimensional *Creative* act of the 5D ego, an uprising of the *Dynamic Force*.

How does the *Force* interact with the *Dynamic Force*?

Let us remind ourselves that the mythical symbol for the *Demon* is the Fall of Lucifer. We learned that, originally, the *Demon* is an *Angel* who falls, that is, a dimension of the *Spirit* that is opposed, **paradoxically**, to the *Creation* of the *Spirit*[459]. That way, the *Demon* was previously a **Spiritual Image**, but after opposing to the *Spirit*, becomes a **perverse power**, *Perverting* the fifth-dimensional spiritual *Creation*. If it is allowed to act freely, it will cause the emergence of "utter darkness" and the "destruction of humanity".

The *Demoniac* perversion will invariably seek power, will have the desire to create alternative realities, *Repetitive* ones, and to achieve this it will use temptation, lies and accusation. It is important to remember that, since the *Pneumatic* reality is *Spirit* and *Body* at the same time, the *Demoniac* uprising acts on the individual both spiritually, spreading terrifying *Pneumatic* images and causing psychological *Unbalance*, as well as physically and materially, causing nefarious events.

To deal with this situation, the 5D ego must be **strongly conscious** of the *Demoniac* uprising, clearly noticing what the *Demon* is doing, spiritually, physically and materially – which, in five dimensions, is the same thing. When the 5D ego has a unified consciousness, maintaining contact with the infinite and, simultaneously, is sufficiently aware of the *Demon*, knowing its Name and its perverse action, the *Force* awakens. The *Force*, with its *Creative* impulse of *Inspiration*, descends.

In its descent process, **the *Force Educates* the *Dynamic Force***. The term "*Educate*" was carefully chosen because it accurately describes the nature of the *Force*. In its perverse state, the *Demon* is invariably crude and rough, it is violent. It lacks aesthetics. It lacks, above all, humanity. The *Demoniac* action is always somewhat awkward. Even though the *Demon* tempts, it does not achieve. Lucifer, for example, is adept of luxury and glamour; but its superstar attitude prevents it from having actual style. Haures seeks beauty but does so through plagiarism. The *Force*, on the other hand, appears beautiful: it is the very force of *Inspiration*. It is extremely elegant, and has the natural poise of true class, true politeness, as does the beautiful lady that delicately holds the mouth of a powerful lion, on the 11th Arcane of the Tarot de Marseille, the Strength. The *Force* gives the Opposer "a containing embrace, one which does not underestimate its danger, nor does it let it run wild and chaotic. But always recognizes him."[460]

The *Force* does not act forcefully – except as a last resource, since violence is also part of Wholeness. The *Force* is all wisdom, originating from the multi-paradoxical consciousness of the infinite: the *Pneumatic Truth*. It does not deny the *Demoniac* but incorporates it in its wisdom. It incorporates the *Dynamic Force* within itself, whereas the 5D ego employs both – *Force* and *Dynamic Force* – in its *Creative* act. It is important to notice that the *Force* is pure spiritual energy that moves towards the *Body*, the materialization. In its path, it finds the *Demon*, who, resisting *Creation*, has no *Body* and refuses to do so. But the use of the *Demon* in the *Creative* act of the 5D ego channels the *Demoniac* dynamism to the *Body*, materializing it. With that, it neutralizes its *Demoniac* potential, its perverse power, now *Embodied*. There is no longer any free energy that can oppose to the *Creation* process. The energy was materialized in the *Body*. "The place for the *Demon* is in the *Body*."[461]

The *Demon*, previously a perverse power that was opposed to the *Creative* act, now guided by the *Inspiration* of the *Force*, starts to **cooperate** with the *Creative* act, adding its **dynamism** to it. The process of *Education* of the *Dynamic Force* by the *Force* also accelerates the achievement of the *Creative* act of the 5D ego, since it is a **Dynamic** *Force* – the *Demon*, who was opposed to the *Creative* act, having been educated by the *Force*, now is *Dynamic Force* and adds dynamism to the *Creation*.

Having come from full wisdom as *Inspiration* and having descended to the instinctual hell, having *Educated* the *Dynamic Force*, integrating it in its *Creation* process, the *Force* has as an ultimate effect the **realization of the Spirit** in the **Body** and **Matter**, creating the opportunity to achieve the *Unus Mundus*.

* * * * *

The total realization of a process of *Force* – the realization of a *Pneumatic Image* in the *Body* and Matter, including the *Education* of a *Dynamic Force* – causes a surplus of positive energy that can be employed in new *Creations*. I call this surplus **Redeemed Throne**. However, the foundations of this term, as well as the detailing of the process of *Education* of a *Dynamic Force*, are beyond the scope of this book and will be part of another book, to be written in due course.

---

[424] RAFF, J. (2000) *Jung and the alchemical imagination.* Chapter 3 "The creation of self" Florida: Nicolas-Hays, Inc. (Kobo eBook version).

[425] *The New Jerusalem Bible.* Mark 15:22.

[426] GOVINDA, A. (1975) *Foundations of Tibetan mysticism.* New York: Samuel Weiser. p. 191.

[427] Ibid.

[428] Ibid. p. 191.

[429] NIETZSCHE, F. (2006) *On the genealogy of morality.* Translated by DIETHE, C. Cambridge University Press. Aphorism 24.

[430] GOVINDA, A. *Foundations of Tibetan mysticism.* Op. Cit. p. 192.

[431] Ibid. p. 129.

[432] Ibid. p. 130.

[433] "The crucifixion was the culmination of Jesus' earthly life. In the course of being crucified, Jesus as ego and Christ as Self merge. The human being (ego) and the cross (mandala) become one. [...] Christ is both man and God. As man he goes to the cross with anguish but willingly, as part of his destiny. As God he willingly sacrifices himself for the benefit of mankind. Psychologically this means that the ego and the Self are simultaneously crucified." EDINGER, E. F. (1992) *Ego and archetype.* Boston: Shambhala. p. 150.

[434] "Matter" is a strange concept to Tibetan Buddhism. The closest idea to this is the "sensory": the perception that the consciousness has of the "matter".

[435] *The New Jerusalem Bible.* Matthew 27: 50, 52-53

[436] *The New Jerusalem Bible.* Luke 23:53

[437] The *Symbolum Apostolicum* is a prayer, considered by the Catholic Church as the faithful summary of the Apostles' faith, and whose verses were originated from biblical verses. Its form has undergone various alterations. One of its most important versions – the Nicene-Constantinople creed – was elaborated in the Council of Nicea (325 A.D.) and Constantinople I (381 A.D.). About the *Symbolum Apostolicum*, Saint Ambrose says: "He is the Symbol kept by the Roman Church, the one where Peter, the first of the Apostles, had his See and to where he took the common expression of faith (Expl. Symb.,7; PL 17, 1158D; CIC §194). Available at: <https://www.cardinalnewman.com.au/images/stories/downloads/The%20Apostles%20Creed.pdf> Access: May 3rd 2020.

[438] *The New Jerusalem Bible.* Luke 3:16.

[439] GOVINDA, A. (1975) *Foundations of Tibetan mysticism.* New York: Samuel Weiser. p.194.

[440] *The New Jerusalem Bible.* Acts 11:5.

[441] NIETZSCHE, F. (2016) *Ecce homo.* "Thus spoke Zarathrusta, a book for all and none". Translated by Ludovici, A.M. and Cohn, P. V. Project Gutemberg ebook. Available at: <http://www.gutenberg.org/ebooks/52190> Access: February 28th 2020. Aphorism 3.

[442] *The New Jerusalem Bible.* Acts 2:1-4.

[443] GOVINDA, A. *Foundations of Tibetan mysticism.* Op. Cit. pp.213 and 214.

[444] See chapter "*Grail*".

[445] Jung mentions this type of psychological situation when he writes about the psychological functions: "The same is true of every function that is repressed into the unconscious. It remains undeveloped, fused together with elements not properly belonging to it, in an archaic condition —for the unconscious is the residue of unconquered nature in us, just as it is also the matrix of our unborn future. The undeveloped functions are always the seminal ones [...]" JUNG, C. G. (1976) *Psychological*

types .Translated by Baynes, H.G. CW VI. Bollingen Series XX. Princeton University Press. §907.

[446] JUNG, C. G. (1975) *The structure and dynamics of the psyche. On the nature of the psyche* Translated by Hull, R. F. C. CW VIII. Bollingen Series XX. Princeton University Press. §427.

[447] BLAKE, W. *The marriage of heaven and hell.* Chapter 1.(Produced by eagkw, Dianna Adair – online) Available at: <http://www.gutenberg.org/files/45315/45315-h/45315-h.htm> Access: 28 April 2020. p. 7.

[448] JUNG, C. G. (1972) *Two essays on analytical psychology. On the psychology of the unconscious.* Translated by Hull, R. F. C. 2nd edition. The CW VII. Bollingen Series XX. Princeton University Press. §195.

[449] JUNG, C. G. (1975) *Psychology and religion: West and East. – Answer to Job.* Translated by Hull, R. F. C. 2nd edition. CW XI. Bollingen Series XX. Princeton University Press. §745.

[450] See chapter *"Macroimage"*.

[451] See chapter *"Demon"*.

[452] GOVINDA, A. (1975) *Foundations of Tibetan mysticism.* New York: Samuel Weiser. p.97.

[453] Ibid. [own author's highlights]

[454] Ibid. p. 139.

[455] Ibid. p. 193.

[456] Ibid. p. 131.

[457] RAFF, J. (2000) *Jung and the alchemical imagination.* [Quoting ALI PULI, *The center of nature concentrated.* (1988). p. 21. Florida: Nicolas-Hays, Inc. (Kobo eBook version).

[458] ANGELINI, H. (2015) *Força.* Unpublished text.

[459] See chapter *"Demon"*.

[460] ANGELINI, H. (2015) *Força.* Unpublished text.

[461] LEITE, P. C. T. (Paula Caju).(2016) *Paula Caju: a obra artística com o diabo no corpo.* Universidade Est. Paulista Júlio de Mesquita Filho, Instituto de Artes. Available at: <http://hdl.handle.net/11449/155477> (2019) *As Possibilidades da Psicologia Analítica para a Voz Cantada na Semana da Psicologia Mackenzie.* Youtube. Available at: <https://www.youtube.com/watch?v=kPOSZ9Shx44> Acess: April 15th 2020. [Not published in English]

INTERFERENCE

The third dimensional universe belongs to the ego.

In that dimension, the 3D Self hides in the unconsciousness and gives the ego the impression that it can move freely. The ego takes advantage of this moment when no other power emerges to dominate and grow. Morals are the only existing system of definition of right and wrong, and the ego chooses the ones it will follow more or less conveniently, always standing on the "right side" of morals. Everything is in the ego's hand: if he gets it right, its his merit, and if it makes any mistakes, it can easily fix it.

Unconscious of the Soul, "soul" for the 3D ego is an abstract concept, a metaphor for its own well-being and satisfaction. If the ego is happy and satisfied, it is a clear indicator that the "soul" is happy and satisfied with it. If the ego is successful, it is a clear sign that it is close to its "soul", because the "soul" is "good", and only brings "good" things to the ego. The "soul" does whatever the ego wants: it brings the desired partner, the dream job, money and the victory of the football team. Given that the moral system defines what is good and bad, that the ego is always on the good side (whatever the definition of "good"), and that the "soul" is "good", it follows that, in the third dimension, **the "soul" is the ego**. For that reason, third dimensional egos behave as though its lives were entirely on their hands.

Such is the state of identification of the third-dimensional ego with the Soul. The consciousness of *maṇipūra* is fundamentally inflated, which is a consequence of the identification with the Soul and also with many other parts of the psyche. With no ethical conflicts (4D) or the responsibility of an actual free-will (5D), the 3D ego has a large quantity of energy arising from these identifications (unconscious contents are generally very energetic), and so it spends this energy as it wants, considering this energy as its own, with no concerns as to the source of such energy. With the fire as a symbol for *maṇipūra*[462], the 3D ego is easily inflamed and has a lot of igneous energy.

The most curious point of this scenario is that none of that is a mistake, but simply the normal functioning of the third dimension. The 3D ego does not notice the Soul because it is evil: it is the Soul who chooses not to show itself to the ego. The 3D ego **is not prepared** to know the Soul. The Soul **allows** the ego to not know it, it **allows** the ego to identify with it and **allows** the inflation to occur. This state of things exists on purpose, so that the ego **can** form itself from those identifications with the various unconscious contents, so that the ego **can** feel the king of its own life, without having to relativize itself in relation to the various unconscious contents with which it is identified or the existence of another psychological centre (the Self), without having to experience ethical conflicts.

At this point in the journey, the third-dimensional ego blindly believes that it has free-will and that all its choices are free, having its destiny entirely on its hand and being entirely responsible for everything it does. It does not suspect that there are extremely complex unconscious patterns determining its opinions, reactions and "choices". It sees its complete automatism as complete freedom.

How joyful is this childish state of "omnipotence"!

The house of cards collapses with the moral defeat. There is now a problem that the ego cannot solve, and following that, the Soul appears, omnipotent, good and evil at the same time. The moral defeat shatters the ego's identification with the Soul. With the changes in the rules, every time the ego insists on its identifications or projections, its symptoms become more serious. The ego realizes that its 'free-will' is negative, because it slowly realizes that the Soul is not an 'exterior entity' – it is an interior entity', it is the very depth of its Being – hence 'disobeying' the Soul is not like rebelling against someone else or another power, but to distance from itself, from the Self. The "free-will" progressively transforms in surrender, surrender to the Divine, to the **interior** Divine.

In the Paradigm of Balance, there is a concept that is fundamental: ὕβρις (*hýbris*). Very well-known in Analytic Psychology, this Greek term is very closely related to μέτρον (from the Greek *métron*: measure). The Greek concept of *métron*, beyond a physical measure, is a "psychological measure". In a civilization where the guidelines of the Apollo Oracle are γνῶθι σ᾽αὐτόν (from the Greek *gnôthi s'autón*: know thyself) and μηδὲν ἄγαν (from the Greek *medèn ágan*: nothing in excess), the psychological measure is essential. The Greek context of knowing oneself is the understanding of not only one's own being, but also the acknowledgement of one's own place in the Cosmos. The Greek context of nothing in excess is the understanding that there are spiritual forces, cosmic – the Gods and Goddesses – who are higher than human beings, and that one should not try to be like them. To remain being who one is, occupying its place in the Cosmos, without exceeding oneself in feelings or acts, is the *métron*.

Nevertheless, there is *hýbris*, whose most basic understanding is the overcoming of *métron*, it is to be beyond its own measure, exaggerating on purpose, in feelings and in acts. Disregarding the Christian notion of sin, an alien concept to the Greek culture, the *hýbris* attracts the rage of the gods, because in committing it human beings get dangerously close to the gods, starting to have purpose, feelings and acts that are reserved to the gods, not to human beings. Extremely aesthetic, the Greek culture is adept of balance, and *hýbris* is dangerous because it breaks the Balance. When nothing is in excess, the Gods are in Balance. But when there is an excess of purpose, feelings or actions, the force that is being expressed through these excesses is undue. In other words, one God is dangerously predominant, and the other Gods are lagging, breaking the Balance. This state of things causes rage in the Gods, particularly Zeus, a God who is always acting to restore the Balance and will do anything to achieve it. In his exposition about the myth of the hero Phaethon, Junito BRANDÃO DE SOUZA says:

> Zeus, the supreme symbol of the spirit, re-establishes the order. Throwing its lightening against Phaeton, puts an end to the destructive work. […] The lightening, the spiritual clarification, inflames mankind in a sublime manner, arousing enthusiasm and productive joy; the affront to the spirit, however, the unwise exaltation of the spiritual attribute transforms the gift in punishment, the clarity in lightning bolt.[463]

There is even a Goddess with the precise aim to punish the *hýbris*.

> NEMESIS, in Greek *némesis*, from the verb *nemeîn*, "distribute", where Nemesis is the "distributive justice", hence the "indignation for the injustice practiced, the divine punishment". The essential function of this deity is, therefore, to **re-establish the balance**, when the justice stops being equanimous, in consequence of the *hýbris*, of an "excess", of an "insolence" practiced.[464] [author's own highlights]

Given the huge importance that the Greek culture places on Balance and cosmic order, it is amazing that the *hýbris* is such a fundamental trait, associated to the psychology of ἥρος (from the Greek *héros*: hero), one of the exponents of this culture.

> [...] what would, after all, constitute the much decanted and proved heroic ambivalence? The hero accumulates [...] contradictory attributes. Of an exceptional, ambivalent and not uncommonly abhorrent and monstrous nature, the hero reveals to be resplendent and sinister, simultaneously good and evil, benefactor and scourge. Dominated by an incoercible *hýbris*, its "*démesure*", its boisterousness does not know boundaries nor limits.[465]

As with any archetypal Symbol, the hero establishes a paradoxical reality. On the one hand, *hýbris* is a mistake that cannot be made, because the human being starts to show disregard for its cosmic place, committing excesses and not observing the *métron*. On the other hand, *hýbris* is a defining feature of the hero's personality.

To make the whole idea even more complex, **the same gods that forbid the *hýbris* are the ones who instil it in the hero.**

> Still as an external factor which, by Zeus' will, acts upon mankind and troubles its mind, we find in Homer the word *Áte*, which could be translated as *blindness of reason*, "**involuntary madness**", whose consequences the hero later regrets. [...]

> It is to the son of Peleus that I wish to express what I think. Examine it well, Argivos, and seek to understand my intention. Often, the Achaeans told me about this and censored me. **I am not to blame, but Zeus, Moîra and Erínia who walk in the shadow, when in the assembly suddenly threw in my spirit a crazy *Áte*,** on the day that I stole the honour gift from Achilles.[466] [author's own highlights]

However, in order to reach a sufficiently reasonable understanding of the relationship between *hýbris* and the hero, two other elements need to be introduced: the Greek notions of ἀρετή (*areté*) and τιμή (*timé*).

> *Agathós* in Greek means good, remarkable, "skilled for any superior end"; the superlative of *agathós* is *áristos*, the most remarkable, the bravest, and the verb formed from it is *aristeúein*, "to behave as the first". Very well, *areté* belongs to the same etymological family as

áristos and *aristeúein* and means, consequently, the "**excellence**", the "**superiority**", which is particularly revealed in the battle ground and the assemblies, through the art of the word. *Areté*, however, is a bestowal from Zeus: it is diminished when one falls into slavery, or it is severely punished when the hero commits a *hýbris*, a violence, an excess, overcoming its measure, the *métron*, and desiring to be equal to the gods. [...]

A logical consequence of *areté* is *timé*, **the honour rendered to the value of the hero**, and which constitutes the highest compensation for the warrior. [...][467] [author's own highlights]

Finally, the author establishes a relationship between *hýbris*, *areté* and *timé*:

Well, such antagonistic attitudes forcedly demand an explanation, which does not seem too difficult. Endowed with *timé* and *areté*, closer to the gods than to mankind, the hero is always in a limit situation, and *areté*, **the excellence, easily leads it to transgress the limits imposed by the *métron*, arousing the excessive pride and insolence (*hýbris*)**. It was necessary that Apollo, in the XXII 8sqq. Chant from Iliad, reminded Achilles, who was advancing like a thunderstorm against Ilion, the unsurmountable abyss that is established between a god and a mortal, albeit awarded with *timé* and *areté*.[468] [author's own highlights]

There are many circumstances that predispose the heroes to *hýbris*. Receiving *areté* and *timé*, from the Gods, the heroes are also at a limit situation with the deities. They are in a partial identity with the gods, since although they are not gods, they are their direct descendants, even called "these *hemítheoi*, these semi-gods, closer to the gods than to mankind, these indispensable intermediaries between the mortals and the immortals".[469] Finally, the gods themselves instil in them a "involuntary madness", through Ἄτη (*Áte*: Goddess of Fatality).

It is unavoidable: the hero will give in to *hýbris*.

A small observation can help understanding. When Analytic Psychology uses the terms **identification** and **projection**, it refers to the relationships between the ego and the unconscious contents. In identification, the ego is overcome by an unconscious content and starts to behave according to it. In projection, the ego sees the unconscious content in another person and believes that they behave according to it.

The important point is that, if the identification and the projection are unconscious, we **cannot** say that "the ego identified" or that "the ego projected". The ego could not identify by its own accord with an unconscious content because, for that to happen, it would need to consciously know the unconscious content and choose to identify with it. In the same way, the ego could not project an unconscious content by its own accord, because, for such, it would need to consciously know the unconscious content and choose to project it in someone else. If the ego knew the identified and the projected contents, they would not be unconscious contents. It is clear that it is **the Soul that causes identifications and projections**, and the ego can simply notice and deal with them, **after** they have occurred. Among many others, I believe this is one of the reasons why JUNG says that projection and identification are unavoidable processes, in that they are **unconscious** processes.[470]

The correct understanding of this mechanism is of utmost importance, because it avoids various negative situations. It prevents, for example, that someone is blamed for identifying or projecting – blame has no purpose from the fourth dimension on. However, even more important is that the identification and the projection are ways through which the unconscious can demonstrate directly to the ego which energies are constellated, and make the ego learn with itself. It is impossible to **explain** to someone something that they are unconscious of. Understanding is **not** integration – a mistake that I observe in various professionals, influenced by the rationality that soars in the current Psychology, as affirmed by RAFF[471]. It is necessary to learn from the unconscious itself.

So, if these types of psychological events – identifications and projections – occur with anyone, it is very understandable that *Áte* occurs with the heroes, that *Áte* is "instilled" in them.

In the Paradigm of Balance, the Hero is a very peculiar archetype, which certainly does not belong to the ego (since it is an archetype), nor is it completely a god, but it is half-way: it is a semi-god. The famous cycle of the hero[472,473] is a model of consciousness development, a model of ego development. It is very close to the ego, closer than any other archetype, and serves as an inspiration for its development.[474]

If the archetype of the Hero is responsible for stimulating the development of the ego, it is natural that the ego identifies and projects, inflates and commits *hýbris*, since it is instilled by the gods themselves. But if the ego is not initially conscious of the identifications and projections, it cannot take responsibility for their existence – the gods cause *Áte* even in the hero. On the other hand, even if the ego does not **cause** identifications and projections, **the ego is fundamental for their**

integration. The ego does not cause identifications and projections, but it must acknowledge them as early as possible and deal with them, disidentifying and taking back the projections, thereby promoting consciousness – the hero does its jobs. Therefore, the *hýbris* is unconscious and unavoidable, but the acknowledgement of this "involuntary madness" must occur as soon as possible, and its consequences are indeed the ego's responsibility. As we have seen several times, **life is indeed unfair**. That is why we grow.

The Paradigm of Sense starts when the Soul is integrated at Crucifixion, at the culmination of the Paradigm of Balance, concluding the process of integrating the archetypes that had been occurring throughout the fourth dimension. From this point forward, there is Balance: metaphorically, the ego sees around it, equidistantly, the archetypes. In the *Universe* of the *Spirit*, the archetypes have been integrated and compose the *Macroimage*, with their various conformations and, **paradoxically**, can be freely chosen by the ego to make part of the images that will go through the process of *Draw*, of fifth-dimensional *Creations*.

One of the archetypes that was **integrated** in the Paradigm of Balance is the archetype of the Hero. The Hero lead the ego since its formation, through the *jobs* that were specifically listed for that ego, until the apotheosis[475,476,477], typical of the hero's cycle, materialized in the crucifixion. As with any other archetype, the fifth-dimensional ego can freely choose from the *Macroimage*, the archetype of the Hero to *Unbalance* and start a *Creative* process of *Draw*, as long as it makes *Sense* to it. The creation of the 5D ego with the archetype of the Hero will certainly include the *hýbris*, **because now the *hýbris* is integrated**.

The integration of one of the archetypes which is closest to the ego – the Hero – means the integration of *hýbris*, one of the fundamental traits of the fifth-dimensional psychological structure. The mythical image of the **semi-god hero** was integrated and manifests as *Spirit*, a coincidence between the consciousness and the unconscious, between **the ego and the Transcendence**. The 5D ego enters the Paradigm of Sense with the archetypes in equal distance among them, makes free choices and can **Unbalance archetypes**, which means that the 5D ego can **use archetypes in its *Creations***. Until the fourth dimension, the archetypes were perceived as divine potencies with autonomous actions over human beings. In the fifth dimension, the archetypes are perceived as part of the coincidence between ego and Soul, as part of the *Macroimage* of the *Spirit*, as *Spiritual Images* that can be chosen, manipulated, *Creatively Drawn* and materialized. What used to happen autonomously before, now happens consciously. What was divine action before is now *Spiritual Action*, that is, a harmonic action between the ego and the Transcendence, since the *Spirit* supports the 5D ego in its *Actions*, with its *Word*.

Let us face the question upfront: **the fifth-dimensional ego is having divine actions, and this is *hýbris***. *Hýbris* is integrated and is now part of the 5D ego. Not just a part of it, but the **whole** *hýbris* is integrated.

It is true that the fifth-dimensional ego is endowed with *areté* and *timé*. Through the long chain of moral defeats, heroic work and surrender to the Soul that takes place in the fourth dimension, the 4D ego has followed the archetype of the Hero and developed a **psychological excellence**, and because it has experienced the psychological development in the body, it manifests this **excellence in actions**, and is **honoured** for it. The 5D ego has integrated *areté* and *timé*. Integrated, *areté* and *timé* manifest as *Force*. Like the hero, endowed with *areté* and *timé*, and always part of the plans and actions of the gods in the world, the fifth-dimensional ego experiences the *Force*, the force of *Inspiration* that *Draws images* of the *Spirit* in the *Body* and matter. To say that the 5D ego has *Force* suits someone who has integrated the Hero, and, therefore, **is a hero**.

But it is also true that *areté* and *timé* mean *hýbris*. Indeed, in face of Balance and the *Retreat of the Soul*, the fifth-dimensional ego **needs** to choose which or how many of the archetypes it will *Unbalance* in order to start the *Creative* process of *Draw*, the ones in which it sees *Sense*. The integrated *hýbris* is now manifested in the *Unbalanced* actions – and **paradoxically**, *Creative* – of the 5D ego. We know the consequences of *hýbris*: the *Balance* must be restored, and for such, the hero must perform its **jobs**, facing monsters, **its own monsters**, provoked by its own *Unbalance*. The integration of the **whole** *hýbris* on the fifth dimension means the integration of the jobs and facing the monsters. Indeed, in *Unbalancing* a spiritual *Image* of the *Macroimage*, an archetype, the 5D ego triggers a process of *Draw*, which, as with any *Creative* fifth-dimensional process, means a *Demoniac* uprising equivalent to the *Creation*. The heroic 5D ego faces its monster: the *Demon*. The heroic 5D ego uses its *Force* as a guiding power for the *Dynamic Force*, and makes it cooperate with the *Creative* process, reintegrating it to the *Spirit* in the fifth dimension, while it re-establishes the Balance in the fourth dimension. The re-established *Balance* is now in a higher dimension, the fifth: it has been realised in *Body* and matter.

The Paradigm of Sense and its characteristic psychological structure have impacting consequences. The fifth-dimensional ego has divine purposes, feelings and acts, and this is sufficiently disturbing. Even more shocking are the implications of this for the human being, because the 5D ego is an individual with divine characteristics whilst living in society;

preferentially, living **normally** in society. In the middle of everyone, there is someone freely choosing *Images* in the *Macroimage*, freely choosing which archetypes they will employ, according only to what makes *Personal Sense*, having divine actions of *Force* with the full support of the *Spirit*, whether these actions are right or wrong – there is someone having fifth-dimensional acts, there is someone having *Interferences*.

The impact of this structure is big because, even if the success of the *Interference* depends entirely on the *Force* of the 5D ego and its skill, and it is *Not Guaranteed*, the *Force* grants the ego a huge spiritual power. The healthy 5D ego is not primarily interested in power (*Śakti*), concentrating its attention on the Wisdom (*prajñā*), obtained through its vision of the *Macroimage* and the realization of this Wisdom on the *Body* and matter. But, although the primary interest is not power, its power is higher than if the primary interest was power:

> [...] The authors of the Tantras knew that knowledge based on vision is stronger than the power of subconscious drives and urges, that ***prajñā* is stronger than *Śakti***. For *Śakti* is the blind world-creating power (*māyā*), which leads deeper and deeper into the realm of becoming, of matter and differentiation. Its effect can only be polarized or reversed by its opposite: inner vision, which transforms the power of becoming into that of liberation.[478] [author's own highlights]

The characteristics of *Interference* are impacting for various reasons, related not only to its divine nature, but also to the fifth-dimensional **paradox**, where the other is simultaneously a dimension of the 5D ego **and** a completely independent person. Based on the views of the *Images* in the *Macroimage*, the *Interference* has access to what is in the unconscious and *Interferes* in the unconscious, and, **paradoxically**, also has access to what is in the unconscious of others and *Interferes* in the unconscious of others. By freely choosing which images of the *Macroimage* it will *Draw* in its *Body* and reality, only according to its *Personal Sense*, **paradoxically**, it freely chooses which images of the *Macroimage* it will *Draw* in the *Body* and reality of the other, only according to the *Personal Sense* of the 5D ego. The *Spirit* will support the creative use of the *Force* and the *Interference*, which will have practical consequences on the life of the 5D ego, and, **paradoxically**, on the life of the other. The choices and the use of *Force* will cause a *Demoniac* uprising, and also the success or failure of the guiding power of the *Force* over the *Dynamic Force*, which will, in turn, determine if the *Demon* will or not be

Educated – all that will have consequences over the life of the 5D ego and, **paradoxically**, the life of others.

The ethical discussion that this arises is huge, because a fifth-dimensional ego uses a strictly personal criterion – the *Sense* – and has access not only over its own unconscious, but also that of the other, and its *Interferences* over itself and the other are supported by the *Spirit*, whether they are right, wrong, ethical or unethical. Considering that the 5D ego will make mistakes just like anyone, and that it is dealing with *Demoniac* potencies, the level of danger is alarming. To make it clear, **the 5D ego *Interferes* independently of the wishes of the other.** We know that the free-will that people have until the fourth dimension is extremely limited, if it exists at all. But the fact that these people's experiences are determined by unconscious facts, and, ultimately, by the Self, is hugely different than the situation where the experience of these people are determined by an *Interference* in their unconscious and in their lives, realized by a 5D ego.

Nonetheless, the criterion of the Paradigm of Sense is **not** ethics. Because it belongs to a previous dimension, **the ethics is regressive** for a 5D ego. The criterion of the Paradigm of Sense is the *Creation*. A 5D ego will *Interfere* in the free-will of other people who have up to four dimensions when it sees *Sense* in it, since it does so *Creatively*. Because there is no separation between I-other in the fifth dimension, the 5D ego will strongly consider the other's opinion, but it will still *Interfere*, independently of the other's wishes. The risk for **abuse of power** is immense, particularly on an individual who is acting in *hýbris* (especially because it is integrated), and if there is risk, there is a possibility of it happening.

Evidently, one can object that such circumstances are tremendously unfair. And it is undeniable that they are; but life is **paradoxically** fair and unfair. That way, despite the unfairness, we cannot avoid admitting that the 5D ego has access to much wider realities than the ego with up to four dimensions. Although I admit that the proportion is much higher in the fifth dimension, I do not consider, however, this to be a fundamentally different situation from a psychologist seeing a patient. The psychologist knows the unconscious psychological process of their patient, and the patient does not know it. Any minimally honest psychologist needs to admit that, given their knowledge of the human psyche, particularly their knowledge about the unconscious, compared to the patient's ignorance of these instances, gives them great power over the patient. A power that perhaps the patient does not even notice. The risk for abuse of power in a therapeutic process is huge.[479] In a society such as ours, that only considers psychological aspects when they are blatant, only the ethical conflict of the psychologist stops them from committing abuse of power.

Nothing guarantees that the psychologist is well-intentioned; and even if they are, the forces of the unconscious are extremely powerful and can push them towards the abuse of power. The same logic can be applied for doctors and patients, since their level of expertise and their decisions can cure or kill a patient; it can be applied to lawyers and clients, since the level of expertise of the lawyer and their decisions can acquit or condemn their clients to life in prison; it can be applied to politicians and nations, since the level of expertise and decisions of the government can create a thriving economy or poverty for many, peace or war; it can even be applied to parents and their children, since the parents' expertise and decisions can form healthy human beings or traumatize their psyches, something the psychologists know well. Life is indeed **paradoxically** fair and unfair.

It is important to also consider that the 5D ego can coexist with other 5D egos, which is extremely positive, avoiding deep levels of loneliness through isolation. In that case, a 5D ego is paradoxically a part of the other 5D ego, and **paradoxically** an independent person; and vice-versa. Both 5D egos notice the *Macroimage*, both make free choices about which *Image* they will *Draw*, based on their *Personal Sense*, both realize *Creative* processes, face the resulting *Demoniac* uprising, *Educate* the *Dynamic Force* and realize the *Spirit* in the *Body* and matter. The harmony between two 5D egos can manifest through their agreement or disagreement – Ἁρμονία (Harmony) is the daughter of Ἀφροδίτη (Aphrodite), Goddess of Love, and Ἄρης (Ares), God of War. If there is agreement, they can even work together in a *Joint Creation*, obviously bigger and stronger than an individual creation. If there is disagreement, particularly if the disagreement causes shocks between them, the intensity of each of their *Force*, their level of *Creativity* and their acts, among other things, can mean the victory of one over the other. The fifth dimension is the Paradise, but the Serpent is also there: to imagine that the fifth dimension is a pink dimension where there is only blessedness is a fantasy typical of those who ignore what it is, in the same way that teenagers, feeling limited by their parents, fantasize that adult life is pure freedom and they can do "whatever they want".

In any case, the integration of the Hero, and with it, of *areté*, *timé* and *hýbris*, is not everything. The integration of the Hero is also the integration of its **tragic dimension**. – Over the hero looms an unquantifiable oppression. Its birth is difficult. It will spend its own life occupying the epicentre of both the conflicts between the Gods and the consequences of this conflict for human beings. The Gods will inflict *Áte* on the hero, only to demand that it repairs the mistakes caused by them. It will have to realize impossible jobs. At the end, it will find death, as anyone.

The typical fantasy about the fifth dimension is that the 5D ego can "do whatever it wants", without consulting anything or anyone, that it is a perfect master and never makes a mistake, that it only lives the good and there is no conflict, and other such nonsense; once again, it is the teenage fantasy of "pure freedom in adult life". Nothing could be more distant from reality.

The situation of a fifth-dimensional ego is **tragic**. Through successive moral defeats, the 4D ego has endured much psychological pain to surrender to the Soul, allowing it to guide until this learning became whole in Crucifixion. In this very acute moment, what it feels is abandonment. The *Retreat of the Soul* puts the 5D ego in the oppressing silence of the fifth dimension: there is no longer any transcendental guidance about what to do. Suddenly, the overwhelming weight of the free choice collapses over it. *There is no Guarantee* that the choice is right, because the moral criteria of right and wrong no longer makes sense, and with no spiritual guidance, there is no way to determine what is ethical or not. The *Personal Sense* is the only ground on which the 5D ego can stand, and given that the 5D ego is not infallible, *There is no Guarantee* that the *Personal Sense* is being correctly evaluated.

Whatever the choice of *Image* to *Draw*, the spiritual *Images* are always huge, much bigger than the fourth-dimensional Symbols, therefore the effort to draw them is colossal and *There is no Guarantee* that it will be successful. The *Creative* process, essential, will cause an extremely dangerous *Demoniac* uprising and *There is no Guarantee* that the *Education* of the *Dynamic Force* will be successful. This whole process, in the unity of the fifth-dimension, involves other people, whether or not they want to participate, given that the *Interference* causes fifth-dimensional acts which reflect in the unconscious of others, leading them to act in a certain direction – the 5D ego knows that.

We must not forget that the myth of the hero directly involves the collective. The *Áte* instilled in the hero leads it to commit crimes that will impact on people[480]. The monsters that the hero faces befall on entire societies[481]. After completing its jobs, the hero must return and re-integrate into society, bringing the benefits and wisdom accumulated during its deeds for the benefit of civilization[482], of which sometimes it will become a ruler[483]. The acts of the hero have a **cultural impact**.

The spiritual *Images* are huge and require many people to be seen and *Drawn*. The fifth-dimensional psychological structure is *Collective* and encompasses other people[484]. That way, although this is not a rule, the spiritual *Images* refer to bigger themes than the individual scope and even bigger than the scope of interpersonal relationships – they are *Collective*. The 5D ego is very strong, and to use its fifth dimensional structure to deal with individual problems or issues related to interpersonal relationship is a bit too much. It can be done, undoubtedly; there is no right or wrong. But it is like using an airplane to cross the road. It costs too much. The 5D ego is a normal person and the realization of a complete process of *Draw* is very complex and spends a lot of energy and time, even if the temporal structure *All-the-times*, typical of the fifth dimension, is used. Individual issues tend to be easily resolved with a third-dimensional structure, and interpersonal relationship issues are resolved with a fourth-dimensional structure. The fifth-dimensional structure is much more adequate for actions of a larger scope, more *Collective*. Therefore, normally, the *Interference* is in fact a *Cultural Interference*. I am referring to *Creative* processes in the various fields of work – Arts, Philosophy, Psychology, Medicine, Business, Economics, Politics, Law or any other – through which *Creations* and advances in any of these areas are realized, capable of incarnating the *Spiritual Image* and have a **Collective** **impact**.

Integrated, the archetype of the Hero means that the *Cultural Interference* of the 5D ego has a *Collective* impact, and even more responsibility is placed on its hands. The *Cultural Interference* means, as in any 5D creative process, the *Education* of a *Demon*. *There is no Guarantee* that the *Education* of the *Dynamic Force* will be successful, and if it is not, the *Demon* will have access to the collective; we already know how the *Demon* likes the masses and the huge damage that the *Demoniac* potencies have caused societies. *There is no Guarantee* that the *Cultural Interference* will be successful, and, with or without success, the responsibility of a *Collective* cultural impact will fall on the 5D ego. The culture over which the 5D ego *Interferes* will become more elevated or viler, more complex or more banal, more advanced or regressed, more human or inhuman? These questions have weight, *with no Guarantee* of an answer, over the shoulders of a 5D ego.

Every fifth-dimensional act is an *Act with no Guarantee*. In fact, the only guarantee is the 5D ego. **The fifth-dimensional ego needs to *Guarantee its own Act*.** With the gravity centre of the fifth dimension completely skewed towards itself, the 5D ego needs to, **alone**, *Guarantee* the integrity of its act, beyond morals, beyond ethics, trusting only on the *Sense* of the act and the *Greatness* of its *Creation*.

This is the tragedy of the 5D ego.

Finally, despite all this oppression that the 5D ego faces over its tragic circumstances, there is the **tragic** social pressure. Society is not used to coexist with psychological structures of such greatness, so it rejects that this quantity of power is invested in a human being and accuses it of crime. Many times, the 5D ego opts for staying silent about its condition, being forced to endure levels of loneliness. Other times, the 5D ego seeks to form relationships, absolutely necessary to the human being, and risks ostracism.

Consciousness is *hýbris*. Consciousness is crime. To be one dimension ahead of the average level of humanity is a very serious crime. An even bigger crime is to be two dimensions ahead. But, when the tragedy is intense and the fifth-dimensional ego questions whether it should have gone so far, the terrible words of Christ echo:

> In all truth I tell you, whoever believes in me will perform the same works as I do myself, and **will perform even greater works**, because I am going to the Father.[485] [author's own highlights]

---

[462] "As long as you are in *maṇipūra* you are in the terrible heat of the center of the earth, as it were. There is only the fire of passion, of wishes, of illusions. It is the fire of which Buddha speaks in his sermon in Benares where he says, 'The whole world is in flames, your ears, your eyes, everywhere you pour out the fire of desire, and that is the fire of illusion because you desire things which are futile.' Yet there is the great treasure of the released emotional energy." JUNG, C. G. (1996) *The psychology of Kundalini Yoga.* Bollingen Series XCIX. Princeton University Press. p. 35.

[463] BRANDÃO DE SOUZA, J. (1989) *Mitologia Grega*, Vol III. Petrópolis, RJ: Editora Vozes p. 230.

[464] Ibid. Vol I. p. 232.

[465] Ibid. Vol III. p. 66.

[466] Ibid. Vol. I. p.142.

[467] Ibid. Vol. I. p. 142.

[468] Ibid. Vol. III. p. 67.

[469] Ibid. Vol. III. p. 69.

[470] "The mechanism of projection, whereby subjective contents are carried over into the object and appear as if belonging to it, **is never a voluntary act**, and transference, as a specific form of projection, is no exception to this rule. You cannot consciously and intentionally project, because then you know all the time that you are projecting your subjective contents; therefore you cannot locate them in the object, for you know that they really belong to you" [...] JUNG, C. G. (1980) *The Symbolic life*. Translated by Hull, R. F. C. CW XVIII. Bollingen Series XX. Princeton University Press. §314. [author's own highlights]

[471] See chapter "*Macroimage*".

[472] BRANDÃO DE SOUZA, J. *Mitologia Grega*, Vol. III. Op. Cit. p.15

[473] DOWNING, C. (1991) *Mirrors of the self – archetypal images shape your life*. J. P. Tarcher

[474] "An image painted by Campbell of this archetypal protagonist, so central to his whole notion of the power of the myth, can be persuasive. In the fairy tales, in the mythical stories, in the religious texts of traditional cultures, as in arts and science, and in the popular means of communication of the contemporary world, warriors, saints and wise-men inspire us, evoking **our admiration and desire to imitate them**." Ibid. [Translated from the Portuguese version: (1991) *O espelho do self.* São Paulo: Cultrix. p. 197] [author's own highlights]

[475] "The initiations of ephebe serve as a shield and support to the great gestures of this life, but the initiation of the Mysteries seem to predispose him to the last adventure, the ultimate agony: death, which, in fact, will transform him into the real protector of his city and fellow citizens." BRANDÃO DE SOUZA, J. *Mitologia Grega*, Vol. III. Op. Cit. p. 51.

[476] "[...] in the so-called cycle of death and apotheosis [...] only the annihilation of the human Heracles allowed the apotheosis of the son of Zeus; [...] This is, however, the great paradox of Heracles: as the son of Zeus and Alcmena, despite so many glorious gestures, he had to climb the mount Eta to purge so many excesses, inherent to his 'hero condition' and detach himself, in flames, of the carnal enclosure; as an 'initiated', escalates the mount Olympus in an **apotheotic** manner, and as reborn from Zeus and Hera, **becomes immortal amongst the Immortals**, in the elation of the feasts. [...] [the] tension that constantly sends Heracles from the death of the mortals to **the death that immortalizes**." Ibid. p. 130. [author's own highlights]

[477] CAMPBELL, J. (2004) *The hero with a thousand faces*. Part I "The adventure of the hero". Chapter II "Initiation". "Apotheosis". Bollingen series XVII. Princeton University Press.

[478] GOVINDA, A. (1975) *Foundations of Tibetan mysticism*. New York: Samuel Weiser. p.104.

[479] GUGGENBUHL-CRAIG, A. (1990). *Power in the helping professions*. Dallas, TX: Spring Publications.

[480] "[...] Ate instils in the human heart an inhuman disregard, both for the traditions and for the consequences of our actions. She causes confusion in our minds and blinds us spiritually in such a way that we not only act with disregard in relation to what is morally correct, but also towards what is ultimately in our own interest. Perplexed with the careless impulses that Ate instils in us, humans, we are led to our supreme ruin. It is not surprising that Ates, together with Ares, the god of wars, was the most hated deity; however, the mortals notice that, nevertheless, they are mortally attracted to her, even

though she leads them inexorably to a dark end." SANFORD J. A. (2018) *Fate, love and ecstasy.* Asheville, NC: Chiron Publications. [Translated from the Portuguese version: (1999) *Destino, Amor e Êxtase.* São Paulo: Editora Paulus. Pág. 75].

481 "When [the Lion of Nemea] left the hiding place, it did so to devastate the whole region, devouring the inhabitants and the herds. [...] [The Stymphalian birds] were anthropophagic and liquidated the passers-by with its acerated feathers, which served as deadly darts." BRANDÃO DE SOUZA, J. (1989) *Mitologia grega*, Vol. III. Petrópolis, RJ: Editora Vozes. p. 98.

482 "The Hero must sacrifice the supernatural benefits of their personal triumph and return with the elixir to the world of the common mortals. This return is the real reason and aim of his whole journey: both the Hero and society need spiritual recovery, and he must bring back the sacred blessing to his fellow mankind, be it the family, the tribe, the nation, or, in the case of Jesus, Mohammed and Gautama Buddha, the whole world." DOWNING, C. *Mirrors of the self – archetypal images shape your life.* Op. Cit. [Translated from the Portuguese version: (1991) *O espelho do self.* São Paulo: Cultrix. p. 19.].

483 "Consecrated, in Corinth, the vessel Argo to Poseidon, Jason returned to Iolcos and delivered the golden fleece to Pelias. From that moment, there are several traditions and variants. Some mythographers affirm that Jason took power in Iolcos in place of his uncle and lived happily in his kingdom [...] BRANDÃO DE SOUZA, J. *Mitologia grega*, Vol. III. Op. Cit. p. 186.

484 See chapter *"Collective ego"*.

485 *The New Jerusalem Bible.* John 14:12.

MANIFESTATION

This chapter is dedicated to the Lama Anagarika Govinda, in appreciation for his monumental work Foundations of Tibetan Mysticism, *fundamental to my encounter with the* Imponderable.

IMPONDERABLE

The understanding of the first dimension, the psychological structure of *mūlādhāra*, is difficult because, both as an era of humanity's history and as a phase of one's psychological development, it corresponds to stages of development before the ego's formation. We find it difficult to imagine a reality with the complete absence of the ego[486]. In any case, the first dimension culminated in the symbolic encounter between Eve and Lucifer, by the Tree of Knowledge of Good and Evil, when consciousness was born at the same time as duality. In that precise moment, the Paradigm of Civilization started, with a very subtle line drawn between the emerging ego and the infinite of the unconscious.

At this moment, having just been formed, the ego is very fragile. The ego exists, but the unconscious is hegemonic and can dissolve it at any point. The unconscious creates the ego, but, ambiguous, constantly threatens its existence. Possible Symbols for the ego and unconscious, Gilgamesh has an intimate relationship with his mother Tiamat; but she transforms into a dragon and tries to kill him when he decides to become independent[487].

In face of the constant sea storm that is the unconscious, the ego must **hold itself**. The unconscious bombards with a profusion of psychological images, irrational, discontinuous, all contradictory among themselves. All that the ego needs to maintain its fragile structure is **continuity**; it is the only thing that can guarantee its safety.

Duality has allowed the birth of consciousness, imposing a **limit** – the Expulsion from Paradise – defining "what I am" and "what I am **not**". This apparently simple psychological operation creates the conditions for **continuity**, vital for the existence of consciousness. Every day the person wakes up, its consciousness emerging again from the unconscious, being the same person, with the same characteristics, the same body, the same name, the same address, the same relationships. The characteristics which are unknown to that ego did not invade it.

During the whole Paradigm of Civilization, society imposes a strict definition of social roles that help the ego define "what it is" and "what it is not". Within the social structure, the ego can be whatever it is, with its own characteristics, and the characteristics unknown to it can be experienced safely through what other members of society are.

Then, during the whole Paradigm of Self-Affirmation, the ego must make an effort by itself. In order to define itself, it constantly exposes "what it is" and "what it is not", seeking to convince itself and other people; it self-affirms. Step by step it builds a personality. The end of the third dimension is reached when the ego is strong and the personality is clearly defined, allowing the ego to build a life for itself, whatever its organization.

At this point, duality is at its maximum. More importantly than the duality that establishes a difference between the ego and other people is the duality that establishes the separation between the ego and the unconscious. This separation is now at its maximum: the ego is completely in charge while the Soul is dozing. With the reins in its hands, the danger of the unconscious dissolving the ego no longer exists; in fact, the ego does not even remember that the unconscious exists. This state of things allows for a **total continuity**. The ego no longer changes, unless it wants to.

But the Soul was waiting for precisely this moment. As soon as the ego is completely strong and in control, as soon as duality is at its maximum, the Soul reappears omnipotent, for the ego's surprise. The Soul shows itself through the appearance of an important problem that the ego cannot solve, however much it tries. The ego cannot solve it because the problem is fourth-dimensional and it does not fit into the third-dimensional ego, seeming like an ambiguity, an irrationality; and it is. To not be able to solve this important problem is a painful defeat for the ego. Defeated, the ego loses control. The reappearance of the Soul is a great **discontinuity**, a miracle, the miracle of Christ's birth, the only miracle that Buddha acknowledges.

[...] It is a new vista, 'a direction of the heart' (as Rilke calls it), an entering into the stream of liberation. It is the only miracle which the Buddha recognized as such and besides which all other *siddhis* are mere playthings.

[...] This revelation does not come about through discursive thought, intellectual analysis, or logical conclusions, but through the complete coming to rest and relinquishing of all thought-activities, whereby we create the necessary conditions under which a direct vision of reality can arise, namely **the intuitive experience of the infinity and the all-embracing oneness of all that is**: of all consciousness, of all life, or however we may call it. For here **end** all names and definitions of **our three-dimensional conceptual world**. Here we become aware of an infinite succession of higher dimensions (in which those we know are contained), for which we have not yet found adequate means of expression, though we may sense the existence of those dimensions and feel them with the yet undeveloped organs of our intuitive consciousness, into which *manas* is transformed, if it turns away from the activities of the outer senses and the discriminations of the intellect.[488] [author's own highlights]

Discontinuity has an inestimable psychological importance.

Consciousness has an inestimable value for the Soul and for the *Spirit*, since the creation and development of the ego are very high investments. For an ego to exist, it is necessary to **separate** a part of the psyche, which by itself goes against the **unified** nature of the unconscious and the Self. The Soul creates a structure – the ego – by which it will progressively be forgotten, to point of being completely ignored in the culmination of the third dimension. So that the continuity of the consciousness can exist, the unconscious and even the Soul must be relegated to second level.

In the peak of the Paradigm of Self-Affirmation, however, the state of continuity is so apparent that it hampers consciousness. Given that the nature of the ego is one of continuity and safety, the 3D ego concludes its formation by producing a watertight personality. The characteristics that it has developed for itself, now imprison it. The definition of personality contained the denial of characteristics that the ego did not include in its organization. These are now automatically barred, at the very least tolerated, at the receiving end of merciless moral judgement and prejudice, at most, considered abominable, ultimately, feared. The ego only knows how to **continue** what it is already doing. At this point, there is no way out. The psychological development has stopped.

Discontinuity is the **transcendental** action of the Soul. To transcend is to go beyond oneself. The ego cannot produce transcendence because the ego is consciousness, and any movement of the ego will always be an elaboration of whatever it already knows, never something entirely new. Therefore, Lama GOVINDA teaches that "this revelation does not come about through discursive thought, intellectual analysis, or logical conclusions"[489]. Ego is consciousness, so going beyond itself is to reach the unconscious dimensions of the being. The hypothetical situation of the ego making a transcendental movement is impossible, because for that to happen it would need to know the unconscious, a *contradictio in adjecto* – at least in the third dimension. Therefore, it is necessary that a centre higher than the ego, a centre that surpasses the ego and the unconscious, the 4D Self, does the **transcendental** action, constellates an unconscious content, irrational, incomprehensible to the ego, whose solution cannot be reached by a higher development of one of the ego's characteristics, or even all of them, an unconscious content that **makes the ego acknowledge** the unconscious – this is the moral defeat. This event is a **discontinuity** because in no way it is a consequence of the ego's development in the first three dimensions, because in no way it continues this development, it is something **entirely new**.

The content of the moral defeat itself is not necessarily such an epic thing, although it feels as much to the third-dimensional ego. Normally, it is a situation of everyday life that strongly contradicts the moral system adopted by that ego, and destroys its pride – a sexual issue, a family or relationship problem, a professional or financial difficulty. This is only perceived as very serious because the 3D ego is strongly identified with its sexuality, its family, marriage, profession, etc.

However, if the content of the moral defeat is not epic, its **meaning** is astounding. For the first time, **the Transcendence is being direct and consciously noticed internally**, without religion, without gurus, without intermediaries of any kind. For the first time, the ego realizes that it is not the centre of the psyche or of its own life, and in fact it is the smallest part of its own being. For the first time, the ego **knows** that something happened in its being that was not caused by it, something **transcendental**, stronger than the ego and that can oppose and even destroy it. The ego's arrogance is immediately defeated, and the Transcendence will grow until it becomes hegemonic[490]. The greatness of the moral defeat is that it is a transcendental discontinuity that, ultimately, opens to the ego – now fourth-dimensional – the path to "The experience of the infinity and the all-embracing oneness of all that is."[491].

The moral defeat is just the first transcendental event that opens an infinite series of new transcendental events. When the problem brought by the moral defeat is solved, through the confrontation with the unconscious and its respective ethical conflict, often the emerging 4D ego behaves as if everything was sorted and so it can return to its old life of egoic continuity, go back to what it was before. This will **never** happen. After the first moral defeat, there will be many others. One by one, the ego's characteristics are relativized by a series of infinite constellated unconscious contents. **The Transcendence is infinite and inexhaustible**. Infinite, the Transcendence transcends the very states it has created: as soon as the ego is made to transcend one of its characteristics, the Transcendence starts a new movement.

Throughout the Paradigm of Balance, the ego is made to transcend all its characteristics. Step by step, the ego realizes that the characteristics which are contrary to its own and those entirely unknown to it do not destroy the characteristics that it already had, but simply relativize it. What is actually destroyed is the partiality of the ego, its unilaterality in the pairs of opposed characteristics, its attachment to a single side of each pair of opposites. The ego realizes that what is seen as opposite is, in fact, a complement. The duality is consciously noticed, it becomes an acknowledged duality. Integrated, the pairs of opposites become paradoxes.

In the horizon of the Paradigm of Balance, the Crucifixion appears. As the Golgotha gets near, the psychological reality reaches unbearable degrees of tension. "In his **anguish** he prayed even more earnestly, and his sweat fell to the ground like great drops of blood."[492] Nearing the multi-paradoxical reality of Crucifixion, the ego no longer has characteristics that **define** it. It cannot be said that the ego is selfish, or altruist, as it is a paradox I-other. It cannot be said that the ego is good or evil, as it is an ethical paradox. It cannot be said that the ego is male or female, as it is an androgynous paradox. Each paradox contains an infinite tension, an energy that keeps it together. One can no longer define the truth for that individual, since having a multi-paradoxical reality, its truth is neither selfishness nor altruism, neither good nor evil, neither male nor female.

"Truth?" [...] "What is that?"[493]

The **philosophic** dimension of this question is colossal. When formulating it, Pilate was facing Christ, contemplating his multi-paradoxical reality. Christ cannot be defined by any characteristic, therefore he is not restricted by any characteristic, since he has **all the characteristics**. In face of such person, how can the truth be defined? Soon after, Christ will be on the cross, **between** Good and Evil. The Eden is reflected in the Golgotha.

The acknowledged duality ends.

The *Soul Retreats* and the psychological direction ceases.

The *Spirit* of the *Truth* descends from heaven, enunciated by Christ[494].

What is the *Truth*?

In the Paradigm of Sense, the *Truth* occupies a central role.

In the Paradigm of Balance, the emergence of successive unconscious contents relativizes any moral system that the ego can follow. With that, we learn that the *Truth* is not linked to either the **good** or the **right**. The *Truth* is **not** a virtue.

Morals overcome, the 4D ego experiences a continual confrontation with the unconscious, where its conscious stances are in an ethical conflict with the unconscious positions. However, who determines which complexes and which archetypes are constellated, in which order and when, is the 4D Self, the Soul. That way, while there is a growing relativization of the conscious contents and, simultaneously, of the unconscious contents, it becomes more and more clear that, beyond this relativization process and the ethical conflict, hovers sovereignly a **direction for the psychological process**, established by the Soul. During the Paradigm of Balance, the truth is **this direction**. However, in Crucifixion, the Soul abandons the ego, it *Retreats*: there is no longer a direction in the psychological development. With that, we learn that the *Truth* is **not** linked to the adequacy of the ego to the Soul's wishes, or, in theological terms, the *Truth* is **not** linked to the adequacy of the human being to God's wishes.

The *Spirit* of the *Truth* has descended from heaven in the middle of a multi-paradoxical reality that was established the moment Christ commits the *Spirit* in the Cross and stays after its *Resurrection*. **The multi-paradoxical reality can be defined as the coexistence of all characteristics, all possibilities, paradoxically organized among themselves.** That way, the *Truth* is **not** "this" or "that". For that reason, Nietzsche cites the *secretum* of the Order of the Assassins: "Nothing is true, everything is permitted."[495] This is true. Since there is not one thing in particular that can be taken as the truth, **the *Truth* is the Wholeness**. This is the first consideration about the *Truth*.

In acknowledging the *Truth* as a Wholeness that the 5D ego already experiences as a multi-paradoxical reality since Crucifixion, we must admit its eternally transcendental character. As already said, to transcend is to go beyond oneself. Including all of the possible elements, the *Truth* is Transcendence because, when in contact with it in the **huge discontinuity** that is the Crucifixion, the 5D ego instantly experiences a much wider reality, one in which it can access and experience any characteristic, much beyond the personality that it had before Crucifixion. The 5D ego is **paradoxically** Total.

Truth as Wholeness – even if we define Wholeness as the coexistence of all characteristics, of all possibilities, paradoxically organized among themselves – is impossible to be understood intellectually, because thought is dual and both *Truth* and Wholeness are unified. In order to establish a minimal understanding of this it is necessary to follow the whole development through the first four dimensions, and undeniably, experience it. Even then, we still need to deal with ever more complex aspects of the *Truth*.

A second consideration about the *Truth* – the relationship between *Truth* and Darkness – can seem somewhat repetitive. However, given the duality and morality firmly established in the human psyche for eras, there is a persistent illusion that needs to be dealt with. The moral human being fantasizes that an exclusively good reality is possible, and at a certain point will be installed. Even if darkness becomes progressively more evident at each step of the psychological development, the fantasy of an exclusively good reality persists and is postponed. The 3D ego fantasizes that the Soul is exclusively good. After entering the fourth dimension, the 4D ego finds a simultaneously good and evil Soul. However, it is possible that the fantasy persists and the 4D ego fantasizes that the *Spirit* is exclusively good, projecting this onto the fifth dimension. It is **not** true. In my opinion, the view of Analytical Psychology is final in that respect: the bigger the light, **the bigger** the darkness[496]. Consciousness (= light) is bigger in the fifth dimension. Therefore, **darkness in the fifth dimension is bigger than in the fourth**. If the fourth dimension integrates the Shadow and evil, the fifth dimension integrates the *Demon* and perversion. Two things are worth remembering. The first is that the **integrated** Shadow, evil, *Demon* and perversion do not even closely resemble the same things **disintegrated**, as in the previous dimensions; without this understanding, 5D (or even 4D) egos will be thought of as great criminals. Let us not forget that consciousness is seen as a crime. The second thing is that to integrate is not to understand, it is to practice.

Why is this so important, to the point of being necessary to see this theme through so many perspectives? Because while there is any kind of resistance to Darkness, whether brought about by Transcendence, or practiced by the 5D ego, there will be duality, there will be thought and in the presence of thought the *Truth* will remain inaccessible.

> It is the truth of **being, beyond right and wrong**; it is **real being** beyond thinking and reflecting. It is "knowledge" pure and simple, knowledge of the Essential, *Veda* (Greek "oida", German "wissen", [English] to know). It is the direct simultaneous awareness of the knower and the known.[497] [author's own highlights]

The fact that "beyond right or wrong" and "beyond thinking and reflecting" there is a "real being" raises attention. We saw above that, according to Lama GOVINDA, experience of the infinity and the all-embracing oneness of all that is", that is, Wholeness, goes beyond "all **names** and definitions of our **three-dimensional conceptual world**". In the same way, Christ says "Mine is not a kingdom of this world"[498] Why are the intellect, the thought and reflection so obstructive to the access to the *Truth*? There are a few reasons.

One of them is that the intellect thinks of the world by establishing **definitions**. The very term "definition" is illustrative. Its etymology comes from the Latin *definire* (de + finire), which means to **limit**, to **terminate**. Establishing definitions is, therefore, to say that something "is this way" and "**not** that way"; we are once again in the realm of duality. That way, the intellect fantasizes a world where **concepts** – what things are and are not is conceptualized – have predominance over **facts**, overwriting them. For the intellect, the interpretation of reality, unavoidably dualist, is more important than the reality.

But the effect of the definitions from the intellect is even more pernicious when they are established about beings (which, in fact, always happens). The intellect defines the being in a certain way and not another, defines which characteristics that being has and which it does not, that way keeping it from its **inherent internal Wholeness**. The intellect is a structured and meticulous barrier against the "true being".

The intellect made its first move on the Eden, on the Tree of Knowledge of Good and Evil, when duality was established. In the presence of the intellect, the first conscious emotion was **shame**. On the Eden, before biting the apple "both of them were naked, the man and his wife, but they felt no shame before each other."[499] The consciousness brought about by Lucifer totally changed this situation.

> Then the eyes of both of them were opened and they realised that they were naked. So they sewed fig-leaves together to make themselves loin-cloths. The man and his wife heard the sound of Yahweh God walking in the garden in the cool of the day, and they hid from Yahweh God among the trees of the garden. But Yahweh God called to the man. 'Where are you?' he asked. 'I heard the sound of you in the garden,' he replied. 'I was afraid because I was naked, so I hid.'[500]

With duality, there is shame. This happens because duality is not applied only to the world view, but also to the being. Therefore, the person starts to define what is good and evil in themselves, what can be expressed and what cannot; ultimately, this defines what can **exist** in them, with the other things being denied. As we have extensively seen, this mechanism is essential to create consciousness and establish **continuity**, of fundamental importance to the ego. On the other hand, the same mechanism **separates the ego from** *Truth*, since the *Truth* is wholeness, and shame establishes that only one **part** will be admitted into consciousness, the other part will be denied. With the doors to Paradise closed, the access to the *Truth* also closes.

Note that the result of shame is to **hide**. The image is clear: the person no longer sees themselves with kind eyes. Even if Jehovah's reaction to Adam and Eve's act was extremely hard, we must acknowledge that they hid **before** they knew the divine reaction, revealing a pre-existing negative opinion about themselves. In duality, **the magnitude of the being is denied** in favour of the admission of the few things that are "allowed". From this point on, the moral judgement is established as the higher power and the human being starts to hide even more. What is hidden is evidently considered evil and dark, otherwise it would not need to be hidden. Contrary to the Christian teaching that the human being was separated from the *Truth* because it separated from Light, the terrible conclusion that can be drawn from all this is that the human being was separated from the *Truth* because it separated from Darkness, denying both. Since the *Truth* is Wholeness, to eliminate Darkness means to leave Wholeness and the *Truth*. Once again, **the** *Truth* **includes Darkness**. The breakdown of this idea is equally terrible: the intellect sets out the moral judgement, which introduces shame and denies the internal Darkness, thereby **hiding the real being**. That way, the intellect separates the being from itself, blocking the access to the real being, who, as the *Truth*, is at once luminous and dark. We will return to this idea in due course.

The fact that the *Truth* is Wholeness, which necessarily includes Darkness, adds a second dimension of Transcendence to it. This is because, besides the fact that the *Truth* allows the 5D ego to experience any characteristic, it can also – **surprisingly and paradoxically** – oppose itself, blocking its own manifestation. This is the *Demoniac* part of *Truth*, **discontinuous** to the Whole that is the *Truth*. The 5D ego will notice this as instances of its being (in the fifth dimension, everything is "**internal**", consciencial) that are opposed to creative processes.

The perception that *Truth* is Totality, simultaneously luminous and dark, evokes the mythical image of Πάν (Pan), the Greek god whose name means Wholeness (from the Greek *pán* = all)[501]. The image of Pan has a strong similitude to the *Image* of Eden. Both relay a paradisiac environment where the relationship with the body and the animal instinct is very high and there is no shame. In a large garden with four rivers, Adam and Lilith were naked and had wild sex[502], even imagining alternative sexual positions. Living in the woods, Pan is a phallic god and is constantly chasing the nymphs around the river springs, masturbating the rest of the time[503].

Pan has a strongly dark dimension, causing **panic**[504] on those who walk alone in the woods at night[505]. The etymology of "panic" is very well known, from the Greek *pán + eikós* = all the images. Note that such etymology points to the fact that Pan is capable of constellating all psychological images at the same time. This is exactly the definition of *Truth* that we have so far: the multi-paradoxical simultaneity of all cosmic possibilities, which is the same as saying that the *Truth* is the multi-paradoxical simultaneity of all *Spiritual Images*, since the universe is entirely composed by *Images*. Note that the access to all *Images* occurs when one is in contact with the Darkness, as the panic occurs in the woods, at night. **Panic** is precisely what someone with up to four dimensions feels, when they face an irruption of the fifth dimension, the *Truth*, in its psyche. The Tibetan Buddhism also highlights this fact:

> If, however, the intellect succeeds in catching occasional glimpses of the true nature of things, then its world collapses and ends in destruction and chaos. To the spiritually unprepared, immature mind, the nature of reality, of unveiled truth, therefore **appears in terrible form**. For this reason, the experiences connected with the

breaking-through towards highest knowledge or awareness of reality, are represented in the terrifying images of 'blood-drinking deities'.[506] [author's own highlights]

The relationship between the *Truth* and the mythology of Pan sheds even more light over the nature of the *Truth* and leads us to the third consideration about the *Truth*. Pan is always presented as a very ancient god, therefore very wise[507,508], connected to the **body** and **nature**. When Adam and Eve are separated from their **nature** through the emergence of the intellect, the shame that they feel is of their **bodies**. It is significant that the Tree of Knowledge and shame are the reason for the separation between humans and Jehovah, **at the same** time as the separation between the humans and their bodies. The breakdown of **unity** is symbolized by the distancing from God, and will result in the Expulsion from Paradise, but the breakdown in unity also means the inferiorization of the body. The negative view of the body and its separation in relation to the rest of the psyche is mythically expressed, for example, both in the "death" of Pan and in the demonization of its image by Christianity[509,510]. With the breakdown in unity, the body has become **evil**.

Our analysis leads us to an important conclusion. If we conclude that the break in unity leads to the exclusion of the body, we must admit that the unity includes the *Body*, and therefore, ***Truth is Corporeal***. This acknowledgement should not be met with surprise, since *Spirit* IS *Body*. However, beyond that, we now have Pan's mythology to guide us. According to it, **the Whole is corporeal and it is sexual**. Therefore, the *Truth* is Wholeness and Wholeness is *Corporeal*. The Tibetan Buddhist image of the *Dharmakaya* is extremely significant, in that sense.

> In the Dharmakaya,[511] [**Dharma = Truth + kaya = body**] the universal principle of all consciousness, the totality of becoming and being is potentially contained - comparable to the infinity of space, which embraces all things and is the *condition sine qua non* of all that exists. Yet we can neither say that space is identical with things, nor that it is different from them. As little as we can become conscious of space without its opposite pole, i.e., form, so the *Dharmakaya* cannot become reality for us without **descending into forms**.
>
> This happens in two ways: in the realm of pure form, or pure mental perception, i.e., in the realm of ideas – and in the realm of action, of individuality, **of materialization or embodiment**.[512] [author's own highlights]

The ascertainment that the *Truth* is a **Body**, simultaneously *Spirit* (universality, completeness, space) and *Body* (form, materialization, incarnation), takes us once again to that which is developed with the progression throughout the fifth dimension, until it involves the whole reality: the *Unus Mundus*, a simultaneously *Spiritual* and *Corporeal* reality.

With the consciousness that the *Truth* is Wholeness, which, therefore obviously includes Darkness and the *Body*, we can advance and contemplate its other aspects.

The ascertainment that the *Truth* is the Wholeness and that the Wholeness is the multi-paradoxical reality, the coexistence of all cosmic possibilities, means that there is nothing outside Wholeness, which is true. A logic interpretation of Wholeness will conclude, therefore, that if all possibilities are included, there is **no longer** *Creation*, since *Creation* leads to the emergence of possibilities beyond those included in the Wholeness, which is a *contradictio in adjecto*. However, we already know that the intellect is not an adequate tool for the fifth dimension, because a dual tool cannot apprehend a unified reality – in this case, for example, the intellect concludes that the *Truth* **either** includes all possibilities and does not create, **or** the *Truth* does not include all possibilities. Yet – and this is our fourth consideration about the *Truth* – a fifth-dimensional conscience knows that, precisely because it includes **all** possibilities, **the *Truth* includes the *Creation***, whose existence is so evident in the whole universe. Contrary to what the intellect could argue, the *Truth* would not be Wholeness if it **excluded** *Creation*.

The inclusion of *Creation* in *Truth* becomes even more encompassing, given that, when the reality of *Creation* is applied to the reality that encompasses all existing possibilities, **the *Truth* proves itself infinite**. In perfect consonance with the Physics of Relativity, which establishes that the whole Universe, the Whole, **paradoxically** expands infinitely, the fact that the Wholeness creates new elements, and more than that, new dimensions, **eliminates** any possibility to **define** the *Truth*.

> The ecstatic figures of heroic and terrifying deities express the act of the *Sadhaka*'s breaking through towards the **'Unthinkable'** (*acintya*), **the intellectually 'Unattainable'** (*anupalabdha*), as mentioned m *Subhuti*'s answer in the *Prajnaparamita-Sutra*, when the Buddha had asked him whether the highest enlightenment (*anuttara-samyak-sambodhi*) could be described, or whether the Buddha had ever taught such a thing: 'As I understand the teaching of the Lord Buddha there is no such thing as *Anuttara-samyak-sambodhi*, **nor is it possible for the *Tathagata* to teach any fixed**

Dharma. And why? Because the things taught by the *Tathagata* **are, in their essential nature, inconceivable and inscrutable**; they are neither existent nor non-existent; they are neither phenomena nor *noumena* [fundamental essences]. What is meant by this? It means that the Buddhas and Bodhisattvas are not enlightened by fixed teachings but by an intuitive process that is spontaneous and natural.'[513] [author's own highlights]

Being impossible to define intellectually, and therefore to fixate, the *Truth* emerges as an eternally moving Wholeness, a creative Wholeness, one that, **paradoxically** increases as a **discontinuous** Wholeness, since new elements appear – an **Infinite Wholeness**. That way, the dimension of Transcendence of the *Truth* explodes in the direction of the Infinite. Regardless of how much the individual develops, there will always be infinitely more, infinite dimensions, infinite complexity. Even more surprising is that, since there is no internal x external dichotomy, the Infinite Transcendental *Truth* is "interior", is the Being itself.

As previously seen, the ***Creation*** is simultaneously a characteristic of the *Spirit* and of the 5D ego, being the meeting point between them. For that reason, the creative dimension of *Truth* is in complete harmony with the *Force*. When we described it, we saw that the *Force* can be understood as an *Inspiration*, whose power inseminates the 5D ego with enough energy to undertake *Creative* work. The *Creative* nature of the *Spirit* is so essential that it is considered a criterion of the fifth dimension, a criterion of harmony between the *Spirit* and the 5D ego. Having considered the universal character of the *Spirit*, and the fact that the 5D ego is conscious, only *Creativity* can be the criterion for a harmonious relationship between them. Without a relationship of *Creative* collaboration, the *Spirit* would preponderate, and the *Free-will* would be eliminated by determinism, or the ego would preponderate, and the *Free-will* would be eliminated by defiance. Through *Creativity*, the *Spirit* can be Wholeness and the 5D ego can equally be Wholeness and interact freely with it. All this *Creativity* is moved by the power of *Inspiration* that is the *Force*. In the *Force*, the contemplation of the *Truth* is the space of *Creation* of the 5D ego.

Finally, our fifth consideration about the *Truth* is the **mistake**. It can seem inadmissible that the *Spirit* of *Truth* makes mistakes, that God makes mistakes. But, if we understand that the *Truth* is Wholeness, we cannot exclude the mistake from the Wholeness.

What makes the notion of mistake so incompatible with the notion of Infinite Wholeness? In one word, the omniscience that is attributed to the Infinite. The meaning of omniscience is to know all. This eliminates the notion of mistake, because it is not possible to make mistakes if one knows all – this would make the mistake intentional, and therefore it would no longer be a mistake, but what was intended in the first place and therefore it is no longer a mistake, it is what was intended. Omniscience means perfection. Commonly, perfection is defined as absence of faults, but it is important to notice that this is a moralist definition, because, after all, something is being considered a fault in comparison to a fixed pattern, and a fixed pattern is invariably a moral pattern. Both omniscience and perfection are considered divine attributes, making it unacceptable that God makes mistakes.

JUNG, however, defines perfection in a completely different way. Considering its etymology (from the Latin *per* = entirely + *facere* = do), perfection is defined as "done entirely", as **completeness**. JUNG's definition for perfection is completely in line with the notion of *Truth* as Wholeness. The mistake **needs** to be included in the completeness. Therefore, the *Truth* includes the mistake and we must accept that God makes mistakes, which in practice is to say that **the Self makes mistakes**. In order to "save" God's image, normally the mistake is attributed to the *Demon*, the representative of the Self's mistakes.

> You utter **fraud**, you impostor, you son of the devil, you enemy of all uprightness, will you not stop twisting the straightforward ways of the Lord?[514] [author's own highlights]

Whoever is mistaken makes mistakes and goes the wrong way. The mistake of the human being is attributed to the *Demon*. We know that the *Demon* was, in the beginning, an Angel. But the Angel is created by God. There is no point in saying that it was the Angel that made the mistake, because this would just shift the problem, since God created an Angel with the **possibility** of making mistake. Once again, we return to the idea that God includes the mistake.

The mistake is, on the other hand, essential. If God had created the Angels and the human beings **without** the possibility of mistake, the determinism would have been absolute. In this case, there would be no free-will. In such circumstances, consciousness would be the cruellest universal characteristic, since it would simply contemplate a sequence of unavoidable events with no possibility of interaction between them, and the universe would end up in the most tedious boredom. We saw that the *Demon* is the dimension of the *Spirit* that resists *Creation*, **paradoxically** creating a **space** for *Creation* to take place and exist[515]. **The mistake is therefore the space of *Creation*.**

Thankfully it is like that. **Without the *Demon*** and the mistake, the fifth dimension would be a state of merging with Wholeness, losing individuality and ceasing to exist (the OM̐ without the HŪM̐). Without the *Demon* and the mistake, the omniscience would reign, the free-will would disappear, the determinism would reach its maximum and the consciousness of an illuminated being would be entirely passive – Christ's and Buddha's biggest problem would be to deal with a mind-bogglingly tedious reality. **With the *Demon* and the mistake**, the **space of *Creation*** appears. Existence is self-evident, individuality is complete, *Free-Will* can reign over determinism. The consciousness of an illuminated being is not associated to omniscience; **the consciousness of an illuminated being is unlimited**, which is completely different. In omniscience, existence is cynical, there is total boredom, there is nothing one does not know, nothing surprises, nothing excites, and nihilism is absolute: the desire for nothing prevails. In the unlimited consciousness there is no omniscience, the illuminated being does not know everything, but **is open to everything that pops up**. (Just as a curiosity, illumination is a reality of the sixth dimension. I have used the image of the illuminated here only for didactic reasons.) What the *Truth* brings to the 5D ego is immediately verified by it. This is not omniscience, but **absence of denial**. The 5D ego does not want to be a god (this desire is totally third-dimensional, it is a projection of power), it does not long for omniscience. The 5D ego, having been through the fourth dimension, has become completely **human**, and in the fifth dimension, makes an effort to remain so, carefully calculating its *hýbris* according to the size of the *Dynamic Force* that it supposes to be able to educate.... And it can be mistaken in this evaluation.

However strange the notion of the *Spirit* making a mistake, of the Self making a mistake, of God making a mistake might seem, it is only so if we contemplate it from a moral perspective, one that fixates a pattern and consider the deviations to that pattern as faults, mistakes. However, as we have seen several times, the *Truth*, the Being and the fifth-dimensionality exist totally **beyond right and wrong**.

This notion bothers deeply in the core of beings because the annihilation of right and wrong means that there is no purpose to the universe beyond completeness, Wholeness. Any purpose considered "right", different from completeness – for example, good, evil, love or any other –, would instantly produce an asymmetry in the Wholeness and establish duality. Nevertheless, if the Wholeness is the only purpose, any purpose is equally valid, and ultimately, there is no purpose. The idea that **life has no**

purpose is an attack on the ego's pride, since it likes to see itself in the centre of the universe, as the purpose of the universe. It is, above all else, an attack on the ego's childishness, who likes to think that there is something in the universe looking after it; or more precisely, that there is someone in the universe looking after it, from where the persistent (and unbearable) idea of the coming of a Saviour arises.

The idea that life has no purpose causes very passionate acts of rebellion in the great majority of people due to the sensation of emptiness that it creates. There follows the accusation of nihilism. It is understandable that this accusation is made because until the fourth dimension, a defined purpose is necessary. In the second dimension, the purpose is civilization. In the third dimension, the purpose is the ego, the power of the ego, is "to be happy". In the fourth dimension, the purpose is the surrender to the Soul, to follow the Soul towards Wholeness. However, in the fifth dimension, the Wholeness has been achieved. Therefore, **the purpose of life was integrated**. The 5D ego is no longer based on society, on the fantasies of power or even on the Soul to define its life purpose.

In the Paradigm of Sense, the integrated purpose of life is called *Sense*. Beyond morals and ethics, beyond any spiritual guidance, the 5D ego defines the *Sense* of life, of choice and action by itself. Nothing is more distant from the *Pneumatic* reality than nihilism: life has no intrinsic purpose because the fifth-dimensional ego has **complete freedom** to define this by itself, defining the *Sense* of life. The 5D ego is in no way dissolved in the cosmic Wholeness, or lost in it. On the contrary, it is in total harmony with the *Truth*, the Wholeness, and, **paradoxically**, calmly allows itself to have its personal interests (which it needs to have, as we will see ahead), and is not interested in moralizing others, instead, only in defining the *Sense* **of its own life**, leaving others free to define the sense in theirs. By the way, the definition of *Sense* changes as frequently as it wants, since any inflexibility will close access to the *Truth*, to Wholeness.

The fact that the *Truth* is Wholeness, includes the Darkness, is a *Creation* with no start and no end, includes the *Demon* and the mistake, elevates its **discontinuity** to Infinite. It is not possible to keep anything in the universe, because keeping immediately closes access to the *Truth*, to Wholeness. **This** level of discontinuity, **this** level of Infinite, means that the ***Truth is Imponderable***. In face of the *Imponderable*, **it is impossible not to make mistakes**. In fact, it is not desirable to not make mistakes because the mistake is the space of *Creation*. **Paradoxically, it is impossible to make mistakes** because there is no standard to which the act can be compared, to define whether or not there is a mistake by deviation from the standard, because life has no purpose *a priori*, from which it can distance itself or approach. **It is impossible to make mistakes because it is the 5D ego that defines its own reality, by choosing which *Images* from the *Macroimages* it will creatively *Draw*, according to the *Sense* defined by that ego.**

And it is fine if its intentions do not come to anything. No result is also part of Wholeness.

KARMA

The first meeting with the *Imponderable* happens with the body suspended on the Cross, the first moment when the Gates of Eden open again, and the unity is directly accessible. The *Imponderable* is of an infinitely complex nature, luminous and dark at the same time, infinitely creative and yet resistant to creation itself, a Wholeness in a vertiginous change process, impacting and mortal *Truth*.

To understand the *Imponderable* – an idea whose even mention seems impossible – requires an extremely developed consciousness. To practice the *Imponderable* seems something beyond impossible. The overwhelming majority of humanity hasn't even gone through the moral defeat, let alone Crucifixion, therefore they fall totally short of understanding this matter, which seems to them more abstract than air; and it is, it is ether.[516]

If nowadays the understanding of the *Imponderable* is extremely improbable, imagine in the aurora of the consciousness development. In fact, the *Imponderable* prevents the first steps of development precisely because of its Wholeness. As we have seen several times, it is impossible to start the development of consciousness through unity, through Wholeness. It is necessary to first eat from the Tree of Knowledge of Good and Evil and embrace duality, leaving behind the unity of the Paradise of Eden, dimension of the *Imponderable*, and only return after Crucifixion, going through Michael's Flaming Sword.

Leaving behind the infinite discontinuity of the *Imponderable*, the Expulsion from Paradise gives access to continuity, a stable ground over which the ego can stand, and the consciousness can develop. Now the ego can affirm itself: "I have such and such characteristics and not such and such". Establishing which are its characteristics, the ego chooses its behaviours and constitutes a personality. Henceforth, the ego will

maintain it, continually. This type of structure is extremely praised by the current third-dimensional structure: to maintain a stable and predictable behaviour is seen as having coherence, and these people are described as "having a personality", as being authentic and trustworthy.

What is being praised is the most common and extremely necessary psychological structure of the third dimension: the neurosis. There are many forms of defining neurosis, all valid. We are interested in two of them. The first is the neurosis as a defence against a deeper unconscious nucleus, particularly, an archetype[517]. This idea is very similar to the idea of defending from the *Imponderable*; the difference is that the *Imponderable* is something much deeper than an archetype. The second is the neurosis as a repetitive mechanism, as a deep-seated habit, exempt of any creativity[518]. The repetitive character of neurosis was evidenced by JUNG, when he stated that the psychological illness does not distinguish anyone, does not make anyone special or individual or creative; this is something that only individuation can achieve[519]. Once again, the similarity is big, as the only way to defend oneself from the *Imponderable* is through continuity, through repetition.

As it is clear, the defence against the unfathomable depth of the psyche and its huge dynamism[520] is very familiar to the Analytical Psychology, being expressed in one of its most basic concepts. The healthy structure of a third-dimensional ego is a very well-orchestrated group of a few dozen neurosis (seen as stable conscious structures, capable of preventing an invasion of contents from the unconscious); this is what is called "personality". This is healthy because it is the price to pay for the development of consciousness, to structure a strong ego, absolutely necessary to enable and support an authentic encounter with the Self. Nevertheless, it vetoes the access to the depth of the unconscious, to the archetypes. A successful individuation process is a fourth-dimensional process through which the 4D ego learns to recognise its neurosis and, through establishing psychological tensions with unconscious complexes and archetypes, overcome its neurosis and ascend to the wider reality of the Self, reaching Wholeness through the contact with this Archetype.

The Paradigm of Sense starts precisely from this point and its objective goes way beyond – the *Unus Mundus*. Whereas the Paradigm of Balance – a process that aims at the second *coniunctio* – seeks to reach the **psychological integration**, the Paradigm of Sense – a process that aims at the third *coniunctio* – seeks to reach the **physical integration**, synonymous with a ***Pneumatic*** integration, since *Spirit* is *Body*. The psychological reality (4D) is transcended by the *Pneumatic* reality (5D). In the same way as the **process** of personality construction (neurosis) of the third-dimensional ego – which denies deeper psychological realities – is transcended by the fourth dimension, the **process** of overcoming neurosis and integrating the fourth-dimensional Self – which denies deeper *Pneumatic* (= physical) realities – needs to be transcended by the fifth dimension. The whole process starts from one state of things and reaches another state, preferentially more complex, if evolutive, through the solution of problems. The Paradigm of Self-Affirmation solves **inconsistencies** of the consciousness and **fragilities** of the ego, in order to reach a coherent personality and a strong stable ego. The Paradigm of Balance solves **neurosis**, denials of the unconscious psychological reality, in order to integrate Wholeness. So, what solves the Paradigm of Sense in order to integrate the *Unus Mundus*? ***Karma***, a denial of the *Pneumatic* (= physical) reality.

In order to understand this Sanskrit word, which I borrowed from the Tibetan Buddhist cultural matrix, we need to first **extinguish** any relationship between this word and Christianity. Western folk tend to see *Karma* as **guilt**, as **punishment**, as atonement for their sins. Such scenario leads to the fantasy that there were "masters of *Karma*", capable of cancelling *Karma*, in the same way as a Saviour could forgive and redeem someone, avoiding the atonement of their sins. **Nothing is more distant from the notion of *Karma* than sin, guilt, punishment and saviours**. Let us exterminate this bent idea.

> Also in the later forms of the *Mantrayana* (as the mantric Schools of Buddhism were called) it was well understood that karma could not be neutralized by merely muttering mantras or by any other kind of religious ritual or magic power, but only by a pure heart and a sincere mind.[521]

In order to correctly define ***Karma***, let us start from the *Imponderable*, the *Truth* (= Dharma)[522].

Given that the *Universe* is entirely built with *Images*, so is the *Imponderable*. It is composed of the Totality of *Images*, an infinitely complex group of *Images*, luminous and dark at the same time, *Spiritual* and *Corporeal* at the same time, vertiginously changing all the time in its infinite *Creative* process. An illuminated consciousness is open for the contact with this constantly transcendental dimension, and can move freely through these *Images*, remaining with them in harmony, while *Creating* with them directly on the *Corporeal* and material level.

Presently, however, the overwhelming majority of people do not have a stable enough consciousness to withstand this level of **discontinuity**, of **Transcendence** – not enough greatness to accommodate so many *Images* flowing. The discontinuity is so vertiginous that the consciousness becomes attached to a few of these *Images* and fixates on them, striving to maintain them **continuously**, thereby acquiring some sort of security. Each *Image* to which it has become attached, making them fixed, is a **Karma**[523].

> How much truth can a certain mind endure; how much truth can it dare? These questions became for me ever more and more the actual test of values.[524]

Karma is not, however, essentially different from the *Imponderable*; both are *Images*. The difference is the relationship one has with the *Image*: one can either coexist with the infinite discontinuous flow, or halt the flow to generate continuity, to generate **Karma**. *Karma* is a way of turning the *Imponderable* **ponderable**, of guaranteeing the existence of the intellect – which is dual, which **ponders**. Far from being a punishment for one's faults, *Karma* is a way of evading the infinite discontinuous flow of *Truth* with which one **cannot** coexist, of leaving the *Truth* behind, with its unbearably *Imponderable* character. The *Karma* is a **protection** against the *Truth*. This is the nature of **illusion**, which is not **opposed** to the *Truth*, only much smaller.

> If we call *māyā* a reality of a lower degree, we do this because illusion rests on the wrong interpretation of a partial aspect of reality. Compared with the highest or 'absolute' reality, all forms, in which this reality appears to us, are illusory, because they are only partial aspects, and as such incomplete, torn out of their organic connexions and deprived of their universal relationship. The only reality, which we could call 'absolute', is that of the all-embracing whole. Each partial aspect must therefore constitute a lesser degree of reality – the less universal, the more illusory and impermanent.[525]

Incapable of internally experiencing the infinite discontinuous flow of *Images*, a consciousness with up to four dimensions automatically rejects it and fixates in certain spiritual *Images*, becoming attached to them. Now, with no flow, the *Images* **no longer change, no longer vary**. Instead of a discontinuous flow of **different and unknown** *Images*, one now sees the return of a few spiritual *Images* which are bearable for that ego, a small **repetitive** group of equal *Images*, which are easy to deal with because they are **familiar**. This repetitive and familiar group of *Images* is the individual's *Karma.*

Note that, once again, it is **not** about punishment for mistakes, associated to blame, but instead a self-imposed group of *Images*, seeking more protection and security. The similarity with a neurosis is evident: both are repetitive situations that seek protection from deeper layers of the unconscious.

Karma can be good or bad; this is irrelevant. One can have a familiar group of spiritual *Images* associated to good situations, such as health, competence, wealth, success, love, acceptance, etc.; this is the good *Karma*. One can also have a familiar group of spiritual *Images* associated to bad situations, such as diseases, hardship, poverty, bankruptcy, fear, rejection, etc.; this is the bad *Karma*. What defines an *Image* as a *Karma* is not whether it is good or bad, but whether or not it is repetitive and familiar, because then, it brings security.

It may seem strange that a bad spiritual *Image* can bring security, and therefore, be desirable. However, it is very common to notice, in clinical practice, that a neurosis – however much a patient expresses unhappiness with it – is a familiar way to behave, and translates into safety, therefore becoming preferred. This is so true that a resistance to psychological treatment is extremely common, and, very frequently, neurotic structures are considered authentic parts of one's personality and background. In face of the options for a change of behaviour in a certain therapy, the patient claims that they cannot change because they "were brought up that way", or they "have always been that way", and list a hundred reasons why "it is not possible to change". In clinical practice, this type of reaction from the patient occurs independently of whether the situations which are "impossible to change" are good or bad. A successful doctor or lawyer are not interested in adding sentiment to their work because this would affect their professional success; a good neurosis. They maintain their success – good – avoiding something that they consider bad, that is, unknown: sentiment. On the other hand, a woman who suffers domestic violence from her husband can refuse to report him to the police because he is "a good man" or because "her religion does not allow it". Someone who was cured from cancer can refuse to return to work or to travel because "they can't". The domestic violence or the illness remain, avoiding something that is considered bad, that is, unknown: a life without aggression, autonomous, and a healthy life. The categories of good and bad are extremely fluctuating and relative. The fact that someone likes or not something they know and choose to repeat indefinitely is irrelevant, because regardless of that, the repetitive situation is **comfortable** for them, since they know how to deal with it.

The scenario that involves the neurosis is the same that involves *Karma* – the difference is simply one of dimension. If the situation experienced is good, the person becomes attached to it because it is familiar, it is comfortable, it is not a threat. If the situation experienced is bad, the person becomes attached to it because it is familiar, it is comfortable, it is not a threat. Therefore, any repetitive situation that occurs in someone's life is karmic, regardless of being good or bad, simply because it halts the discontinuous infinite flow of the *Imponderable*. Whatever the repetitive situation, however benevolent or malevolent, it halts the Whole, halts the infinite, halts the discontinuous change.

> For character is nothing but the tendency of our will, formed by repeated actions. Every deed leaves a trace, a path formed by the process of walking, and wherever such a once-trodden path exists, there we find, when a similar situation arises, that we take to this path spontaneously. This is the law of action and reaction, which we call *karma*, the law of movement in the direction of the least resistance, i.e., of the frequently trodden and therefore easier path. It is what is commonly known as the 'force of habit".[526]

Much more adequate to the Paradigm of Sense than the Olympic generation of gods, the Τίτανες (Titan) generation offers a mythical image that adheres to the notion of *Karma*: Κρόνος (Cróno).

> Krono, in Greek *Krónos*, without a definitive etymology so far. For a simple play of words, for a type of forced homonymy, Krono was identified several times with the personified Time, since, in Greek, *Krónos* is the time. If, in fact, *Krónos*, Krono, has no etymological connection with *Krónos*, the Time, the semantic identification is, in a way, valid. Krono devours, at the same time as it breeds; by mutilating Uranus, it staunches the sources of life, however becoming itself a source, fecundating Rhea.
>
> The fact is that **Uranus, as soon as its children were born, returned them to the maternal breast, certainly fearing being dethroned by them**. Gaea then decides to free them and asked her children to vindicate and free her from her husband. They all refused, except for the youngest, Krono, who hated the father. Gaea gave him a scythe (a sacred instrument that cuts seeds) and when

Uranus, "avid for love", laid down, at night, over his wife, Krono cut off his testicles. All the blood from Uranus wound, however, fell over Gaea, who conceived, for that reason, sometime later, the Erinyes, the Giants and the Meliae Nymphs. The testicles, thrown in the sea, formed, with the foam that leaked from the divine organ, a big froth, from which Aphrodite was born. With that, the youngest of the Titans vindicated his mother and freed the siblings. [...]

As for Krono, after he possessed the governance of the world, turned into a worse despot than his father. Fearing the Cyclopes, whom he had freed from Tatar at Gaea's request, were again thrown into the darkness, together with the Hecatoncheires. Since Uranus and Gaea, as depositories of mantic, that is, the knowledge of the future, had **predicted that he would be dethroned by one of the children that he would have with Rhea, he started to swallow them, as they were born**: Hestia, Demeter, Hera, Hades or Pluto, and Poseidon. Only Zeus escaped. Pregnant with the latter, Rhea run away for the island of Crete, where she secretly gave birth to the youngest, in the Dicta mount. Involving a rock in linen cloths, she gave that to her husband, as if it was the child, and the god immediately swallowed it.[527] [author's own highlights]

The reality of Krono is to see his father Ὀυρανός (Uranus) vetoing the growth of his children, avoiding being uncrowned. Apparently, Krono fights against this reality, castrating his father. However, as soon as possible, he takes the familiar place and lives the only reality he knows: he becomes the father who vetoes his children's growth, avoiding being uncrowned. His destiny is the same as that of his father: he is betrayed by his wife and dethroned by his son. Krono **is simple repetition**. As we will see later, the fact that Krono **separates Heaven from Earth** and is the **God of Time** is very revealing.

Although he is part of the generation of Olympic gods, more adequate to the understanding of the Paradigm of Balance, the God Ἅιδης (Hades) also contributes with insights about *Karma*. Let us see the myth of Tantalus:

It all started with the *harmatia* of Tantalus, son of Zeus and Pluto, who reigned in Phrygia or Lydia, over Mount Sipylus. Extremely rich and liked by the gods, he was admitted in their feasts. Twice Tantalus had betrayed the friendship and trust of the immortals: in one of them, he revealed to mankind the divine secrets, and in another, he stole nectar and ambrosia from the gods, to offer his mortal friends. The third *harmatia*, terrible and hideous, granted him eternal condemnation. Tantalus, wishing to know whether the Olympus

[gods] were indeed omniscient, sacrificed his own son Pelops and offered him to them as a delicacy. The gods, however, recognized what was being offered, except for Demeter, who, beside himself due to the kidnapping of his daughter Persephone, ate one of Pelops' shoulder. The gods, nevertheless, reconstituted him and brought him back to life.

Tantalus was thrown in the Tatar, condemned forever to the torment of thirst and hunger. Immersed up to the neck in clear and fresh water, when he tries to drink, the liquid spills through his fingers. Trees heavy with tasteful fruit hang over his head; starving, he extends his crinkled hands to fetch them, only for the branches to abruptly rise. There is a variant of great symbolic value: the king of Phrygia was condemned to stay forever over a huge rock about to fall and where he would have to remain in eternal balance.[528]

The myth of Sisyphus is also enlightening:

Sisyphus, the most shrewd and audacious of mortals, managed to **escape Death** twice. When Zeus captured Aegina, daughter of the river Asopus, he was seen by Sisyphus, who, in exchange of a source granted by the river-god, told him who was the raptor of his daughter. Zeus immediately sent Thanatos, however the astute Sisyphus confused him in such a way which allowed his capture. As nobody else died, and Hades rich and dark reign was becoming poor, answering a complaint by Pluto, Zeus intervened and freed Thanatos, whose first victim was Sisyphus. The astute king of Corinth, however, before dying, asked his wife not to carry out the funeral honours. Arriving to Hades without the habitual "cover", that is, not as an eidolon, Pluto asked him the reason for such sacrilege. The shrewd son of Eolus deceitfully blamed the wife of wickedness and, after much pleading, was permitted to briefly return to earth in order to severely punish his partner.

Once in his kingdom, the king of Corinth no longer cared to keep his word with Pluto and allowed himself to stay, living until old age. One day, however, Thanatos came to collect him for good and the gods punished him mercilessly, condemning him to roll an immense boulder up a hill. However, after barely arriving at the top, the boulder rolls back down, dragged by its own weight. Sisyphus starts again, repeating the action for **eternity**.[529] [author's own highlights]

Besides these two myths, there are several others that include the idea of a situation that lasts forever – Ixion rotates fixed to a wheel for all eternity.

Narcissus still tries desperately to see himself in the dark waters of the Styx. Danaïdes eternally fill a bottomless cistern. A situation that lasts forever has as its main characteristic an **infinite repetition of the same Image**; such is the nature of *Karma*.

It is important to note that the repetition is triggered by the **denial of wider realities**. Tantalus, being well-regarded amongst the gods, denies the self-evident reality of the gods' omniscience and attacks them with his intellect, **testing them** (intellectually), to gauge whether (a dual perspective) they really were omniscient. Sisyphus denies the reality of death. Ixion gets lost in fantasies (Hera-cloud) and denies the movement of Wholeness (rotating wheel). Narcissus denies the reality of other people. Danaïdes deny a dimension of femininity. To deny a wider reality is an idea which is very close to denying the omniscient reality of the *Imponderable* – precisely the nature of the Gods denied by Tantalus.

The denial of a wider reality, therefore, appears much more evidently in the myths of Tantalus, Sisyphus and Ixion. We know that the wide culmination of the Paradigm of Balance is symbolized by the gods on Balance, equidistant from consciousness, central, in coincidence with the Soul – the same situation enjoyed by Tantalus, well-regarded **among** the gods. Because this wide reality is denied by Tantalus, because Ixion denies the movement of Wholeness and because Sisyphus denies the wide reality of death, they are all placed in a repetitive situation of **balance**.

The denial of death, maybe the bigger **discontinuity** in the life of a human being, is symbolically the denial of the *Imponderable*. Remember that Christ achieves the *Imponderable*, dying on the skull (Golgotha), and that the *Imponderable* is reached when the palace of *Ḍākinī* skulls (a "blood-drinking deity") is accessed. Death is an excellent symbol of the *Imponderable*, given the infinite discontinuity character of both, in face of which it is impossible to keep one's personality, circumstances or even own body. In face of the Golgotha or *Ḍākinī*, of the *Imponderable*, the only possible destiny is death. That way, just as Sisyphus, Orpheus denied the imponderable character of death:

> When returning from the Argonauts expedition, married the nymph Eurydice, who he loved deeply, considering her a *dimidium animae eius*, as if she were his soulmate. But one day [...] the beekeeper Aristaeus tried to molest the wife of the singer from Thrace. Eurydice, when trying to escape her persecutor, stepped on a serpent and was bitten by it, causing her death. Inconsolable with the loss of his wife, the great bard decided to descent to Hades' darkness, to bring him back.

> Orpheus, with his zither and divine voice, enchanted the chthonic world in such a way that even the Ixion wheel stopped going round, Sisyphus' rock stopped oscillating, Tantalus forgot his thirst and hunger and the Danaids rested from their eternal labour of filling bottomless barrels. Touched by such proof of love, Pluto and Persephone agreed to return his wife. However they imposed one extremely difficult condition: he would go in front, and she would follow his steps, but whilst they walked through the infernal darkness, whatever he heard, whatever he thought, Orpheus ***should never look back*** until the couple had walked beyond the empire of the shadows. The poet accepted the imposition, and was almost reaching the *light*, when a **terrible doubt** assaulted his spirit: **what if** his beloved was not behind him? **What if** the gods of Hades had fooled him? Bitten by impatience, uncertainty, longing, "neediness" and an invincible *póthos*, for the great desire for the presence of an absence, **the singer looked back**, transgressing the order of the sovereigns of darkness. In turning, he saw Eurydice, who disappeared forever in a shadow, "dying a second time..." He still tried to go back, but the ferryman Charon did not allow.

> [...]

> In fact, **the great mismatch of Orpheus in Hades was to have looked back, to have returned to the past**, to have been attached to the material, symbolized by Eurydice. An authentic orphic, as it will be seen later on, **never "returns"**. **They detach, completely, from the viscous concrete** and leaves, no longer returning.[530] [author's own highlights]

The nature of the *Imponderable* is to **never return**. The Transcendence is absolute: no situation, however small, **never returns, is never repeated**. Being infinitely discontinuous and creative, why would the *Imponderable* need to repeat itself? Therefore, the illuminated consciousness "they detach, completely, from the viscous concrete", always moving, changing, going forward. An illuminated consciousness dies constantly.

To look back is to seek the past, in order to **repeat it**, evading from the **present** time of the *Imponderable*. To look back is to repeat, it is *Karma*. While walking resolutely **towards death**, Orpheus moved freely, and even other people's repetition ceased. But looking back imprisoned him. Looking back inevitably leads to Hades and imposes the paradox of God: Hades imposes eternal repetition until his Mystery is understood – the Mystery of Death – never repeat, never return.

MANIFESTATION

The smaller and repetitive reality of *Karma* is not exempt from the laws of the *Imponderable*. The fact that the *Universe* is entirely built by *Images* also applies to *Karma*. If every reality in the *Universe* appear through the *Manifestation* of spiritual *Images*, the smaller and repetitive *Image* of the *Karma* will also *Manifest*, exactly according to its nature, smaller and repetitive. Therefore, those whose consciousness are imprisoned by *Karma* will see that everything in their lives repeat. They start off by boasting that they have a very defined personality, which is coherent and stable, thereby always acting in the same way, reliably, predictably. They have friends who agree with them and are also similar. Although they fall in love with people who are completely different from them – by force of the God Ἔρως (Eros) – they try to make their relationships stable, and as soon as they can, argue incessantly with their partners to make them agree and change, giving in, until they are entirely conformed. Their friends are all similar amongst themselves, and if they start a new loving relationship, their next partner will be very similar to the previous one – as the saying goes, "all men are the same, they only change address". Their life situation, at work, their finances, their leisure, repeat until exhaustion. In the English language, people often express dissatisfaction by saying "I'm not comfortable with that"; they prefer what is comfortable. People always complain about the repetitive situations of life, however the perspective of change is fanatically denied, even if not explicitly. For the consciousness imprisoned in the *Karma* it is preferable to endure the monotony of *Karma* than to face the constant death of the *Imponderable*.

One of the many possible interpretations for the myth of Uranus and Kronos is useful for our understanding of *Karma*. Uranus and Γαῖα (Gaia) are in perpetual union, Heaven and Earth in perfect unity – an *Image* of *Unus Mundus – Spirit* IS *Body*. However, Kronos castrates Uranus and **breaks the unity**, separating the spiritual reality from the physical reality, which no longer reflect each other. **Outside unity**, Kronos starts repetition, *Karma*. Now, it is no longer the reality of unity in constant movement and change (Uranus, Heaven) that is manifested in a creative consciousness and life situations (Gaia, Earth), but the smaller reality of *Karma* that is manifested on a defined personality and comfortably repetitive situations.

With Time (Chronos), the *karmic* reality is **the only known reality**. The person "was brought up that way", and the world "has always been this way". Ignorant about the *Imponderable* and its infinite possibilities, the person understands that the "truth" is what they see in their everyday lives, that the world functions that way, that the laws of physics, biology, sociology, economics, politics, psychology, etc. – in summary, the laws of the Universe – function that way. **This** functioning of the Universe is the **only** way of functioning that they see since they were born, it is the **only functioning that there is**.

Note that it is not about **beliefs**, but **certainties**. Someone who **believes** that God forbids sexuality may [one day] no longer bear the prohibition that their belief imposes on them and give in to sex; this is common. But when someone is **certain** that the law of gravity exists, it does not follow that they "cannot bear" the certainty of such existence and decide to throw themselves from the top of a building; this does **not** happen. Beliefs easily accept exceptions; certainties **will not admit any exception**. The fact that *Karma* is an illusion, in the sense that it is only a miniscule part of the infinite *Truth*, does not prevent it to be perceived as a **certainty**[531]; one is **certain of the illusion**. However, in fact, as demonstrated by the Relativity of Einstein, there is no "law of gravity", it is just an illusion created from the lack of understanding of a wider dimension: the curvatures of the space-time, fourth-dimensional. But the illusion of the law of gravity works brilliantly: apples fall, and people will die if they jump from buildings. Therefore, **certainties about reality will produce a reality compatible with those certainties, making the imprisonment inexpugnable**.

Convictions are more dangerous enemies of truth than lies.[532]

Someone who is imprisoned in the *Karma* is incapable of perceiving other realities. In my experience, when I come across someone imprisoned in *Karma* and I express to them the existence of different realities from the one they perceive, the reaction is that of a fanatic and passionate stubbornness. The person is visibly disturbed, something between unbelieving and irritable, and employs all their energy in proving that they are right, that the reality they live in is the only one there is, the only one possible, and that the reality that I see is fantasy. They respond with **facts** that "prove" the reality which they are sure of. More than that, they present **physical facts** – emotional reactions that they **cannot change**, situations that have occurred **several times**, people who **always** act the **same way** – to demonstrate the veracity of their reality. **The worst part is that they are right**. The partial *Image* of the *Karma* reflects relentlessly in the reality of that person, from top to bottom, from the most abstract levels to the most physical levels, in every detail, revealing to be entirely real, manifesting through the numerous **facts** that serve as arguments; endless arguments. For that reason, the *Karmic* imprisonment is inexpugnable: **nothing** in the reality of that person shows any sign that their certainties are **not** the **only** reality of the universe. Therefore, they do everything in their reach to prove that the other realities are non-existent, that they are **impossible**. Perhaps that is why there are so many stories about *Bodhisattvas* who suggest meditations for people and then disappear, returning after decades[533]. Fortunately, the *Bodhisattvas* also have an infinite patience.

When this situation is noticed, by reading a text like the present one, the reality of the *Karma* may seem horrible, because the repetition and monotony become blatantly obvious, and at least in speech, people claim to be averse to imprisonment. However, it is important to notice that *Karma* is a **protection** against the *Truth*, against the terrible characteristics of *Truth*, since the *Truth* is destructive for the ego and its world as it is – the *Truth* first appears to the ego as a **disaster**. Therefore, although the reading of this text might cause horror in face of the view of oneself as described herein, almost certainly **the person will not change**. This is not so because they want to. They do want to change, given that the perspective of being imprisoned to any situation is repulsive. This happens because the person **cannot** access the *Imponderable*.

Consciousness cannot be based on nothing. For the same reason that nothing will convince a healthy person to throw themselves in the abyss, a consciousness imprisoned in *Karma*, not knowing another reality other than their *Karma*, will remain **automatic and inexorably** based on *Karma*, regardless the amount of effort they make to leave, regardless the technique they use. Techniques are useless in freeing someone from *Karma*. Saviours are equally useless.

One could argue that the consciousness could stop being based on *Karma* and start to be based on the *Imponderable*. But this is impossible, because the central characteristic of the *Imponderable* is that it is imponderable, therefore the conscience cannot reach it. We will see why:

The *Imponderable* is **transcendental**. The individual has a consciousness, and whatever their level of development, this consciousness has an extent. Everything beyond that – everything that the individual does not know – is **transcendental**. When an individual approaches an unknown content, a **transcendental** content, they can work with it and, in due course, integrate it to their conscience, becoming conscious about that content. However, the *Imponderable* is infinite, so although the individual has become conscious about that specific content, they have the infinite ahead of them. When the individual becomes conscious of a content, the *Imponderable* remains *Imponderable*, never repeats. For that reason, all attempts to **define** the *Imponderable* are in vain, because the *Imponderable* is **infinite**. The attempt to reach the *Imponderable* is as effective as trying to hold on to the void.

Evidently, once the need to use *Karma* as a protection against the *Truth* is overcome, it is not desirable to remain imprisoned to *Karma*. But trying to reach the *Imponderable* is impossible and all attempts to define the *Imponderable* are simple fantasies of the ego about it, fantasies about how the ego **would like** the *Imponderable* to be. In trying to define the *Imponderable* through its personal taste or current "spiritual" fads, once again the ego will be creating partial egoic realities, creating more *Karma*, since now, besides all existing limiting certainties, one more limiting certainty has appeared about how the *Imponderable* is. An **impasse between the *Karma* and the impossible** has been established.

How to overcome this impasse?

Consciousness cannot be based on nothing. Instead of trying to define the *Imponderable*, of trying to cover it with egoic definitions of "good", of fantasizing about the absolute unknown, it is more intelligent to accept the reality, the smaller reality of the *Karma*, the petty, ugly and unpleasant reality of the *Karma*. To dislike the *Karmic* reality, to avoid it, even if the goal is to "reach the *Imponderable*", is to simply deny it and sink deeper in fantasy. Being the *Imponderable* unachievable, one is left to accept *Karma*.

The truth is that ***Karma* is the only reality that the consciousness has**, at least to start with. The limitations of the personality itself, the limitations of people and life are much more accessible. To define the *Imponderable* is impossible; it is much easier to notice the limitations of other people, it is much easier to complain about life, and with some degree of honesty, it is even possible to be bothered by one's own limitations – pettiness is always accessible. It does not matter if these limitations are considered "good things" (i.e. "I have always been rich and I have no idea of what poverty is") or considered "bad things" (i.e. "I have always been poor, and I have no idea of what it is to be rich"). Regardless of that, they are limitations. And although the moral system forbids one to complain about life, people or even about oneself, it is better to admit that we do that, because in order to break the *Karma*, it is fundamental to first admit it. Denying reality has **never** helped anyone to advance in their consciousness development. On the other hand, who is willing to admit being envious, selfish, manipulative, a betrayer…. In one word, "bad"? Or, even worse, who is willing to admit that their self-esteem, their selflessness, their integrity, their loyalty, among other qualities considered good, are unilaterally "good", missing all its darker counterparts? Nobody wants to admit their own reality, either because it is ugly and bad and they want to eliminate it, or because it is beautiful and good, and they want to keep it. Nobody wants to admit their own *Karma*. It is much more interesting to watch several spiritual talks and get to know "the latest definition of Truth", renew their fantasies, than to make the effort to admit to each certainty they have about reality, each miniscule piece of their *Karma* and effectively get to know oneself.

Only when one realises that **there are no Saviours**, that **there are no Masters of *Karma*** and **no miraculous techniques**, when one gets tired of fantasizing and decide to opt for a self-redemptive action, only then it is possible to finally dedicate to accepting reality, the **entirely *Karmic*** reality in which they live. It will still not be the transcendent reality of the *Imponderable*; but at least the denial that there is *Karma* and that there are specific characteristics of a personal *Karma* will cease. Only then one can break the first layer of fantasy.

The type of consciousness that appear is typical of the Paradigm of Sense – a different type of consciousness whose most appropriate name, as will see later, is *Manifestation*. Having experienced the *Imponderable* at least once, in Crucifixion, one no longer completely believes in the partial reality of the ego, the *Karmic* reality. It is still a long way from a total break from the *Karma*. Being a structure of endless repetition, *Karma* has an inertial nature – like a pendulum, once in movement, *Karma* takes a while to stop oscillating. But the penetrating consciousness of a fifth-dimensional ego – its *Manifestation* – admits reality as it is, pleasant or unpleasant, and **knows** that this reality, this *Karmic* reality, is only a smaller reality than the absolute reality of the *Imponderable*. The fifth-dimensional consciousness accepts the facts of reality, the physical facts, **noticing that they are illusory**, i.e., that they are **real**, but their reality is **smaller** than the absolute reality of the *Imponderable*.

> We, therefore, can touch 'matter' as little as we can touch a rainbow. And just as a rainbow, though being an illusion, is by no means an hallucination, because it can be observed by all who are endowed with a sense of sight, can be recorded by cameras and is subject to certain laws and conditions; so in a similar way all inner and outer objects of our consciousness, including those which we call 'material' and which make up our apparently solid and tangible world, are real only in a relative sense (in that of an 'objective' illusion).[534]

Paradigm of Sense

Let us make a small digression.

Why am I calling the typical consciousness of the Paradigm of Sense of *Manifestation*, why use another name? The answer is because its nature is fundamentally different. We saw that consciousness is born under the Tree of Knowledge of Good and Bad and develops until Golgotha. During this whole journey, consciousness has a dual character, always separating reality in two, with one of the main separations being between the "psychological" and the "material", or, as it is usually called, between the "interior" and the "exterior". However, in the Paradigm of Sense, the whole reality loses the dual character. There is no separation between the "psychological" and the "material", nor between the "interior" and the "exterior". In the Paradigm of Sense, *Spirit* IS *Body, Spirit Manifests Body*.

Consciousness has developed until Crucifixion, and in Golgotha, in the *Ḍākinī* palace of skulls, the ascendant current of consciousness finds its estuary and drains in *Force* – this peak of energy causes the *Force* to awaken, the descendant current of the *Force*, the descent of *Spirit*. However, what comes after conscience? Through the unifying action of the *Inspiration* of the *Spirit* – the *Force* – consciousness is transformed, becoming fundamentally unified. The unified consciousness, united with reality, perceives reality in an equally unified manner. No longer separating realities into "interior" and "exterior", it perceives reality as an immediate coincidence between the *Spirit* and the *Body*, and the consciousness of this coincidence is called *Manifestation* (Uranus united with Gaea). Although this seems "just" a terminology, this perspective is very different because, from a dual perspective, consciousness is external to the phenomena it realises, therefore it perceives an "interior" reality manifesting in an "exterior" reality. However, from a unified perspective, there are no phenomena external to consciousness: consciousness is the **only** phenomenon, perceiving **itself** as simultaneously spiritual and corporeal, as consciousness **is** *Manifestation*.

Note that the *Force* is a descendant current. Why is it that, after completing ascension, the development needs to turn downwards?

> But Jesus, again crying out in a loud voice, yielded up his spirit. And suddenly, the veil of the Sanctuary was torn in two from top to bottom, the earth quaked, the rocks were split, the tombs opened and the bodies of many holy people rose from the dead, and these, after his resurrection, came out of the tombs, entered the holy city and appeared to a number of people.[535]

In face of Crucifixion, the veil that covers reality is removed **from top to bottom**, and Christ's death in the Skull causes the **resurrection of bodies at the bottom**. This **dead body**, this **body destitute of *Spirit*, is again *Inspired* by the *Spirit* and *Resurrects***. The body destitute of *Spirit*, the body separated from the *Spirit*, is the ***Karma*** (Chronos castrates Uranus, separating it from Gaea). The *Force* redirects consciousness downwards, rendering it *Manifestation*, which assumes the job of entirely breaking the *Karmic* structure, eliminating all points of separation between *Spirit* and *Body* one by one, culminating in the third *coniunctio*, the *Unus Mundus*.

Manifestation, the fifth-dimensional consciousness, accepts the facts of reality, the physical facts, **realising that they are illusory**, i.e., that they are **real**, but that their reality is **smaller** than the absolute reality of the *Imponderable* [536]. The fifth-dimensional consciousness looks at itself, seeking internally for each one of its certainties, knowing that **its certainties are false, because having certainties is impossible in face of the *Imponderable***. After all, what is the use of a certainty? None at all, except to defend itself from the *Imponderable* and generate *Karma*, a safety measure. The *Manifestation* is a peak of conscience that accepts bluntly the illusory nature of certainty, the *Karma*. Consciousness had certainties, and for that reason, the whole reality behaved that way. *Manifestation*, in turn, knows that its certainties are false and the whole reality cracks – the earth quaked, the rocks were split. Reality is not immediately annihilated because the nature of *Karma* is inertial: consciousness must be entirely transformed for reality to be entirely different. It is necessary that the fifth-dimensional consciousness remains aware at each instant when the certainty on which *Karma* is supported is manifested, and acknowledges its repetitive, illusory character. At each acknowledgement, the cause is removed, and therefore, the consequence. ***Karma* becomes a practical path for freeing the consciousness**.

To that end, practicing *Manifestation* requires courage. More than that, it requires *hýbris*. It is important to remember that what is *Imponderable* for the freed consciousness is **impossible** for the consciousness imprisoned to *Karma*. Knowing **only one** reality, the consciousness imprisoned to *Karma* considers other possibilities impossible. Only someone who has **integrated *hýbris*** is willing to realise an impossible task, going in the direction of the *Imponderable*.

Besides that, knowing **only one** reality, the consciousness imprisoned to *Karma* is certain that by going in different directions to the only one it knows is madness, and that, fatally, it will go **wrong**. If "going wrong" means to produce a different result to the expected, the familiar, the predicted, then it will really go wrong. On the other hand, it is important to notice that, in face of the *Imponderable*, it is impossible that something will work out, since what is being dealt with is imponderable. The fact that getting it right is impossible, means that it is impossible to define the mistake, therefore deems the concepts of "right" and "wrong" redundant. In the **Pneumatic reality, the mistake is the space of *Creation***, and the *Manifestation* is successful because it is placed **beyond right and wrong**, beyond morals, beyond ethics.

Without denying *Karma* or being deterred in face of the impossible, overcoming right and wrong, the ethical and the anti-ethical, the *Manifestation* is at ease with the *Imponderable*. It is not omniscient, nor does it desire such bore. It is simply entirely open to the transcendent infinite that constantly flows towards *Manifestation*.

Supported by the *Imponderable* and inspired by the *Force*, the *Manifestation* is the simultaneity *Spirit-Body*. With the progressive removal of the *Karmic* limitations, the reality of the individual's life transforms entirely. Step by step, the relativization of certainties completely destabilizes the life situations, as concrete as they are repetitive, and they start to collapse. Progressively, the personality is relativized through the contact of the fifth-dimensional consciousness and the *Imponderable*. It no longer makes sense to maintain the characteristics of that personality, because **all** other characteristics become accessible and start to become available in the array of eligible behaviours for that being. The characteristics that are part of that personality are still available and can be translated into behaviour, but they are no longer exclusive, coexisting with all the others, including its opposites and, if used, only reflect a preference, never a habit. Other people, in face of this level of change, tend to accuse them of lack of authenticity, lack of personality, of having changed (!), of no longer behaving as they always did. They are right; this is exactly what is happening. Little do they know that, being themselves part of the **Pneumatic reality** of the fifth-dimensional ego, they are paradoxically changing too, even if they do not realise, and their behaviour towards the 5D ego is different. The decrease of the *Karmic* repetition means not only a change in other people's behaviour, but also no longer attracting the same type of person to the life of that 5D ego, therefore the variability becomes staggering. In the same way, progressively, the repetitive patterns that were manifested in the life situations of that ego are also emptied, giving way to an **absence of pattern**, a new and **always new** sequence of imponderable life situations. The *Manifestation* causes the emergence of entirely new situations, in continual and creative change, perfectly reflecting the *Imponderable*. The *Manifestation* promotes the experience of the *Pneumatic* reality, which is constantly renovated, in an eternal creative flow. The *Manifestation* eliminates certainties, which become obsolete, and instils in its place the surprise, the shock and the enthusiasm for life.

With no intellectual certainties, the *Manifestation* frees the path and the *Force* of the *Spirit* descends to the *Body*. Whereas the self-exile of Lilith and the instinctual contention were fundamental to the ascension of the conscience, the *Manifestation* requires the **presence** of Lilith, so the experience of the *Instincts* in Paradise is allowed and desirable. The effects of the descent of the *Spirit*, of the *Body* being now full of Fire, are vitality and lust. The *Manifestation* transforms Krono, the God of *Karma*, in Saturn, the regent God of the Champs Elysées and the *Saturnalia*, where everything is permitted, "everything is allowed".

> So, in order to celebrate this paradisiac state and obtain the blessings and protection from the god on the vegetation and seeds thrown on the soil, the *Saturnalia* was celebrated, every year. [...]
>
> The *Saturnalia* were, ultimately, a reminiscent of *aetas aurea*, that is, of abundance, equality, freedom. They would start, in Rome, in the morning. After removing the woollen strip that covered, throughout the whole year, the pedestal of the statue of Saturn, there was later on a public feast, which at the end was marked by the chanting of distension: *Io Saturnalia!* Everything stopped: the senate, the tribunals, the schools, work. **Joy, orgy and freedom reigned. Any prohibition was eliminated**. The hierarchization of the proud Roman society was broken: the slaves, temporarily in total freedom, were served by the lords, who, not uncommonly, were insulted and had their vices, cruelty and turpitude thrown at their faces.[537]

ALL-THE-TIMES

> Time in itself consists of nothing. It is only a modus cogitandi that is used to express and formulate the flux of things and events, just as space is nothing but a way of describing the existence of a body.[538]

The reality of *Karma* is very narrow: always the same personality, always the same people, always the same behaviour. However, this extreme limitation is even bigger. The reality of *Karma* imprisons people in time and space.

Time is commonly perceived as a third dimensionality: a group of past, present and future, which unravels linearly. Given these three possibilities, people believe that they live in the present, with their past extending before that and the future coming afterwards. However, this reality is only valid in the Paradigm of Self-Affirmation (3D), whose base is **causal**, therefore the past has caused the present, which in turn causes the future.

In the Paradigm of Balance, the linear structure of time is strongly relativized as time is perceived as a psychological structure, as a **psychological time**. In this structure, time is still perceived linearly, as past, present and future. However, there are severe exceptions.

In face of the psychological reality that the fourth dimension opens, the certainty of living in the present is relativized. The perception of the psychological complexes – markedly the maternal and paternal complexes – show that, in various moments of the "present", one is in fact living in the "past". An extremely simple example is the adult who, when near the parents is easily regressed, behaving as they did when they were children or teenagers[539]. Besides, it is already known that a neurosis is a repetitive behaviour. What does the neurosis repeat? The neurosis repeats a pattern of behaviour from the **past**, formed in the past and brought to the present. To cite a stronger example, a sexual trauma created by a past experience has consequences in the present, keeping the person imprisoned to strong sexual limitations. The **psychological time** of that person, concerning their sexual life, is stalled in that trauma, in that past. **Psychologically**, that person is living in the present, but in the sexual sphere they are living in the past. However, this sexual trauma is not the only neurosis on that hypothetical person's psyche. People – all people – have various neurosis in their psyche, and these are manifested in their behaviour. Each neurosis was formed at a different time in the past, and therefore, each behaviour that this person has in the "present" is in fact an expression of various times "in the past". Therefore, in the **psychological time** of the fourth dimension, what we call **present** is a **composition of times in the past**.

The perception one has of the future also radically changes. In the third dimension, people believe that they have an unrestricted free-will and that they can build their future the way they want. We have seen, however, that free-will in that dimension is zero. Let us remember JUNG's sentence: "Free will is doing gladly and freely that which one must do."[540] Therefore, as Oedipus found out, what we normally call "future" is, in fact, a destiny we cannot avoid. We can, at most, experience this future with more or with less consciousness, with more or with less quality. Once destiny is determined by unconscious factors, it can only be altered to a certain degree through the process of individuation, which alters the economy of the unconscious. On the one hand, individuation leads to the integral admission of the personal destiny; on the other hand, it leads to the partial alteration of this destiny, through the increase in size and quality of consciousness. That way, the free building of the future based on free choices in the present of the third dimension is replaced by the **psychological perception** that **changes in the future** can only be partially achieved if substantial **psychological changes** are realised.

The mechanism of abreaction, for example, deals directly with these temporal realities. Abreaction is defined as a situation where the patient re-lives in the **present** a **past** situation, adding a new meaning, that way finding a cure[541]. Through this process, the psychological element of the past that prevented the experience of the present is overcome, and the person arrives in the present. As they have been cured, their future will be different.

In the Paradigm of Sense, the **psychological time** is progressively relativized as it is perceived as a *Pneumatic* **reality**, as a **present time**. After the rational and causal reality of the third dimension is overcome, the linearity of time explodes. Besides that, after the psychological reality of the fourth dimension is overcome, the determination of time by psychological factors explodes.

We have seen that one way to define *Karma* is as a certainty that protects against the *Imponderable*. It happens that this certainty was acquired at some point in the **past** and raised into a *Karma*. Henceforth, the past is repeated indefinitely in the present. In fact, the past overwrites the present, given that situations that appear in the present are not experienced, not even noticed, by the consciousness that is occupied with living in the past, protecting itself against the present.

It happens that people do not just have one certainty. On the contrary, consciousness is a group of certainties, therefore people's reality is entirely *Karmic*. Consequently, in the Paradigm of Sense, we arrive at the daunting perception that **we all always live entirely in the past – more than that, in a remote past, one which we cannot even remember – and will never know the present.**

The future is even more abstract. Usually, people say that the future has not yet happened. They try to influence the future through "present" choices. However, we have just seen that no one knows what the present is. From this perspective, it is easy to notice that the psychological relationship that one has with the **future** is a group of projections created from past elements, that one wishes to keep for they have pleased the ego, or from past elements that one wishes to alter for they have not pleased the ego. Therefore, **the future is again, the past.**

Although it is not pleasant to admit, **while one is entirely immersed in the *Karmic* reality, one lives entirely in the past.**

The Paradigm of Sense opens an entirely new reality. The *Manifestation* is a peak of consciousness, is a contact with the *Imponderable*, which ascertains *Karma*. The fifth-dimensional ego **no longer** sees *Karma* as a **past** experience, once it acknowledges its effects in the present. It is no longer necessary to remember the circumstances around which that *Karma* was formed, or remember the past, to break the *Karma*. Looking to the past will lead even more into the past. It is more intelligent to notice that the *Karma* is **present, it exists now**. *Karma* as a past experience lived in the present is directly accessible to the fifth-dimensional conscience, which, in contact with the *Imponderable*, no longer needs the *Karma*, and can remove it.

> In Buddhist parlance, karma loses its power and is dissolved in the light of perfect knowledge. As long as karma remains the force of the dark and impenetrable past, it is a fixed and unalterable magnitude, which we feel as 'the power of fate', against which we struggle in vain. In the moment of profound intuition or enlightenment, **the past is transformed into a *present* experience**, in which all the moving forces and circumstances, all inner and outer connections, motives, situations, causes and effects, [...] the very structure of reality, is clearly perceived. In this moment the Enlightened One becomes master of the law, the master-artist, in whom the rigid necessity of law is transformed and dissolved into the supreme freedom of harmony.[542] [author's own highlights]

This is what happens when we look at **one** *Karma* (if that is even possible): the past concerning that *Karma* is relativized, and with it, also the projections into the future, whether they are desires to repeat the past, or desires to avoid it. The consequence is that that specific *Karmic* point that used to keep consciousness imprisoned to the past or to a future projection is relativized – at that point the *Imponderable* flows again and the consciousness is returned to the **present**.

When this process is performed continually and the series of relativized *Karmas* is increased, the past progressively loses its ascendance over consciousness, and the future is no longer fantasized as an escape route from unacceptable realities. What consciousness **used to be** is replaced by what consciousness **is**. Consciousness lives ever more in the **present**, with **no** past and **no** future. There is always an instant in this process where the structure of time collapses, exploding the linear time and the psychological time. **Time is transcended in favour of the present.**

Nonetheless, it is essential to know that **the present is not known** – it was only very rarely experienced in sparse experiences of *kairós*[543] that may have taken place – since the consciousness imprisoned to the *Karma* was always imprisoned to the past. What characteristics does the present have?

In order to answer that question, however, we must not give in to the temptation of considering the present a concept. Let us remember: in this phase, the intellect was transcended, it no longer directs the consciousness therefore abstract concepts no longer make sense. The present is a state of fifth-dimensional consciousness.

Its main characteristic has been exhaustively exposed: **the present is *Imponderable***. On one hand, this means that **all** events in the present are entirely new, derived from the creative current of the *Spirit*. On the other hand, it is completely unpredictable, anything can happen. With no need for safety, the experience of the present is pure excitement and pure enthusiasm in face of the entirely new, of the entirely **transcendent**. In the experience of the present, put in harmony with the *Creative* current of the *Spirit* by the *Force* of *Inspiration*, **the fifth-dimensional ego transcends itself at each instant.**

Moreover, *Karma* kept consciousness linked to the past, which worked as a distraction of consciousness in relation to the present. Looking continuously at the past, consciousness imprisoned to the *Karma* managed to avoid dealing with the *Imponderable* in the present. The relativization of the *Karma* destroys the **conscious sensation of past**, illusory, and, in the present, the level of **attention to the real** increases exponentially. Without the weight of the *Karma*, the fifth-dimensional consciousness becomes agile and can deal with growing levels of perceptions. As the attention to the real increases, the **speed** of the consciousness increases, and **each instant "lasts" gradually longer**. Or, to put it another way, as the attention to the real increases, consciousness can realise more operations at any given instant. The fifth-dimensional consciousness experiences the present as a progressive temporal distension, whereas, relatively, consciousness with structures up to four dimensions are shocked with the immense speed of action of the 5D ego. The distension becomes so large that the instant starts to be seen as an interval of "time" when it is possible to enter, contemplate, create, act and leave. Metaphorically, it is as if consciousness could "pause" each instant, perform a number of actions (this number increases with the increase in speed of the consciousness), and then free the instant so that it can pass. However, it is just a metaphor with didactic reasons, since "pausing time" would mean evading the infinite current of the *Imponderable*, and this is not the objective of the 5D ego. Therefore, **the present is an instant whose duration is directly proportional to the speed of consciousness.**

As one advances in the Paradigm of Sense, the relationship between the past and the present changes. Note that it is not possible to "destroy *Karma*". *Karma* is a smaller reality than the reality of the *Imponderable*, but it is still a **reality**. A hypothetical destruction of a *Karma* would lead to the loss of a part of reality, a limitation of the *Imponderable*; this is totally undesirable. The process of liberation from *Karma* enforced by *Manifestation* is a **relativization** – the character of absolute certainty is deducted, but the smaller reality of the *Karma* is reintroduced in the bigger reality of the *Imponderable*, being acknowledged as **relative** to it. That way, one is no longer imprisoned to the reality of *Karma*, but that reality has not become forbidden, constituting one more of the infinite parts of the Whole. When people use the expression "break the *Karma*", what they mean is that the repetitive sequence of life situations is interrupted, making space to the infinitely *Creative* and discontinuous current of the *Imponderable*. Therefore, the realities (events) which were previously considered as past do **not** stop existing, they are simply **relativized**. On one hand, this means that they will not be summarily forgotten. But this is not enough. What this really means is that these realities, as with *Karma*, are no longer **attached to the past**, because the very notion of past is being relativized. **The past realities become present realities.** Since nothing in the fifth dimension is theoretical, it is a **practical situation: the past realities become accessible in the present**. We will soon return to this point.

The relativization of the past promoted by *Manifestation* eliminates the expectation of keeping the past existing in the future, as well as the desire to deny the past and build the future opposed to it. That way, the relativization of the past results in a relativization of the future. However, the future is more than a group of projections based on the past. The notion of **Destiny**, as we find in Analytical Psychology, is in a very close relationship with the notion of future. According to it, the archetypal dimension defines each person's destiny, establishing their future[544,545]. There are even Goddesses who specialize in that, the Μοῖραι (Moiras):

[...] For a start, we will face *moîra* or *aîsa*, the great conditioner of life. The Greek word *moîra* comes from the verb *meíresthai*, to obtain or inherit, obtain by luck, share, from where *Moîra* is part, plot, portion, that which each was awarded by luck, destiny. Associated with *Moîra* is, as synonym in the Homeric poems the arctic-Cypriot voice, one of the dialects used by the poet *Aîsa*. [...] Destiny was never personified, and, consequently, *Moîra* and *Aîsa* were not anthropomorphised: they hover, sovereign, over the gods and mankind, without having ever been upgraded to the category of distinct deities. **The *Moîra*, the destiny, in theory, is fixed, immutable, and cannot be altered even by the gods.** There is, however, those who make serious restrictions to this affirmation, and fall for the extreme opposite: "In the eyes of Homer, *Moîra* is mistaken with the wishes of the gods, especially *Zeus*".[546]

In the Paradigm of Balance, the ego is unconscious of the archetypes and will therefore be inexorably determined by them; the implacable Moira establishes the destiny. However, in the Paradigm of Sense, there is a coincidence between consciousness and unconscious, changing the relationship between the ego and the archetypes. The archetypes are integrated and acknowledged, no longer making sense to impose themselves in order to be acknowledged. Besides, the archetypes are in Balance, constellated with equal intensity, and in the reality emanated by the *Spirit*, by the 5D Self, **it is demanded of the 5D ego that it chooses which archetype it will *Unbalance*.** In other words, in harmony with the *Spirit* and inspired by the *Force*, the 5D ego will need to choose with which archetype it makes *Sense* to create. It is not about **controlling** an archetype, as would a 3D ego, intellectually interpreting the fifth dimension. It is about being in such a great state of harmony with the *Spirit*, acknowledging its laws and learning to operate them, and that way, performing a masterpiece. There is no opposition, there is *Creation*.

If beyond the projections of the past, the future, the Destiny, is determined by the archetypes, and the 5D ego is in a position to acknowledge the archetypes and their laws and *Create* with them, the 5D ego is able to *Create* its future. If above all, the Self is the great creator of the human being's Destiny and the 5D Self does not guide the 5D ego, then the 5D ego **needs** to define its own Destiny. As the 5D ego has access to the archetypal dimension and creates with it, we can affirm that the actions taken by the 5D ego in the fifth dimension are perceived in the previous dimensions **a while later**, at what the linear structure of time calls "future". For that reason, one of the types of fifth-dimensional action is called *Actions in the Future*.

As we have seen so far, in the Paradigm of Sense, **past** is the name given to a group of situations entirely accessible to the 5D ego in the **present**. **Future** is the name given to a group of situations that the 5D ego is creating in the **present**. **Present** is the name given to the conscious sensation of experiencing the present **instant, which passes. Instant** is the name given to the duration which is proportional to the speed of the fifth-dimensional consciousness. All the times are available to the 5D ego in the **now**. For that reason, the temporal structure typical of the Paradigm of Sense is *All-the-Times*. This temporal structure has its centre in the **instant** of the **present**, which gives access to the whole **past** and the whole **future**. Placing itself in the centre of *All-the-Times* – the **instant of the present** – the fifth-dimensional conscience develops, therefore, in an *Instantaneous Presence*, around which there are all the times: the past, the present and the future. This is the **sensation** experienced by the fifth-dimensional ego: the *Manifestation*.

MULTI-DIMENSIONALITY

The **space** is perhaps the most third-dimensional structure, commonly noticed as width, height and depth, which relate to each other perpendicularly. Given these three possibilities, one believes that in order to reach anywhere it is necessary to move towards it through space. However, this reality is only valid in the Paradigm of Self-Affirmation (3D), where the ego is the agent of all reality, and, being the only causing agent, only this ego can produce the necessary movement, taking itself from one place to the next.

In the Paradigm of Balance, the structure of space is strongly relativized as the space is perceived as a psychological structure, as a **psychological space**. In this structure, the space is still perceived as an extension, as width, height and depth. However, there are serious exceptions.

In face of the psychological reality that the fourth dimension opens, the certainty that the spaces are separate, that there is distance between the here and there, needs to coexist with the irruption of events **here**, which previously only occurred **there**. One could argue that this is perfectly common; indeed, there is nothing surprising about events of a different nature suddenly starting to occur in a certain place. However, what in fact changes is that the perception of this phenomenon as **casual** is replaced by the perception that changes in the organization and economy of the

Unconscious – unconscious complexes and Archetypes – are reflected in changes on the type of event which normally occurs in a certain place.

Let us look at an extremely simple example. The denial and consequent projection of an anger complex by person A can lead the unconscious to start attracting aggressive persons B, C and D, in order to compose the social circle of person A, thereby forcing the consciousness to acknowledge anger as a valid psychological energy. Note that **attracting** means to bring persons B, C and D into the space of person A's life. It was not person A who sought persons B, C and D. Strictly speaking, by denying anger, that person would rather not have B, C and D in their life. But the reality is that, if person A does not manage to integrate anger and eliminate persons B, C and D from their life, the Unconscious will select other aggressive persons from the environment, E, F and G, bringing them into the life of person A, and so on, until person A integrates anger. If, on the other hand, person A, through therapy or any other expedient, manages to integrate anger, aggressive people will stop invading their space. This is not about a **causal** phenomenon. What is seen as **casual** is, in fact, caused by the Unconscious, a subjacent dimension to the third-dimensional space of consciousness, metaphorically a fourth dimension, subjacent to the three dimensions of space. Although this may seem magical for someone with no understanding of how the Unconscious works, it is a technical knowledge. A good Jungian psychologist can predict the occurrence or the ceasing of phenomena in a patient's life, simply by observing their dreams, as dreams cause the person's reality.

The psychological space is, therefore, a composition of people, things and situations automatically assembled by the Unconscious, from its organization. More than that, the conscious use of techniques from Analytical Psychology makes the composition of people, things and situations accessible to the consciousness, and enables it to alter that composition through changes in the organization of the Unconscious. If they are accessible, they can be experienced again.

Given that the fifth-dimensional consciousness is based on the *Imponderable*, its amplitude is much higher and tends towards the infinite. Therefore, its perspective in relation to the "past" situation, re-lived in the present, is entirely different. The 5D ego can re-live "past" situations in an unaltered form or **with alterations**.

In the Paradigm of Sense, the **psychological space** is progressively relativized as it is perceived as a ***Pneumatic* reality**, where the "interior" reality is identical to the "exterior" reality – *Spirit Manifests Body*. Having overcome the rational causal reality of the third dimension, the third-dimensional space explodes. Besides that, having overcome the psychological reality of the fourth dimension, the determination of space by psychological factors also explodes.

What changes in the perception of space of the Paradigm of Sense is the notion of ***Body***. In the previous dimensions, the body has **finite dimensions**, it occupies a **finite space** and finds itself in a **specific position**. In the fifth dimension, however, duality is entirely overcome, and the *Spirit* coincides with the *Body*. Without duality, it makes no sense to separate the "interior" reality from the "exterior". More than affirming that there is a correspondence between the Symbols of the "interior" reality and the events of the "exterior" reality (a 4D approach), we can affirm that the "exterior" reality is "interior". That way, the *Body* of the 5D ego is **paradoxically** its *Spirit*. People are independent and **paradoxically** part of the 5D ego. Situations occur according to the laws of physics, chemistry and biology, and **paradoxically**, are situations occurring "within" the 5D ego. However, the 5D ego does **not** perform "interior" or "exterior" modifications: it performs modifications in the global *Pneumatic* reality, **paradoxically** *Spirit* and *Body*, unified.

However, when we consider the *Pneûma* and the *Macroimage*, the notions of third-dimensional space and psychological space explode. Being a dream with five dimensions, the structure of the *Pneûma* is **physical**, so it is not possible to distinguish a *Pneumatic Image* from a physical event. **The 5D ego is conscious** within the *Pneûma*, as it would be in "any" physical event, since the *Pneûma* **IS** a physical event. Let us look at the example of the individual who is in bed with his wife, and dreams, awake (!), that he is on the top of a mountain with a hooded skeleton – this is the experience that Jeffrey RAFF tells us in *Jung and the alchemical imagination*[547]. How could he have been **physically and instantaneously transported** to the top of the mountain? Or, worse, how could he, awake, be physically and **simultaneously** in two places? These questions do not proceed, not because the experience is not possible or real – I believe in RAFF. They do not proceed because in the fifth dimension, although the space exists, there is no separation between the various locations. If the structure of a *Pneûma* if physical, **a *Pneûma* is a specific location**.

An addition of all *Pneumata* (plural of *Pneûma*), an addition of all – and **paradoxically** infinite – *Images* of the *Universe*, **the *Macroimage* includes the space of the whole *Universe***. This means that the fifth-dimensional ego has access to any location of the Cosmos whose *Pneûma* it can access, whether by "dreaming", imagining or having visions. There are no barriers or distances between the various locations of the Cosmos. In the Paradigm of Sense, **the space is formed by contiguous locations,**

by contiguous realities, since its *Images*, which are physical, can be accessed sequentially or even simultaneously.

Considered together, the *Macroimage* and the *All-the-Times* take us to an absolutely shocking perception: in the Paradigm of Sense, **any reality of any time – any dimension – can be accessed here and now**, as long as one has access to its *Image*, obtained either by *Pneumata*, by vision or even in the physical *Image* seen awake[548]. **In the Paradigm of Sense, the *Pneumatic* reality is the *Multi-Dimensionality*.**

> To the enlightened man [...], **whose consciousness embraces the universe**, to him the universe becomes his 'body', while his physical body becomes a manifestation of the Universal Mind, his inner vision an expression of the highest reality, and his speech an expression of eternal truth and mantric power.[549] [author's own highlights]

Let us take as an example, or preferably, as a metaphor, the experience that Jesus had with Moses and Elijah.

> Six days later, Jesus took with him Peter and James and his brother John and led them up a high mountain by themselves. There in their presence he was transfigured: his face shone like the sun and his clothes became as dazzling as light. And suddenly Moses and Elijah appeared to them; they were talking with him. Then Peter spoke to Jesus. 'Lord', he said, 'it is wonderful for us to be here; if you want me to, I will make three shelters here, one for you, one for Moses and one for Elijah.'[550]

The scene is described from the perspective of Jesus, who receives in his environment Moses and Elijah, third-dimensionally separate from them by several centuries and great distances, but, fifth-dimensionally, all three are going through contiguous realities. For that reason, it is important to know that, from Moses' perspective, Jesus and Elijah were visiting his reality, maybe in the Pharaoh's palace, maybe crossing the Red Sea, maybe in the desert. In the same way, from Elijah's perspective, Jesus and Moses were visiting his reality, maybe in the Horeb Mount. They all see each other, talk, touch. For them all, the three realities make sense. In the *Multi-Dimensionality*, realities – supposedly separate by centuries and kilometres – reveal to be contiguous and can be physically accessed through their *Images*.

Beyond being a transcendence of time and space, the *Multi-Dimensionality* is the very structure of the Universe. On one hand, it is a whole organized in different parts. It is important that the parts are distinct, so that we can identify them. Without that, everything would end up in confusion, in nothing, in nihilism and chaos. On the other hand, all different parts are united among themselves, and are contiguous realities – all contiguous with all – and the total sum is the *Imponderable*, which, **paradoxically**, is larger than the total sum. Without that, it would all end up in the illusion of separation and of *Karma*.

> Thus we discern in the figure of the Buddha three 'bodies' or principles:
>
> 1. that, in which all Enlightened Ones are the same: the experience of completeness, of universality, of the deepest super-individual reality of the *Dharma*, the primordial law and cause of all things, from which emanates all physical, moral and metaphysical order;
>
> 2. that which constitutes the spiritual or ideal character of a Buddha, the creative expression or formulation of this universal principle in the realm of inner vision: the *Sambhogakaya*, the 'Body of Bliss' (rapture or spiritual enjoyment), from which all true inspiration is born;
>
> 3. that, in which this inspiration is transformed into visible form and becomes action: the *Nirmanakaya*: the 'Body of Transformation', the human embodiment or individuality of an Enlightened One.
>
> In the *Dharmakaya*, the universal principle of all consciousness, the totality of becoming and being is potentially contained – comparable to the infinity of space, which embraces all things and is the *conditio sine qua non* of all that exists. Yet we can neither say that space is identical with things, nor that it is different from them. As little as we can become conscious of space without its opposite pole, i.e., form, so **the Dharmakaya cannot become reality for us without descending into forms**.[551] [author's own highlights]

The *Multi-Dimensionality* is the maximum exponent of *Manifestation*. There, the *Imponderable* is the **Body** of the totality of the *Universe*, and in contact with it the consciousness tends to the infinite and constantly transcends itself. There, the *Force* is the **Body** of *Inspiration* of the *Spirit*, and in contact with it the consciousness builds its *Creative* work. There, *Manifestation* is the **Body** of transformation, where the *Spirit* manifests continually. *Manifestation* is *Body* in every dimension, from the most imponderable (abstract) to the most transformative (concrete, corporeal). The *Manifestation* is the perfect **Corporeal** reflection and connexion of all dimensions in every dimension. The *Manifestation* is the **Corporeality** of the *Multi-Dimensionality*.

---

[486] I suggest the reading of Erich NEUMANN's, *The Origins and History of Consciousness*. (1962. New York: Harper Torchbooks.) Part II "The Psychological Stages in the Development of Personality", item A "The original unity".

[487] "In Babylonia, the male-female unity of the uroboros is constituted by Tiamat and Apsu, who are the primordial chaos of the water. But Tiamat is the actual principal of origination: mother of the gods and possessor of the table of fate. [...] Tiamat survives the death of Apsu and when she is finally defeated by Marduk, the patriarchal sun god, the upper vault of heaven and the lower vault of the underworld are fashioned from her body. [...] But Tiamat, whose open gullet seeks to devour Marduk, the solar hero, is not only evil; she is also the generative cave-womb of the Great Mother. [...] Therefore, Tiamat is far from being only the abysmal, nocturnal monster that the later patriarchal world of the victorious Marduk saw in her. She is not only the generatrix but also the true mother of her creatures [...]". NEUMANN, E. (1963) *The great mother - an analysis of the archetype*. Translated by Manheim, R. 2nd edition. Bollingen series XLVII. Princeton University Press. pp. 213-214.

[488] GOVINDA, A. (1975) *Foundations of Tibetan mysticism*. New York: Samuel Weiser. pp 75 and 77.

[489] Ibid.

[490] This process is masterfully described by Carl JUNG in *Psychology and religion: West and East. – Answer to Job*. (1975) Translated by Hull, R. F. C. 2nd edition CW XI. Bollingen Series XX. Princeton University Press.

[491] GOVINDA, A. *Foundations of Tibetan mysticism*. Op. Cit. p. 77.

[492] *The New Jerusalem Bible*. Luke 22:44.

[493] Ibid. John 18:38.

[494] Ibid. John 15:26.

[495] NIETZSCHE, F. (2006) *On the genealogy of morality*. Translated by DIETHE, C. Cambridge University Press. Aphorism 24.

[496] "First, the message that there is na autonomous power of evil that is beyond man's control. Second, the message that there is a balance of opposites in life; that light must

be opposed by darkness, and that the more the light, positive side is stressed and personified in the figure of a beneficent diety, the more inevitable it becomes that the dark side will likewise appear in a god or goddess who is as evil and malevolent as the light deity is good and well intentioned." SANFORD, J. A. (1998) Evil: *The shadow side of reality*. The Crossroad Publishing Co. pp. 22-23.

[497] GOVINDA, A. *Foundations of Tibetan mysticism*. Op. Cit. p. 18.

[498] *The New Jerusalem Bible*. John 18:36.

[499] Ibid. Genesis 2:25.

[500] Ibid. Genesis 3:7-10.

[501] "The gods gave him the name of Pan, meaning 'All Things', not only because **all things** are to some extent like him in their greed, but also because **he is a universal tendency incarnate**. He was the god of All Things, doubtless indicative of the procreative current charging All Things, All Gods or All Life." CHEVALIER, J. and GHEERBRANT, A. (1996) *A Dictionary of Symbols*. Translated by Buchanan-Brown, J. UK: Penguin. p. 734. [author's own highlights]

[502] "The Garden of Eden has certain features of a mandala with four rivers flowing from it and the tree of life in its center. The mandala garden is an image of the Self, in this case representing the ego's original oneness with nature and deity. It is the initial, unconscious, animal state of being at one with one's Self. It is paradisal because consciousness has not yet appeared and hence there is no conflict." EDINGER, E. F. (1992) *Ego and archetype*. Boston: Shambhala. p. 17.

[503] "Pan, the sheperd's god, had half-human, half-animal shape; bearded, horned and hairy, lively agile, swift and crafty, he expressed *animal cunning*. He preyed sexually upon nymphs, and boys indifferently, but his appetite was insatiable and he also indulged in solitary masturbation." CHEVALIER, J. and GHEERBRANT, A. *A Dictionary of Symbols*. Op. Cit. p. 734.

[504] "He gave his name to the word 'panic', the terror which fills all terror and all beings when the feeling that this god is there disturbs the spirit and bewilders the senses. Ibid.

[505] "Pan, like other gods who dwelt in forests, was dreaded by those whose occupations caused them to pass through the woods by night, for the gloom and loneliness of such scenes dispose the mind to superstitious fears. Hence sudden fright without any visible cause was ascribed to Pan, and called a Panic terror." BULLFINCH, T. (2002) *Bullfinch's mythology*. Chapter 22, "The rural deities and Erisichthon Rhoecus, the water deities Camenae Winds." "The rural deities" (Online) Available at: <http://l-adam-mekler.com/bulfinch.pdf> Access: January 27th 2020.

[506] GOVINDA, A. *Foundations of Tibetan mysticism*. Op. Cit. p. 176.

[507] "Pan, the old philosopher, the wise, a "simple pastor", attached to the earth, to the animals and nature, also having a fortune telling powers [...]" BRANDÃO DE SOUZA, J. (1989) *Mitologia grega*, Petrópolis, RJ: Editora Vozes. p. 236.

[508] "Pan, the god of the countryside, sat on the river's brow with Echo, the mountain goddess, in his arms, teaching her to make melodious answer to sounds of every kind. [...] The goat-footed god called Psyche to him gently, for she was bruised and swooning, and he knew moreover what had befallen her [...]" NEUMANN, E. (1971) *Amor and psyche: the psychic development of the feminine*. Translated by Manheim, R. Princeton University Press. p. 28.

509 "Neoplatonist and Christian philosophers made Pan the synthesis of paganism. Plutarch records the legend of sailors on the high seas hearing mysterious voices proclaiming "great Pan is dead!". No doubt the voices mourning among the waves foretold the death of the pagan gods, epitomized in Pan and the birth of a new age and one which made the Greco-Roman world shiver with fear." CHEVALIER, J. and GHEERBRANT, A. *A Dictionary of Symbols*. Op. Cit. p. 734.

510 "(There is) an early Christian tradition that when the heavenly host told the shepherds at Bethlehem of the birth of Christ, a deep groan, heard through all the isles of Greece, told that the great Pan was dead, and that all the royalty of Olympus was dethroned and the several deities were sent wandering in cold and darkness. So Milton in his "Hymn on the Nativity" [...] BULLFINCH, T. *Bullfinch's mythology*. Op. Cit. Chapter 22, "The rural deities, Erisichthon Rhoecus, the water deities, Camenae Winds." "The rural deities."

511 Although the terminology "psyche" is used, more adequate to the fourth dimension, Jung deals with this reality in his work: The psyche is therefore all-important; it is the all-pervading Breath, the Buddha-essence; it is the Buddha-Mind, the One, the *Dharmakaya*. All existence emanates from it, and all separate forms dissolve back into it." JUNG, C. G. (1975) *Psychology and religion: West and East*. Translated by Hull, R. F. C. 2nd edition. CW XI. Bollingen Series XX. Princeton University Press. §771.

512 GOVINDA, A. (1975) *Foundations of Tibetan mysticism*. New York: Samuel Weiser. pp. 213 and 214.

513 Ibid. p. 199.

514 *The New Jerusalem Bible*. Acts 13:10.

515 See chapter "*Demon*".

516 "[...] So if one speaks of *viśuddha*, it is of course with a certain hesitation. We are stepping into the slippery future right away when we try to understand what that might mean. For in *viśuddha* we reach beyond our actual conception of the world..." JUNG, C. G. (1996) *The psychology of Kundalini Yoga*. Bollingen Series XCIX. Princeton University Press. p. 4.

517 "Neurosis [...] [is] a dividing line drawn by the power of the ego consciousness to **resist the break-through of unconscious content**. [...] Complexes of the personal unconscious are less to be feared in this connection; the conscious mind can somehow deal with them. For the explosive dynamic of their "nucleus" is sufficiently insulated by the layer of personalistic, environment-conditioned experiences around it, which serve as a kind of buffer in its encounter with consciousness. Only when this "layer" is worn out, or when it is very thin to begin with (as is the case in many individuals threated by psychosis), can the threat become really effective. For this reason, the danger and the corresponding anxiety are greatest when the confrontation is with complexes of the collective unconscious, whose "explosive charge" can act as an earthquake, shattering everything around it." JACOBI, J. (1959) *Complex/Archetypes/Symbol in the Psychology of C. G. Jung*. Translated by Manheim, R. Bollingen Foundation, Inc. pp. 28-29. [author's own highlights]

518 See in previous note: "the conscious mind can somehow deal with them. For the explosive dynamic of their "nucleus" is **sufficiently insulated by the layer of personalistic, environment-conditioned experiences around it**, which serve as a kind of buffer in its encounter with consciousness." Ibid. [author's own highlights]

[519] "Thus the theory of repression, whose validity in a definite field of pathology is incontestable [...] as been extended to creative processes, and the creation of culture relegated to second place, as a mere replacement product. At the same time the wholeness and healthiness of the creative function is seen in the murky light of neurosis, which is of course an undoubted product of repression in many cases. In this way creativity becomes indistinguishable from morbidity, and the creative individual immediately suspects himself of some kind of illness, while the neurotic has lately begun to believe that his neurosis is an art, or at least a source of art. [...] True productivity is a spring that can never be stopped up. [...] Creative power is mightier than its possessor. [...] Disease has never yet fostered creative work; on the contrary, it is the most formidable obstacle to creation. No breaking down of repressions can ever destroy true creativeness, just as no analysis can ever exhaust the unconscious." JUNG, C. G. (1981) *The Development of personality.* Translated by Hull, R. F. C. CW XVII. Bollingen Series XX. Princeton University Press. §206.

[520] "Since the Apocalypse we now know again that God is not only to be loved, but also to be feared. He fills us with evil as well as with good, otherwise he would not need to be feared." JUNG, C. G. (1975) *Psychology and religion: West and East. – Answer to Job.* Translated by Hull, R. F. C. 2nd edition. CW XI. Bollingen Series XX. Princeton University Press. §747.

[521] GOVINDA, A. (1975) *Foundations of Tibetan mysticism.* New York: Samuel Weiser. p. 34.

[522] *Dharma*, law, truth, guidance, is said to be "nowhere save in the mind." JUNG, C. G. (1975) *Psychology and religion: West and East. Western religion.* Translated by Hull, R. F. C. 2nd edition. CW XI. Bollingen Series XX. Princeton University Press. §822.

[523] "The East, on the other hand, compassionately tolerates those "lower" spiritual stages where man, in his blind ignorance of karma, still bothers about sin and tortures his imagination with a belief in absolute gods, who, if he only looked deeper, are nothing but the veil of illusion woven by his own unenlightened mind". Ibid. §771.

[524] NIETZSCHE, F. (2016) *Ecce homo.* Preface. Translated by Ludovici, A.M. and Cohn, P. V. Project Gutemberg ebook. Available at: <http://www.gutenberg.org/ebooks/52190> Access: 28 February 2020. Aphorism 3.

[525] GOVINDA, A. *Foundations of Tibetan mysticism.* Op. Cit. p. 217.

[526] Ibid. p. 243.

[527] BRANDÃO DE SOUZA, J. (1989) *Mitologia grega*, Vol. I. Petrópolis, RJ: Editora Vozes. p. 198.

[528] Ibid. p.79.

[529] Ibid. p. 226.

[530] Ibid. Vol. II. p.142.

[531] "The 'thought-forms' appear as realities, fantasy takes on real form, and the terrifying dream evoked by karma and played out by the unconscious 'dominants' begins." JUNG, C. G. (1975) *Psychology and religion: West and East. Western religion.* Translated by Hull, R. F. C. 2nd edition. CW XI. Bollingen Series XX. Princeton University Press. §850.

[532] NIETZSCHE, F. (1910) *Human, all too human.* London: T. N. Foulis. (eBook) Available at:

<https://digitalassets.lib.berkeley.edu/main/b20790001_v_1_B000773557.pdf>
Access: January 27th 2020. Aphorism 483.

533 "With these words he poured a heap of jewels into a corner of the room, made the pupil sit down before it, and left him to his meditation. [...] Thus his former pride and elation turned into dejection, and when the Guru returned after twelve years and asked the pupil how he was faring, he told the Master that he was very unhappy." GOVINDA, A. (1975) *Foundations of Tibetan mysticism.* New York: Samuel Weiser. p. 55.

534 Ibid. p. 68.

535 *The New Jerusalem Bible.* Matthew 27:50-53.

536 "With this final vision the karmic illusions cease; consciousness, weaned away from all form and from all attachment to objects, returns to the timeless, into a state of the *Dharmakaya.*" JUNG, C. G. *Psychology and religion: West and East. Western religion.* Op. Cit. §853.

537 BRANDÃO DE SOUZA, J. *Mitologia grega*, Vol. I. Op. Cit. p. 341.

538 JUNG, C. G. (1976) *Letters*, Vol. II. Translated by Hulen, J. Bollingen Series. Princeton University Press. p. 176.

539 "Should this more developed activity meet with an obstacle that forces it to regress, the regression will be to an earlier stage of development." JUNG, C. G. (1976) *Symbols of transformation.* Translated by Hull, R. F. C. CW V. Bollingen Series XX. Princeton University Press. §206.

540 "Free will is doing gladly and freely that which one must do." Carl JUNG. JUNG, C., JUNG, E. and WOLF, T. (January 11, 2020) *A collection of remembrances.* [online: weblog]. Available at: <https://carljungdepthpsychologysite.blog/2020/01/11/carl-jung-on-free-will-anthology/#.Xoc-kP1Khdg> Access: January 22nd 2020.

541 Carl JUNG acknowledges the importance of the process of ab-reaction: "Hence one could easily represent the trauma as a complex with a high emotional charge, and because this enormously effective charge seems at first sight to be the pathological cause of the disturbance, one can accordingly postulate a therapy whose aim is the complete release of this charge. Such a view is both simple and logical, and it is in apparent agreement with the fact that abreaction – i.e., the dramatic rehearsal of the traumatic moment, its emotional recapitulation in the waking or in the hypnotic state often has a beneficial therapeutic effect". JUNG, C. G. (1985) *The Practice of psychotherapy. Ab-reaction, dream analysis and transference.* Translated by Hull, R. F. C. 2nd edition. CW XVI. Bollingen Series XX. Princeton University Press. §262.

However, he says that this mechanism is not, on its own, enough for the psychological cure, since the psychological problem is not just a repressed emotional load, but a **psychological split**, so the reason for the relationship with the doctor (frequently, a relationship of transference) becomes essential: "The rehearsal of the traumatic moment is able to reintegrate the neurotic dissociation only when the conscious personality of the patient is so far reinforced by his relationship to the doctor that he can consciously bring the autonomous complex under the control of his will." Carl JUNG. *Ab-reaction, dream analysis and transference.* Ibid. §271. [author's own highlights]

542 GOVINDA, A. *Foundations of Tibetan mysticism.* Op. Cit. p. 267.

543 "Taking the astrological constellation into consideration is what is meant by this idea of *kairikai baphai. Kairos* therefore at that time and in this connection means **the astrologically right time, the time when things can turn out successfully.**" von FRANZ, M. L. (1980) *Alchemy: an introduction to the symbolism and the psychology.* Inner City Books. p. 44. [author's own highlights]

544 "Every dream is a statement of the psyche about itself. [...] The answers to the secrets of the day and the solutions to the riddles are all contained in its primordial womb. That is why there is always something fateful about the images and symbols that arise from it. 'Perhaps – who knows? – these eternal images are what men mean by fate.'" JACOBI, J. (1959) *Complex/Archetypes/Symbol in the Psychology of C. G. Jung.* Translated by Manheim, R. Bollingen Series LVII. Bollingen Foundation, Inc. pp. 197-198.

545 Synchronicity appears as another Jungian concept which is determining in the individual destiny: "Chance appears to play an important role in the working out of the purpose in the seed of individuality. It, however, needs to be a *meaningful* chance, what Jung terms a "meaningful coincidence". The coming together by apparent chance of factors that are not causally linked but that nevertheless show themselves to be meaningfully related is at the very heart of the process by which the purpose of the individuals life unfolds and becomes his 'fate'." PROGOFF. I. (1973) *Jung, synchronicity and human destiny.* New York: Delta. p. 64.

546 BRANDÃO DE SOUZA, J. *Mitologia grega.* Vol. I. Op. Cit. p.140.

547 RAFF, J. (2000) *Jung and the alchemical imagination.* Florida: Nicolas-Hays, Inc.

548 "[...] **the form is not other than the spiritual being itself**; on the contrary, **it is identical** with it, even if it is found in a thousand places, or in all places and is diverse in shape.' [quoting Ibn ARABI]. In other words, **the form that a psychoidal being assumes in the psyche, the inner figure in which it manifests, is identical with the psychoidal entity**. There is no difference between the spiritual being, itself, and the imaginal form in which one experiences it. Active imagination with such a figure therefore relates one to the world beyond the psyche, to the spiritual domain and reality in which the divine resides. Though it may never be possible to experience that reality in and of itself, one can experience it through the form that it assumes. Since that form is no different than the thing itself, the imaginal encounter with the form is the encounter with the divine entity from which it originates." RAFF, J. (2000) *Jung and the alchemical imagination.* Chapter 1 "Jung as a spiritual tradition" "psyche and psychoid". Florida: Nicolas-Hays, Inc. (Kobo eBook version). [author's own highlights]

549 GOVINDA, A. *Foundations of Tibetan mysticism.* Op. Cit. p. 225.

550 *The New Jerusalem Bible.* Matthew 17: 1-4.

551 GOVINDA, A. *Foundations of Tibetan mysticism.* Op. Cit. p. 213.

EVOLUTION

This chapter is dedicated to Rúbia Mattos, in whom I saw the Evolution *for the first time. She was fighting for the* Grail.

PLENITUDE

The *Spirit* is Most High. Realities such as the *Macroimage*, the *Word*, the *Demon*, the *Force*, the *Manifestation*, the *All-the-Times* and the *Multi-dimensionality* are extremely complex and way beyond common life. Beyond all these realities, and including them, there is the *Imponderable*, eternally challenging the understanding. In such a **transcendent** scenario, to remain sane is to remain human. More than that, the human being occupies a unique position in the Universe – Self-awareness – the human being is a Self-aware Universe[552].

Christianity led us to adopt a position of false modesty in face of the Most High, as if we should place ourselves way below the Most High. There is a degree of truth hidden in this. GALILEO showed us that we are not the centre of the Universe, DARWIN showed us that we are not the main species of this planet, FREUD showed us that the ego is not the totality of the psyche. We must agree that, in a Universe where we observe billions of galaxies, some billion light-years from us, how can we sustain any level of grandiose fantasy? To sustain this would be ridiculous.

Nevertheless, **paradoxically**, the *Universe* – the *Imponderable*, the *Macroimage*, the *Word*, the *Demon*, the *Force*, the *Manifestation*, the *All-the-Times* and the *Multi-dimensionality* – and dimensions much higher than these – converge to the Self-Aware Universe, to the human being. In the Paradigm of Sense, the infinite potencies of the Universe exist "**within**" the human being, since there is no "outside". The human being is *Imponderable*.

Having the Infinite "within" itself, the hardest objective to be reached is to **remain human**, reaching an even higher level of purity, therefore of *Evolution*. The fifth-dimensional realities are infinite potencies and their convergence towards the human being tend to cause identifications. In a dimension where the *hýbris* is integrated and the identification is structural, where one of the realities is the *Demon* and its continuous and tempting suggestion of identification, to remain human is a herculean job. Even so, it is necessary to give everything to reach this objective, to maintain the **purity**[553], which, as we will see, is the essence of *Evolution*. One might believe that giving in to the *Demon* and elect as the main goal to absorb the divine potencies makes the human being powerful. Indeed, this occurs for a while – sometimes, for too long. However, to put power above everything else disconnects the human being from its most essential characteristic – humanity – dehumanizing them and turning them into a sort of **monstrosity**. It is not about punishment, but consequence. Those who prioritize power only do so because they, fanatically and obsessively, seek certain specific objectives in detriment of others, they magnify certain characteristics in detriment of others. To overly glorify the importance of certain characteristics leads to deformation. Noting is more horrible than **inhumanity**.

It is true that the Paradigm of Sense includes the *hýbris* and the exercise of power in *Unbalance*. However, at least to those who wish to remain sane, the highest desire is the wisdom, the Wholeness, not power. The exercise of power in *Unbalance* of the fifth-dimensional ego stems from the Balance and the *Force*, it settles its *Unbalance* with the *Demon* (cosmic potency of the *Unbalance*), and as soon as possible, re-establishes the Balance, at a higher level. It is something completely different.

Not only is the identification with a specific infinite potency a great risk, the identification with the *Imponderable* also is. There are those who mistake the self-aware experience of the *Imponderable* with **dissolving** in the *Imponderable*. In the Paradigm of Sense, the self-aware experience of the *Imponderable* does not include the loss of ego or the loss of individuality. Being the centre of the Self-conscious Universe, **the ego always grows**; it only loses the characteristic of separation and duality, which were only necessary until it was sufficiently defined and strong to the point of enabling the experience of the *Imponderable*. To dissolve in the *Imponderable*, to leave human life, leads to a loss of consciousness, loss of humanity, and ultimately, the worst monster of all – the **nihilism** – the maximum expression of contempt by what one is[554]. JUNG **never** advocated in favour of the ego's death. On the contrary, it keeps affirming the absolute need for a strong ego for the consciousness development[555].

The self-aware experience of the *Imponderable* needs to be experienced as a human being – this is its greatness. The challenge inherent to this experience is to remain in the infinite and discontinuous flow of spiritual *Images*, and operate it in practice in human life, placing the infinite in the finite, the OM in the HUM. That way, the *Imponderable* converges towards the human being[556]. That way, the human being is *Imponderable*. That way, **humanity**, as a characteristic of the human being, occupies a central position in the Paradigm of Sense. The movement that allows individuals to remain human in the Paradigm of Sense is *Evolution*.

Having said that, we must return our attention to the **human experience** of the Paradigm of Sense, prioritizing the understanding of the **experience** of the fifth-dimensional realities.

> Life and spirit are two powers or necessities between which man is placed. Spirit gives meaning to his life, and the possibility of its greatest development. But life is essential to spirit, since its truth is nothing if it cannot live.[557]

The Paradigm of Sense starts with a first experience of the *Imponderable*, on the Cross. This first experience causes an indelible mark on the individual, making the individual fifth-dimensional. However, the experience on the Cross is too excruciating to be bearable, and fortunately, the individual is returned to their daily life, **human**. The 5D ego has experienced the *Imponderable*, now they need to experience it in their daily life, **human**.

The *Imponderable* is an infinite and discontinuous flow of spiritual *Images*. This idea is extremely complex. Instead of adhering to the **idea**, let us turn our attention to the **human experience** of the *Imponderable*. We know that the *Universe* is entirely built by *Images*, which manifest in life situations. Therefore, an infinite and discontinuous flow of spiritual *Images* are manifested in an infinite and discontinuous sequence of life situations. 3D egos experience this as a sequence of random facts, as "things of life", as "things that happen". 4D egos experience this as a sequence of physical facts that relate **significantly** with psychological facts, produced by the Self. 5D egos experience this as a ***Pneumatic reality***, where physical facts are spiritual facts. Regardless of how many dimensions does the ego experiencing this has, it will be an infinite and discontinuous sequence of life situations.

In face of this experience, 3D egos select, according to their preferences, which life situations they want to experience and which they want to avoid, denying the latter and relegating it to others. 4D egos observe the directions given by the Self in order to define which situations foster psychological integrations and which situations are regressive, that way, selecting how to behave.

The **experience** of the 5D egos is entirely different because they have already **experienced** the *Imponderable*, and have their consciousness based on that. In *Evolution*, **5D egos simply include everything and live all experiences**, pleasant or unpleasant, splendid or atrocious, luminous or dark, good or evil, ethical or unethical, fair or unfair – in sum, all experiences. The 5D ego lives in a ***Pneumatic* reality**, where there is no "internal" separate from the "external", where the life situations **are** aspects of the being. Therefore, to deny a life situation is to deny an aspect of oneself, which by itself is very negative, but that, even worse, causes an immediate disconnection from the *Imponderable*. It is not worth it. It is better to live **all** experiences, which are evidences of their own being, as that way they gain access to the reality of their own being, that way it is possible to "see oneself deeply, see all of one's sides, notice each detail, each reaction of the Being."[558]

Evidently, "not everything is beautiful, harmonious and balanced"[559]. Life has an infinite ability to be horrible. The 5D ego has no obligation to like everything. It is not being suggested here, in any way, the complete **acceptance** of all life situations. This would lead to an attitude of indifference in face of life. We often see much falsehood on those who call themselves spiritualists: passive aggressiveness, false elevation, false love, **false acceptance**. It is clear to whoever wants to see, that everything in that being rejects the unpleasant experience, but they force themselves to accept it, simply because they heard that this is an "evolved" attitude, unaware that **the *Truth* about oneself is simultaneously beautiful and horrible and this is infinitely more desirable than hypocrisy**. As very well expressed in a sentence frequently attributed to FREUD: "We could be much better if we did not wish to be good."[560] The *Truth* about oneself and about life (the same thing) **hurts**. The 5D ego "lets it hurt"[561], since it prefers the *Truth*. The 5D ego **acknowledges** all of life situations, but it does not feel obliged to **accept** them. To recognise is to admit its existence and experience it in their reality, as it is. The reaction in face of a situation, however, is totally their choice. In front of an offense, for example, that ego can opt for a higher spiritual understanding and forgiveness, it can decide that they have no time for that offender at that moment in time and ignore it, or it can feel a huge anger and punch them. The 5D ego takes part in all situations, but the role it plays on them is their choice; in contact with the *Imponderable*, it has **all** options at its disposal. However shocking this may seem, there is no right or wrong. Recognising is one thing, accepting is another.

Therefore, in order to gain access to the reality of life, one needs to lose naivety. Those spiritualists who force themselves to accept and love are as childish as infants who cover their eyes with their hands and say that reality has "disappeared". To close eyes to evil, for example, will not extinguish evil; on the contrary, it will contribute to its increase, once it will only leave it freer to act. To believe that you, just you, are a good person, different from the rest of humanity and life, is to be either naïve or deceptive. Now, to believe that there is no evil in life is stupidity. Such spiritualists **mistake purity with childishness** and exempt themselves from the terrible problems of the world, leaving them to the grown-up spiritualists to solve (and maybe it is better that way).

Purity is something entirely different.

> Baptism is, in its essence, a ritual of purification that washes away one's impurities, both literal and spiritual. The washings were frequent preliminary procedures in religious ceremonies. – for example, the Eleusinian Mysteries. Psychologically, the dirt (or sin) washed by baptism can be understood as unconsciousness, shadow qualities that we are not aware of. Psychological cleaning does not mean literal purity, but instead a **consciousness of the one's own dirt. If one is psychologically clean, one will not contaminate one's environment with shadow projections**.[562] [author's own highlights]

In *Evolution*, the experience of life is the evidence of the being: **the reality of life is identical to the reality of oneself**. Both are terrifying. This will not change. In an *Imponderable* scenario, each human being has all characteristics, from the most beautiful to the most awful. If the interior unconscious situation occurs outside, as a fate, it is necessary to choose where to put the dirt: in the consciousness or in the world. Purity is to find the dirt **within** oneself, where, consciously, it is possible to experience it in integration with the Whole, *Creating* with it, **humanizing it**. More than that, purity is to consciously integrate any energy within oneself, since any conscious psychological energy, dirty or not, has a much superior quality than the unconscious ones, as it has been humanized.

These perceptions lead us to a deeper understanding about *Evolution*, which is a **humanizing** fifth-dimensional force. The *Imponderable* converges concurrently towards the human being. We saw that purity is the internalization of any type of psychological energy. Adding everything up, *Evolution* is **purity**.

Regarding the *Imponderable*, purity, in *Evolution*, is to include everything and to live all life experiences that appear. The fact that the being acknowledges all experiences and all characteristics is experienced in *Evolution* as *Plenitude*, a feeling of being whole, of being complete, of nothing lacking, therefore of integrity – from the Latin *integritat*: entire. In *Evolution*, the *Imponderable* is *Plenitude*.

From the point of view of *Plenitude*, each life situation that is denied locks the infinite and discontinuous flow of life, whereas living the flow allows it to run freely. Since, in the *Pneumatic* reality, the reality of life is identical to the reality of oneself, to deny a situation of life is to deny oneself, which delays the development; whereas to include everything and to live all experiences of life is to rapidly recognise oneself. For that reason, the development of the fifth-dimensional consciousness in *Evolution* is a movement with an exponential speed.

Let us not forget, however, that *Evolution* is part of the *Imponderable*, therefore its ground zero is Wholeness. The infinite and discontinuous flow of life situations, integrally experienced, promotes the development of the being, promotes a development which is **larger than Wholeness**. However strange this might seem to the common consciousness, it is possible for something to be larger than Wholeness, since when Wholeness unfolds into life situations which are experienced integrally by an individual, Wholeness interacts **creatively** with that specific individual, therefore new dimensions appear in that individual, and consequently, in Wholeness itself. So, strangely, **the feeling of *Plenitude* grows**, in the same way that the Universe is everything there is but still expands.

Finally, *Plenitude* brings an exponential gain of **self-esteem**. Someone who is willing to experience all life situations that appear, identical to all the dimensions of the being that emerge with those situations, is someone whose *Greatness* grows exponentially, and with it, self-esteem. To put it simply, failures in self-esteem are related to difficulties with aspects of oneself considered inferior or unacceptable. What one cannot live with, one cannot love. Being a human being like any other, the 5D ego has self-esteem problems. However, the progressive inclusion of all life situations and all dimensions of the being tends to decrease the number of situations and characteristics considered unacceptable, causing an exponential gain of self-esteem. Moreover, it is extremely difficult to offend a fifth-dimensional ego in *Evolution*, since any name-calling, however sordid, will be recognised as **real**, having been found by that ego itself in some part of its being, seen as integral and growing parts. It is extremely difficult to scratch the self-esteem of such an individual. The *Plenitude* of *Evolution* produces a shameless self-esteem.

RELATIONSHIP

The *Imponderable* can be understood as an infinitude of relationships between the infinite elements of the growing Wholeness. If the fact that the fifth-dimensional consciousness is based on the *Imponderable* makes it include everything and experience all life situations that appear, the relationships between the various individuals present as elements of extreme importance. If, in the *Pneumatic* reality, simple events such as to break a glass or to lose a wallet are *Pneumatic* events, at the same time physical and spiritual, imagine a relationship with another individual, an infinitely complex reality.

Some of JUNG's texts show that images of people are used by the unconscious to represent qualities of the soul, and, reflexively, images coming from the soul, can be projected onto other people. This exchange of psychological contents and people is very familiar in Analytical Psychology:

> [...] anima, or inner attitude, is represented in the unconscious by definite persons with the corresponding qualities. Such an image is called a "soul-image." [...] (when) the soul accordingly is unconscious, the soul-image is transferred to a real person.[563]

The relationship with the mother, for example, originates the mother complex, whereas the relationship with the father originates the father complex[564]. Other complexes, in turn, relate to other people; above is an example where an anger complex attracts relationships with aggressive people. An unconscious complex is directly related to a person – the unconscious complex and the person are **similar**, but **not identical**[565]. JUNG says clearly that the projection we make on someone else has a "hook"; that is, the content projected is, **to an extent**, found in that person[566]. However, the projection is not entirely real, because the unconsciousness in relation to the projected content necessarily means a misunderstanding about that content, normally presenting a degree of **exaggeration**. So, if we project aggressiveness on someone, certainly that person has aggressiveness as a personality trait – without which it would be impossible to see aggressiveness in them – but also, certainly, that person is not as aggressive as we suppose, since our unconsciousness about aggressiveness makes us have an exaggerated perception of aggressiveness. In the Paradigm of Balance, relationships are very important paths of development, once projections are one of the most frequent means of relationship with unconscious contents. It is worth remembering that, besides projecting unconscious complexes, it is possible to project archetypes, whose size is much larger, creating opportunity for proportional integrations.

In the *Pneumatic* reality of the Paradigm of Sense, however, people are independent and **paradoxically** *Images* from the consciousness of the fifth-dimensional ego. Therefore, people are no longer **approximately** what is projected in them, and, **paradoxically**, start being **exactly** identical to the *Images* of the fifth-dimensional ego.

This paradox is practically unacceptable for the current level of consciousness of humanity. Through a huge effort of consciousness and the essential action of the transcendent function, however, this reality is reached as early as the Paradigm of Balance, as its final product, from then on becoming the *Pneumatic* reality of the Paradigm of Sense. For that reason, the following is on the illustration IX of *Rosarium Philosophorum*:

> The "soul" which is reunited with the body is the One born of the two, the vinculum common to both. [The Soul] **is therefore the very essence of relationship**. Equally the psychological anima, as representative of the collective unconscious, has a collective character.[567] [author's own highlights]

This idea is very shocking to people. It is very common, especially in non-spiritualist environments, that people believe that they have very good relationships with people, but they have no idea of what the Soul is. The opposite is also common, especially among spiritualists: to believe that they have an excellent relationship with the Soul, despite having a terrible relationship with people. Both beliefs are false, since the internal relationship is **identical** to the external relationship.

Knowing that, it makes no sense to stop relating to whoever it is – including **all** people is the **purity** in the *Relationship*. To not relate to someone is identical to not relating to a dimension of oneself, to deny a part of the *Imponderable*, "externally" and "internally". More than that, it makes no sense to have a superficial relationship with whoever it is, as this would be a superficial relationship with oneself.

Obviously, by now, it is already possible to understand that relating to all people is to **love** all people, however one does not need to **like** them. To **love** is to recognise the reality of the other, whatever it is, and relate to them. This is relatively easy for a 5D ego. Having reached Balance and integrated various archetypes, particularly the Shadow, having included everything and knowing that all life situations that it experiences are aspects of itself, the 5D ego knows many of its own characteristics, from the most sublime to the most sordid. Since the 5D ego knows these realities in itself, it becomes very natural to this ego to see others having the same characteristics, from the most sublime to the most sordid, or similar characteristics. The reality of the other, as its own, is very accessible and recognised by the 5D ego, and it becomes capable to deeply love the others.

To **like**, is something else. To like is to want to be around those whose characteristics are compatible with our preferences (even if this compatibility is produced by a passion). Let us remember that to force oneself to love or accept is to evade the reality of oneself. Therefore, to love someone is to recognise their reality and deeply relate to them. However, the characteristics of this relationship can be freely chosen, from the feeling of liking or not someone or any other emotion that appears. For that reason, this deep relationship of love can be indeed experienced through a solid friendship, or a romance, but it can also be experienced as aggression, vengeance, repulsion, loathing or even separation. Whatever it is, however, the type of relationship that is established, the reality of the other does not stop being recognised and the relationship is deep and intense.

Moreover, the *Pneumatic* reality is "transpsychic"[568] and the 5D ego has access to the *Truth* of the *Spirit*. Therefore, the relationship with the other is much less determined by psychological projections and the access to the reality of the other is much higher. JUNG says that it is only possible to get rid of illusions and know the reality of others when projections are integrated[569]; this is common in the Paradigm of Sense.

Beyond projections, in a "transpsychic" (=*Pneumatic*), reality, in *Evolution*, the other is me. It is important to notice that the affirmation "the other is me", in the fourth dimension, means that the other reveals to me my own unconsciousness; this is psychological. However, in the fifth dimension, the affirmation "the other is me", from Oswald de ANDRADE[570], has a different meaning: the other is **identical** to the conscious dimensions of my being; this is *Pneumatic*. In the Paradigm of Sense, the 5D ego knows that it is the Whole, as the *Imponderable* converges to the human being. But this does not mean that it **wants** to *Manifest* the Whole all the time, occupying all positions of life all the time, performing alone all functions of life at the same time, relating only to itself – this would be dehumanizing. Selfishness has already been overcome in this dimension. Although it can remain in the Whole, the 5D ego can choose a specific position in life, a specific role, giving others the space to exist in its life, occupying other positions and performing other roles, and relate to them. This is much **richer**. To deeply coexist with all the others, with **all** parts of the others, is to deeply coexist with all parts of oneself.

Beyond projections, in a "transpsychic" (=*Pneumatic*) reality, **paradoxically**, the other is the other, existing entirely in its own reality, different from me. This dimension of the other is entirely **singular** (6D) and can only be understood by me if I have access to my own **singularity** (6D) – and even then, it is about understanding something **different**. The position of the other, whether they know it or not, is absolutely unique. For that reason, in *Evolution*, the other is Another *Universe*.

When one acknowledges that the other is Another *Universe*, the richness of the relationship is bigger than the infinite. Contemplating the *Plenitude* of *Evolution*, we saw that the *Imponderable* converges to the human being, and that the experience of life situations leads to the development of the infinite Wholeness, and consequently, of the being. Now, realising that the other is Another *Universe*, we have an *Imponderable* converging to a human being in the development of an infinite Wholeness, in *Relationship* with an *Imponderable* converging to **another** human being in **another** development of the infinite Wholeness. The possibilities of development are now much more than infinite. Such is the richness of the human being.

HUMANITY

Christ's characteristic that I find most endearing is his **humanity**. With all the **greatness** that there was in that being, with all the **divinity** that inhabited in him, it is astonishing that he managed to remain so **human**. He loved unequally, having John as his most loved one[571]. Lied to his brothers[572]. Lost his temper and mistreated people[573]. Physically assaulted people[574]. Fought with his own family[575]. Called the Pharisees "brood of vipers and whitewashed tombs"[576,577], possibly the equivalent of telling someone to "fuck themselves" in current terms. He was negligent with his friends[578]. His agony in the Gethsemane[579] and his pain in the Golgotha are specially moving.

However, for me, his humanity reached the peak when he met his disciples, and in face of Thomas' lack of faith, shows him his holes[580]. Christ had already resurrected and soon would ascend to the heavens. With at least a fifth-dimensional structure, he could have proved himself through any of his many capabilities, including the miraculous ones. However, he preferred to be physically touched by Thomas, specifically in his holes, where it was probably his most sensitive point. After experiencing the unity with the *Imponderable* on the Cross, Christ returns to the human experience.

Despite the huge cultural differences, we saw the same movement happening in Greece, where the hero returns to his city after his deeds and contributes towards civilization, and again in the Tibetan Buddhism, where the universality of the OM is followed by the integration and humanity of the HŪM.

These *Images* evidence precisely the turn of the Paradigm of Balance to the Paradigm of Sense in the process of human development. During the whole fourth dimension, the human being turned completely towards the Self, sacrificing to the Self its very right to choose, in order to harmonize with it. In the peak of this experience, the individual experiences a contact with the Self, with the whole *Universe*, with the *Imponderable*. The human development could stop precisely here, in this beautiful and Most High image.

However, it does not stop there. It not only does not stop there, but it takes an ugly turn. It is shocking that something so brutal follows such a beautiful reality. Crucifixion only made sense while it was realized in the presence of God, so that the amplest surrender to Divinity could take place, one that is realised even in face of certain torture and death. The moment the Divinity abandons Christ, there is an imminent collapse. He to whom Christ had surrendered – God – was no longer there. From that moment on, Christ's surrender was no longer justified by fulfilling the Father's wishes[581] or fulfilling the Scriptures[582]. When Christ gave these reasons for his Crucifixion, he was **certain** that the Father would be with him until the end. For that reason, he is surprised with the *in-extremis* abandonment by the Father, and, more human than ever, **complains**[583] - in fact, given the circumstances, he was extremely respectful. Without the great meaning of his experience, Christ had every right to protest and finally leave the Cross.

But he did not do that. In face of the abandonment, Christ remained on the Cross. With no metaphysical reason to be there, the only possible motivator of the experience **was his own will**. At that precise moment, Christ transcended the need for a God to govern his choices. At that precise moment, **Christ chose by himself to be Crucified**. As darkness fell over Earth, expired[584].

At that precise moment, Christ transcended the meaning of his action and understood the *Sense* of his action, **choosing** to realise it. From what is known, this was his first contact with an overwhelming **emptiness** of experiencing the *Sense*. It is no longer possible to project his own divinity in whoever it is, not even God. There is no longer any transcendent indication of which action to take or how to do it. It is no longer possible to rely on the meaning of the experience, since it is the human being who defines the *Sense* of the action.

The abandonment by the Divinity, the *Retreat of the Soul*, is the revelation of its savagery in the highest degree. However, **paradoxically**, its last affront is the most generous. In abandoning his own Son on the verge of a psychological chaos, the Divinity gives him the terrible choice of throwing himself into despair and the demoniac rebellion, OR of giving *Sense* to the action and affirm himself as the Author of his own story, experiencing the *Free-Will* for the first time. We know which was Christ's choice, since the *Sense* of his action inaugurated an era for humanity which, with all its excellence and excrescence, has been going on for two thousand years. The abandonment by the Divinity gave the human being, finally, its biggest characteristic: its **humanity**.

However, the *Evolution* has its focus on the human **experience**, the human experience of *Humanity*.

For someone who was willing to die on the Cross and surrender to God – for the current Christs who, like JUNG, surrendered their lives to the realization of the Self – to face the complete absence of God's will, the complete absence of transcendent guidance, is distressing. The first reaction is one of disbelief, of complete disorientation. For me it was also like that. It took me years to admit that the psychological "rules" that I so meticulously followed and experienced no longer described all the phenomena that occurred with me, neither the "interior" ones nor the "exterior" ones. And, when I finally admitted it, I sought a new type of transcendent guidance, a "higher Soul", which I could follow. I sought to re-establish the relationship of priority of the Self in relation to me, however much I hated the Self for having abandoned me – I sought to re-establish the Paradigm of Balance somehow. I never succeeded; my ability to find the flow of the libido, to understand the Symbols, to know which

Archetype was constellated, no longer worked. The understanding that I had to give *Sense* to the action and to accept this was extremely difficult at the time, and it still is now.

Perhaps it is the irresistible tendency of human beings to always blame someone, and the relief that this brings, that leads us to desperately seek someone to tell us what to do, whether it is the third-dimensional moral system, or the fourth-dimensional Self. If the action goes wrong, there will be someone to blame.

But this game of blame and guilty ones is a silly and outdated sham, an element of the old era that masks the real conflict: the absolute panic that we feel about our own *Greatness* as *Humans*.

In *Evolution*, the *Human*, is the centre of convergence of the *Imponderable*, therefore, of immeasurable *Greatness*. This is the most terrifying element of the human experience – the fact that we are, every and each one of us, **infinite**.

We tend to oppose this abysmal point of view with all our faults, all our mistakes, all our pain, all our unconsciousness. We claim that, if we possess these obscuring traits, we are in no position or even have no right, to exercise our infinite *Greatness*. This point of view is a self-inflicted act of hatred, and ultimately, of nihilism, because it presupposes that in order to be *Great*, we must not possess these obscuring traits. But the vicious cycle that is implicit in this world view is that, in order to be *Great*, we could not be *Human*, since the faults, mistakes, pain and unconsciousness are undoubtedly components of the human being. In opposition to this, people create an exterior God, totally inaccessible, to be the depositary of *Greatness*.

Evolution, however, includes everything, experiences everything, and causes an exponential gain of self-esteem. It overcomes the dualist doctrines such as the *summum bonun*[585] and knows that the *Imponderable* is the Wholeness and as such, in its **perfection**, **paradoxically** includes the imperfection, the faults, the mistake, the pain, the unconsciousness and so many other difficulties – all the atrocities in the world are evidences of that. Both the *Imponderable* and the *Human* have faults, mistakes, pain and unconsciousness, with no duality between them. This recognition is deeply unsettling for the dualist consciousness, because it is entirely beyond good and evil, beyond right and wrong and **beyond the Divine and the *Human***, since, if the *Imponderable*, the Transcendence, has exactly the same characteristics of the *Human* and is in unity with it, the very definitions of right and wrong **disappear**, and it becomes virtually impossible to say that something is wrong.

In no way, however, acceding to *Greatness* eliminates the anguish of the fifth-dimensional ego. Because it includes its faults, its mistakes, its pain and its unconsciousness – or because it realises that it is not possible to define anything as a mistake, if you prefer – **the anguish grows.** The relativization of the notion of mistake relativizes in equal proportion the notion of success. **There is no way of knowing for sure which is the correct action to take.** The decision is **entirely** down to the fifth-dimensional ego and it will be the one it sees *Sense* in. But the consequences are, as everything else in life, *Imponderable*. Invariably, other people will be involved in the fifth-dimensional action and will experience pleasant and unpleasant, excellent and atrocious consequences. The 5D ego also feels responsible for its own actions, not only because of the unrestricted love it feels in the *Relationships* of *Evolution*, but also because it knows that its *Word* is *Creative*, and will be supported by the *Spirit*, therefore its world will be entirely conformed to its decisions. Being *Imponderable*, the consequences of its actions, luminous and dark, are the definitions of its own reality. It is not possible to eliminate the anguish, an element of the *Imponderable*. The *Evolution* includes the anguish as a factor of humanization, a balancing dark factor in the face of the unquantifiable potencies converging towards the 5D ego, and it does the only thing possible in this scenario: **it takes the risk**. In *Evolution*, the anguish is the risk inherent to the human *Creation*.

> At this point I can no longer evade a direct answer to the question, how one becomes what one is. And in giving it, I shall have to touch upon that masterpiece in the art of self-preservation, which is *selfishness*. Granting that one's life task – the determination and the fate of one's life task – greatly exceeds the average measure of such things, **nothing more dangerous could be conceived than to come face to face with one's self by the side of this life-task**. The fact that one becomes what one is, presupposes that one has not the remotest suspicion of what one is. From this standpoint even the blunders of one's life have their own meaning and value, the temporary deviations and aberrations, the moments of hesitation and of modesty, the earnestness wasted upon duties which lie outside the actual life-task.[586] [author's own highlights]

The search for Transcendence led the ego to notice the Paradigm of Sense – a reality where one finds out that the Transcendence does not make decisions for them and does nothing more than support them in their decisions, which is good enough. Nor are there Saviours. At some point one needs to stop needing "dear God" – overcoming the illusions that "someone is responsible for everything", that "someone is looking out and taking care of everything", that "someone will guide me about what I need to do", that "someone will save me", that "someone will punish the culprits" – to spiritually become an adult and admit to one's own *Greatness*, taking responsibility for their own actions.

At that point, the *Human* notices the *Pneumatic* reality: he is the Soul itself and the *Spirit* is the Whole around it, including himself. At that point, the *Human* sees the infinite light and the infernal abyss, the archetypes are around them. The realities are infinite, and the possibilities are infinite. Everything converges towards the *Human* and the convergence increases with the increase in consciousness, in the same way that the curvature of the space-time increases with the mass increase of a Star. However, the *Spirit* awaits; it awaits the *Human* being. In the middle of the absolute equivalence of all realities and all possibilities is the *Human* being and its tragic characteristic: **choice**. The *Force* inspires but it does not determine. **It is down to the *Human* being to choose and give *Sense* to the action.** This act belongs only to them. In *Evolution*, the *Human* gives *Sense* to the Action. In *Evolution*, the *Human* Hero breaks the Cosmic Balance and causes a **movement forward**, in the direction that makes *Sense* to them, and gets into ***Action****, with no Guarantees*.

The *Human* being is the only creator of their own reality, as well as that of others, and can choose from the most imprisoning karmic realities to the most supreme *Creative* freedom of the *Imponderable*. Their reality is what they are and what they chose to create, at their own risk.

EVOLUTION

The *Spirit* is Wholeness. The *Force*, it inspires the *Creative* process of incarnation of the *Spirit*. The *Macroimage*, it produces all *Images* and with them, builds the whole *Universe*. An *All-the-Times*, its time extends from the most remote past until the most unimaginable future; its time is circular. The *Multi-Dimensionality*, it connects all realities, from any space and time, making everything contiguous. The *Manifestation*, it is consciousness of all dimensions and intrinsic unity of them all. *Imponderable*, it is infinite and pure Transcendence – it transcends itself continuously, **always** beyond the restricted and dual individual understanding.

The Wholeness of the *Spirit* is absolute – there are no exceptions, there are no deforming theological subterfuges. The Wholeness of the *Spirit* includes the *Demon*, a dimension of the *Spirit* who resists *Creation*, resists incarnation. More than that, the *Demon Perverts* the energy of the *Spirit*, using it to purposes contrary to those for which they were emanated. For that reason, the *Demon* is so systematically avoided in the process of consciousness development – Lilith chooses the exile. Even the Tibetan Buddhism, a more mature world view, capable of seeing the phenomena of the *Universe* with a much lower degree of histrionics, does not concentrate directly on power, the *Śakti*, does not seek power above everything; it understands power from the wisdom of Wholeness and Humanity. Even then, when consciousness is sufficiently large, when knowledge is sufficiently mature, it will be necessary to comprehend the *Demon*, admitting its presence in the Wholeness of the *Spirit*, as in it lies the **dynamism**, essential to incarnation, to the realisation of the *Spirit* in the *Body*, in the Matter. The *Demon* is the *Dynamic Force*.

The unity, the universality, consists in **experiencing** the light of the *Spirit* and the *Demoniac* darkness as one **single** reality, as a **harmonic** composition of the **same** *Image*, as a painting from Rembrandt. The relationship between Light and Darkness defines the various dimensions – the contrast of Darkness, giving **dimension** to Light, **infinite**. An image in two dimensions is the **contour** (darkness) of a certain **area** (light). In order to reach an image in three dimensions, we must add the contrast of the **shadows** (darkness) to the figures and spaces (light). In order to reach an image in four dimensions, we must add the backstage of the Unconscious (darkness) to the consciousness (light). In order to reach an *Image* in five dimensions, we must add the *Demon* (darkness) resisting the *Body* (=*Spirit*, light). Often, we can only understand the dimension of what we are doing through the opposition caused. In the Paradigm of Sense, the *Demoniac* uprising is proportional to the size of the spiritual *Creation* that one is undertaking. In the unity of the fifth dimension, it is **desirable** that the *Demon* appear, since the *Image* of *Creation* proceeds from the *Spirit*, the *Inspiration* of *Creation* proceeds from the *Force*, the **Energy** of *Creation* proceeds from the *Demon*.

Evil is the active springing from Energy.[587]

The *Human* finds themselves precisely in the **middle** of the Infinite – between the *Spirit* and the *Demon* – the *Imponderable* converges towards them. It is the *Human* who will give, alone, the *Sense* of the action. For such, the *Human* in *Evolution* **includes everything**.

> Do not try to be better than you are; otherwise, the demon will be wrathful. Do not try to be worse than you are; otherwise, God will be wrathful. Try to be what you are; this is sufficiently acrobatic.[588]

The *Spirit* goes in front of the *Human* and shows extreme complexity – a *Multi-Dimensional Macroimage* in *All-the-Times*, *Imponderable*. The Sun of the *Spirit* emanates its blazing *Truth*. Its *Truth* is **evident**. To be in the presence of the *Spirit* is very difficult, because the situations that appear are very clear. All its characteristics, all its details, are there to be seen, from the most excellent and exuberant to the most atrocious and obscure. The people, with all their characteristics, from the most noble to the feeblest, are there to be seen. The 5D ego can easily see, and if it does not, is because it is tired or being dishonest with itself. If it wants to see, it will.

Completely beyond duality, the 5D ego has no moral or ethical criticism to make. If people are admirable or abominable, they are being exactly who they are. The 5D ego itself is like that, simultaneously admirable and abominable. If the situation is wonderful or atrocious, if it is productive or unsustainable, it is a fact, identical to the situation of the 5D ego itself. There is nothing to deny. It makes no sense to transgress the **evidences**. To deny them would only return it to duality, halting the infinite and discontinuous flow of the *Imponderable*, delaying (never avoiding) that experience – a waste of time. The view of the *Spirit* is the *Obvious*.

From the perception of reality as it is – from the perception of the *Images* of the *Spirit*, of the 5D ego itself, of the people involved and the situation as a whole, as they are – magnificent and sordid and everything else – **including everything** – the *Human* Hero in *Evolution* sees *Sense* in one of the *Images* and immediately gets into *Action*, explodes in a **movement forwards**. The individual has started a *Creative* process that will *Draw* a spiritual *Image* in the *Body*, in the matter.

The *Demon* goes behind the *Human* and resists the *Spirit* and the *Human*. In the *Universe* of the *Spirit*, the *Demon* is the *Verse*. An undisputed expert in the *Instinct*, the *Demon* **tempts**, offering realities that deviate the 5D ego from its *Creation* process. The temptation is only effective if the **desires** it offers to satisfy are **real**. In the *Demoniac* uprising, the tempting reality can seem more interesting, more valuable or more pleasurable than the process of spiritual *Creation* in which the 5D ego sees *Sense*. If the *Demon* were to offer anything that was not an object of desire, it would be met with indifference, it would not cause any discomfort. The possibility of having something it has always wanted, of living something it has always dreamt of, this presents an element of conflict.

An undisputed usurper of the mind, the *Demon* **accuses**, pointing faults, mistakes, blames and unconsciousness that remove the *Force* to act from the 5D ego. The accusation only resonates with the 5D ego if it is consistent and points to **real** faults, mistakes, blames and unconsciousness. In the *Demoniac* uprising, the accusation can seem stronger and uglier than the Self-image that the 5D ego has of itself. If the *Demon* were to make an accusation that was not related to that ego, it would be met with indifference and laughed at. The real accusation, that one has the potential of destabilizing the ego to the point of stopping its action.

In *Evolution*, the *Demon* speaks the truth.

> [...] one thinks of the devils mentioned by St Athanasius in his life of St Anthony, who talk very piously, sing psalms, read the holy books, and – worst of all – **speak the truth**. The difficulties of our psychotherapeutic work teach us to take truth, goodness, and beauty where we find them. They are not always found where we look for them: **often they are hidden in the dirt or are in the keeping of the dragon**. "In stercore invenitur" (it is found in filth) runs an alchemical dictum—nor is it any the less valuable on that account. But, it does not transfigure the dirt and does not diminish the evil, any more than these lessen God's gifts. The contrast is painful and the paradox bewildering.[589] [author's own highlights]

If the *Demon* is using real desires to tempt, what good would it do to deny this reality? Denying the reality, whichever it is, returns things to duality and unconsciousness. In the Paradigm of Sense there is no truth, and everything is allowed. In *Evolution*, everything is included. The fifth-dimensional consciousness is based on the *Imponderable* and Lilith's self-exile has ended. All the archetypal prohibition to the satisfaction of instincts or desires has ended. **It makes no sense at all to deny one's own *Instincts* or one's own desires**. When listening to the *Demon* tempting them with the satisfaction of his *Instincts* and desires, the *Human* in *Evolution* understands that **the *Demon* is right**, and their immediate reaction is to **satisfy their desires**. It is not necessary that the *Demon* leads the 5D ego to experience its *Instincts* and desires, the 5D ego does so by its own accord, satisfies them and returns home satisfied. In the end, it feels grateful to the *Demon*, because it revealed *Instincts* and desires that up to then were unknown, but which are now sources of *Corporeal* (= spiritual) pleasure.

If the *Demon* is using real faults, mistakes, blames and unconsciousness to accuse, what good would it do to deny this reality? To deny the reality, whichever one it is, would return things to duality and unconsciousness. In the Paradigm of Sense, the reality is *Imponderable*, it is beyond right and wrong. In *Evolution*, the *Imponderable* converges towards the human being, who is beyond right and wrong. All moral conceptualization and all ethical conflict have been overcome. **It makes no sense at all to deny one's own faults, mistakes, blames and unconsciousness**. In listening to the *Demon* accusing them with the denial of their own faults, mistakes, blames and unconsciousness, the *Human* in *Evolution* understands that **the *Demon* is right**, and their immediate reaction is **not** to correct them – this would be to deny their own reality. In *Evolution*, the *Demon* offers excellent diagnoses and it is worth listening to them. In *Evolution*, our faults, our mistakes, our blames and our unconsciousness are undeniable parts of ourselves and perhaps our most **interesting** parts. To correct them would perhaps produce a human being too perfect, too divine... boring. After all, "correct" them according to which standard of "truth", "virtue" and "correctness"? Knowing that the mistake is the space of *Creation*, the *Evolution* creates a way to **re-establish its movement forward**, using the faults, mistakes, blames and unconsciousness as they are, as elements of *Creation*. As every artist knows, adverse situations are excellent stimulus to creation.

However, if in *Evolution* the *Demon* speaks the truth, why is it said that the *Demon* **lies**? Indeed, it lies. The *Demon* lie is not in the content of what it says, but in the relationship of this content with the Wholeness. If, for example, the *Demon* tempts the 5D ego with power, he is right. The 5D ego does feel the need for power and the only sane thing that it can do is to conquer power. However, the *Demon* lies because wanting power is **only one characteristic of the 5D ego, in the middle of infinite other characteristics of the *Imponderable* that flow towards it**. Or, if the *Demon* blames the 5D ego for faulting their partner, it is right. But the 5D ego is not only "someone who faulted their partner", this is **only one action of the 5D ego in the middle of the infinite others that it practices**. The *Demon* speaks the truth regarding the content of its temptations and accusations but **lies** in relation to the Whole. The *Demon* presents its temptations and accusations as **absolute truths**, when in fact, they are **relative truths**, partial. Said in a different way, the *Demon* is excellent to reveal the *Verse* of the 5D ego and its *Pneumatic* reality, showing hidden desires, unconscious faults, mistakes and blames, but cannot reach the *Universe* of the *Spirit* – the *Demon* tries, but does not succeed.

> Seen from the consciousness of the Dharmakaya, all separate forms of appearance are *māyā*. Maya in the deepest sense, however, is reality in its creative aspect, or the creative aspect of reality. Thus *māyā* becomes the cause of illusion, but it is not illusion itself, as long as it is seen as a whole, in its continuity, its creative function, or as infinite power of transformation and universal relationship. As soon, however, as we stop at any of its creations and try to limit it to a state of 'being' or self-confined existence, we fall a prey to illusion, by taking the effect for the cause, the shadow for the substance, the partial aspect for ultimate reality, the momentary for something that exists in itself.
>
> It is the power of *māyā* which produces the illusory forms of appearance of our mundane reality. *Māyā* itself, however, is not illusion. **He who masters this power, has got the tool of liberation in his hand, the magic power of yoga, the power of creation, transformation and re-integration**. (Skt.: laya-krama; Tib.: rdzogs-rim.)[590] [author's own highlights]

The *Demon* is the great partner of *Evolution*.

The *Evolution* includes everything, which results in **purity**: the fundamental energy of *Evolution* **is** purity[591,592]. When the *Demon* invests against the 5D ego, it finds purity, which includes all. Purity also includes the *Demon* and everything that the *Demon* does is dynamically used by the *Evolution* to produce movement forwards, to accelerate. In *Evolution* the *Demon* is the fuel of *Action*. In *Evolution* the *Demon* is the source of *Corporeal* pleasure. In *Evolution* the *Demon* offers excellent diagnoses. In *Evolution*, the lies of the *Demon* are relative truths that help compose the Total *Truth*, the *Imponderable*. In *Evolution*, the *Demon* contributes towards more purity and action.

For that reason, the confrontation between *Evolution* and the *Demon* is a question of self-esteem. The bigger the self-esteem, the easier it is to include everything, to become shameless and to deal with all offenses, temptations, desires, accusations, mistakes, faults, blames, unconsciousness, lies and everything else that turns up, whatever it is, with the most absolute lightness and naturality. Everything that gets into contact with the *Evolution* is absorbed by its field of purity, becomes purer and explodes into a movement forwards, into *Action*.

A *Demoniac* attack imposes a relative truth that quickly grows, turning the consciousness, especially the mind, imprisoned to this alternative reality (smaller reality), which, suddenly, seems to be the whole universe. If this reality becomes the only thing that the 5D ego can see, it will stay imprisoned in this reality and a total possession will have occurred. In *Evolution*, the self-esteem allows that, in the face of a *Demoniac* attack, the 5D ego **can remember (which is extremely difficult) that the lie that the *Demon* is telling is a relative truth, not the Wholeness of the *Truth*, and then create with it.** That way, the alternative reality returns to be relativized, the *Demon* enters *Evolution*, takes part in the *Creation* and takes that which it most wants – the *Body*.

$$* * * * *$$

In its all-inclusive movement, creative and forward, the *Evolution* creates formulations that prompt it. Below there are some examples that I created whilst writing the text. The list is infinite.

In *Evolution*, the *Imponderable* is the *Plenitude*.

In *Evolution*, the life experience is the evidence of the being.

In *Evolution*, the other is me.

In *Evolution*, the other is another *Universe*.

In *Evolution*, the *Human* is the centre of convergence of the *Imponderable*.

In *Evolution*, anguish is the risk inherent to human creation.

In *Evolution*, the *Human* gives *Sense* to *Action*.

In *Evolution*, the *Demon* says the truth.

In *Evolution*, the *Demon* is source of *corporeal* pleasure.

In *Evolution*, the *Demon* offers excellent diagnoses.

In *Evolution*, the *Demon* is the fuel of *Action*.

In *Evolution*, the lies of the *Demon* are relative truths that help compose the Total *Truth*, the *Imponderable*.

552 GOSWANI, A. (1995) *The self-aware universe.* Tarcher Perigee.

553 "Hence the *mundificatio* – purification – is an attempt to discriminate the mixture, to sort out the *coincidentia oppositorum* in which the individual has been caught. The rational man, in order to live in this world, has to make a distinction between "himself" and what we might call the "eternal man." Although he is a unique individual, he also stands for "man" as a species, and thus he has a share in all the movements of the collective unconscious. In other words, the "eternal" truths become dangerously disturbing factors when they suppress the unique ego of the individual and live at his expense. [...] it is absorbed by the unconscious to such an extent that the latter alone has the power of decision, then the ego is stifled, and there is no longer any medium in which the unconscious could be integrated and in which the work of realization could take place. The separation of the empirical ego from the "eternal" and universal man is therefore of vital importance, particularly today, when mass-degeneration of the personality is making such threatening strides. [..]" JUNG, C. G. (1985) *The Practice of psychotherapy. Ab-reaction, dream analysis and transference.* Translated by Hull, R. F. C. 2nd edition. CW XVI. Bollingen Series XX. Princeton University Press. §502.

554 Various movements that appeared in the West in the last decades declared themselves based on Buddhism and allege being based on it in order to preach the "death of the ego" dissolving it. Lama GOVINDA, however, shows that this understanding is not correct: "The Buddhist, therefore, **does not endeavour to 'dissolve his being in the infinite'**, to fuse his finite consciousness with the consciousness of the all, or to unite his soul with the all-soul; his aim is to become *conscious* of his ever-existing, indivisible and undivided completeness. To this completeness nothing can be added, and from it nothing can be taken away. It may only be experienced or recognized in a more or less perfect way. [...] *Mani* has been interpreted poetically as the 'dew-drop in the lotus', and Edwin Arnold's 'Light of Asia' ends with the words: 'The dewdrop slips into the shining sea.' If this beautiful simile is reversed, it would probably come nearer to the Buddhist conception of ultimate realization: it is not the drop that slips into the sea, but the sea that slips into the drop!" GOVINDA, A. (1975) *Foundations of Tibetan mysticism.* New York: Samuel Weiser. p. 80. [author's own highlights]

555 The self in its divinity (i.e., the archetype) is unconscious of itself. It can become conscious only within our consciousness. And it can do that only **if the ego stands firm**." JUNG, C. G. (1973) *Letters*, Vol. I. Edited and translated by Hull, R. F. C. Bollingen series XCV. Princeton University Press. pp. 336-336. [author's own highlights]

556 "Man is the central seat of all created things. Through the force of his imagination (this being the focal point of everything), all things in the world must obey him, as before the fall". RAFF, J. (2000) *Jung and the alchemical imagination.* Chapter 2 "The alchemical imagination". "Alchemy and imagination". Quoting AL PULI, (1988) *The center of nature concentrated.* Florida: Nicolas-Hays, Inc. (Kobo eBook version). p. 21.

557 Carl JUNG. *On the nature of the psyche.* CW VIII. §648

558 MATTOS, R. G. (2013). *Evolução.* Unpublished text.

559 Ibid.

560 This sentence is frequently cited and attributed to FREUD, however no evidence was ever found that it is, in fact, his.

561 MATTOS, R. G. (2013). *Evolução.* Unpublished text.

562 EDINGER, E. (1991) *Anatomy of the Psyche: Alchemical Symbolism in Psychotherapy.* Chapter 3. Open Court Publishing Company.

563 JUNG, C. G. (1976) *Psychological types.* Translated by Baynes, H. G. CW VI. Bollingen Series XX. Princeton University Press. §808.

564 In the present work, the terms "mother complex" and "father complex" refer to unconscious complexes originated in the relationship with the human mother and father, whereas simultaneously based on the Archetypes of the Great Mother and of the Father. As complexes, these invariably contain both positive and negative traits, and can strongly tend towards one side or the other. In the present work, however, the terms do not necessarily have the pathological connotation that sometimes is attributed to them.

565 "Conscious adaptation to the person representing the soul-image is impossible precisely because the subject is unconscious of the soul. Were he conscious of it, it could be **distinguished** from the object, whose immediate effects might then be mitigated, since the potency of the object depends on the projection of the soul-image." JUNG, C. G. *Psychological types.* Op. Cit. §808. [author's own highlights]

566 "Experience shows that the carrier of the projection is not just *any* object but is always one that proves adequate to the nature of the content projected – that is to say, it must offer the content a 'hook' to hang on." JUNG, C. G. (1985) *The Practice of psychotherapy. Ab-reaction, dream analysis and transference* Translated by Hull, R. F. C. 2nd edition. CW XVI. Bollingen Series XX. Princeton University Press. §499.

567 Ibid. §504.

568 RAFF, J. (2000) *Jung and the alchemical imagination.* Introduction. "The beginnings of alchemy". Florida: Nicolas-Hays, Inc (Kobo eBook version).

569 "For example, about the projections that involve the anima: "[...] as the result of a long and thorough analysis and the withdrawal of projections, the ego has been successfully separated from the unconscious, the anima will gradually cease to act as an autonomous personality and will become a function of relationship between conscious and unconscious. So long as she is projected she leads to **all sorts of illusions about people and things and thus to endless complications**. The withdrawal of projections makes the anima what she originally was: an archetypal image which, in its right place, functions to the advantage of the individual." JUNG, C. G *The Practice of psychotherapy. Ab-reaction, dream analysis and transference.* Op. Cit. §504 [author's own highlights]

570 ANDRADE, O. (1928) *Manifesto antropófago.* Revista de Antropofagia. Ano 374 "da deglutição do Bispo Sardinha". Available at: <https://pib.socioambiental.org/files/manifesto_antropofago.pdf> Access: April 28th 2020.

571 "Near the cross of Jesus stood his mother and his mother's sister, Mary the wife of Clopas, and Mary of Magdala. Seeing his mother and the disciple whom he loved standing near her, Jesus said to his mother, 'Woman, this is your son.' Then to the disciple he said, 'This is your mother.' And from that hour the disciple took her into his home." *The New Jerusalem Bible.* John 19:25-27.

572 "After this Jesus travelled round Galilee; he could not travel round Judaea, because the Jews were seeking to kill him. As the Jewish feast of Shelters drew near, his brothers said to him, 'Leave this place and go to Judaea, so that your disciples, too, can see the works you are doing; no one who wants to be publicly known acts in secret; if this is what you

are doing, you should reveal yourself to the world.' Not even his brothers had faith in him. Jesus answered, 'For me the right time has not come yet, but for you any time is the right time. The world cannot hate you, but it does hate me, because I give evidence that its ways are evil. Go up to the festival yourselves: I am not going to this festival, because for me the time is not ripe yet.' Having said that, he stayed behind in Galilee. However, after his brothers had left for the festival, he went up as well, not publicly but secretly." Ibid. John 7:1-10

[573] "Jesus left that place and withdrew to the region of Tyre and Sidon. And suddenly out came a Canaanite woman from that district and started shouting, 'Lord, Son of David, take pity on me. My daughter is tormented by a devil.' But he said not a word in answer to her. And his disciples went and pleaded with him, saying, 'Give her what she wants, because she keeps shouting after us.' He said in reply, 'I was sent only to the lost sheep of the House of Israel.' But the woman had come up and was bowing low before him. 'Lord', she said, 'help me'. He replied, "It is not fair to take the children's food and throw it to little dogs.' She retorted, 'Ah yes, Lord; but even little dogs eat the scraps that fall from their masters' table.'" Ibid. Matthew 15:21-27

[574] "Making a whip out of cord, he drove them all out of the Temple, sheep and cattle as well, scattered the money changers' coins, knocked their tables over" Ibid. John 2:15.

[575] "Now his mother and his brothers arrived and, standing outside, sent in a message asking for him. A crowd was sitting round him at the time the message was passed to him, 'Look, your mother and brothers and sisters are outside asking for you.' He replied, 'Who are my mother and my brothers?' And looking at those sitting in a circle round him, he said, 'Here are my mother and my brothers. Anyone who does the will of God, that person is my brother and sister and mother.'" Ibid. Mark 3:31-35

[576] "You brood of vipers, how can your speech be good when you are evil? For words flow out of what fills the heart." Ibid. Matthew 12:34

[577] "Alas for you, scribes and Pharisees, you hypocrites! You are like whitewashed tombs that look handsome on the outside, but inside are full of the bones of the dead and every kind of corruption." Ibid. Matthew 23:27.

[578] "Martha said to Jesus, 'Lord, if you had been here, my brother would not have died'" Ibid. John 11:21

[579] "Then he said to them, 'My soul is sorrowful to the point of death. Wait here and stay awake with me.'" Ibid. Matthew 26:38

[580] "Thomas, called the Twin, who was one of the Twelve, was not with them when Jesus came. So the other disciples said to him, 'We have seen the Lord', but he answered, 'Unless I can see the holes that the nails made in his hands and can put my finger into the holes they made, and unless I can put my hand into his side, I refuse to believe.' Eight days later the disciples were in the house again and Thomas was with them. The doors were closed, but Jesus came in and stood among them. 'Peace be with you', he said. Then he spoke to Thomas, 'Put your finger here; look, here are my hands. Give me your hand; put it into my side. Do not be unbelieving any more but believe.' Thomas replied, 'My Lord and my God!' Jesus said to him: You believe because you can see me. Blessed are those who have not seen and yet believe." Ibid. John 20:24-29

[581] "'Father,' he said, 'if you are willing, take this cup away from me. Nevertheless, let your will be done, not mine.'" Ibid. Luke 22:42

582 "After this, Jesus knew that everything had now been completed and, so that the scripture should be completely fulfilled, he said: I am thirsty." Ibid. John 19:28

583 "And at the ninth hour Jesus cried out in a loud voice, 'Eloi, eloi, lama sabachthani?' which means, 'My God, my God, why have you forsaken me?'" Ibid. Mark 15:34

584 "It was now about the sixth hour and the sun's light failed, so that darkness came over the whole land until the ninth hour. The veil of the Sanctuary was torn right down the middle. Jesus cried out in a loud voice saying, 'Father, into your hands I commit my spirit.' With these words he breathed his last." Ibid. Luke 23:44-46

585 AUGUSTINE of HIPPO, (+/- 495 A. D.) *De natura boni.* Translated by Newman, A. H. (on line) Available at:
<http://www.documentacatholicaomnia.eu/03d/0354-0430,_Augustinus,_De_Natura_Boni_Contra_Manichaeos_[Schaff],_EN.pdf> Access: April 30th 2020.

586 NIETZSCHE, F. (2016) *Ecce homo.* Translated by Ludovici, A.M. and Cohn, P.V. Project Gutemberg ebook. Available at: <http://www.gutenberg.org/ebooks/52190> Access: February 28th 2020. Aphorism 9.

587 BLAKE, W. *The marriage of heaven and hell.* "The argument" (Produced by eagkw, Dianna Adair – online) Available at: <http://www.gutenberg.org/files/45315/45315-h/45315-h.htm> Access: April 20th 2020.

588 JUNG, C. G. (1998) *Visions: Notes on the Seminar Given in 1930-1934.* Routledge. p. 235.

589 JUNG, C. G. (1985) *The Practice of psychotherapy. Ab-reaction, dream analysis and transference.* Translated by Hull, R. F. C. 2nd edition. CW XVI. Bollingen Series XX. Princeton University Press. §384.

590 GOVINDA, A. (1975) *Foundations of Tibetan mysticism.* New York: Samuel Weiser. p. 219.

591 "They were incorruptibly pure and without stain.' I would understand this to mean that **the eternal body is not contaminated with unconsciousness**. The symbolism of purity, in psychological terms, means that **we are conscious of our own dirt**, not that we don't have dirt but it's purified dirt because we're conscious of it. and that makes all the difference." EDINGER, E. F. (1994) *The mystery of the coniunctio: Alchemical image of individuation.* Picture 10 "Resurrection of the united eternal body". Inner City Books. [author's own highlights]

592 EDINGER, E. F. (1991) *Anatomy of the Psyche: Alchemical Symbolism in Psychotherapy.* Chapter 7: "Separatio". Open Court Publishing Company.

.

COLLECTIVE EGO &
SYMBOLIC EGO

Main thought! The individual himself is a fallacy. Everything which happens in us is in itself something else which we do not know. 'The individual' is merely a sum of conscious feelings and judgments and misconceptions, a belief, a piece of the true life system or many pieces thought together and spun together, a 'unity', that doesn't hold together. We are buds on a single tree – what do we know about what can become of us from the interests of the trees! But we have a consciousness as though we would and should be everything, a phantasy of "I" and all "not I". Stop feeling oneself as this fantastic ego! Learn gradually to discard the supposed individual! Discover the fallacies of the ego! Recognize egoism as fallacy! The opposite is not to be understood as altruism! This would be love of other supposed individuals! No! Get beyond 'myself' and 'yourself'! Experience cosmically![593]

The structure of the ego is eternal, as is everything else in the universe. The unconscious would not have made an investment of eras in building a structure only to throw it away. The Paradigm of Self-Affirmation has the formation of a strong ego as its final objective. As opposed to the nihilist spiritual movements and their psychotizing proposals of a life without an ego, I am an admirer of a strong ego. I consider the ego one of the most beautiful things of the UNIVERSE, since it is the structure on which the consciousness – better still, the self-aware consciousness – was developed.

However beautiful is the construction of a strong ego in the Paradigm of Self-Affirmation, the third-dimensional structure of the ego imprisoned in selfishness and duality must be overcome – everything that is in the universe must be overcome. In the Paradigm of Balance, the structure of the ego is violently attacked and relativized by the appearance of an infinitely higher divine centre, the 4D Self, the Soul. In contact with the Soul, the 4D ego learns that the reality it knows is not the only one there is. The 4D ego realises that what it has always been is just a group of conditionings learned since childhood, and it does not even have its own personality. A reductive therapy can help this ego to achieve its own personality. But the fourth dimension is extremely vast, and a reductive therapy is just an introduction to the unconscious psyche. An archetypal dimension follows, with extremely transcendent realities in relation to the reality of that ego. If it is strong enough to resist the very powerful movement caused by the instinct of individuation[594], this ego will reach a final confrontation with the Self, on the Cross.

During its journey through the Paradigm of Balance, the 4D ego starts, very slowly, to leave the imprisonment inside itself, through the removal of projections that its Soul places on others. As its prejudices fall, the 4D ego realises that those things which are different from itself are not worse, and moreover, those characteristics in others which it furiously or cynically criticised, were just parts of itself that it did not recognise. With the proximity of the end of the fourth dimension, particularly after integrating the contra-sexual archetype *Anima/Animus*, the fourth-dimensional **paradox** me-others is inevitably formed. We have discussed it several times in the present work. It is about the perception that the other is a reflex of extracts of the 4D ego's psyche, therefore alterations made in the psyche of the 4D ego psyche are instantly reflected in the others and raises the question: is the other a psychological image of the 4D ego or are they an independent person? The **paradoxical** response is: both. It starts to become clear that the notion of **me** is strongly linked to the notion of **other** in a transcendental manner, beyond the desires or the control of the ego.

In the Paradigm of Balance, the ego receives at least three violent blows against its pride: the succession of moral defeats (particularly the return of projections), the me-other paradox and the perception that it is not the whole of the psyche, but the Self is. Even then, during the whole fourth dimension, the ego maintains the illusion that it is a "separate unity" from the rest of people and the universe. This illusion is maintained until the Cross, when the ego is entirely destroyed by the IMPONDERABLE. This moment is extremely special, because it is when a human being reaches complete union with the Soul, with the IMPONDERABLE, and becomes **divine**. At the same time, the Soul completes its process of incarnation and becomes **human**. The second *coniunctio* has occurred – the connection between the ego and the Self has become stable.

The Paradigm of Sense makes its first movement with the abandoning by God, the RETREAT OF THE SOUL on the Cross. But it is the RESURRECTION that completely opens the horizon of the fifth dimension, and from there the resurrected ego (5D) will realise that several of its characteristics have changed. Its fifth-dimensional consciousness is a coincidence between what in the fourth dimension was known as "consciousness" and "Unconscious". The 5D ego has overcome the psychological reality and is now in the *Pneumatic* reality, perceiving the SPIRIT directly in its BODY and in the reality that surrounds it. These circumstances reveal to the ego completely new facts about itself: its structure is entirely different.

In the Paradigm of Balance, the ego has coexisted with the Soul, and realised that the Soul was way beyond it. Among the various characteristics that made the Soul bigger, one is of particular interest to us: its ability to manage the relationship of the 4D ego with other people, attracting people who were suitable to its intention regarding the development of the 4D ego, and repelling others, at the same time that the coexistence with the 4D ego was important to the development of the people who had been attracted to it. The arrangements and rearrangements of relationships made by the Soul during the whole fourth dimension are evidence that **the Soul is not individual, it is an encounter of individuals.**

The understanding of the Soul as "my Soul" is shallow and third-dimensional. Indeed, in the Paradigm of Self-Affirmation, the Soul allows the ego to be sovereign of the psyche whilst it was being developed and becomes strong enough to meet the Soul. Therefore, the ego assumes that the "soul" is satisfied when it is satisfied, that the "soul" will get the partner it wants, the job it wants, the money it wants and the victory of its football team, as long as the ego prays for the Soul, communicating its own wishes. The ego believes that the "soul" will never harm it, that is, will never contradict its expectations, since every ego considers itself to be good, whatever their definition of good. Above all, as the 3D ego sees itself as an **independent and separate** person from all the others, and, in this paradigm, the ego is the "soul", the ego understands that the "soul" is its stronger mark of separation between itself and the others. In the third dimension, the "soul" is the **identity** of the ego, what separates it from the rest, forever – the "soul" is "**mine**".

When entering the Paradigm of Balance, the Soul systematically destroys the separation between the 4D ego and other people, forcing it to see itself in others (projections), and no longer managing its relationships according to the ego's convenience, but according to its own intentions, markedly the instinct of individuation. The Soul does that so that the ego can develop to a point if understanding the nature of the Soul: the transcendence of the personal to the relationship. It is not about denying the fact that each person is a unity, an individual – the third dimension will be eternally valid. But the Soul is a **paradox** between the individual and everyone else. It is not by chance that the expression *Anima mundi*, the Soul of the world, appears several times in alchemy, which scope includes **all** people. So, although each person is an **individual**, and in the fourth dimension they experience the instinct of **individuation**, the terms "individual" and "individuation" have an entirely diverse meaning and **include all others**[595]. If the second *coniunctio* means the integration of the Sun and the Moon to the fourth-dimensional consciousness, to reach this *coniunctio* necessarily means to be a wholly developed individual, **to have become what it is** (Sun), and, **paradoxically, to include all others inside** (Moon).

It happens that, in the Paradigm of Sense, the fifth-dimensional ego has **integrated the Soul**. This fact is **experienced** by the ego after its Resurrection, when it finds itself in the ***Pneumatic* reality**. The **sensation** of opening one's eyes and **knowing in one's own Body** that the people one sees around are parts of oneself, are elements of the unified *Pneumatic* reality, and that, ultimately, **all the others are myself, including 'myself'**[596] – this **sensation** is absolutely fantastic. In the beginning, it is almost unbelievable, but the 5D ego cannot avoid the **evidence** that proves itself again and again: people behave **exactly** as the spiritual Images seen by the 5D ego. In a kind of constant synchronicity, everything that the 5D ego experiences is being experienced by people around it. If it is writing a text, people around it will be talking about that subject. If it needs an information, someone nearby will bring it. If it is feeling any pain, people around will be experiencing similar problems. If it experiences lack of confidence, its peers are there to question or challenge it. During its sleep, it experiences a Pneûma, and the next day it will find that a friend dreamed with the continuation of its Pneûma. Whether the situation of the 5D ego is positive or negative, whether it is *Dharma* or Karma, people around are sharing **exactly** the same situation, as if they were characters of a fourth-dimensional dream, where every detail is precisely positioned to contribute to the meaning, the only exception being that the *Pneumatic* reality is **not** symbolic and does **not** need to be interpreted: its Truth is **evident and obvious, explicit** as the Sun.

As if all this was not enough, since the 5D ego lives in the temporal structure of All-the-Times, the **precision** between its consciousness and people's behaviour is maintained even when the 5D ego acts in different times to the **present**. If, when in contact with the MULTI-DIMENSIONALITY, it accesses a "past" situation and relativizes a "past" KARMA, experiencing it in the present, the past is altered. This alteration causes a **complete rearrangement of the *Pneumatic* reality**, since the "past" has changed. This rearrangement includes people leaving the 5D ego's lives, and others arriving, but more than that, it includes an immediate change in the behaviour of all those who stay in the 5D ego's life, **with no apparent reason and without them even noticing it**. It is as if "history" had been re-written since the past, now altered, until the present, and that it had always been that way, therefore no one has changed their behaviour, people were always like that. What the 5D ego perceives as present, even if they are spiritual IMAGES from the "past", other people will see as "past", and even then, the timings of the 5D ego and that of others will be synchronized.

On the other hand, the 5D ego has conscious access to the archetypical dimension, and its choices cause an UNBALANCE on one or another archetype, DRAWING their IMAGE in the BODY and in the matter. Given that the archetypical reality determines Destiny, the events which will happen in everyone's lives, the 5D ego, in contact with the MULTI-DIMENSIONALITY, when acting in the archetypal dimension, has *Actions in the Future*, actions which will take place in the "future". To much surprise, what is noticed is that these actions actually do take place and involve the 5D ego and everyone around it. What the 5D ego perceives as present, even if they are spiritual *Images* of the "future", other people perceive as "future", and even then, the timings of the 5D ego and that of other people are still synchronized.

The same rationale is valid for different spaces. If, in the *Multi-Dimensionality*, the 5D ego has actions in *Images* from the *Macroimage* which are manifested in distant places from where the 5D ego lives, the implications of these actions will be felt in these distant places, even if the 5D ego has never been there physically, because it has been there "physically" (= in *Spirit*), during a *Pneûma* or an imagination, for example.

On the verge of the absurd, the **paradox** is that, despite all this **precision** between the *Pneumatic* reality of the 5D ego and the behaviour of other people, **the other people are other people, "independent", and can make decisions as freely as their level of *Free-Will* allows**. It is not necessary for the 5D ego to impose this reality on people – although it can do that through the various kinds of *Interference* possible. Quite simply, in the *Pneumatic* reality, the reality of the 5D ego is **exactly** adjusted to the "independence" of everyone else.

The **precision** between the *Pneumatic* reality of the 5D ego and the "independent" reality of everyone else is known as *Collective Ego*, and this is the description of a fifth-dimensional ego. The *Collective Ego* is, therefore, more a "**we**" than a "**me**".

Although, so far, we have appreciated the perspective according to which the behaviour of other people is identical to the *Pneumatic* reality of the 5D ego, and they are still independent, the interaction between the 5D ego and other people is even more profound. In this scenario, it is important to say that the *Collective Ego* **experiences** the "we" as a "me". This means that, just as in the *Pneumatic* reality, where the "interior" world of the 5D ego IS the "exterior" world where people circulate, the "interior" world of people is manifested in the *Pneumatic* reality of the 5D ego, which feels it from "inside". That way, the 5D ego opens itself to feel inside itself the needs, sensations, feelings, thoughts and even the unconsciousness of other people, in the same way that it feels its own, with no mixture between them, but union. For that reason, the 5D ego is extremely sensitive to realities which are transcendent to its own, whether they are the realities of other people or realities of the collective. In the 5D ego, its own "interior" events – its needs, sensations, feelings, thoughts, Unconscious, etc. – and the "interior" events of other people are distinct, but they are experienced from a single common base, an even bigger movement: **the collective movement**. As this is conscious to the 5D ego, it experiences itself as a *Collective Ego*.

Let us contemplate the situation from an instinctual perspective, since the fifth dimension is fundamentally instinctual. There is a huge quantity of instinctual discharges which are strongly individual, particularly the survival instinct. The 5D ego is conscious of these *Instincts*, and differently from the way it used to do in previous dimensions, it feels entirely free to satisfy them. Therefore, it **satisfies** them, which makes it feel a **satisfied** and **accomplished** person. It is noticeable how much a satisfied person, particularly instinctually satisfied, is much more stable, has much more self-esteem and feels much more accomplished than a dissatisfied person. Passionate, given that it is fundamentally instinctual, with its *Instincts* freely satisfied, the 5D ego is solid and has a high self-esteem, therefore **able** to dedicate to issues that transcend it, the issues of others, and more than that, the **collective** issues.

The very structure of the *Spirit* is collective. Let us build on this idea.

In a 3D ego, there is **no space** for a psychological image because there is not enough **psychological space**. This happens because every psychological image is paradoxical, and, from a dual perspective, has "two sides". As the 3D ego only has "one side", no psychological image can consciously fit, therefore it identifies with "one of the sides". Let us take as an example the psychological image of androgyny. The two sides of this image are the masculine and the feminine. A 3D ego cannot consciously be androgynous, man AND woman at the same time, so it chooses one side, either man OR woman. The other part will be projected on other people and remain unconscious.

A 4D ego has enough psychological space to fit psychological images (**Soul** images). This happens because the 4D ego has discovered that it has an unconscious. Therefore, "one side" of the image can remain in its dual ego, whereas the "other side" can remain in the unconscious. As we have seen several times, the unconscious is manifested directly through the other people, particularly through the mechanism of projection. To put it another way, as there is no "my soul", the Soul – *Anima mundi*, the Soul of all – accommodates a psychological image in a couple of people. This is what Christ, symbol of the Soul, refers to when he says "For where two or three meet in my name, I am there among them."[597]. If we continue the androgyny example, now in four dimensions, the Soul accommodates the image of the man in the 4D ego and the image of the woman in another person, or vice-versa. The coexistence between these two people leads to the progressive awareness of the psychological image, and eventually, there will be integration, both ascending to the reality of androgyny, overcoming the opposites man and woman[598]. Therefore, **a psychological image needs at least two people** to be manifested and integrated. Self-help has no chance of success.

The *Pneumatic Images*, even the smallest ones, **do not** fit into just two people.

Pneumatic Images (*Images* of the *Spirit*) are not just paradoxes (4D), they are spiritual *Truths* (5D). Beyond the fourth-dimensional paradox, a pair of opposed and simultaneously valid energies, the smallest possible *Pneumatic Images* have at least two more poles, the *Instinctual* poles of the paradoxical energies. In our example, a *Pneumatic Image* of androgyny has the archetypal masculine pole, the feminine archetypal pole, the masculine *Instinctual* pole and the feminine *Instinctual* pole. One could argue that the *Instinctual* poles already exist in four dimensions. It is a fact; they do. However, these poles are secondary and can only be assimilated through the archetypal dimension, as taught by JUNG[599]. In the fifth dimension, the archetypal sphere is already integrated, and the *Instinctual* pole of the archetype becomes priority, never secondary. Therefore, it is a different configuration.

Evidently, the structure of the 5D ego is different and the fact that it needs the participation of other people in order to receive a *Pneumatic* image is not necessarily related to an unconsciousness in relation to some of the poles (parts) of the *Image* (although unconsciousness can exist in the 5D ego, given that the fourth dimension is eternally valid). Its need of participation of other people is preferential because it is very hard and time-consuming to realise all parts of the *Pneumatic Image* with only one (physical) *Body* – it would be like swimming with only one arm, which is possible, but not desirable. It is better to realise the *Pneumatic Image* with several (physical) *Bodies* – to swim using two arms and two legs – which is much more efficient. For that reason, it is ideal that there are at least four people receiving the most basic type of *Pneumatic Image* there is. Assuming that these people are united for this purpose, the 5D ego is androgynous (masculine and feminine at the same time), and *Pneumatic* (spiritual and corporal at the same time), and could, in a given situation, *Corporally* perform all four functions, which would be complicated, lengthy and tiring. Instead, it performs corporally only one function, let us say, an *Instinctual* female, whereas other people perform other functions.

However, our example described a simple *Pneumatic Image*, with just four poles, four types of basic "information". There are infinitely larger *Pneumatic Images* in the *Macroimage*. A *Multi-Dimensional Image*, for example, can include several environments (spiritual dimensions, spiritual spaces), in several times of the *All-the-Times*, involving several people, each one with their consciousness, their histories, their thoughts, their feelings, including the *Image*'s unconscious, in its personal and collective dimensions, sometimes several levels of the unconscious, etc. In the chapter *Manifestation*, (in *Multi-Dimensionality*), I showed the example describing Christ's encounter with Moses and Elijah. Note the **huge complexity** of this *Image*, considering the encounter of these three **gigantic icons**, each with their consciousness, their history, "their" Unconscious, the collective Unconscious of the Hebrews, the collective unconscious of humanity, each with their culture, their position in space, their position in time, their interpersonal relationship. Besides the greatness of these three icons, Christ's friends participated clearly in the *Image*, and undoubtedly, if we knew Moses' and Elijah's perspectives, we would see that their friends also took part.

Adding this all up, **Pneumatic Images can only be received in group, and the size of a *Pneumatic Image* received depends on the size of the group that receives it, both in terms of the capacity of each fifth-dimensional ego involved, a *Collective Ego*, and in terms of the number of members of the group.**

Also note that the **interest** about a *Pneumatic Image* is markedly **collective**. On one hand, a fifth-dimensional ego is someone who has worked very hard to complete their being, to satisfy and realise itself – they have lived through the third and fourth dimensions to achieve that. Therefore, almost every time, when the 5D ego wants to complete even more its already complete being (a **paradox** that exists, given that the fourth dimension continues to exist after the opening of the fifth dimension), when it wants to be further satisfied and realised, the 5D ego "deals" with these questions by using its completely developed 3D and 4D structures. On the other hand, *Pneumatic Images* are too large to relate only to one person; it would be like writing a whole book to describe one single pencil. Therefore, the *Pneumatic Images* that are received by the *Collective 5D Ego* are of **collective interest**. For example, the *Pneumatic Image* of the encounter between Christ, Moses and Elijah are of collective interest, largely surpassing the "strictly individual" scenario of each one of them, however complex they might have been. In another example, of a completely diverse culture, the problem faced by a Greek hero is never strictly personal. Oedipus faces the pest that is spread around the **whole of Thebes**, he is not the only one ill; strictly speaking, he is not. In the works of Heracles, the monsters have names that include their region: the Lion attacks Nemea and Hydra attacks Lerna, regions of the Peloponnese, and not where Heracles lives. As it can be seen, it is about collective problems[600]. An avatar or a hero, being the child of a god or goddess, with super-human powers, simply worrying about personal issues, would be even more selfish and deluded than a normal person. **The *Collective Ego* experiences in itself its own reality AND the reality of other people, and its experiences involve many people. In the interim, many people have their experiences through the experience of the *Collective Ego*.**

Even though the collective interest prevails in the *Pneumatic Image*, the personal interest is equally **indispensable**. Let us not forget that the *Collective Ego* includes itself as one of those who compose the collective. When there is no personal interest, there is an identification with the collective ideals, causing dehumanization. In this situation, the 5D ego ignores itself as a human being and identifies itself as the representative of the collective. This behaviour does not consider its own humanity, therefore dehumanizes that ego. Similarly, there is also the risk of considering itself a "saviour", falling for the illusion that it can "develop the other". In both cases, collective archetypal images – **titanic** archetypal *Images*, as it is typical of the fifth dimension – will be manifested through the fifth-dimensional ego dehumanized, brutal, prioritizing power instead of wisdom, and every kind of monstrosity can be manifested. The fifth-dimensional ego is divine when it is inspired (by the *Force*), but it is *Demoniac* when prioritizes power (by the *Dynamic Force*). The fifth-dimensional *Collective Ego* will have to make its choices based on what makes *Sense* to it, never forgetting that it must **first** make *Sense* to it.

* * * * *

The Paradigm of Sense is a long process, a **creative** process. As its end gets near, it is necessary that the *Collective Ego* has been dedicated to a **great creation**, the creation of something concrete, that will remain for a long time in the world, to the benefit of humanity, in the same way that a hero, after completing its work, **returns and becomes the patron of a civilization**[601].

In the start of the paradigm, the ego is much more focused on learning the characteristics of that paradigm, it is experimenting. Further along the journey, it dedicates to various *Creations*, based on several *Pneumatic Images* in which it has seen *Sense*. While it is dedicated to these, it is also occupied with the integration of the titanic generation of Greek gods, typical of that paradigm, and educates *Demons* (*Dynamic Forces*), taking care not to fall into *Demoniac* imprisonments. Close to the end of the paradigm, however, besides the various *Creations* that it might be undertaking, it is common that, being more mature, it prefers to dedicate to one or only a few bigger, more complex *Creations*, whose *Sense* is wider, and that the ego likes more (preferences are desirable). Such bigger and more complex *Creations* are, as with any fifth-dimensional *Creation*, based on great *Pneumatic Images* and involve many people, causing a great concreteness, a great incarnation, of great value to society.

At the end of the Paradigm of Sense, the *Collective Ego* evolves to a *Symbolic Ego*. The association in the long term between the 5D ego and the *Pneumatic Image* allows that the former perfuse the latter. Being a *Pneumatic Image*, the 5D ego and the incarnation of both in a concrete creative work become an organic whole, only one thing. People who report to that *Creative* work will always have that 5D ego as a **reference**. In this case, the 5D ego, which is an integrated Soul, **humanized, symbolizes** the *Creative* work – at the same time protecting everyone from the light and blazing heat of the Sun of the *Spirit* (the total *Pneumatic Image*), and allowing that the *Image* and the *Creative* work are **understood** by all. In this scenario, the 5D ego incarnates the **Symbol** of its *Creative* work: the *Symbolic Ego*.

593 NIETZSCHE, F. *Kritische studienausgabe.* (on line) Available at: <https://www.goodreads.com/quotes/8010169-main-thought-the-individual-himself-is-a-fallacy-everything-which> Access: February 28th 2020.

594 "Throughout life, the Self is constantly putting pressure on the ego, both to make it face reality and to make it take part on the individuation process. The Self does this with or without the ego's consent, however the compensations against the resisting ego (nightmares, accidents, physical symptoms) tend to be more severe than the complementary relationship of an ego that is trying its best to consciously participate in the individuation process." Hall, J. A. *Jungian dream interpretation* [translated from the Portuguese version: (1997) *Jung e a interpretação dos sonhos.* São Paulo: Cultrix. p. 127.]

595 "Individuation is an at-one-ment with oneself and at the same time with humanity, since oneself is a part of humanity." JUNG, C. G. (1985) *The Practice of psychotherapy. General problems of psychotherapy.* Translated by Hull, R. F. C. 2nd edition. CW XVI. Bollingen Series XX. Princeton University Press. §227.

596 NIETZSCHE, F. *Kritische studienausgabe.* Op. Cit.

597 *The New Jerusalem Bible.* Matthew 18:20

598 This example, specifically, is dear to Analytical Psychology, because it describes the therapeutic mechanism of transference and countertransference, as described by Carl JUNG. JUNG, C. G. (1985) *The Practice of psychotherapy. Ab-reaction, dream analysis and transference.* Translated by Hull, R. F. C. 2nd edition, CW XVI. Bollingen Series XX. Princeton University Press.

599 See chapter "Instinct".

600 See chapter "Interference".

601 See chapter "Interference".

GRAIL

BETRAYAL

On his way towards the Cross, to the *Imponderable*, Christ externally embraced all the relationships he came across, internally embracing all the psychological energies he came across. He had a relationship with the purest mother, Mary, and had a relationship (in my opinion, sexual) with a prostitute, Mary Magdalene – Christ is pure and promiscuous. He had a relationship with the fishermen who had nothing and with Joseph of Arimathea, a rich man – Christ is poor and rich. He had a relationship with the self-righteous Pharisees and with Pontius Pilate, who asked one of the most profound questions of a total philosophical amplitude – "Truth? What is that?"[602] – Christ was a hypocrite and sought the *Truth*. We could continue on a long list of characteristics. Each and every relationship can be found in Christ and each and every characteristic can be found in Christ.

This is the only way to be complete, because to be complete means just being complete, therefore anyone who wishes to reach completeness must be *de facto* complete – there are no deforming theological or psychological subterfuges. Reaching the *Imponderable* means having the bravery of possessing **all** possible characteristics.

In his all-inclusive journey, the Christ managed the feat of being loved by all and hated by all. In the beginning, his ability to see the other as they were, in the same way as he saw himself as he was, with no moral judgement, caused the others to feel loved and understood; they loved him back, perhaps surprised by being completely loved for the first time.

However, later on, it became difficult to have a relationship with someone who had **all** characteristics. In the third dimension, the correct thing is to have certain characteristics and not others; one must choose a side. Having all characteristics is something inconceivable in three dimensions. As humanity still has three dimensions, having all characteristics is still inconceivable and very probably many people were shocked when they read the first paragraph of this chapter. Having all characteristics is a fourth-dimensional structure, therefore it **does not fit** in three dimensions. The interpretation of a posterior dimension by a previous one is always deforming.

Initially, the 3D egos interpreted the paradoxical personality of the 4D Christ as "lack of personality", of "authenticity", as "not choosing a side" – sentences such as "pay Caesar what belongs to Caesar – and God what belongs to God"[603] and "your left hand must not know what your right is doing"[604], perfectly natural paradoxes in four dimensions, are very shocking in three dimensions. Later on, the confrontation became deeper. As Christ got closer and closer to the Soul, becoming one with the Father, its divine nature became apparent[605]. It became clear the situation which humanity, at all times, considered the most unacceptable, the most atrocious, the most repugnant, the one which simultaneously arises the biggest hatred, disbelief and contempt: **the fact that the human being is truly divine**. It was this fact that finally distanced Christ from the population – on Palm Sunday everyone cheering him as a King, and on Maundy Thursday everyone abandoned him, including God on Good Friday.

> The Jews replied, 'We have a Law, and according to that Law he ought to be put to death, because he has claimed to be Son of God'.[606]

This fact also led him to be judged:

> The men who had arrested Jesus led him off to the house of Caiaphas the high priest, where the scribes and the elders were assembled. Peter followed him at a distance right to the high priest's palace, and he went in and sat down with the attendants to see what the end would be. The chief priests and the whole Sanhedrin were looking for evidence against Jesus, however false, on which they might have him executed. But they could not find any, though several lying witnesses came forward. Eventually two came forward and made a statement, 'This man said, "I have power to destroy the Temple of God and in three days build it up." The high priest then rose and said to him, 'Have you no answer to that? What is this evidence these men are bringing against you?' But Jesus was silent. And the high priest

said to him, 'I put you on oath by the living God to tell us if you are the Christ, the Son of God.' Jesus answered him, 'It is you who say it. But, I tell you that from this time onward you will see the Son of man seated at the right hand of the Power and coming on the clouds of heaven.' Then the high priest tore his clothes and said, 'He has blasphemed. What need of witnesses have we now? There! You have just heard the blasphemy. What is your opinion?' They answered, 'He deserves to die'.[607]

The logical rationale is that Christ caused a conflict with the Judaic orthodoxy. Claiming to be the Son of God, Jesus presented himself as a **divine** human being, and this was considered a blasphemy, because for the Jews, only God is divine. To attribute this conflict to the Judaic orthodoxy, however, is stupid. Our current society would react with the same contempt in the face of someone who explicitly claimed to be the "Son of God", "In unity with the Father", "Perfect" and able to perform "Miracles". No psychological or mythological proof are necessary to test this, it is enough to do the experiment. Say these things to your friends, with conviction, and pay attention to their reaction. Maybe the current reaction would stop at contempt, since our society seems to be more sceptical and more cynical than the Judaic society of two thousand years ago. However, if someone's declaration of divinity was persistent and seemed consistent, I doubt whether reactions would not be violent, after all, the horrors of the twentieth century seem to be even darker than those from the start of the Christian Era.

We judge people from "that time" as very inferior to ourselves, as if currently we would have a different attitude to theirs in the face of Christ, as if his arrival among us could be immediately understood. I do not believe it would. Christianity is an evidence of that. Christ says that he would send the *Holy Spirit* to the people, and that they would do bigger things than he did. But if someone declares to have the *Holy Spirit* in their *Body* and take the *Word*, saying different things than what is written in the "Scriptures" they would be discredited[608]. Why we would need the *Holy Spirit* to repeat the words in the "Scriptures" is a question that, for me, has no answer. Perhaps it would be wiser to learn with Peter that people who swear not to betray Christ are those who would systematically do just that[609].

The all-inclusive path of Christ led him to being betrayed by the whole population. It is very illogical that the love for all has led to betrayal by all, but that is how irrationality works. The affirmation that Christ has been betrayed **by all**, which, evidently, includes **all**, is so unbearable, so unacceptable, that it is necessary to use someone as a scape goat, as the epitome of betrayal – Judas. Through this shameful mechanism, it seems that just this sinister character, Judas, has betrayed Christ, whereas all others were there to support him and give their lives for him. With that, Judas hangs himself[610], instead of the whole of humanity hanging themselves, one by one, as it would perhaps be much fairer.

Although the betrayal of all towards Christ happened for the reasons described above, it is more superficial when compared to Judas' betrayal, much more complex.

> According to John 13:26f Judas is given his terrible fate at the Last Supper. After Christ announces that one of his disciples will betray him, he is asked who it will be. He replies, "He it is, to whom I shall give a sop, when I have dipped it. And when he had dipped the sop, he gave it to Judas Iscariot, the son of Simon. And after the sop Satan entered into him."
>
> Certain medieval pictures show Satan as a tiny demon entering the mouth of Judas as Christ gives him a morsel. [...] It is as though Christ fed Judas his assigned destiny at that moment and Judas dutifully carried it out. **This may explain why the betrayal is accomplished with a "kiss" and why Christ calls Judas "friend" as he receives the kiss**. It is an act of love to lead a person to his proper destiny. It was Christ's destiny to be crucified. Therefore he calls Judas "friend" and reacts angrily when Peter suggests he could avoid that fate:
>
> Jesus began to make it clear to his disciples that he was destined to go to Jerusalem and suffer grievously at the hands of the elders and chief priests and scribes, to be put to death and to be raised up on the third day. Then, taking him aside, Peter started to remonstrate with him. "Heaven preserve you, Lord;" he said. "This must not happen to you." But he turned and said to Peter, "Get behind me, Satan! You are an obstacle in my path, because the way you think is not God's way but man's." (Matt. 16:21-23, Jerusalem Bible)[611] [author's own highlights]

It is evident that Christ **wanted** to be betrayed, calling his "traitor" friend, rejecting more than once those who wanted to "protect" him, as mentioned above and as happened in Gethsemane[612]. The all-inclusive behaviour of Christ also must include betrayal, without which there would be a limitation in his being, a barrier between him and the *Imponderable*. In part, this explains why the traitor is a friend and the kiss is the betrayal.

However, betrayal is not just any dark element, it has a special characteristic: **it is the extreme opposite of the all-inclusive behaviour**. Therefore, Judas' betrayal seems so horrendous in a third-dimensional scenario, and let us be honest, even in a fourth-dimensional scenario. To betray someone is considered something horrible (3D), but to betray someone whose love is transcendental, someone who would understand **anything** (4D), seems as unreasonable as it is unbelievable, and it causes violent reactions of contempt – in Brazil, the burning of Judas is a cultural custom practiced to this day (*malhar o Judas*, in Portuguese).

The transcendent love between Jesus and Judas is **strongly paradoxical**, well-fitting at the end of the Paradigm of Balance. On one hand, considering the point of view of Edward EDINGER, Jesus helps Judas to fulfil his Destiny, and Judas helps Jesus fulfil his Destiny. On the other hand, Jesus throws Satan inside Judas' body and Judas delivers Jesus to the fatal torture.

However, there is an even more extreme paradox. On one hand, Christ's action would only be **absolutely** all-inclusive if it embraced betrayal, the extreme opposite of the total inclusion. Christ realises this by being friends with Judas, and Judas realises this by kissing Jesus. However, **Christ himself** could not betray, because if he did, his all-inclusive action would not be complete. It was necessary that he loved **all** and conducted **all**; and that is what he did. But there was an exception, **paradoxically necessary**: Judas.

> While I was with them, I kept those you had given me true to your name. I have watched over them and not one is lost except one who was destined to be lost, and this was to fulfil the scriptures.[613]

Therefore, Jesus does not compromise his all-inclusive action by becoming a traitor, and fulfilling the compulsory reflex between interior and exterior, typical of the fourth dimension, Jesus abandons Judas, now the son of damnation, throwing the *Demon* inside his *Body*, and Judas abandons Jesus to torture. Judas did the only thing that Christ could not do, to betray, without which Christ's action would not be complete and all the work would be in vain.

Jesus' action towards Judas is abominable, and Judas' action towards Jesus is abominable. For this very reason they were actions of **extreme love**. They both had the courage to do for one another something that no one else would. **That way, all** the energies were included, **without** practicing betrayal, allowing Christ's action to reach plenitude and became available in the Collective Unconscious of the whole humanity, opening a New Era.

Nevertheless, this is not enough to understand the joined action of Jesus and Judas. We can describe the situation that they experienced as **extreme love**, as **extreme courage**, therefore fourth-dimensional. But we cannot deny that the **paradox was not** established between two opposed energies simultaneously valid, **both included**, as it is typical of the Paradigm of Balance. The paradox was established between two opposed energies simultaneously valid, with **one included and the other excluded**. More still, this energy that was excluded from Christ's all-inclusive love, experienced by Judas, established a ***Demoniac* possession**, with the consent of Christ himself: Christ consciously allowed the *Demon* to enter Judas' mouth. This action, which used an energy that had not been included in the multi-paradoxical all-inclusive behaviour of Christ, a *Demoniac* energy, was **fifth-dimensional**. Through this action, this **betrayal**, this absolutely **necessary anti-ethical** action, therefore with strong *Personal Sense*, Judas opened the access to the Paradigm of Sense.

In opening his mouth for the *Demon* to enter, as it was Christ's wish, Judas opens himself to receive Christ's **Shadow**. Christ, however, integrates in his path from Bethlehem to the Last Meal, the **whole** Shadow, becoming himself a Symbol of Wholeness, a Symbol of the Self. How can we, then, speak of Christ's Shadow at this point? Knowing that Christ could only arrive at the Last Meal and at Golgotha because he integrated the whole Shadow, the Shadow of the fourth dimension, then the Christ's Shadow at this point is what at that moment was at a deeper level of the unconscious, the fifth dimension. As Christ concluded the whole psychological process of the fourth dimension, his action towards Judas constellated the 5D Shadow, the *Demon* itself, **opening the access to the fifth dimension**. Opening the Paradigm of Sense, therefore, means adjusting the course of humanity's spiritual history to the next destiny, to the fifth dimension, to the encounter with the Anti-Christ, Christ's Shadow, the internalization, the admission of the ***Demoniac* element**. That way, Judas was the necessary precursor of the Anti-Christ, the Anti-Christ wished by Christ in the Last Meal: the precursor of the Anti-Christ is called a **friend** by Christ. I cannot end this part without asking myself who is this person, this very special person, this person of admirable expertise, this friend of extreme loyalty, who Christ trusted with this abysmal task. This kind of person is precisely the type 'burned' by the rest of humanity, as Judas still is in Brazilian folklore.

ENIGMA

The Paradigm of Sense is a tightrope between the *Spirit* and the *Spirit*: between the *Spirit* of *Truth* and the *Spirit* of the Abyss, between the *Spirit* and the *Demon*. The *Spirit* resists itself. This is what opens the space for consciousness and creation.

The Fire of *Spirit* burns the ego with its *Truth*, explicit and bitter, dazzling and caustic, divine and infernal. Besides, the *Spirit* crushes the fifth-dimensional ego with the infinitely complex *Multi-Dimensionality*, only minimally bearable in groups sufficiently large to receive the *Pneumatic Images*. Finally, the *Spirit*, in conjunction with the freedom of *Free-Will*, places the colossal weight of decision over the ego's shoulders, which it will support, whether the ego is right or wrong. This decision will have an effect on other people, who are unconscious of this. The *Spirit* imposes only one limit: one cannot sin against the *Spirit,* "blasphemy against the Spirit will not be forgiven"[614], one cannot err knowingly.

If the *Spirit* was not enough, there is more *Spirit* – the *Demon*. The *Demon* is precisely an "intellectual substitute for instinct"[615]. Displacing the unquantifiable *Instinctual* energy to the rational mind, the Demon *Perverts* the energy, usurping it for mental control instead of allowing its free *Instinctive* flow. The mind becomes hypertrophied and alternative realities, non-immediate (as are the *Instinctual* realities), are built.

The *Demon* resists creation and the incarnation of the *Spirit* through temptation, through accusation and through lies. In union, the fifth-dimensional ego and the *Spirit* are *Creating* through a *Pneumatic Image* of the *Macroimage*, and then comes a *Demon* opposing contrary images – the *Spirit* is *Universe* and the *Demon* is *Verse*. In practice, the healthy 5D ego knows the *Truth* of the *Spirit* which it works on, and the *Demon* wants to argue intellectually with it. For example, in order to perform an action of a spiritual nature, the Christ goes to the desert (with its blazing Sun) to meditate. The *Demon* quickly appears and starts to **argue** with Christ, **discussing** the Scriptures with him, causing **polemic** about the meaning of those texts.

A more mundane and personal example might help understand this dynamic: a situation that I experienced.

Writing *Paradigm of Sense* was a fifth-dimensional process. I had already been working on this career for 18 years and had been 8 years since I discovered the Paradigm of Sense when a *Pneûma* appeared in the *Macroimage*, showing the writing of a book. I was already partially conscious of several psychological issues that stopped me from writing. The dream was the last straw. It made *Sense* to me that I had to overcome all this and finally write my *Creative* work.

My *Creative Choice* immediately triggered a *Demoniac* response and a great crisis in my life.

A few months before the dream, I had decided to move to Berlin to study German, and in due course, work. It became evident that I would not be able to write a book with this degree of complexity and, at the same time, start a new life in a new country with a language that was unknown to me. I knew that, if I wanted to write the book, I had to sacrifice my new life in Berlin and return to Brazil. The insidious speech of the *Demon* started:

Demon: Are you going to sacrifice your new life in Berlin to write this book?

Me (5D ego): Yes.

Demon: But this will hurt you.

Me (5D ego): Yes.

Demon: You are going to sacrifice a new life in a new country for the second time? Changing countries is something you have always wanted.

Me (5D ego): Yes, I am.

Demon: You are going to sacrifice your personal objectives to realise a great spiritual work? You are going to do that again? How many times are you going to do this?

Me (5D ego): Yes, I am.

It is very important to make clear that speeches from the *Demon* are extremely painful and cause great confusion in the consciousness because they point to psychological realities, even if partial. Remaining firm in the *Pneumatic Image* that I chose because I saw *Sense*, as I answered the *Demon*, was extremely difficult. Each answer came after the great pain of acknowledging the reality of the internal conflicts that the *Demon*, very informedly, pointed to.

But the worse was still to come. When I returned to Brazil, I went to visit my parents. A discussion with my father during one of the family meals was the trigger for another action from the *Demon*: psychological wounds from childhood were used.

Demon: The concepts that you are going to publish in the book are very controversial and will never be accepted publicly.

Me (5D ego): It is perfectly possible that this will happen. But without boldness, nothing new can be created.

Demon: How do you know that what you are creating is new?

Me (5D ego): It is impossible to know for sure, but everything that I have studied in the last 20 years is very distant from what I am going to write.

Demon: What do you mean "everything you have studied"? You have never been to university.

Me (5D ego): True. My education is based in my self-taught studies, in everything I have tested and the results I have analysed.

Demon: You cannot even convince your father...

At that point, the pain was too great, and I could no longer answer the *Demon*. Temporarily, it won. Only days later I noticed that my objective in writing *Paradigm of Sense* was not to "convince my father". However noble and loving the relationship with the father, to "convince the father" is a childish expectation that, in an adult, shows huge lack of confidence and low self-esteem. My objective, infinitely more difficult, possibly impossible, is to build a psychological paradigm that can positively contribute to the psychological and spiritual development of the **whole humanity**. It was **this** 5D Shadow that I was denying and that the *Demon* was using to accuse me.

The tendency is that *Demoniac* accusations such as those described in Christ's life and in my personal life will last forever.

One could argue that this type of mental discussion occurs with anyone in any dimension. And it does. In dimensions previous to the fifth, the mind, as a psychological organ, really usurps the energy, particularly in the *maṇipūra* level. As these dimensions are smaller and the mythical extract on which they are based **is not titanic**, as there is an **Olympic** protection for the ego, the *Perversion* does not reach geometric progressions. In the Paradigm of Self-Affirmation, people are protected by the huge limitation imposed by their mental beliefs, by the narrowmindedness of their psyche. In the Paradigm of Balance, people are protected by their contact with the Transcendence, the 4D Self, whose directions they follow and can always allege, for their own safety: "I am doing what the Transcendence ordered me to".

In the Paradigm of Sense, however, the spiritual potencies concern the ego directly, the Titans leave the Tartarus and have free access to the consciousness, and the 5D ego is facing **power** upfront. In this new scenario, the *Demoniac* allegations are **not** considered implausible (as they would be in previous dimensions, incapable of perceiving this level of Darkness); on the contrary, they are perceived as truths. The huge energy usurped from the instinctual instance of the being makes the partial truth brought by the *Demon* grow incredibly, seeming very real for the 5D ego, threatening to overtake the whole reality, leading to failure and despair. Only with much *Force*, the 5D ego can remain wholesome and continue its *Creative* work. Only with much *Evolution*, the 5D ego can absorb that energy, transforming it in fuel to dynamize the movement forwards. The difference in sensation between listening this type of mental discussion in the dimensions previous to the fifth and participating in the same type of discussion in the fifth dimension is the same as between watching a film about World War I on the sofa in your house and being at the front in the Maginot Line.

It is extremely difficult for the 5D ego to participate in a circumlocution with the *Demon*, as it takes a huge amount of energy to give it an answer. For such, this ego must penetrate a barrier created by the *Demon* through the exponential increase of the partial reality, fed by the huge input of *Instinctual* energy flowing towards this mental creation. Both the *Force* – through the beauty of its *Inspiration* and the firmness of its action –, and the *Evolution* – through the capacity of its purity to include and thus turn the *Demoniac* energy positive – are extremely useful to deal with *Demoniac* arguments. Indeed, when an answer is finally given and the usefulness of the *Demoniac* energy takes a step forward, the quantity of *Pneumatic* energy received is bigger than that spent to transpose the barrier – it is worth it.

However, it is essential to notice one fact. It is not worth arguing with the *Demon* – this is exactly what it wants to happen. By *Perverting* the huge wealth of instinctive energy, the *Demon* has an enormous mind. Arguing with it is a waste of time and it will always win, because its argumentation is infinite and very well constructed. In fact, as the philosophers know well, **any point of view can be refuted**, therefore any discussion can become infinite if it is well constructed, and the *Demon* has a special talent for that. The mind is dual, and any point of view has its opposite.

However, when it is said above that one "answers" the *Demon*, in no way this refers to mental answers, whether verbalized or silent. A fifth-dimensional ego must answer the *Demon* with **actions**, actions **filled with Sense**. The need for the answers to be given through actions not only prevents one from falling into *Demoniac* mental games, falling prey to alternative realities, but also channels the *Demoniac* energy to the *Body*. **The *Demon*, in the *Body*, is *Educated* and no longer resists the *Spirit*, or poses a risk to the 5D ego; on the contrary, it contributes to the**

dynamism of the *Creative* work, which can now move quicker. That way, the hypothetical answers of the fifth-dimensional ego from the example above are given through actions, in this case, by writing a book, channelling the *Demoniac* energy towards the book. The *Demoniac* energy is channelled towards the book through channelling the **content** of the conflict with the *Demon* towards the *Creative* work. We must not forget that the *Demon* is *Spirit*, the part of the *Spirit* that resists itself, which does not make it **dispensable**. On the contrary, the *Demon* is all Darkness, ugliness, deformity and *Perversion* that tend to be kept out of a *Creative* work, and, ignored, end up precluding the *Creative* work. Many pieces of work die that way. Besides, with the inclusion of the dark dimensions of the *Spirit*, the *Demon*, the whole *Creative* work becomes infinitely more **beautiful**, as every good artist knows.

The progression of the discussion with the *Demon* – the *Creative* actions of the 5D ego interspersed with the rationalizations of the *Demon*, even if the 5D ego manages not to be imprisoned in any of the alternative realities constructed by the *Demon* – tends to be exponential and grows dangerously. In a given moment, an unbearable level is reached. The *Creative* actions of the 5D ego generated an impressive *Creative* (at this point, given its concreteness, it can be called a **construction**), but all this construction is entirely relativized by the *Demon*, and seems real (spiritual) and unreal (demoniac) at the same time. In this instant, there is an impasse, something like a technical draw at a chess game, caused by a mutual check.

This impasse is called *Enigma*.

The tension is immense – the *Spirit* is measuring *Force* with the *Demon*, through the *Human*. It is very important to understand that the huge intuitive intelligence of the 5D ego has been vertiginously extended and the huge relativist rationalization of the *Demon* continues to extend. If the 5D ego does not make a **radical** move, the *Demon* will swallow it, as, without a *Body*, the *Demon* becomes progressively bigger.

Had we been in the fourth dimension, this moment of maximum tension was overcome by the Transcendent Function. However, in the fifth dimension, there is no transcendental assistance, only the support that the *Spirit* gives to the **choice** and the **action**. In the fifth dimension, the ego precedes the *Spirit*.

Without any transcendental guidance and with its creative work entirely relativized by the *Demon*, the fifth-dimensional ego **has no guarantee** of success. There is no correct answer. The 5D ego **knows** that there are no guarantees, no saviours. In this instant of conscious unquantifiable intensity, and therefore, very long duration, the 5D ego must see what makes *Sense* to it, and consequently to others, **and *Act*, completely *Without Guaranteee* (*Action Without Guaranteee*), in the direction of the conclusion of its *Creative* work. It is its own guarantee, it must guarantee by itself that the action will be completed.**

IF the 5D ego is sufficiently *Strong* (= expressing *Force*), if it is sufficiently *Evolving* (= dynamic), the *Demon* will enter the *Body* and, educated, will start to contribute to its *Creative* work, dynamizing it. There will be a *Manifestation*.

If the *Demon* is stronger and more dynamic, the 5D ego will fall into a *Demoniac* prison, will believe in that alternative reality and stay stuck, since it is a *Demoniac* prison for the consciousness, therefore there is no way out because the consciousness forgets what freedom is and no longer wants to leave. In this case, it is essential that the 5D ego have 5D friends...

GRAIL

In any dimension, these are attributes of the ego: **to have consciousness, to choose and to act**.

It is highly probable that these three attributes have been developed in the first dimension, since they are in the sphere of meanings of the root *cakra*, *mūlādhāra*, which is exactly what Adam and Eve did under the Tree of Knowledge of Good and Evil (end of the first dimension). Since then, these characteristics have become the very nature of the ego. Being the centre of consciousness, it is its job to have consciousness (obviously). The Self and the Unconscious are Whole and ambiguous, since they have all energies available, and always tend towards the Whole, towards the circle, not prioritizing any particular direction; therefore, it is the ego, dual, that needs to choose. Finally, it is the ego who exerts the strongest domain over the physical body, particularly during vigil and over that which is voluntary (although there are also many involuntary expressions in the body); therefore, it is the ego who must act.

During the whole fifth dimension, the ego learns to add new meanings to these attributes. Its **consciousness** is in coincidence with the Unconscious, and, for the first time since it was formed at the end of the first dimension, **unified**. For this reason, it turns to the ***Pneumatic reality***, whose starting point is multi-paradoxical (a state reached in

Crucifixion), and whose objective is the *Multi-Dimensionality*, the *Imponderable*, simultaneously spiritual and physical. *Inspired* by the *Force*, transcendental and *Instinctual*, consciousness becomes progressively more *Corporeal*, more physical, more *Instinctual*. The 5D consciousness is *Manifestation*.

The **choice** goes through the most radical transformation since the consciousness became possible. There is no longer an unconscious determination of choices typical of the second and third dimensions, nor the "free choice" that had to be in consonance with the constellations of the Unconscious, typical of the fourth dimension. In the fifth dimension, there was a *Retreating of the Soul*, and the *Spirit* appears as an all-encompassing Wholeness, always stable in its wholeness, never guiding the ego about what decision to take, even if it makes mistakes. However abyssal the anguish that it feels in face of the silence from the Transcendence **regarding choice**, the 5D ego will need to make its own choices and take responsibility for them, with an aggravating factor: in this dimension, every choice will mean an *Unbalance*, therefore an uprising of *Dynamic Force*, which will need to be educated. The ego will no longer be able to say, "I have nothing to do with this". The end of Lilith's self-exile teaches the ego to be **free in relation to the Transcendence and everything else**, which, in this dimension, in no way means an opposition to the *Spirit*, but harmony, i.e., *Force*. The free choice is the element that puts everything in movement in the fifth dimension and it is of fundamental importance – it is based on the *Personal Sense*, precisely the element that the Paradigm of Sense wants to develop, its objective.

Finally, the **action** is the main milestone of the fifth dimension, of which the *Unus Mundus*, pure *Spirit* (i.e., *Corporeal*, material) is the finishing line. The *Instinctive* action is precisely the dimension of the ego that allows it to progressively and more deeply access the unified *Pneumatic* reality and participate in it. After overcoming duality, now the consciousness is **inspired by the *Force***, both unified, and for that reason, in the fifth dimension, **the action is *Creation*** (the criterion of this dimension). At the end of the Paradigm of Sense, the fifth-dimensional ego is occupied with a **Great Creation** that it has chosen for itself. The 5D ego will complete the paradigm by generating a *Manifestation* of a *Multi-Dimensional Creation* in *All-the-Times*.

The size of the fifth-dimensional creation is **dimensioned** by the size of the *Demoniac* uprising that it causes – the bigger the strength of the *Demoniac* uprising, the bigger the dimension of *Creation*. Therefore, the *Great Creation* that will mark the end of the Paradigm of Sense will cause a generalized *Demoniac* uprising, all the infernal potencies in activity against the fifth-dimensional ego, which will be tempted in every way possible, accused in every way possible, and will hear lies of every kind. It is impossible to reach the end of the paradigm without facing the *Enigma*. At that point, when the *Demoniac* uprising is using all its power, everything will seem unreal, false. The fourth dimension tends to become powerfully regressive and the 5D ego will want the Transcendence to point to a certain direction, as well as feeling terrified by realising that its choices were often anti-ethical – since the criteria of the fifth dimension is *Creation*, which transcends ethics. But there is no return – the consciousness only advances. The ego will doubt the very structure of the fifth dimension: its vision of *Pneumatic Images* in the *Macroimage*, its immediate perception of the *Pneumatic* reality with its various elements, its accesses to the *Multi-Dimensionality* and to the *All-the-Times*, sometimes too fantastic. The very *Sense* will seem "merely personal", egoic and inferior, when he feels himself as a farce. The 5D ego feels as though it is hallucinating, schizophrenic, that everything its experiences is a psychotic outbreak. Maybe, the *Enigma* is the worse aspect of the *Imponderable*, as the *Demoniac* uprising makes all and every reality of the **Being** (*Spirit*, Total *Truth*) seem as **no-being** at the same time (*Demon*, false = partial reality). At no other time the *Spirit* manifests its dimension of **danger** so directly – in an experience of the *Enigma*, the risk of the consciousness being imprisoned by a *Demoniac* dimension is maximum.

Precisely in the middle of an *Enigma*, the fifth-dimensional ego needs to gather all its *Strength* to realise the very lesson of the Paradigm of Sense: to maintain itself standing, **alone**, **only** trusting its *Personal Sense*, and consolidate its *Creation*.

It is a tragic moment, because the *Spirit* is at the same time *Truth* and *Abyss*, and the *Enigma* is the fact that both dimensions grow vertiginously, as progressive **multi-paradoxes**. **The *Enigma* has no solution**. It is useless to look for one, and also counter-productive, because any solution, the prevailing of any principle over another, even if the *Spirit* prevails over the *Demon*, would be a solution in some way moralist and hopeful. The perception of the *Imponderable* has shown that the *Spirit* includes the *Demon*, therefore the prevailing of the former over the latter would, ultimately, be the prevailing of the *Spirit* (*Truth*) over the *Spirit* (*Demon*), in other words, ridiculous. There is no need to create a theological subterfuge.

In the middle of the infinite complexity of the *Enigma*, where the *Truth* is Whole to the point of including all of its own "contraries" – as simultaneously **the same thing** and its **contraries**, like the point of a circumference diametrically opposed to another is simultaneously a

point of the same circumference and an **opposite point** – the *Human* and its *Sense* become the point of overtaking, through an *Action Without Guaranteee*. **In this tragic moment**, of infinite risk, the fifth-dimensional ego discovers that it is, now, a deity on earth, an incarnated deity, a **Son of God**, extremely *Human*, walking in the **Paradise of Eden that is Earth**, for the shock of those who believe that the Son of God is the only begotten, to the shock of those who believe in the separation between *Spirit* and *Body*, to the shock of those who believe that *Body* and Earth are inferior and would not be a dignified enough place for a *Spirit* to manifest, to the shock of those who believe that the human being is inferior and would never have the *Spirit* inside, or even better, **be** the *Spirit* – to the shock of those who are nihilist. If the *Enigma* puts us in front of our own Abyss, it also puts us in the heights of the *Spirit*, and if on one hand we have to face the terrifying reality of our infinite *Perversions*, on the other hand we have to face the equally terrifying reality that we are all incarnated deities. The *Enigma* is tragic because of its infinite intensity, but also for making it so clear that there is no one "out there", "outside" ourselves, to be made responsible, let alone to blame. There is nothing besides ourselves, only ourselves (the Transcendence is 'interior')

> [...] Thus men forgot that all deities reside in the human breast.[616]

The image of an incarnated Son of God, extremely controversial and considered the maximum crime, is directly manifested in Christ, extensively dealt with in this work, and in the image of Διόνυσος (Dionysus), whose mythology reveals the climax of the Paradigm of Sense,

> [...] from the love of Zeus and Persephone, the first Dionysus was born, most commonly known as Zagreus. **Favourite of the father of gods and mankind, he was destined to succeed him in governing the world**, but destiny decided the contrary. To protect the son from the jealousy of hiswife Hera, Zeus trusted him to the care of Apolo and the Curetes, who hid him in the Parnassus forest. Hera still found the whereabout of young Zeus and **asked the Titans to kidnap and kill him**. With their *faces covered in plaster* to avoid being recognised, **the Titans attracted the little Zagreus** with *mythical toys*: little bones, spinning tops, whirligig, "*crepundia*" and mirror. In possession of Zeus' son, Hera's envoys *tore him into pieces: cooked his flesh in a caldron* and ate it. Zeus fulminated them and from their ashes, mankind was born [...]

> [...] indeed, Zagreus came back to life. Athena, others say Demeter, saved his heart which was still beating. Swallowing him, the Theban princess Semele became pregnant of the second Dionysus. The myth has variants, especially the one according to which it was Zeus who swallowed the son's heart, before impregnating Semele. [...]
>
> [...]
>
> [...] Semele became pregnant of the second Dionysius. Hera, however, was watchful. When she learned of the intimate relationship between her husband and Semele, decided to eliminate her. Transforming into the maid of the Theban princess, advised her to ask the lover to present himself in all his splendour. The god warned Semele that such a request was fatal, since a mortal, revested by matter, does not have the structure to support the epiphany of an immortal god. However, as he had sworned by waters of the Styx to never deny her wishes, Zeus presented himself with his lightenings and thunders. Semele's palace caught fire and she died, charred. The unborn child, the future Dionysius, was saved by a dramatic gesture of the father of gods and mankind: Zeus quickly took from his lover's womb the unfinished fruit of their love and placed it in his thigh, until the gestation was complete. [...] Fearing a new plan from Hera, Zeus transformed the son in a ***goat*** and asked Hermes to take him to the Nisa mount, where **he was trusted to the care of the Nymphs and the Satyrs**, who inhabited a deep cave.
>
> Even much later, Dionysus was known as *Pyrigenés*, *Pyrísporos*, which means "born or conceived in fire", in that case from the lightening[617] [author's own highlights]

The myth shows a serious confrontation between the Τίτανες (Titans) and Dionysus, surrounding his birth. The mythology of the Titans, as we said, is very useful to the understanding of the Paradigm of Sense, because they are the Gods who inhabit the Inferior Worlds, specifically the Tartar, the infernal level of the great criminals, eternal. That way, the Titans have several characteristics which are compatible with the dimension of the *Spirit* that we have been calling *Demon*, or *Dynamic Force*, particularly its **resistance to the *Spirit***. It is not just about that, obviously, but also the break of unity, the union between Ὀυρανός (Ouranós) and Γαῖα (Gaia), and the lack of **cosmic** beauty, that is, of connection with the Cosmos.

Supporting, in face of the Titans, the unbreakable symmetry of the *Imponderable*, we find that Dionysus, **favourite of Ζεύς (Zeus) and mankind**, shows more easily some of the characteristics of the most positive dimension of the Paradigm of Sense. Dionysus is a clearly fifth-dimensional *Image*, as after the sacrifice typical of the fourth dimension, it lives its **Resurrection in the Body** (5D), becoming **Spirit** in the *Body*, incarnated *Spirit*, deity and **also** human being, being son of the gods Zeus and Περσεφόνεια (Persephone) and **also** son of the god Zeus and the **human** Semele.

Dionysus is the God of the *Imponderable*, the Whole *Truth*, "god of the [continuous] *metamórphosis* [transformation], internally and externally: 'Dionysus scares because of the multiplicity and novelty of his transformations. He is always in movement; penetrates all places, all lands, all communities, all religions, ready to be associated to various deities, even the antagonic ones".[618] But being "only" the God of the *Imponderable*, of the Whole *Imponderable* and the continuous Transformation, i.e., of the Transcendence, in the "spiritual" level, abstract, does **not** make Dionysus an *Image* of the fifth dimension. The undisputed proof that Dionysus is an *Image* of the Paradigm of Sense is the fact that it experiences the *Imponderable*, the Whole *Imponderable*, the Transcendence, **in the *Body***.

> Dionysus devouts, after the vertiginous dance mentioned, colapsed semi-awake. In that state, they believed to have been off from themselves through the process of *ékstasis*, ecstasy. Being off from themselves implied *a dive of Dionysus into his adorer* through *enthousiasmós*, "enthusiasm". The *man*, mere mortal, *ánthropos*, in *ecstasy and enthusiasm*, in communion with immortality, became an *anér*, that is, a *hero*, a male who overcame *métron*, the measure of each one. Having overcome its mortal measure, **the *anér*, the hero, transforms into *hypocrités*, the one who responds in ecstasy and enthusiasm, namely, the actor.**
>
> This overcoming of *métron*, by *hypocrités*, takes the form of *hýbris*, na overblow, a "démesure", a *violence*, commited to oneself and the immortal gods, which unleashes *némesis*, the punishment for the practiced injustice, the divine *jealousy* [...]
>
> [...] through this state of semi-unconsciousness, those adept of Dionysus believed to be off from themselves through the process of *ékstasis*, the ecstasy. This being off from themselves meant overcoming the human condition, an overcoming of the *métron*, **the discovery of a total liberation, the conquering of a freedom and a spontaneity that the other human beings could not experience. Evidently, this overcoming of the human condition and this freedom, acquired through the *ékstasis*, constituted, *ipso facto*, a liberation from prohibition, taboos, regulations and conventions of an ethical, political and social order [...]**

> The *ékstasis*, however, was just the first part of the integration with the god: the *being off from themselves* implied a dive into Dionysus and of the latter into his adorer through *enthousiasmós, entheós*, that is, "animated from a divine transport", *en* being "inside, in the core", and *theós*, "god", that is, **enthusiasm means having a god within oneself, to identify with it, co-participating of its divinity**. And if of the Maenads or Bacchantes, and both terms mean the same, *the possessed*, that is, **in *ecstasy* and *enthusiasm*, theirs, as of the adorers of Dionysus, the mania possessed, "the sacred madness, the divine possession", and the *órguia*, "possession of the divine in the celebration of the mysteries, orgy, uncontrollable agitation" was realized the communion with the god.**

> [...]

> It is important, therefore, to not mistake this explosion of the Dionysian or human Maenads (as happens in the gigantic euripidean tragedy The Bacchantes) with "psychopathic fits", because the *manía*, sacred madness and the orgy, uncontrollable agitation, animic inflation, undoubtedly possessed the value of a religious experience.[619] [author's own highlights]

The Ἔκστασις (ecstasy), being out of oneself, is the Dionysian *Image* for the complete transposition not only of the third-dimensional ego entirely limited to itself, but also of the fourth-dimensional ego still in the process of union with the Soul, to a fifth-dimensional ego, a *Collective Ego*, who, being *Spiritual* (= *Corporeal*), has **all** the characteristics and is itself and other people. Dionysus, therefore, is **not** the *Image* of a "state of semi-consciousness", as BRANDÃO DE SOUZA wants[620]; Dionysus is the *Pneumatic Image* of the coincidence between consciousness and Unconsciousness, which has enough **capacity (space)** to have its own characteristics (personality) **and also all the others**, *conditio sine qua non* to make **space** to a God the size of Dionysus, a God large to the point of "[penetrating] all places, all lands, all communities, all religions".

The *Collective Ego* is large enough to be himself, **and to also leave itself**, making space for Dionysus to "enter" the ἐνθουσιασμός (enthusiasm). God of Dithyramb, God of Tragedy, God of Theatre, Dionysus is pure *Spirit* (= *Body*), pure Divine *Inspiration, Force*. **Let us not be fooled**. The ecstasy and enthusiasm necessarily mean "a liberation from prohibition, taboos, regulations and conventions of an ethical, political and social order". It is impossible to manifest a God as great as Dionysus and respect ethics at the same time. For that reason, the criterion of the fifth dimension is **not** ethics, but a criterion much more adequate to the God of Tragedy:

creation. Without euphemisms, fifth-dimensional actions are sometimes anti-ethical and very badly regarded socially; but they are *Creative*.

Resembling directly the archetype of Lilith, whose self-exile has ended, Dionysus leads the fifth-dimensional ego to experience a "total liberation, the conquering of a freedom and a spontaneity that the other human beings could not experience". With a "god within onself", the 5D ego "overcomes its mortal measure", the μέτρον (*métron*), and becomes a **hero**. With the ὕβρις (*hýbris*) integrated, "transforms into *hypocrités*, the one who responds in ecstasy and enthusiasm, namely, the **actor**". Filled with Dionysus, **the actor acts**; and its action is *Action Without Guarantee*. Filled with Dionysus, **the actor acts in *hýbris***; and its action is *Interference*.

Let us not be fooled. The action of the *Spirit* is *Imponderable*, Total *Truth* and Transcendent; in the *Body*, it can only be equally *Imponderable*, Total *Truth* and Transcendent. The ecstasy and the enthusiasm **in the *Body*, in action**, are total liberation and will exceed all measures. If Dionysus leads to the overcoming of *métron*, the measure imposed **by the Gods and Goddesses themselves**, what will he do with morals and ethics, with the egoic and social limits? Why does he care about common sense, good customs, good manners, "good people", religious dogmas and all other limitations created for the "good of society"? These structures are indeed necessary for the previous dimensions, but for those Freed fifth-dimensional beings this is totally irrelevant. The ecstasy and the enthusiasm **in the *Body*, in action** in the fifth dimension, **will be *manía* and will be orgy**. If an action is fifth-dimensional, it will invariably and deeply bother those who want to maintain any kind of *status quo*, because in that action the *Imponderable* is in the *Body*, therefore a **Son of God** is acting, and the action will seem too divine to be human or too *Demoniac* to be human; people are crucified for considering themselves Sons of God.

Being the Son of God and having the *Holy Spirit* in the *Body* are maximum crimes because, as it was in the times of Judaic orthodoxy, **even today the type of action performed by a Son of God is considered a social and a theological scandal**. A Son of God does **not** 'forgive the prostitutes' for being who they are, while he remains separate from them, with an "evolved" stance of disgust and distance; if he is indeed a Son of God, he is as human as they are and there is no separation: a **Son of God is a male whore that has sex with female whores**. It also has sex with male whores, with men, women, as a couple, as a threesome, a foursome, with how ever many men and women it wants to, according to its preferences. A Son of God does **not** 'forgive those who surrender to the pleasures of the flesh', while remaining distant from such pleasures and the people who commit them. This type of "forgiveness" is a refined and disgusting kind of **hypocrisy**, of **false love**. It is exactly the type of pharisaic attitude that Christ **cursed** as "brood of vipers and whitewashed tombs"[621]. Our current society IS the "Judaic orthodoxy". In the western democracies, it is forbidden to stone people, but stones continue to be thrown; they are just not material stones.

With the *Spirit* in the *Body*, in ecstasy and enthusiasm, the Son of God overcomes all limitations and experiences total liberation – there is no space for any kind of asceticism (except, as with everything else, temporarily as the manifestation of an *Image* of asceticism that might exist in the *Imponderable*). In *Evolution*, a Son of God experiences the spiritual ecstasy in its maximum intensity, and the carnal ecstasy in its maximum intensity **at the same time because they are the same thing**. The **extraordinarily *Creative*** presence of the God Dionysus in the *Body* overcomes any positivity and any negativity and this is what we see exploding into a **frenzy** in those who surrender to Dionysus in its procession. This same creative presence, beyond all positivity and all negativity, exists nowadays, for example, as **Axé**, an *Intense Happiness* that is manifested as a deep simultaneous spiritual and corporeal ecstasy, as known to the people of Bahia, in Brazil. The epitome of Axé is the **carnival**, the "party of the flesh", when the people from Bahia, also known as *baianos*, are strongly spiritualized and *Creative*, expressing all this in a corporeal party, which goes on for several days, with several hours of dancing, drugs and sex, wearing costumes that make fun of all social conventions. This *Intense Happiness* evidences the presence of the *Spirit* among the *baianos*, as this feeling is particularly hard (if not impossible) to pretend: "Joy is the litmus test."[622] Dionysus and its procession – as it happens with the *Axé*[623,624] and its carnival – with all its positivity **AND** its negativity[625], but always with **intensity** – get very close to the type of experience that the fifth-dimensional ego experiences daily.

What is the difference between **the ecstasy and the enthusiasm, the frenzy**, of Dionysus and Christ? The answer is stentorian: **none**.

It is true that, when the Dionysian cult is compared to Christianity, in the way we know it currently, the difference is great. But Christ is one thing, and another very different thing is Christianity. Friedrich NIETZSCHE, in his monumental works *The Anti-Christ*[626] *On the Genealogy of morality*[627], widely demonstrated how Christianity was created based on the sacerdotal world view, particularly that of Paul of Tarsus, a view which is totally different from that found in the Gospels: "The very word "Christianity" is a misunderstanding—at bottom there was only one Christian, and he died on the cross."[628]

[...] one might actually call Jesus a "free spirit" [...] The idea of "life" as an experience, as he alone conceives it, stands opposed to his mind to every sort of word, formula, law, belief and dogma."

[...]

In the whole psychology of the "Gospels" the concepts of guilt and punishment are lacking, and so is that of reward. "Sin", which means anything that puts a distance between God and man, is abolished – this is precisely the "glad tidings". Eternal bliss is not merely promised, nor is it bound up with conditions: it is conceived as the only reality – what remains consists merely of signs useful in speaking of it.

The results of such a point of view project themselves into a new way of life, the special evangelical way of life. It is not a "belief" that marks off the Christian; he is distinguished by a different mode of action; he acts differently. [...]

The life of the Saviour was simply a carrying out of this way of life – and so was his death... He no longer needed any formula or ritual in his relations with God – not even prayer. He had rejected the whole of the Jewish doctrine of repentance and atonement; he knew that it was only by a way of life that one could feel one's self "divine," "blessed," "evangelical", a "child of God". Not by "repentance", not by "prayer and forgiveness" is the way to God: only the Gospel way leads to God – it is itself "God!" – What the Gospels abolished was the Judaism in the concepts of "sin", "forgiveness of sin", "faith", "salvation through faith" – the whole ecclesiastical dogma of the Jews was denied by the "glad tidings."

The deep instinct which prompts the Christian how to live so that he will feel that he is "in heaven" and is "immortal," despite many reasons for feeling that he is not "in heaven": this is the only psychological reality in "salvation." – A new way of life, not a new faith...[629]

There is an insurmountable abyss between Christianity and Christ. According to NIETZSCHE, the main notions of Christianity – sin, blame, punishment, reward, remission of sins, faith, salvation through faith, penitence, prayer for forgiveness, dogma – are exactly the elements that what the Gospels *abolished*, are exactly the things Christ **destroyed with his life**. Christianity depends on the distance between God and mankind, which justifies its very existence as a necessary religion to transpose this distance – and with that, **two** realities are created, one where God is, and

another reality, the reality of the world where we live, perceived as vile. Christ, on the other hand, acknowledges only [one] reality in this world, with no distance between the reality of this world and another reality, where God would be, simply because **this other reality does not exist, it is a complete fantasy**. In Christ's eyes, the reality of this world, **the world we live in**, is one of **beatitude**. In our world, we can feel "in heaven", we can feel "eternal". **There is no need for other realities. Our world is a reality that allows us to be perfectly 'blessed'. Above all, our world is the place where we can be "divine".** Due to living entirely in the **only** reality of **this world**, Christ dedicates to the experience of life, to practice. That way, **Christ shows that to be "divine" is something that can be practical**. Calling him the **joyful messenger**, NIETZSCHE shows how Christ lived according to his world view and was a "free spirit".

It is perfectly understandable that Christianity is a valid psychological reality, moreover, archetypically valid – JUNG analyses it brilliantly in *Psychology and religion: West and East*[630]. No movement that lasts two thousand years and has influenced a whole hemisphere, perhaps the whole world, can be considered an entire fantasy. Christianity was, in fact, the climax of the archetype of the Celestial God and of its separation from the archetype of Lilith, which caused her self-exile. However, besides the fact that Christianity is showing evident signs of exhaustion, its validity as an expression of an archetypal reality does not mean that its dogma is identical to the good news of Christ. On the contrary, what NIETZSCHE shows with a wealth of details is that **Christianity is the extreme opposite of what Christ lived.**

Removing Christianity, we see Christ as a free spirit. Independently of any organized religion, Christ lives the reality of a blessed, divine and eternal being. This world is the only reality and his characteristic is beatitude. Christ is **joyful**. Above all, Christ professes that **we can all live the same reality as his**. For this reason, Christ says: "You are gods."[631] Therefore, removing Christianity, Christ appears as a *Pneumatic image* which is extremely similar to Dionysus.

We could trace a long parallel between Christ and Dionysus, but this is beyond the scope of this book. For now, let us dedicate to the point that interests us centrally: the **Cup**.

> Another important line of symbolic connections links the blood of Christ with the grape and wine of Dionysus. The original reference is in the Gospel of John where Christ says of himself: "I am the true vine, and my father is the vinedresser. Every branch of mine that bears no fruit, he takes away, and every branch that does bear fruit he prunes,

that it may bear more fruit ... I am the vine, you are the branches." (John 15: 1-5 RSV). From this it is only a short step to the identification of Christ with the grape which is crushed to make wine. [...]

The miracle at Cana which transformed water into wine (John 2: 1) established Christ as a wine-maker, and wine with its indwelling spirit is analogous to the "living water" which Christ offered the woman of Samaria. (John 4: 10). Living water or elixir vitae is a term used much later by the alchemists. The chalice of Antioch in the Cloisters of the Metropolitan Museum, dating back probably to the fourth century A.D., shows Christ surrounded by clusters of grapes. As Jung says: "The wine miracle at Cana was the same as the miracle in the temple of Dionysus, and it is profoundly significant that, on the Damascus chalice, Christ is enthroned among vine tendrils like Dionysus himself."[632]

The Grail as an *Image* of Dionysus and Christ, places the latter immediately in the Dionysian sphere of **ecstasy** (being outside of oneself), and particularly, of **enthusiasm** (god inside). Now, it is possible to see the *manía* in the Christ expelling the sellers from the Temple with a whip and the **orgy** in his relationship with Mary Magdalene, the whore. Now, Christ is truly divine and human at the same time.

Regarding Christ, the Cup is the *Grail* (whose importance to us is huge, since the Paradigm of Sense observes *Pneumatic Images* that occur especially from Crucifixion onwards, connected to Christ and the *Holy Spirit*). From data found in the Gospel and the Arthurian tales of Grail, we know that the story of the Grail starts at the Last Meal. Christ prepares to fulfil his Destiny of Supreme Sacrifice in the Cross, in Golgotha, ending the spiritualization of humanity and enabling the descent of the *Holy Spirit* in the *Body*. With the Grail, Christ offers his blood to be drank, his life, to the Twelve Disciples, simultaneously human beings and the various aspects of Wholeness. It was probably in the Grail where Christ dunk the piece of bread that he gave to Judas, from where the *Demon* entered, through the mouth. In Crucifixion, the Grail is used by Joseph of Arimathea to collect the blood and the water that dripped from Christ's wound, caused by the *coup de grâce* by Longinus. Since then, the Grail has disappeared.... It became the objective of the spiritual journey from Knights of the Round Table.

Emma JUNG and Marie-Louise von FRANZ show the Grail as the Symbol of an insoluble problem.

> [...] But the wihdrawal of the Grail symbol into heaven [at the end of the legend] [...] indicates that the integration of this symbol and all that it signifies could not be achieved in the consiousness of medieval man. This is related no doubt to the fact that Chrétien's story was unable to reach an unequivocal ending, and the various continuators propounded different possibilities because there was uncertainty as to which conclusion was actually the correct one. The story of Perceval anticipates psychic problems reaching so far into the future that it could not be wholly comprehended by the medieval attitude. First of all *the psychic assimilation of the Christian symbol had to proceed further.* [...][633]

According to the authors, the ascent of the Grail to heaven means that this Symbol is returning to the unconscious, because the conscience is still not ready to deal with it. It is not ready because "the psychic assimilation of the Christian symbol had to proceed further". As it is written, it seems like the authors believe that the Grail is a Symbol that comes after the Christian Symbol. They are correct. The very sequence of facts corroborates that: the Grail is **formed** in the Crucifixion and its story occurs **after** Crucifixion; therefore, this *Image* points to something that occurs **after** the level of psychological development reached in Crucifixion. Personally, I believe that the spiritual *Image* projected by the life of Christ is strong enough to reach its psychological aims, and it is not necessary that the Grail repeats the whole Christian Symbol. Therefore, the Grail needs to point to a more advanced spiritual reality than Crucifixion; and, as the "Christian symbol" was still being "assimilated", it was impossible to take another step so soon.

> [...] While lingering at thecourt, Perceval asks at the evening meal about the meaning of the empty place and begs permission to seat himself there, threatening departure should this be denied him. The King finally gives in to his importunities; but no sooner has Perceval settled himself than the stone seat splits with such a terrifying din that everyone present imagines the world is coming to an end. A great darkness falls and a voice reproves Arthur for having violated Merlin's commandment. "This Perceval", the voice says, "has undertaken the most harzadous enterprise that any man has yet ventured. From it the most arduous tasks will ensue, both for him and for all those at the Round Table." [...] The voice further informs them – as Merlin too had prophesied – that one of Arthur's knights is destined to find the Grail. [...]

[...] Merlin has already advised Arthur concerning the establishment of the Round Table; he has also mentioned the motif of Judas and has said that the empty seat, the *siége perilleux,* will be occupied for the first time by a knight who has found the Grail. By seating himself on it before accomplishing this deed, Perceval has disobeyed Merlin's command, as it were, and it is for this reason that the stone is sundered.

As is clear from the context, the empty place at the table, **the dangerous seat reminiscent of Judas, symbolizes na unsolved problem, as unanswered question within the spiritual world of Christian chivalry. This unresolved question has to do with the problem of evil and the betrayal of Christ**. When Perceval sits in this seat he us unwittingly putting himself in the place of Judas, and this was obviously not intended. Even though he has to solve a problem related to the integration of evil, he was not meant to fall into its power unconsciously. Therefore, the stone seat splits under him. i.e. this occurrence is a miraculous portent which advises him of the fact that a split threatens the domain of the Christian knights of the Round Table, a spli which can only be reconciled by the redemption of the Grail region.[634] [author's own highlights]

The *Image* of the Grail is strongly projected here: the very formative structure of the Grail, the table of the Last Meal, reaches a more advanced structure and now appears as the Round Table. King Arthur takes Christ's place, and the knights take the place of the disciples. The *Image*, however, changes in what regards Judas, of all people. In the Last Meal, Judas is present. But, in the Round Table, the "dangerous seat", although equivalent to Judas' seat, is different because it is vague, and can only be occupied by the one who finds the Grail. That way, the only person who can occupy this seat is the one who can do so while conscious of what it represents. Perceval tries to own it without such consciousness, and in doing so, causes a series of misfortunes.

Which is, however, the **danger** associated to this seat? We **cannot** attribute the problem of the Shadow or the problem of the evil to this seat, because this problem **has already been resolved by Christ** and by the Christian Symbol: the Shadow (4D) and the evil (4D) have already been integrated, therefore, to affirm that the Grail is doing the same thing would make it redundant.

On the other hand, we know that this is **Judas' seat**. Judas, at the Last Meal, was **not** dealing with the problem of evil (4D), the Shadow having already been included by Christ in Crucifixion – **he was dealing with the *Demon* (5D), the Shadow (5D) excluded by Christ**. Judas was opening the path of the **Antichrist**. Therefore, the danger associated to this seat is **not** the evil, but the *Demon*. **This** question was not answered "within the spiritual world of Christian chivalry" because the process of "assimilation of the Christian symbol" was still taking place, and because this answer only exists in a fifth-dimensional structure and the structure available at that time was still fourth-dimensional. It would take a Judas, with enough dimensions, to answer a question of this magnitude.

[...] On this occasion Arthur is seated at the Round Table with his companions when a loud crash frightens the exceedingly. The store which had split under Perceval is now joined together again. The assembled company does not know what this can mean, until Merlin appears and explains. "Know, Arthur, that in thy time the most sublime prophecy that was ever made has been fulfilled; for the Fisher King is healed, the spell under which Britain has languished is broken, and Perceval is become Lord of the Grail. From now on he will renounce chivalry and will surrender himself entirely to the grace of his Creator." When the King and his knights heard this they began to weep with one voice, and to pray God that He would bring it to a favourable conclusion.

The knights are distressed that the wonders and adventures have now come to an end. They feel superfluous; they consider that there is no point remaining at Arthur's court; they would sooner go overseas to seek fresh fame. [...] Arthurs nephew Mordred is named regent during the Kings absence. On the march to Rome, news arrives that Mordred has seized power, as well as the Queen, for himself. This naturally occasions great consternation. The knights are ordered back to the fatherland, to punish the traitor Mordred, who has allied himself with the Saxons and is preparing a bloody reception for the returning forces. In long and terrible battles, every knight of the Round Table meets his death. Finally Mordred also falls. Arthur mortally wounded is brought to Avalon where he is said to have been healed by his sister Morgana, who would appear to be one of the fairies of that island. [...]

It is surprising that Perceval's discovery and possession of the Grail should have such a disastrous result as the abolition of the Round Table. It is a feature peculiar to this form of the story that **the Round Table is thought to be the third of the three tables which, taken together, represent the Trinity**. The discoverer of the Grail, in this case Perceval, is the tierz hom the third guardian of the Grail and therefore representative of the Holy Spirit, whose era [...] was awaited in the thirteenth century and in our story was expected to dawn with the finding of the Grail. How then does it make sense that the first result of this discovery is that this "third table", the Round Table, is abolished. [...]

The fame and the ideal quality os the Round Table undoubtedly sprang from the union of the secular aspect with the spiritual [...]

At that time, Merlin had prophesied that the empty place at this table would at some future time be occupied by that best and most virtuous knight who should succeed in finding the Grail. Our author appears to have quite lost sight of this idea, for he does not return to it or explain why the prophecy was not fulfilled. Instead of occupying *siège périlleux*, Perceval remains in the Grail castle, renouncing chivalry in order to submit himself entirely to the grace of God [...]. He thus becomes a holy man; [...]

This solution would be an appropriate one for that time, although not in conformity with the tendencies outlined in the beginnings of the story which raised expectation that Perceval would occupy the seat and take the role of earthly representative of the Holy Spirit. Because he does not do this, the Round Table is to a certain extent deprived of the Spirit. No wonder, therefore, that the knights weep when they hear this; **the inevitable result is the fatal drifting apart of the opposites of spirit and world**, which became so evident just precisely in the Middle Ages. Because Perceval turns entirely to the spiritual, the Round Table becomes altogether worldly. **The quest of the Grail, by which the world, i.e. chivalry, and the spirit, i.e the life vowed to God, were to have been brought together**, now loses its objective and in its place there appears a destructive striving after purely temporal power. The realm which Arthur wished to establish was neither that of the Grail nor of the Holy Spirit, but a material world dominion; [...]

Perceval does not occupy this seat [the *siège perilleux*, the dangerous seat], because as a holy man far from the world, he is quite unable to do so. He could only have occupied it if in some way the had consciously taken upon himself the role of Judas, whose place it is, or if he had allied himself with the latter. As the opposite of Christ, the absolute Good, Judas incarnates the principle of Evil. It is not, however, a question of identifying with one or two mutually exclusive principles; what has to be redeemed is the hidden man, the Anthropos. In this Perceval does not succeed because, by choosing holiness instead of humanity, evil as the opposite of good, is constellated anew. This is promptly manifested in the traitor Mordred again a kind of Judas who brings about the downfall of Arthur and his world - and his own ruin at the same time [...]

> [...] The awaited Third Kingdom, that of the Holy Spirit, likewise remains an unfulfilled ideal.[635] [author's own highlights]

The Round Table is annihilated. "[...] every knight of the Round Table meets his death". Arthur is "mortally wounded". Even the traitor Mordret goes down. This is the type of grim destiny that occurs in the face of an unrestrained *Demoniac* uprising. Be aware: the *Demon* is **really dangerous**. The seat is dangerous. There is either a Judas, capable of consciously betraying, capable of holding the *Demon* (the beast) by the mouth, or there is an unconscious traitor, a Mordret, that gives way to the *Demon*, without *Education*, opening the way to a generalized disgrace. Being a **legitimate** Antichrist is not for just anyone: only with five dimensions it is possible to be that **without** disrespecting the Spiritual Law. To synthetize Christ and the Antichrist in one being is the fifth-dimensional task of the *Enigma*.

> [...] [There is an] incompatibility of the Christian spirit with that of alchemy, since in Christ, God became man by his own will, whereas the philosopher's stone is evolved into a new light-bringer through human intention and skill. "In the former case", says Jung, "the miracle of man's salvation is accomplished by God; in the latter, the salvation or transfiguration of the universe is brought about by the mind of man - *'Deo Concedente*; as the authors never fail to add. *In the one case man confesses 'I under God' in the other he asserts 'God under me'*. Man takes the place of creator. Medieval alchemy prepared the way for the greatest invention in the divine world order that man has ever attempted: *alchemy was the dawn of the scientific age*, when the daemon of the scientific spirit compelled the forces of nature to serve man to an extent that had never been known before." **It is the demonism of this spirit which destined Merlin for the role of Antichrist.** *He did not take on this role*, however, because he withdrew from the world and its power politics and resolved to serve only God, in his "Calidon." [...][636][author's own highlights]

That is why the Round Table was the "third table", the table of the *Holy Spirit*, **not** a repetition of the Last Meal, the "second table", Christ's table. The "discoverer of the Grail" should be the "representative of the *Holy Spirit*", not Christ's representative. These are **different** realities, and to say that the *Grail* is a Symbol of the Soul, of the 4D Self, is to not realise that, is to make the same mistake made by Perceval. **The *Grail* is a *Pneumatic Image* of the *Spirit***, of the 5D Self, and only a representative of the *Holy Spirit* has enough dimensions and power to educate the *Demon* and find the *Grail*, seating, **afterwards**, in the "dangerous seat" of Judas.

Pneumatic Image of the *Spirit*, the *Grail* and the Round Table do **not** point towards elevation, do **not** point towards a fourth-dimensional prevalence of the Symbol over the *Instinct*, do **not** point towards an abstract spirituality, removed from the world. The *Spirit* tends to the *Ununs Mundus*, a perfect union between the *Spirit* and the *Body* – more than that, the *Spirit* is *Body*. For that reason, when the *Grail* is found by someone who stops being a knight – stops mastering the **animal**, the *Instinct* – in order to become a **saint**, a fourth-dimensional psychological structure, both the *Grail* and Perceval rise to heaven. The *Grail* is found by someone who does not have the right structure to be its Guardian, and **is lost again...**

To be the Guardian of the *Grail*, one must be a **knight**, master their own *Instincts*, master the *Demon*, so that it remains *Educated*. A knight does **not** need to be removed from the world in order to be spiritual. A knight is able to live in the world. They **like** to live in the world. They have **no** issue with the "profane", because in the Paradigm of Sense, there is **nothing** that can be described as profane. The *Pneumatic reality* is **entirely spiritual**. Even the *Demon*, who, without *Education*, expresses itself in a profane way, is the *Spirit* that resists creation and can be *Educated*; and it is. Saints have **no** *Force* to seat in the "dangerous seat"; Knights do because they find the *Grail* when they reach the *Unus Mundus*. Knights – fifth-dimensional egos – are **extremely spiritual** when they dedicate themselves to complex actions of *Multi-Dimensional Manifestations* in *All-the-Times*, when they dedicate themselves to professional actions in corporate environments and when they dedicate themselves to have sex in a whorehouse. The *Truth* is that "Nothing is true, everything is permitted"[637]. Just as the *Pneumatic reality*, a fifth-dimensional ego is invariably spiritual, therefore *Corporeal*.

More than being just a *Pneumatic Image* of the *Unus Mundus* – *Spirit* is *Body* – the *Grail* is an image of **pleasure**. One of the etymologies of "grail" shown by Emma JUNG and Marie-Louise von Franz deals directly with pleasure as the central meaning of *Grail.*

> Another interpretation, cited by Helinandus, but more as a popular meaning, derives *graal* or *greal* from *gratus* (pleasing, acceptable) and *gratia* (pleasantness, satisfaction, goodwill grace, reward), the French *agréable* (agreeable) from *gré* (wish).[638]

With that, we are ready to return to the connection between Dionysus and Christ.

Dionysus Chalice and the *Grail* are filled with wine – in fact, with any psychoactive substance. As such, they will cause all kinds of trances and experiences, *Pneumatic Images* of Wholeness that they are. However, whatever the type, the experience will always have an **extreme** character, a strong **intensity**, since it is the experience of ecstasy and enthusiasm. The experience varies from the extremely luminous of the spiritual ecstasy until the extremely dark of butchery and cannibalism.

In this scenario, the *Grail* appears as the *Pneumatic Image* of the climax of the Paradigm of Sense: a **Dionysian experience**. Its circular form and is opening upwards evidence that it receives the Totality of the *Spirit*. But the *Grail*, as *Image* of the *Spirit*, is not a vase that contains, but **a vase that overflows** – Christ offers his blood to drink, Dionysus offers his wine. Extremely luminous, the *Grail* is the *Spirit* of *Truth*; extremely dark, the *Grail* is the *Demon*. Around it, all the legitimate spiritual potencies and all the *Demons* in Fall sit equally, all attracted by the growing wholeness of the *Spirit*. Around it, all seats are occupied, including the "dangerous seat".

In the climax of the Paradigm of Sense, the fifth-dimensional ego **experiences** the *Grail*.

The *Grail* is the image of Totality of the Paradigm of Sense – a *Pneumatic Image* of the *Spirit* fully realised in the *Body* – involving all of its diverse aspects. This energy is at the same time *Force* and *Education* of the *Dynamic Force*; it is at the same time *Plenitude, Relationship, Humanity* and *Evolution*. In the middle of all this energy the fifth-dimensional ego is the *Imponderable* that converges to itself. It is the 5D ego who will **freely** choose which *Image* to *Draw*, who will **freely** choose the Direction that the *Spirit* will take, tying up on Earth what will be tied up in Heaven, in complete harmony with the *Spirit* – Lilith has been integrated. It is the 5D ego who will **freely** choose because it owns the *Action Without Guarantee*. From this choice, it can *Manifest* its *Great Creation, Multi-Dimensionality*, in *All-the-Times*.

The **experience** of wholeness of the *Grail* is primarily a **sensation** of **fulfilment** that **grows** in the Being. The starting point of this experience is the *Enigma*. Extremely luminous, the 5D ego sees in the *Spirit* of *Truth* a myriad of *Pneumatic Images*. Extremely dark, it sees in the *Demon* temptations, accusations and lies, relativizing the *Unus Mundus*. **All** energies are equidistant from the *Grail*, which is in the centre, with no difference in value between the most elevated and divine, and the most abysmal and demoniac; they are all aspects of the *Spirit* and point to practical aspects of daily "mundane" life in the *Pneumatic reality*. The exuberance and the horror are part of the *Grail*, and, in its face, are in total harmony. Around the *Grail*, the *Plenitude* arises from one energy potentializing another **infinitely**, reaching the **multi-paradoxical Pneumatic Reality** of the climax of the Paradigm of Sense, the *Unus Mundus*.

The *Grail*, however, includes its own, specific reality. It goes beyond the "simple" sum of all elements of the fifth-dimensional Totality, even though the Totality is infinite. The *Grail* was built at the peak of Golgotha, by the blood that **overflows**. The *Grail* overflows downwards, it is *Spirit* realised **in the *Body*** – the *Grail Draws*. In face of the *Grail*, the 5D ego experiences a discharge of energy, a discharge of *Spirit* that is felt as an **Instinctual satisfaction**. In face of the *Grail*, the *Spirit* is **ecstasy and enthusiasm**. The 5D ego experiences an **intense lust for life in its *Body* of Resurrection**.

Therefore, in the presence of the *Grail*, one experiences the *Intense Joy* of being in the Paradise of Eden, in face of the Tree of Life, in the *Unus Mundus*. This *Joy* is a **silliness** (Perceval was a silly), and often ends up in uncontainable laughter, the result of blessing and the fact that a Freed being will invariably laugh at themselves, incapable of taking themselves seriously, since their own being is *Imponderable*. This *Joy* is a **madness**, a conscious experience of the *Pneumatic* reality that perceives the physical world as a **hallucination**, "people" and "things" as *Images* filled with numen. In the *Unus Mundus*, the *Pneumatic reality* is a "dream".

The climax of the Paradigm of Sense is the *Unus Mundus* – a plenitude of harmony between the fifth-dimensional ego and the *Spirit*. The ego realises its *Great Creation* in the world for one single reason: because it wants to. In harmony with this ego, the *Grail Draws*: *Spirit* IS *Body*, **an extreme (irrepressible) lust, a wild orgasm.**

---

[602] *The New Jerusalem Bible.* John 18:38.

[603] Ibid. Luke 20:25.

[604] Ibid. Matthew 6:3.

605 Ibid. John 10:28-30.

606 Ibid. John 19:7.

607 Ibid. Matthew 26:57-66.

608 "Anyone who dares to establish a connection between the psyche and the idea of God is immediately accused of "psychologism" or suspected of morbid "mysticism". JUNG, C. G. (1975) *Psychology and religion: West and East. Eastern religion.* Translated by Hull, R. F. C. 2nd edition. CW XI. Bollingen Series XX. Princeton University Press. §771.

609 *The New Jerusalem Bible.* Matthew 26:33-35, 69-74.

610 Ibid. Matthew 27:3-5.

611 EDINGER, E. F. (1987) *The Christian archetype.* Inner City Books. p. 83.

612 *The New Jerusalem Bible.* Matthew 26:51-52.

613 Ibid. John 17:12.

614 "And so I tell you, every human sin and blasphemy will be forgiven, but blasphemy against the Spirit will not be forgiven. And anyone who says a word against the Son of man will be forgiven, but no one who speak against the Holy Spirit will be forgiven either in this world or the next." Ibid. Matthew 12:31-32.

615 "By means of 'active imagination' we are put in a position of advantage, for we can then make the discovery of the archetype without sinking back into the instinctual sphere, which would only lead to blank unconsciousness **or, worse still, to some kind of intellectual substitute for instinct.**" JUNG, C. G. (1975) *The structure and dynamics of the psyche. On the Nature of the psyche.* Translated by Hull, R. F. C. CW VIII. Bollingen Series XX. Princeton University Press. §414. [author's own highlights].

616 BLAKE, W. *The marriage of heaven and hell.* (Produced by eagkw, Dianna Adair – online). Available at: <http://www.gutenberg.org/files/45315/45315-h/45315-h.htm>

617 BRANDÃO DE SOUZA, J. (1989) *Mitologia grega,* Vol II. Petrópolis, RJ: Eitora. Vozes. pp.117-121.

618 Ibid. Quoting ELIADE, M. p. 138.

619 Ibid. pp. 132, 136 and 137.

620 Ibid.

621 *The New Jerusalem Bible.* Matthew 12:34; 23:27

622 ANDRADE, O. (1928) *Manifesto antropófago.* (Revista de Antropofagia. Ano 374 "da deglutição do Bispo Sardinha". Available at:
<https://pib.socioambiental.org/files/manifesto_antropofago.pdf>

623 "Axé is vital force, life's principle, sacred force from the. Axé is the name given to the parts of the animals which contain these forces of live nature, which are also in the leaves, seeds and sacred fruit. Axé is blessing, greeting, good luck wishes and and anotherword for Amen. Axé is power. Axé is the group of material objects which represent the gods when they are incorporated, fixed in their particular altars in order to be worshiped. It is the rocks and iron from the orixás, their material representation, symbols of a tangible and immediate sacredness. Axé is charisma, is wisdom about saint things, is seniority. Axé is something one has, uses, spends, replaces, accumulates. Axé is origin, is the root

that comes from the ancestors, is the community of the candomblé grounds. The great carriers of axé, who are venerable mothers and fathers of saint, can pass on axé through hand imposition; through the saliva, which leaves the mouth with the word, through the face's sweat, which the old orixás in trance clean off their foreheads and, kindly, rub on the faces of their favourite. Axé is earned and lost." PRANDI, R. (1991) *Os candomblés de São Paulo*. São Paulo: Editora Hucitec Univ. de São Paulo.

[624] "The good evangelist, to get freed from eternal damnation, needs to destroy their most hidden desires; the good son or daughter of saint needs to realize all their desires so that the axé, the sacred force of their orixá, of whom there are the continuity, can expand and become stronger. Accepting the world as it is, candomblé accepts humanity, situating it in the centre of the universe, presenting it as a religion specially endowed to the narcissistic and selfish society in which we live." PRANDI, R. (1996) *Herdeiras do axé*. São Paulo: Editora Hucitec (Univ. de São Paulo).

[625] One of the carnival songs, for example, says: "My father Oxalá is the King, / Come make me worthy / And the old Omulú / Atotô abaluayê" (MORAES, V. e TOQUINHO (1979) *Meu pai Oxalá*. Song. Available at:
<https://www.google.com/search?gs_ssp=eJzj4tFP1zcsNM1KLsqrMDJg9OLLTS1VKEj MVMivSMw5vBAAklwKbA&q=meu+pai+oxal%C3%A1&oq=meu+pai+oxal%C3%A1&a qs=chrome.1.69i57j46j0l6.5744j0j7&sourceid=chrome&ie=UTF-8. Acess: April 19th 2020.) Oxalá and Omulú are Orixás, ioruhá deities, brought to Brazil with the blacks who were enslaved in the region close to the south of present Nigeria, currently worshiped particularly in the Brazilian religions known as Candomblé and Umbanda. Oxalá is the Orixá of supreme light, of the white, of peace, of faith. Omulú – sang to in the same song, almost regarded as the same being as Oxalá – is the Orixá of darkness, death, of the contagious diseases and convulsion.

[626] NIETZSCHE, F. (2006) *The antichrist*. Translated by Mencken, H.L. Project Gutenberg ebook. Available at:
<https://www.gutenberg.org/files/19322/19322-h/19322-h.htm> Access February 28th 2020.

[627] NIETZSCHE, F. (2006) *On the genealogy of morality*. Translated by Diethe, C. Cambridge University Press.

[628] NIETZSCHE, F. *The antichrist*. Op. Cit. Aphorism 39.

[629] Ibid. Aphorisms 32 and 33.

[630] JUNG, C. G. (1975) *Psychology and religion: West and East*. Translated by Hull, R. F. C. 2nd edition. CW XI. Bollingen Series XX. Princeton University Press.

[631] *The New Jerusalem Bible*. John 10:34.

[632] EDINGER, E. F. (1992) *Ego and archetype*. Boston: Shambhala. p. 235.

[633] JUNG, E. and von FRANZ, M. L. (1998) *The Grail legend*. Princeton University Press. p. 300.

[634] Ibid. pp. 380-381.

[635] Ibid, pp. 381-387.

[636] Ibid. p. 392.

[637] NIETZSCHE, F. *On the genealogy of morality*. Op. Cit. Aphorism 24.

[638] JUNG, E. and von FRANZ, M. L. (1998) *The Grail legend.* Princeton University Press. p. 117.

BIBLIOGRAPHY

ANDRADE, O. (1928) *Manifesto antropófago*. Revista de Antropofagia. Ano 374 "da deglutição do Bispo Sardinha". Available at: <https://pib.socioambiental.org/files/manifesto_antropofago.pdf>
——— *Manifesto da poesia pau-brasil.* (eBlog). Available at: <https://www.passeiweb.com/estudos/livros/manifesto_pau_brasil>

ANGELINI, H. (2015) *Força.* Unpublished text.

Apostles' Creed. (2008) Available at: <https://www.cardinalnewman.com.au/images/stories/downloads/The%20Apostles%20Creed.pdf>

AUGUSTINE of HIPPO, (+/- 495 A. D.) *De natura boni.* Translated by Newman, A. H. (on line) Available at: <http://www.documentacatholicaomnia.eu/03d/0354-0430,_Augustinus,_De_Natura_Boni_Contra_Manichaeos_[Schaff],_EN.pdf> Access: April 30th 2020.

BLAKE, W., *The marriage of heaven and hell.* (Produced by eagkw, Dianna Adair – online) Available at: <http://www.gutenberg.org/files/45315/45315-h/45315-h.htm>

BRANDÃO DE SOUZA, J. (1989) *Mitologia grega*, Petrópolis, RJ: Editora Vozes

BRINTON PERERA, S. (1986). *The scapegoat complex – Toward a mythology of shadow and guilt.* University of Toronto Press, Canada.

BULLFINCH, T. (2002) *Bullfinch's mythology.* (Online) Available at: <http://l-adam-mekler.com/bulfinch.pdf >

CAMPBELL, J. 2004) *The hero with a thousand faces.* Bollingen series XVII. Princeton University Press.

CHEVALIER, J. and GHEERBRANT, A. (1996) *A Dictionary of Symbols.* Trans. Buchanan-Brown, J. Penguin. UK

DOWNING, C. (1991) *Mirrors of the self – Archetypal images shape your life.* J. P. Tarcher.
— Portuguese version also used: (1991) *O espelho do self.* São Paulo: Cultrix.

DRISCOLL, J. P. (1992). *The unfolding God of JUNG and Milton*. Glossary. University Press of Kentucky.

EDINGER, E. F. (1991) *Anatomy of the Psyche: Alchemical Symbolism in Psychotherapy*. Open Court Publishing Company.

— Portuguese version also used: (2008) *Anatomia da psique*. São Paulo: Cultrix.

——— (1992) *Ego and archetype*. Boston: Shambhala Publications.

——— (2002) *Science of the soul: a Jungian perspective*. Canada: Inner City Books.

— Portuguese version also used: (2004) *A ciência da alma*. São Paulo: Editora Paulus.

——— (1987) *The Christian archetype*. Inner City Books.

——— (1984) *The creation of consciousness*. Canada: Inner City Books.

——— (1994) *The mystery of the coniunctio: Alchemical image of individuation*. Inner City Books.

— Portuguese version also used: (2008) *O Mistério da coniunctio*. São Paulo: Editora Paulus.

Bruno ERNST. *The magic mirror of M. C. Escher*. 1976. Ballantine Books. New York. Available at: <https://www.articons.co.uk/escher.htm>

von FRANZ, M. L. (1980) *Alchemy: an introduction to the symbolism and the psychology*. Inner City Books.

——— (1980) *On divination and synchronicity*. Inner City Books.

——— (1995) *Shadow and evil in fairy tales*. Boston: Shambhala Publications.

— Portuguese version also used: (1985) *A Sombra e o mal nos contos de fada*. São Paulo: Editoras Paulinas.

FREUD, A. (1993) *The ego and the mechanisms of defense*. London: Karnac Books.

GALLBACH, M. R. (2006) *Learning from dreams*. Published by Daimon Verlag.

GORRESIO, Z. *A ética da individuação: um estudo sobre a ética do ponto de vista da psicologia jungiana*. e-text, Available at: <http://www.hypnos.org.br/revista/index.php/hypnos/article/view/284/301>.

GOSWANI, A. (1995) *The self-aware universe*. Tarcher Perigee.

GOVINDA, A. (1975) *Foundations of Tibetan mysticism*. New York: Samuel Weiser.

GUGGENBUHL-CRAIG, A. (1990). *Power in the helping professions*. Dallas, TX: Spring Publications.

HALL, J. A. *Jungian dream interpretation* [translated from the Portuguese version: (1997) *Jung e a interpretação dos sonhos*. São Paulo: Cultrix]

——— *The jungian experience* [translated from the Portuguese version: (1995) *A experiência jungiana.* São Paulo: Cultrix.]

HANNAH, B. (2006) *The archetypal symbolism in animals.* Lectures Given at the C. G. Jung Institute, Zurich, 1954-1958., Wilmette, IL: Chiron.

HOLLIS, J. *On this journey we call our life.* [*translated from the Portuguese version:* (2004) *Nesta jornada que chamamos vida.* São Paulo: Paulus]

——— (1995) *Tracking the gods The Place of Myth in Modern Life Studies.* Los Angeles: Inner City Books

JACOBI, J. (1959) *Complex/Archetypes/Symbol in the Psychology of C. G. Jung.* Trans. Manheim, R. Bollingen Series LVII. Bollingen Foundation, Inc.

JUNG, C. G. *Complete Works.* (CW) Edited and translated by Adler. G. and Hull, R. F. C., Bollingen Series XX. Princeton University Press. Complete Digital Edition:

——— (1976) *Symbols of transformation.* CW V.

——— (1976) *Psychological types.* Translated by Baynes, H. G. C W VI.

——— (1972) *Two essays on analytical psychology.* CW VII.

——— (1975) *The structure and dynamics of the psyche.* CW VIII.

——— (1977) *The archetypes and the collective unconscious.* CW IX, part 1.

(1979) *Aion - researches into the phenomenology of the self.* CW IX, part 2.

——— (1978) *Civilization in transition.* CW X.

——— (1975) *Psychology and religion: West and East.* CW XI.

——— (1980) *Psychology and alchemy.* CW XII

——— (1983) *Alchemical studies.* CW XIII.

——— (1977) *Mysterium coniunctionis.* CW XIV.

——— (1971) *The Spirit in man, art and literature.* CW XV.

——— (1985) *The Practice of psychotherapy.* CW XVI.

——— (1981) *The Development of personality.* CW XVII.

——— (1980) *The Symbolic life.* CW XVIII.

——— ETH Lecture 26 Jan 1940.

——— (1973) *Letters*, Vol. I. Edited and translated by Hull, R. F. C. Bolingen series XCV. Princeton University Press.

——— (1976) *Letters*, Vol. II. Trans. Hulen, J. Bollingen Series. Princeton University Press.

——— (1964) *Man and his symbols.* New York: Anchor Press Doubleday (ebook) Available at:
 <https://antilogicalism.com/wp-content/uploads/2017/07/man-and-his-symbols.pdf>

——— *Memories, dreams and reflexions.* Translated by Winston, R. and C. Revised Edition. Vintage Books. (ebook) Available at:

<http://www.venerabilisopus.org/en/books-samael-aun-weor-gnostic-sacred-esoteric-spiritual/pdf/200/265_jung-carl-memories-dreams-reflections.pdf>
— Portuguese version also used: (1981) *Memórias, Sonhos e Reflexões.* Rio de Janeiro: Ed. Nova Fronteira.
——— (1933) *Modern man in search of Soul.* London: Kegan Paul, Trench, Trubner & Co LTD. (ebook) Available at:
<https://archive.org/details/in.ernet.dli.2015.218430/page/n7>
——— (1996) *The psychology of Kundalini yoga.* Bollingen Series XCIX. Princeton University Press
——— (1998) *Visions: Notes on the Seminar Given in 1930-1934.* Routledge.
——— (1998) *Zarathustra seminar.* Bollingen Series XCIX. Princeton University Press
JUNG, C., JUNG, E. and WOLF, T.(January 11, 2020) *A collection of remembrances.* [online: weblog]. Available at:
<https://carljungdepthpsychologysite.blog/2020/01/11/carl-jung-on-free-will-anthology/#.Xoc-kP1Khdg>
JUNG, E. and von FRANZ, M. L. (1998) *The grail legend.* Princeton University Press.
KAPLAN, A. (1997) *Sêfer Yetsirá – The book of creation – in theory and practice.* Revised edition. Boston: Weiser Books.
Koran. (2015) Translated by Mawlavi Sher'Ali. Islam International Publications Ltd.
LAPLANCHE, J. and PONTALIS, JB. (2018) *The Language of Psychoanalysis.* Routledge.
LEITE, P. C. T. (Paula Caju). (2016) *Paula Caju: a obra artística com o diabo no corpo.* Trabalho de Conclusão de Curso. Universidade Est. Paulista Júlio de Mesquita Filho, Instituto de Artes. Available at:
<http://hdl.handle.net/11449/155477> (2019) *As possibilidades da psicologia analítica para a voz cantada na semana da psicologia mackenzie.* Youtube. Available at:
<https://www.youtube.com/watch?v=kP0SZ9Shx44>
LIMA FILHO, A. P. (2002) *O pai e a psique.* São Paulo: Editora Paulus.
MATTOS, R. G. (2013). *Evolução (Evolution).* Unpublished text.
Meditations on the Tarot. (1980) Massachussets: Element. (online) Available at:
<http://tarothermeneutics.com/tarotliterature/MOTT/Meditations-on-the-Tarot.pdf>
Merriam Webster Dictionary. (11th ed.) Springfield, MA: Merriam-Webster.

MILTON, J. *Paradise lost.* Edited by Armstrong, E. (online) Available at: <https://www.yorku.ca/earmstro/text/ParadiseLostBk1.pdf> (44-line 85; 64 – line 263)

NEUMANN, E. (1971) *Amor and psyche: the psychic development of the feminine.* Translated by Manheim, R. Princeton University Press.

——— (1963) *The great mother - an analysis of the archetype.* Translated by Manheim, R. Bollingen series XLVII. Princeton University Press.

——— (1994) *The fear of the feminine: and other essays on feminine psychology.* Princeton University Press.

——— (2002) *The origins and history of consciousness, Vol I.* Translated by Hull, R. F. C. London: Routledge. Kindle eBook. Available at: <https://www.amazon.com/Origins-History-Consciousness-International-Psychology-ebook/dp/B019P2PSDM>. Access: April 26th 2020.

——— (1962) *The origins and history of consciousness, Vol II.* Translated by Hull, R. F. C. New York: Harper Torchbooks. Available at: <https://archive.org/details/originsandhistor017897mbp/page/n3/mode/2up> Access: April 26th 2020.

NIETZSCHE, F. (2016) *Ecce homo.* Translated by Ludovici, A.M. and Cohn, P.V. Project Gutemberg ebook. Available at: <http://www.gutenberg.org/ebooks/52190> Access: February 28th 2020.

——— (1910) *Human, all too human.* London: T. N. Foulis. (ebook) Available at: <https://digitalassets.lib.berkeley.edu/main/b20790001_v_1_B000773557.pdf>

——— *Kritische studienausgabe. (on line) Available at:* <https://www.goodreads.com/quotes/8010169-main-thought-the-individual-himself-is-a-fallacy-everything-which>

——— (2006) *On the genealogy of morality.* Translated by Diethe, C. Cambridge University Press.

——— (2006) *The antichrist.* Translated by Mencken, H. L. Project Gutenberg ebook. Available at: <https://www.gutenberg.org/files/19322/19322-h/19322-h.htm> (Last access: February 28th 2020)

——— (2016) *The birth of tragedy.* Translated by Haussmann, W. A. Project Gutenberg ebook. Available at: <https://www.gutenberg.org/files/51356/51356-h/51356-h.htm>

——— (2012) *The dawn of day.* Trans. Kennedy, J. F. Project Gutenberg ebook. Available at: <http://www.gutenberg.org/files/39955/39955-pdf.pdf>

——— (1999) *Thus spoke Zarathustra.* Trans. Common, T. Project Gutenberg etext. Available at: <http://www.dominiopublico.gov.br/download/texto/gu001998.pdf>

PEREIRA, I. (1990) *Dicionário grego-português e português-grego.* São Paulo: Apostolado da Imprensa Martins Fontes

PRANDI, R., (1996) *Herdeiras do axé.* São Paulo: Editora Hucitec (Univ. de São Paulo)

——— (1991) *Os candomblés de São Paulo.* São Paulo: Editora Hucitec Univ. de São Paulo.

PROGOFF. I. (1973) *Jung, synchronicity and human destiny.* New York: Delta.

RAFF, J. (2000) *Jung and the alchemical imagination.* Florida: Nicolas-Hays, Inc (Kobo eBook version).

ROTHENBERG, R.E. (2004) *A Jóia na Ferida.* São Paulo: Editora Paulus.

SANFORD, J. A. (1998) *Evil: The shadow side of reality.* The Crossroad Publishing Co.

——— (2018) *Fate, love and ecstasy.* Asheville, NC: Chiron Publications.
— Portuguese version also used: (1999) *Destino, Amor e Êxtase.* São Paulo: Editora Paulus.

——— (1991) *Soul Journey: A Jungian Analyst Looks at Reincarnation.* Crossroads Publications

SARTRE, J. P. (2011) *No Exit* (online) Available at: <https://archive.org/stream/NoExit/NoExit_djvu.txt> (Access: February 28th 2020)

Septuagint Bible. Translated from Portuguese. Available at: <https://bibliaonlinesnt.blogspot.com/2012/08/septuaginta.html

SICUTERI, R. *Lilith, la luna nera* [Not published in English. Translated from the Portuguese version: (1985) *Lilith, a lua negra.* 3ª ed. São Paulo: Editora Paz e Terra]

SPINOSA, B. (2009) *Ethics.* Translated from Latin by ELWES, R. H. M. Project Gutemberg eBook. Available at: <http://www.gutenberg.org/files/3800/3800-h/3800-h.htm>

STEIN, R. (1973) *Incest and human love.* Dallas, TX: Spring Publications.

The Hammurabi Code. (2011) Translated by L. W. King. (Online) Available at: <http://www.general-intelligence.com/library/hr.pdf>

The New Jerusalem Bible. (ebook) Available at: <https://www.bibliacatolica.com.br/new-jerusalem-bible/genesis/1/>

WHITMONT, Edward C. (1969). *The symbolic quest.* Princeton University Press. New Jersey.

THE AUTHOR

Cavalher dedicates his career to the development of consciousness in people. He has surpassed the common understanding that the human psychological structure is subjective and hard to apprehend and presents human consciousness and the unconscious to people with clarity and precision, enabling them to apply it to practical situations. His methods allow the elimination of professional blind spots, and the development of new intelligences, new capabilities, and unique talents. Above all, he enables people to live lives that make *Sense*.

For 30 years, Cavalher has been on a journey of self-taught studies in Analytical Psychology, the Philosophy of Nietzsche and symbols present in the Mythology of various cultures, in Astrology and Alchemy. He specialized in the interpretation of dreams, which enables him to map, with precision, the psychological algorithms present in the unconscious mind, optimizing them to achieve results. He created an entirely original style of Kinesiology, which allows immediate and safe access to information present in the unconscious mind, and its re-writing.

The continued work with clients in advanced stages of individuation lead him to the perception of a deeper layer of the human psychological structure, and a new psychological discovery: the *Paradigm of Sense*. It describes reality in 5 dimensions: a multidimensional and multi-paradoxical reality where people experience the freedom to be and the capacity to edit their own reality.

He co-founded, with Valerya Carvalho, the School of Sense©, focused on the creation and implementation of new paradigms. At the School, people and organizations unlearn attitudes that always produce the same results and learn methods to develop innovative potentials to find the path to live lives fulfilled with *Sense* and realization. The School teaches to *Create oneself*.

For 14 years, Cavalher has been conducting talks, courses and workshops in São Paulo and New York about the structure of the human consciousness, of the Unconscious and symbols. These themes are timeless and surpass the recent superficial, repetitive, fanciful and disappointing proposals of self-help and esotericism.

In the last 20 years, Cavalher has been dedicated to the comprehension of the unconscious mind and the construction of the super-consciousness in entrepreneurs, CEOs of various companies, film directors, actors, doctors, barristers, intelligence officers, dancers, judges, professors, advertising executives, real estate executives, fashion stylists, economists and psychologists in São Paulo, Rio de Janeiro, Vitória, Belo Horizonte, Curitiba, Nova York, London and Berlin.

THE TRANSLATOR

Born in London to Brazilian parents, Fabíola Conceição was educated both in Brazil and in the UK. Having returned to Brazil at a very young age in the 70s due to her father's research job, she became bilingual as a child, proficient in both Portuguese and English languages. After returning to England to complete her education, Fabíola graduated in Social Sciences in the UK, and after a ten-year spell in Brazil, where she acquired an MBA and a master's degree in Public Health whilst working as a civil servant for the Ministry of Health, Fabíola returned permanently to the UK in 2012. Here, she acquired further qualifications and worked as a translator and court interpreter for many years, now also working as Tutor of English as a Foreign Language and English for Academic Purposes.

Paradigm of Sense